STRANGE ENEMIES

THE CULTURES AND PRACTICE
OF VIOLENCE SERIES

Series Editors
Neil L. Whitehead, University of Wisconsin, Madison
Jo Ellen Fair, University of Wisconsin, Madison
Leigh Payne, University of Wisconsin, Madison

The study of violence has often focused on the political and economic conditions under which violence is generated, the suffering of victims, and the psychology of its interpersonal dynamics. Less familiar are the role of perpetrators, their motivations, and the social conditions under which they are able to operate. In the context of postcolonial state building and more latterly the collapse and implosion of society, community violence, state repression, and the phenomena of judicial inquiries in the aftermath of civil conflict, there is a need to better comprehend the role of those who actually do the work of violence—torturers, assassins, and terrorists—as much as the role of those who suffer its consequences.

When atrocity and murder take place, they feed the world of the iconic imagination that transcends reality and its rational articulation; but in doing so imagination can bring further violent realities into being. This series encourages authors who build on traditional disciplines and break out of their constraints and boundaries, incorporating media and performance studies and literary and cultural studies as much as anthropology, sociology, and history.

STRANGE ENEMIES

INDIGENOUS AGENCY AND SCENES

OF ENCOUNTERS IN AMAZONIA

Aparecida Vilaça

Translated by David Rodgers

DUKE UNIVERSITY PRESS

Durham and London 2010

Originally published by Editora UFRJ as *Quem somos nós.*
Os Wari' encontram os brancos (Rio de Janerio, 2006)

All rights reserved
Printed in the United States of America on acid-free paper ∞
Designed by Amy Ruth Buchanan
Typeset in Arno Pro by Achorn International, Inc.
Library of Congress Cataloging-in-Publication Data
appear on the last printed page of this book.

TO ANDRÉ, FRANCISCO, HÉLIO,

TEMIS, AND PALETÓ

Porque a vida,
a vida,
a vida,
a vida,
só é possível
reinventada.

—CECÍLIA MEIRELES

CONTENTS

ILLUSTRATIONS

MAPS

FIGURES

ACKNOWLEDGMENTS

This book, published in Portuguese by Editora UFRJ in 2006, is a modified version of my doctoral thesis, completed in the Graduate Program in Social Anthropology (PPGAS) of the Museu Nacional (Universidade Federal do Rio de Janeiro) in 1996. I thank my former lecturers and now colleagues for their support over the years, especially Gilberto Velho, Luiz Fernando Dias Duarte, Otávio Velho, and Roberto DaMatta. Carlos Fausto deserves special thanks for his consecutive readings of my manuscripts and his friendship. Eduardo Viveiros de Castro was my thesis supervisor and responsible for my training in ethnology; his work comprises a central reference point for my own, as will become evident to the reader. It is a privilege to have been able to count on his intellectual generosity and his friendship throughout all this time.

Lisa Stuart helped very generously with all stages of producing the book, while David Rodgers was the translator of my dreams. I thank Neil Whitehead, the editor of the series, for his comments and suggestions. Anne-Christine Taylor, Artionka Capiberibe, Beto Barcellos, Bruna Franchetto, Cesar Gordon, Cristiane Lasmar, Dušan Borić, Elizabeth Pissolato, Joana Miller, Joaquim Pais de Brito, José Antônio Kelly, Manuela Carneiro da Cunha, Marcela Coelho de Souza, Márcio Silva, Marco Antônio Gonçalves, Márnio Teixeira-Pinto, Neila Soares, Oiara Bonilla, Patrick Menget, Peter Gow, Philippe Descola, Philippe Erikson, Tânia Stolze Lima, and Terence Turner, colleagues and friends, contributed ideas, readings, advice, and comfort over twenty years of field research with the Wari'. Julie Coimbra, Marilyn Strathern, Simeran Gell, and Stephen and Christine Hugh-Jones made my stay in Cambridge intellectually and emotionally unforgettable. Peter Rivière is the book's godfather, while Marshall Sahlins gave me essential advice during some of its final stages, as well as providing, through his work, the book's starting point and inspiration. I also thank the late Claude Lévi-Strauss for his interest and comments on the Brazilian version of the book.

Beth Conklin, who began her research among the Wari' a year before I did, became an interlocutor, partner, friend, and *comadre*. In these twenty years we have lived through many important things together and throughout Beth has shown herself to be the most generous person I have known.

My field research among the Wari', began in 1986, was funded by the Ford Foundation, FINEP, the Wenner-Gren Foundation for Anthropological Research (Pre-doctoral Grant and International Collaborative Grant) and, since July 2007, by the John Simon Guggenheim Foundation. CNPQ and CAPES funded my postgraduate studies through study grants; CNPQ has awarded me a research fellowship since 2003 and CAPES provided a post-doctoral grant in 2004.

Current and former employees of FUNAI in Guajará-Mirim contributed in innumerable ways to the success of the research. I especially thank Dídimo Graciliano de Oliveira, Juscileth Pessoa (Preta), Francisco das Chagas Araújo, Francisco Peixoto, Jozélio and Luzia Cunha, Cirilo Ferreira de Menezes and Luzineth Diniz, Francisca Fernandes and her son Maxmilliano, and Lucia Carneiro and her family. I also thank the teachers Dulce Ana Deicke and Evanir Kich.

The team of the Diocese of Guajará-Mirim also provided inestimable help. I especially thank Dom Geraldo Verdier, the bishop of Guajará-Mirim, the late Dom Roberto Gomes de Arruda, and in particular Gilles de Catheau, for his interest and friendship.

My family is an essential part of my work. Temis and Hélio Vilaça, my parents, Eduardo and Mônica Vilaça, my brother and sister-in-law, and Luiz and Rodrigo, my nephews, have encouraged and supported me from the outset. Likewise Waleska, Concita, and Zezé. My late grandparents Olga Vilaça and Manoel and Maria do Carmo Neiva led me to Amazonia, and I am eternally grateful for this. My sons, Francisco and André, have accompanied me to the Wari' since they were little. Their happiness and enthusiasm for our life in the village, and their interest in my work, have been a constant source of support. Together we form a team, and this book is dedicated to them.

My Wari' family is a central part of the story of this book and the history of my life. My father Paletó, one of the most brilliant people I have met, is a constant presence in this work and I owe him more than can be imagined. It always touches me to see him pamper my sons like only a grandfather can, going to the forest to fetch the assai so adored by Francisco, patiently teaching André how to shoot an arrow and, when necessary, rushing to search for forest remedies to cure them. To'o Xak Wa, his wife, possesses an enchanting sobriety and beauty. My brothers Orowao, Abrão, Main, Davi, A'ain Tot, and Ja all have the same keen intelligence as their father. It is a pleasure to be with them. As Paletó often says, living together had made us true kin. I thank all the other Wari' too for their lessons in life, especially Orowao Xik Waji, Hwerein Pe e', Ko'um, Orowam, A'ain Kaxun, A'ain Xit Kao Tokwe, Jap, Dina, Topa' Jam, Wao Tokori, Topa', Xatoji and Maxun Hat, and the late Wan e', Jimon Pan Tokwe and Wem Parawan.

ORTHOGRAPHY

All Wari' words, apart from proper names, are written in italics. The orthography used in this book is based on the phonetic transcription system for Wari' developed by the New Tribes Missions (NTM), the only difference being that I use the letter *k* instead of *c* to represent the phoneme /k/. The approximate values of the sounds are as follows.

VOWELS

a – like *a* in cat

e – like *e* in echo

i – like *ee* in seen

o – varying between *o* in cot, or *oo* in soon

u – like *u* in French *fumer*

CONSONANTS

k – like *c* in cat

h – like *h* in hat

j – varying between *j* in just, or *y* in you

m – varying between *m* in mat, or *b* in bat, with light prenasalization

n – varying between *n* in not, or *d* in dot, with light prenasalization

p – like *p* in pot

r – like *r* in Portuguese *parado* (flap)

t – like *t* in time

w – like *w* in wonder

x – varying between *ch* in chat, or *sh* in shine

The symbol ' indicates a glottal stop. Since I find it very difficult to discern this sound, I have retained the notation only in those words where I am sure I have been able to identify the sound clearly.

INTRODUCTION

Como começar pelo início, se as coisas acontecem antes de acontecer?
(How to start at the very beginning if things happen before they happen?)
—Clarice Lispector

FIRST ENCOUNTERS

About fifty years ago, in 1956, in the state of Rondônia near the border with Bolivia, a group of Wari' (speakers of a Txapakura language) experienced their first peaceful contact with whites—Protestant missionaries from the New Tribes Mission (NTM) and agents from the Brazilian government's Indian Protection Service (SPI).[1] For decades the latter had been attempting to pacify these renowned warriors, who were much feared by the local population. On this occasion a group of Wari' men had ventured as far as the cleared area of forest surrounding the attraction post. Here the men shouted out that they wanted metal tools, which the whites duly handed over. On returning to their villages, the warriors reported: "We touched their bodies!" The message from the whites to their own people was somewhat different: "The region's most warlike tribe has entered the pacification phase!"

This was not actually their first contact, though. Written documents suggest that the Wari' were first sighted at the start of the nineteenth century on the Pacaás Novos, an affluent of the Mamoré River (and the source of the name Pakaa-Nova by which the people became known in the literature), although at that moment no kind of contact was established. The first real contacts between the Wari' and whites[2] date from the beginning of the twentieth century. Initially these encounters took the form of warfare—violent confrontations that stemmed either from the Wari' desire to pursue this type of relationship, when "the whites liked us, but we didn't like them," or from their wish to revenge and repel the violent incursions into their territory made by rubber tappers and their bosses. When the Wari' finally decided to ally with the whites, they were persuaded by a complex set of motives that extended beyond their practical interest in metal tools: above all, the Wari' wanted to rebuild their society, which had been destructured by the territorial invasions, and they believed that the whites would help them achieve this.

The first and subsequent encounters between the Wari' and whites form the ethnographic framework for this book. However, its central theme is inevitably much broader: understanding these encounters means immersing ourselves in the world of Wari' relations with others in general, objectified in the form of affines, foreigners, animals, and enemies. As we shall see, the whites fall into the latter category. Consequently—and remaining faithful to Wari' narratives—my analysis of the Wari' encounters with whites is preceded by an account of their encounters with a wide variety of others in both everyday circumstances and mythic accounts.

What I refer to here as categories of otherness primarily consist of positions within a specific relational context—a topic covered in the first part of this book, "Other Becoming." These positions comprise the primary channels for processing new events and absorbing new people and collectivities. Hence, the foreigner—a member of another of the Wari' subgroups—is a distant relative who can be consanguinized through cohabitation and marriage. Enemies, for their part, are ontologically Wari': foreigners who moved far away and ruptured the exchange cycle of festivals and women. Reversing this movement can turn them back into Wari'. Whites, when they arrived, were also taken as a type of enemy and thus Wari' in origin too.

Classification of the same group of people varies according to the context and the form of relation, and it is always linked to a specific point of view. For the OroEo subgroup, for example, the OroNao' who arrived with the whites to help them pacify the uncontacted Wari' were classified as enemies—coinhabitants and kin of the whites, since they traveled, ate, and slept with them. Later, when communication between the groups became easier, the OroNao' were reclassified as "foreign Wari'." In the native logic, therefore, Wari' and enemy function as interchangeable positions.

In his study of Yanomami perceptions of contact with whites, Bruce Albert (1992) adopts a similar procedure to my own by showing how the native etiological system associated the newcomers with various categories of others. These categories shifted over time. The Yanomami identified whites with specific pathogenic powers, continually reclassifying these new agents in response to their perceptions of the latter's actions: malevolent spirits from the depths of the forest, potential enemies, real enemies, orphans and refugees, as well as other evil spirits—insatiable cannibals—that originated from the cities rather than the forest.

In similar fashion, Teixeira-Pinto (2000) shows how the Arara (a Carib people) initially classified members of the FUNAI[3] "attraction team" as malevolent spirits. Made up of whites and Kayapó Indians, the team initially pursued the group through the forest in an attempt to force contact: their sagacity, cunning, and persistence convinced the Arara that they were spirits who had reappeared in the form of enemies as part of an eternal divine punishment. Later, under new leadership, FUNAI's strategy switched to offering the Arara presents left on *tapiri* shelters in the forest: the whites were consequently reclassified as *ïpari*, "someone with whom one fought in the sky, but who, once on the ground, accepted the rules of mutual conviviality, despite their differences" (Teixeira-Pinto 2000, 417).

A comparable dynamic is evident in Sahlins's classic study of the encounter between Hawaiians and Europeans. By relating intimately with women (especially by eating with them) and by becoming exchange partners, the strangers became secularized, transforming from gods into humans (Sahlins 1981, 53–55). The book edited by Schieffelin and Crittenden (1991b) on the first encounters between native peoples of Papua New Guinea and Australian colonial patrol officers also shows that the whites were reclassified with each new development. These new classifications depended not only on the specific actions of the newly arrived strangers but also on the circumstances in which they occurred: mythic heroes coming back to their lands of origin, or the dead returning to their living kin.

Gods, malevolent spirits, creator heroes, enemies: in each situation, native symbolic systems were able to accommodate these new actors, proving dynamic enough to revise their classifications in accordance with the perception of events (see Fausto 2002b). It is precisely the possibility of exploring the dynamic of native thought that makes the study of first contact with whites so interesting (Albert 1992, 151–52). This is especially so since by revealing their astonishing technological power, introducing highly effective curing methods, and acting in unusual ways, these new actors assumed the position of "superlative Others" (Albert 2000, 13), effectively speeding up reclassification and raising important pragmatic questions in the process. We also have to pay close attention to what Schieffelin and Crittenden (1991b, 4–5) call the "existential dimension" related to the element of surprise involved in the encounter. Although for whites the contact was anticipated, and indeed very often formed the purpose of their expeditions, the natives were frequently taken by surprise by the sudden irruption of these beings into their world—an asymmetry compounded by numerous other factors, including the quickly perceived military superiority of the invaders.

All of these factors reveal the singularity of the encounter with the whites in the overall context of indigenous relations with others (see Ramos 1988, 227), and hence the importance of studies on the theme. Over the last few decades, the discovery of many new documents and the increased sophistication of research tools, based on a constant dialogue between the written sources and ethnography,[4] have helped produce solid analyses of the colonial process and its apprehension by native peoples themselves, as well as a better understanding of the reciprocal implication of the different cultural schema and individual agencies in the repercussions of the encounter.[5]

First published in 1971, Wachtel's book *The Vision of the Vanquished: The Spanish Conquest of Peru through Indian Eyes, 1530–1570* is pathbreaking in the emphasis it gives to native views of the encounter. The author based his research on documents produced by the Spanish from native accounts and on the examination of modern-day indigenous folklore referring to the events of the Conquest (1971, 31). Salomon (1999, 52) comments on the pioneering nature of Wachtel's work and observes that, in contrast to the Peruvian context where "oral testimonies embedded in Iberian chronicles" are abundant, accounts from native witnesses are much more scarce in Amazonia (23). According to the author, "beyond the Andean region, it is harder still to recapture 'Indian history,' even where missionary authors did penetrate" (41).[6] The same observation is made by Caravaglia (1999, 2) concerning the documents describing the European invasion in the Prata Basin: "Only rarely do we hear the direct voice of the natives. Usually native voices are heard through many filters, so that the original is almost completely muffled by a complicated series of transcription and translation."

The particularity of the Wari' case resides in the fact that the first face-to-face contacts with whites occurred a relatively short time ago, in the first decades of the twentieth century. This means that some of the oldest people can remember the stories recounted by their parents of episodes that happened in their childhoods, when they were captured by the whites for a few days, or when the latter had been killed after trying to approach. At all events, the Wari' insist that until the 1950s they never allied with the whites, not even as occasional exchange partners. When not fleeing from them (and being killed), the Wari' were seeking the whites out to kill them, or simply to steal their tools.

Consequently, it was only during the episodes of pacification that many people saw living examples of this enemy for the first time. This especially applied to Wari' women and children. Previously they had only known parts of their bodies, which the warriors had taken back to the villages to be roasted and eaten. For most adult men, it was the first time that they accepted communication with whites, but, above all, the first time they had touched their living bodies. The Wari' retain a rich memory of these events, and I had the chance and luck to be able to meet and interview these protagonists at length between 1992 and 1996. Furthermore, while documentation of the earlier encounters is sparse, the pacification process is well documented in the reports and radiograms of the Indian Protection Service (SPI), which allows us to apprehend the viewpoint of the whites present at the time, filling a lacuna in their testimonies since many have already died or were unable to be located.

Although the ethnohistorical literature has clearly shown that encounters between particular indigenous groups and whites did not occur within a linear timescale, but with the alternation of phases of contact and isolation, and above all that the effects of colonialism were felt long before the first contacts properly speaking (see Salomon and Schwartz 1999; Ferguson and Whitehead 2000; Fausto and Heckenberger 2007b), I wish to insist on the category of first encounters used in the present text. Although an in-depth study of the initial processes of colonization of the area occupied by the Wari' would undoubtedly provide important insights in terms of comprehending the encounters described in this book, I have opted to focus my analysis on the discourse of my interlocutors concerning this theme.[7] The instances of first contact cited in this text are understood from the indigenous perspective: that is, they refer to encounters that the Indians themselves conceive to be their first contact with whites. The focus of my study, therefore, is on the first contacts with whites as experienced by a specific group of native people whose life histories and genealogies can be reconstituted.

The number of works approaching the topic in this way are relatively few, especially because in many of the ethnographic areas studied those who encountered the first whites—and often their immediate descendents—are no longer alive to recount the histories. In the case of Amazonia, an important exception is the collection edited by Albert and Ramos (2000) on the first contacts between indigenous groups of northern Amazonia and Europeans, evocatively titled *Pacificando o branco* (Pacifying the whites). Indigenous

narratives on the first encounters with whites can be found in other collections. I highlight those compiled by the Instituto Socioambiental (2000,
20–48) and analyzed, in the same volume, by Viveiros de Castro (2000b, 14,
49–54).[8] This is also the theme of chapters from a number of recent mono-
graphs and theses (see Fausto 2001; Kelly 2003; Grotti 2007; Bonilla 2007;
Costa 2007). However, as far as I know, and in terms of Amazonia, there is
no other anthropological monograph dedicated to the theme that is based
on native testimonies.

In relation to other ethnographic areas, I highlight the previously mentioned book edited by Schieffelin and Crittenden (1991b) on the contacts
made by the Australian colonial patrols in 1935 between the Strickland and
Purari rivers in the southern Papua New Guinea highlands. As in the case
of the Wari', this work deals with relatively recent examples of first contacts
(with different groups from the same area), which enabled access to narratives from people who themselves took part in the encounters, or from those
who heard about them from their parents and grandparents.[9]

Sahlins's books (1981, 1985, 1995) exploring the encounter between the
Cook expedition and the Hawaiians in the eighteenth century constitute a
case apart. My reading of *Historical Metaphors and Mythical Realities* (1981)
during a stay among the Wari' was decisive in defining my research object;
likewise, the theoretical approach developed by Sahlins in this book and subsequent works is essential to my analysis of the ethnographic material on
the encounters between the Wari' and the whites. Although these texts are
based on documental analysis, Sahlins's methodology provided an invalu-
able framework: the reading of sources via properly ethnographic questions,
the constant recourse to myth, and the apprehension of the initial contacts
and the relations subsequently established with whites within a wider socio-
cosmological schema that extends beyond the immediate context of the encounter enable a heightened perception of the native point of view, which
is then compared with the perspective of the whites. This is precisely what I
have looked to undertake in this work.

INDIGENOUS PRAGMATISM

As I suggested earlier, although encountering the whites for the first time, the
Wari', along with the Yanomami, the Arara, the Hawaiians, and many others,
quickly found a place for the newcomers in their classificatory system—even
though in some cases the initial impact of the encounter had to be overcome

in order for the system to be activated, as Schieffelin and Crittenden remind us (1991b, 4). In many cases, the starting point for classification is myth. It is unsurprising, therefore, that most anthropological works on the encounter between native peoples and Westerners concentrate on exploring the connections between myths and events, since this is precisely what our informants do.[10]

For the Wari', myth is a constant source of inspiration. Indeed, the central role played by myths in the present work is indissociable from their continuing presence in the life of these Indians. As we shall see in the third part of the book, the Wari' often echoed the actions of mythic figures during the episodes of pacification. This reenactment was not just a way of comprehending dramatic events. The Wari' often use small fragments of myths or entire accounts to explain aspects of everyday life, meteorological events, and other phenomena. When Paletó, my Wari' father, visited Rio de Janeiro in 1992, I discovered firsthand the importance of myth in making new experiences intelligible. Since it was the first time he had traveled further than the small city of Guajará-Mirim, I took pains to minimize his culture shock by explaining the many new and strange things around him. But I was the one to be astonished. This man, then around sixty years old, who spoke no Portuguese and had never had access to magazines or television, absorbed everything unperturbed. For example, watching an enormous mechanical digger at work one day, Paletó exclaimed that white people's objects act by themselves, as though alive, because our ancestors had not burst into laughter at the sight of these animated objects. The ancestors of the Wari', by contrast, had laughed wildly when baskets filled with maize began to walk through the forest on their own to spare women the heavy load; the women's laughter caused the baskets to desist forever.

As the studies cited above show, the fact that myths provide a starting point for understanding new experiences does not mean that the originality of the latter passes unnoticed, or that the dynamic of events cannot be processed, or indeed that indigenous peoples are incapable of strategically calculating their actions. The relationship established by the Wari' between mythic and historic accounts (both of which are called "stories of the ancestors") is logical rather than historical. Myth and event are related because they are structurally similar, not because the event is confused with the mythical episode.[11]

This point needs to be underlined given the polemic surrounding this topic. This debate has been primarily concerned with affirming the "historical consciousness" of native peoples (Hill 1988b; Friedman 1988; Obeyesekere 1992). I do not share this concern—and not merely because it strikes me as somewhat obvious. More importantly, many of the authors making this claim rely somewhat unreflexively on the opposition between *mythos* and *logos* that founds Western thought, in particular its modern versions (see Latour 2000). Furthermore, this opposition provides us with no insight into the thinking of the native peoples studied.[12] At an ethnographic level, various authors involved in this polemic have demonstrated the overlapping of mythical and historical accounts, or the blurring of mythic thought and historical agency, in much the same way as I shall do here. In fact, their argument has largely depended on sustaining a theoretical conflict—in general, with the structuralism of Lévi-Strauss—which is, I believe, largely counterproductive.[13]

The fact that myths are not the same as events does not mean that their central figures cannot overlap. As various studies make clear, in some encounters the Europeans or strangers were perceived as returning mythical beings. Sahlins observes that with Cook's arrival "everything transpired as if centuries of Hawaiian sacrifice had finally paid off" (1985, 4). Viveiros de Castro (1992a, 30–31; 2002, 183–264) emphasizes a similar point in analyzing the Tupinambá association of Europeans with powerful supernatural figures. The gods and humans were attributed the same origin, while their separation resulted from contingent events, meaning that the gods could return at any moment.[14] Sahlins's observation concerning the Hawaiians can be extended to other contexts: "Hawaiian thought does not differ from Western empiricism by an inattention to the world but by the ontological premise that divinity, and more generally subjectivity, can be immanent in it" (Sahlins 1995, 6–7).[15]

This does not mean that the practice of associating strange new peoples with legendary figures is exclusive to native groups. As various authors have shown, Westerners involved in these encounters were also motivated by preconceived ideas about indigenous peoples. In his book on the invasion of America, Todorov examines the importance of "beliefs" for Columbus: "Colombus does not believe in Christian dogma alone: he also believes (and he is not the only one to do so during his era) in cyclops and mermaids, Amazons and men with tails, and his belief, as strong as that of Saint Peter, allows him to encounter them" (Todorov 1983, 16).

Overing (1995, 2) echoes this observation, recalling that when the Europeans arrived in the Americas, their imagination had already been shaped by medieval books telling of ogres and cannibal giants. As we shall see later, the different agents involved in pacifying the Wari' also acted in response to preconceived ideas about Indians. The fundamentalist missionaries and the Catholic priests, who played an especially active role in the pacification process, saw them as children of God unaware of their condition, thereby perpetuating the traditional view of Indians as one of the lost tribes of Israel (see Shapiro 1981, 146). A newspaper report on the Wari' from the period of pacification illustrates this point: "They are human, though products of a different field and in our view a kind of hybrid creation" (*O Imparcial*, January 8, 1961).

Obeyesekere devotes an entire book to this topic. For this author, the deification of Cook, a great explorer transformed into a hero, is a European myth rather than a Hawaiian one (1992, 8–10). Furthermore, Obeyesekere argues, by attributing "mythical models" exclusively to natives, we ignore the fact that we ourselves—Westerners and anthropologists—are also informed by our own myths, including those of the wild or prelogical native (18).[16]

Mythical figures abound on both sides, then. What should draw our attention, though, is the considerable hierarchical difference in how the whites and the natives perceived each other: gods and powerful shamans on the one hand; animalized, infantilized, or monstrous beings on the other. Certainly this difference is closely related to the typically spectacular way in which the strangers arrived, along with their large military and material power and their potent medicines. Moreover, as Sahlins noted in the Hawaiian case, the idea of divine immanence on which many native cosmologies are based enabled identification of these unknown strangers with gods. This stands in diametrical contrast to the centrality of the notion of divine transcendence in modern Western thought (see Latour 2000, 38–39). As we shall see in the following chapters, the key point is that this asymmetry in the indigenous and Western classificatory hierarchies is essential in defining the later developments of the encounter.

STRUCTURES AND CONTINGENCIES

Schieffelin, Crittenden, et al. (1991, 285) note that the significance of the first contact for native peoples tends to vary according to the importance of the cultural ideas through which the event is apprehended (which in turn depends on the historical circumstances of the encounter itself). Generally speaking, they argue, when native peoples associate the arriving whites with key figures in their cosmology and ritual practices, as occurred in Hawaii, their advent acquires a deeper meaning and provokes revaluations in the cultural system. But when the whites are associated with mythical figures of little importance, or without much significance in ritual life, the initial impact of this encounter on the symbolic system is less pronounced. In Papua New Guinea, for example, the whites first appeared to the Bosavi in a place without much mythical or ritual meaning: hence their arrival was considered an isolated event. For the Huli, though, the whites were associated with sacred sites and the *dama* spirits, central beings in their cosmology and ritual activities, because they had approached from a specific location (285–87).

The setting of the encounter is fundamental to determining not only which classificatory categories are used, but also the subsequent actions. The case of the Etoro from the same region of Papua New Guinea illustrates this point. According to their origin myth, the creator heroes gave birth to both white-skinned and dark-skinned children. They subsequently left with the light-skinned children, also taking a number of strange items, later associated with clothing, metal tools, and other Western goods. When the colonial patrol set up to explore the region arrived in the 1930s, offering metal objects in an attempt to lure the Etoro, the latter assumed that the creator heroes were returning. Their creation myth told that the world would end when these beings returned to the place of origin. Hence the Etoro wanted the whites to go away, desiring as little contact with them as possible. The offer of metal objects had the opposite effect to what the patrol members had expected (Schieffelin 1991, 64–66). Similar examples can be found in tropical South America. As I have already mentioned, during the expeditions to pacify the Arara, the identification of the whites with the Kayapó—real-life enemies of the Arara—led the latter to associate whites with the primordial enemies described in their origin myth. As a result, the Arara avoided any kind of encounter (Teixeira-Pinto 2000).

Synthesizing their findings, Schieffelin and Crittenden (1991a) suggest that the initial encounters between cultures involve at least three dimensions: "existential," "sociocultural," and "historical," the latter two coinciding with those analyzed by Sahlins (1981, 1985) in his study on the encounter between the Hawaiians and Captain Cook. For the authors, the existential dimension refers to "the raw shock of Otherness" (Schieffelin and Crittenden 1991, 4), which, although especially relevant in situations of first contact, "is present to some extent in all encounters with other people" (Sartre 1966, cited in Schieffelin and Crittenden 1991b, 4). Moreover, "The full impact of the experience is usually short-lived, since cultural categories are quickly marshaled to rationalize it" (Schieffelin and Crittenden 1991b, 4). The second, "sociocultural" dimension refers precisely to this operation, since the encounter is "always shaped by the local social and political structures and framed in prevailing cultural values, categories and understandings" (5). The historical dimension emerges when we consider the importance of contingencies for this process of categorization, revealing "how particular accidents of circumstance, structures of relationship, particular individual personalities, and differing agendas are involved in shaping a set of events at a particular time" (5).

As these authors observe—and as I briefly illustrated at the start of this introduction with the examples of the Wari', the Yanomami, and the Arara— the fact that the cultural categories chosen to classify the new figures and their actions are largely determined by contingent factors leads to a dynamic process of transformations. This is the phenomenon analyzed by Sahlins in his study of Cook's arrival in Hawaii. Sahlins (1981, 1985) argues that events tend to provoke structural transformations; in other words, earlier classifications are revised, displacing the meaning of some of them and producing a different arrangement of categories that become related in new ways. In Hawaii, for example, the relationships between chiefs and commoners, and between men and women, became redefined by their relationship with Europeans (Sahlins 1981, 35). As we shall see later, the same kind of process occurred among the Wari' in the context of the relationship between coinhabitants, foreigners, and enemies.[17] At each historical moment we are faced by a "structure of the conjuncture," a synthesis between structure and event (Sahlins 1981, 33, 38). To understand Sahlins's proposal, we need to note that *all* structures are conjunctural. The idea of an a priori structure, the starting point for transformations, would only be possible if the encounter with Europeans comprised a founding moment of their history. This is not the case, however. As Sahlins observes, "The same kind of cultural change, externally induced yet indigenously orchestrated, has been going on for millennia" (Sahlins 1985, viii).[18] What the arrival of the whites on the scene appears to imply is that this change, though of the same kind, acquires another dimension.

DIFFERENCE

Although we have examined some of the reasons for the asymmetry in the encounter between native peoples and whites, a central question remains if we wish to comprehend this phenomenon adequately in the context of the New World. This concerns the productivity of the notion of difference for its inhabitants. I shall discuss the issue briefly here, returning to it in more detail in chapter 4 and the conclusion. As Lévi-Strauss argues (1991), the real conflict in this encounter of worldviews resides in how each people conceive and deal with difference. On the one hand, the Europeans valued—and even obsessed over—identity, either wishing to transform the Indians into equals (echoing the conceptual importance of "identical twins" in Indo-European mythology) or destroy them completely. This applied to Columbus, for example. According to Todorov, the explorer wanted the Indians to be like himself, "unconsciously and ingenuously assimilationist. . . . The desire to make the Indians adopt the customs of the Spanish is never accompanied by justifications; after all, it is entirely logical" (1983, 41). On the other hand, the Indians manifested a structural need for difference, an interest in precisely what made the European invaders distinct.

However, it is crucial to emphasize that this difference was preserved by the indigenous peoples in a very particular form, one that at first suggests a convergence between the actions of the Europeans and those of the natives. In other words, while the former wanted to transform the Indians into replicas of themselves, the latter seemed happy and willing to accept the project of the invaders. Like the Europeans, the Indians seem to have wanted to annul this difference; yet they did so in the opposite direction, since instead of wishing the Europeans to become like them, they apparently wanted to transform themselves into Europeans. Examining this kind of phenomena in his study of Tupinambá conversion to Christianity, Viveiros de Castro asks: "So why did the savages want to be like us? . . . Which religion and which system of beliefs were these that contained within themselves the desire for their own perdition?" (1992a, 26; 2002, 193–94). The answer encountered by the author lies not in the apparent eccentricity of the native logic, but in the concept of culture used by ourselves in analyzing their customs. In his words, "Our usual idea of culture projects an anthropological landscape peopled by marble statues. . . . We believe that every society tends to persist in its own being—culture being the reflexive form of this being—and that violent and massive pressure is needed for it to become deformed and transform. . . . But perhaps for societies founded on the *relation with the other*, rather than *coincidence with self*, where relations predominate over substance, none of this makes the least bit of sense" (1992a, 26–27; see also 2002, 195).[19]

While indigenous peoples wanted to be like Europeans, they wanted to become so in their own way—and had no wish to remain so forever. This point highlights a radical divergence in the way in which the two cultural logics deal with difference. As Viveiros de Castro (1992a, 2002) noted, what really surprised the missionaries was the "inconstancy of the savage soul": the rapid way in which the indigenous peoples returned to their old customs. For indigenous peoples, difference means a difference of position: the possibility of experiencing this other position—which involves transforming oneself into an other in order to acquire the other's point of view—does not imply erasing this difference. On the contrary, the transformation is only desirable when reversible; though, again, this reversibility does not presume the existence of an original point of view or culture to which one must return. Just as shamans transform into animals to acquire a supplementary capacity, derived precisely from this alteration, so indigenous peoples wanted to turn into whites. I return to this point in the book's conclusion.

CHANGE, VIOLENCE, AND FORGETTING

The Wari', as far back as they can remember and until the period of pacification, were always warriors, and the killer had an important social role, especially in the definition of gender relations. They did not wage war among themselves, only with Indians from other ethnic groups who were invariably classified as enemies. From the beginning of the 1900s, the Wari', especially people from the OroNao' subgroup, were left practically without enemies to attack, since their neighbors had been exterminated by the whites or had fled to remote areas in the attempt to survive. Living on the shores of small rivers and creeks, up until then unfrequented by the whites, the Wari' kept themselves relatively immune to this invasion. As they did not maintain peaceful exchange relations with any other indigenous group, neither did they experience the known effects of indirect contact with whites, such as the access to tools and other goods, or the suffering from epidemics caused by unknown diseases. However, the disappearance of their enemies became a serious problem. The men went as far as to say that they were turning into women, since they could not become full men without being able to acquire the status of a killer.

When the whites finally reached their territory, the Wari' delighted in the possibility of resuming their warfare expeditions. And they did so immediately. According to them, these new enemies arrived with peaceful intentions, ready to offer presents, and in military terms were completely incapable. They lacked guns and simulated rifle shots with slaps on their thighs, which made them easy prey for the Wari'.

The situation changed after the 1940s with the second rubber boom, when the rubber tappers penetrated in large numbers into the more remote area occupied by the Wari'. At this time, especially from 1950 onward, the Wari' began to be killed en masse, sometimes with machine guns, just before dawn while still asleep in their houses. In chapters 2 and 3, I reproduce the narratives of some of these episodes. Occasionally, the whites stayed near the site of the massacre for several days with the aim, the Wari' say, of preventing them from taking the corpses so that they could provide them with an adequate funeral through ingestion. During this period they were filled with hatred of the whites and lived on the run, sometimes unable to make swiddens. Even so, after a period of mourning, they left in search of whites, any whites, in order to exact revenge.

What we can conclude from this brief exposition is that the invasion of the whites provoked two opposite types of effects on Wari' warfare: its initial suppression, due to the disappearance of their enemies, and its later intensification with the beginning of the massacres in the villages. I should make clear that the intensification does not refer to the emergence of internal warfare, since the Wari' never made war among themselves, but to an increase in the deaths from killings by whites, and the Wari' expeditions to these new enemies in search of vengeance.[20] However, the transformation in warfare was rather qualitative than quantitative. As we shall see in chapter 2, Wari' warfare was conceptually very different from the warfare practiced by whites since it took place between full subjects, whether animals (cinegetic predation was a kind of warfare), Indian enemies, or, later, white enemies. The idea of exterminating a naturalized, dehumanized other was inconceivable for them.[21] The other had to exist as a subject for the act of killing to be productive. Killing enemies was not intended to annihilate them, but to enable the extraction of symbolic resources for the constitution of persons and relations, a central objective of warfare. As Fausto observed (2001, 331): "The capacity to extract much from so little seems to be a general fact of Amerindian warfare, distinguishing it radically from the war of extermination or conquest. . . . The logic of quality prevails over that of quantity."

From the Wari' point of view, the massacres clearly indicated that there was a different logic at work. This war was different. The terms used by a man to describe that moment dispense with the need for additional explanations: "It was as though we were animals, as though the whites saw us as peccaries."

In terms of internal social relations, the invasion of the whites initially provoked an increase in the tension between the Wari' subgroups, a consequence of the first experiences of alien diseases, which they attributed to sorcery or poisoning caused by foreigners. The suspicions led to retaliations through the same methods and temporary ruptures in contact between the groups involved (see Conklin 1989, 96–97).[22]

The postpacification epidemics inaugurated a new phase with the recognition of the whites' pathogenic qualities. The Wari' were victims of epidemics of influenza, pneumonia, and measles, which, added to the massacres, wiped out an estimated two-thirds of the population. People died in their dozens and the survivors, weak and sick, found themselves unable to provide the dead with a funeral, abandoning the bodies of their kin to the vultures, which repulsed and saddened them even further. In contrast to the armed attacks, the Wari' did not perceive these illnesses as an active aggression but as something involuntary, caused, among other things, by emanations from white people's bodies (especially through odors).[23] They traced the cause of their suffering to taking the wrong decisions: for approaching the whites too closely, or failing to move away quickly when they felt ill, or refusing the medicines that were offered to them.

All of these themes are examined in depth during the course of the book. My wish here is to call attention to what seems to be a strange forgetting of violence, allied with a pronounced valorization of the positive effects of the encounter with the whites. Paletó once told me that had they accepted the invitations of the whites from the outset, today they would be like the Makurap (a Tupi group of Rondônia), completely white. According to him, the first whites were good: rather than desiring conflict, they merely wanted to persuade the Wari' to live with them. They came with many gifts, but the Wari' killed them. So the whites became angry and decided to wage war. The Wari' had not thought straight in attacking them: if they had, they would be whites now and would know how to build airplanes.

Without wishing to deny that some whites encountered during the initial period had indeed peaceful intentions, some of these contacts, as we shall see in chapter 3, involved episodes of capturing Wari' women and children, whose violence is downplayed in their narratives while the benefits are high-lighted, especially the metal tools and other objects that the women who es-caped were able to bring with them. The narratives also show the fascination over the women's accounts of the life of whites, in particular their strange foods.

Undoubtedly we should entertain the possibility that this peculiar per-ception of the initial encounters is the outcome of comparing them with later events, characterized by the massacre of entire villages. But it is also clear that we are faced with an active manipulation of forgetting, a phenome-non already observed with numerous other Amerindian peoples. As various studies show, forgetting is a central factor in Amazonia, not only to instill the necessary separation between the living and the dead but also to enable the continual appropriation of cultural goods from the outside, such as songs, objects, myths, and technologies.[24] In these cases, forgetting had the effect of making the "alterity entirely their own," as Fausto has demonstrated (2007a, 91) in analyzing the appropriation of Christian symbols by the Guarani (see too Santos-Granero 2007, 61).

This is not exactly the case of the Wari'. Most of the time they affirm the alien origin of a wide range of cultural goods, including maize beer, the bev-erage central to social life, as well as funeral song and Christianity (see Vilaça 2009). In the specific case of white technology, its superiority is usually as-sociated in Wari' narratives with a wrong choice on their part. This is clear in Paletó's statement concerning the refusal to accept the overtures of the first whites (and that today they would know how to build airplanes) and the ex-planations, mentioned above, for the heavy mortality caused by epidemics.

The association of the technological inferiority of the Indians with a bad choice is a common theme in Amazonian mythology. The Yanesha example illustrates this. According to Santos-Granero (2007, 55), both the technologi-cal capacity of whites ("the white men have extraordinary creative powers and can invent marvelous things, such as cars and other machines") and their reproductive capacity ("the white men multiply, while the Yanesha grow fewer each day") are attributed in the myth to the wrong behavior shown by the Indians in response to the demands posed by the divinities (in contrast to the correct behavior of the whites). Among the Barasana, we find a formu-lation shared by numerous other groups: a culture hero gives the Indians the choice of firearms or bows. They choose the latter, leaving the whites with the former, whose greater effectiveness was unknown to them (see S. Hugh-Jones 1988, 144).

Viveiros de Castro (1983, 252–62; 2000b, 49–54; 2002, 203–5) observes that these myths comprise a variant of a set of myths called by Lévi-Strauss (1994 [1964]) "myths of the short life." In these, the origin of mortality is associated with a bad choice arising from an error related to the use of one of the senses (either not hearing well, or speaking too much, and so on). According to Viveiros de Castro, the mythic motive of weapons involves a "modulation of this code. Instead of errors related to the senses, we find a lack of good sense" (Viveiros de Castro 2000b, 52). Although the Wari' do not strictly speaking have a myth of this type (see chapter 7 for a discussion of this theme), as in the narratives mentioned above, mythic fragments such as the walking baskets recalled by Paletó in order to explain the agency of white people's objects relate directly to the theme of the bad choice.

Rather than being related to the technological superiority of the whites, or the exterior origin of their cultural goods, Wari' forgetting seems to be related specifically to overlooking the violence of these enemies. What the Wari' seek to forget is precisely the predatory capacity of whites (who had no firearms, who were full of good intentions). In this way, they make this capacity their own, positively marking their own action, not only in the first encounters with whites but in the later developments.[25] This is not a dispute for power, as appears to have been the case with the Yanesha, who, Santos-Granero (2007, 58) tells us, "seem to omit any suggestion that the others are superior." They "obliterate power differences that place them in a subordinate position. . . . By forgetting, the Yanesha disempower the others to empower themselves" (62). In the case of the Wari', the issue is ontological. In the context of an extended conception of humanity, which includes animals and enemies, predation comprises a core differentiating act, momentarily separating predators and prey and classifying these two positions as human and nonhuman, respectively. Assuming the active role in the act of predation forms the privileged means of making oneself human. I return to this theme in chapter 2.[26]

There is more, though. As I suggested earlier, forgetting the violence inflicted on themselves is also related to a highly positive view of transformation. In other words, everything experienced in the past is forgotten in the face of the outcomes in the present. Gow's ethnographic studies (1991, 2001) on the history of the Piro provide an excellent example. According to Gow (2001, 6), although enslavement and many instances of brutality and injustice meant the process of change was difficult and painful for the Piro, they generally perceive contact with whites as positive, since it allowed them to turn from Indians of the forest into civilized people. And the author asks: "But if they did experience this transition as disastrous, why was that memory not transmitted to their descendents. . . . Memory is selective, but this looked like collective amnesia of a startling kind. . . . I reasoned that Piro people could only act in this way if they experienced their being in the world as inherently transformational" (9).[27]

Among the Wari' too, not only does the violence involved in the process of contact with the whites appear to have been forgotten, the cultural transformations set in motion by living alongside whites are also seen as highly positive. The Wari' continually astonish me by the way they systematically ignore, or sometimes even positively assess, everything that strikes me as a "cultural disaster." For example, they tranquilly remark that their children and grandchildren do not know the myths or how to conduct the festivals that were once so important in their social life. Nowadays, young people want white festivals, fueled by *forró*, a musical genre present throughout this region of Brazil. In response, older people simply say, "That's what they're like," or "That's their way." Such changes seem to be easily comprehended as inherent to life, necessary to its continuity. I shall return to this theme throughout the book.

To conclude this section, it is important to stress that by citing the viewpoint held by some Indians today, I do not want to relativize the brutal, irresponsible, and criminal way in which they were treated in the past, and in some cases are still treated today.[28] As Sahlins emphasized at the start of his essay on the cultural transformations experienced by some native peoples due to the so-called advance of the West: "What follows, therefore, should not be taken as a sentimental optimism that ignores the agony of entire peoples caused by disease, violence, slavery . . . and other miseries which western 'civilization' has spread across the planet. Here, on the contrary, I offer a reflection on the complexity of these forms of suffering, especially in the case of those societies that were able to extract from this ill fate their present conditions of existence" (Sahlins 1997, 53).

THE RESEARCH

Around 2,800 Wari' live in seven villages next to the indigenous posts run by FUNAI, or in the smaller villages linked to the posts. These villages continue to multiply as a consequence of the movement of dispersion coordinated by the Wari' and encouraged by FUNAI. Today just one village is administrated by the Indians themselves: Sagarana, a former religious mission located within the officially demarcated Wari' territory, previously run by the Catholic diocese of Guajará-Mirim. Today all of the five Wari' indigenous areas are officially demarcated and registered: Ribeirão, Lage, Pacaás Novos, Rio Negro–Ocaia, and Sagarana (maps 1 and 2).

My fieldwork was conducted in three phases. The first period totaled eight months between 1986 and 1989. I spent most of this time at the Rio Negro–Ocaia village and made some visits to the Tanajura, Santo André (a.k.a. Pacaás Novos), and Lage villages.[29] At the end of this period, in 1989, I handed in my master's thesis at the Graduate Program in Social Anthropology of the Museu Nacional, Universidade Federal do Rio de Janeiro. This work was published three years later.[30]

At the start of 1990, having already begun my doctorate, I returned to the Wari' and stayed at the Rio Negro–Ocaia village for two months. Following the birth of my son Francisco at the end of the same year, I was only able to resume fieldwork in 1992: accompanied by him, I stayed with the Wari' for a total of six months between 1992 and 1994. I returned again in 1995 and 1996 for quick visits of about a month each. During this second phase of research, I also lived for most of the time at the Rio Negro–Ocaia village, while spending a few weeks visiting the Lage, Ribeirão, Santo André, and Tanajura villages, as well as Sagarana, located on the Guaporé River. These trips were undertaken in order to meet and interview some of the protagonists of the episodes of pacification discussed in the book. All of the testimonies were recorded in the native language and translated by myself into Portuguese.

In December 1992, Paletó, my Wari' father, and his son Abrão, sixty and thirty years old, respectively, at the time, came to stay in Rio de Janeiro for two months. This proved to be one of the most intense periods of fieldwork I have ever experienced. Paletó seemed compelled to speak, narrate myths, and tell stories (we recorded thirty-six hours of cassette tapes). He asked to be recorded and told me to drink coffee when, already late at night, my eyes would droop as he spoke. Some of the best versions of the myths used in the book were obtained during this period, along with various war narratives.

The third phase of research began in 2001 and continues today through annual visits to the Wari' lasting about a month, and some trips undertaken with them, accompanied by the anthropologist Beth Conklin, to areas where they made villages, cleared swiddens, and trekked widely before pacification. My current research is linked to two projects: one of them looks to study Wari' notions of space and locality, involving the production of maps of

Map 1. Brazil.

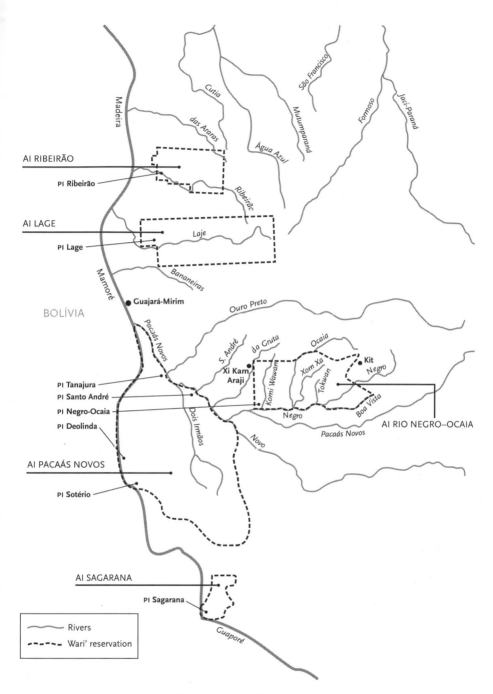

Map 2. Detail of facing page.
Wari' reservations and indigenous posts (PI).

traditionally occupied areas. Some of the data from this research have been included in the book, especially in the form of notes, enriching the information obtained in the 1990s. The second project, to which I have been devoting special attention, aims to study the conversion of the Wari' to Christianity.

THE BOOK

The book is divided into three parts: "Other Becoming," "In Myth," and "We Want People for Ourselves: Pacification." In the first part, I describe and discuss the ways in which the Wari' conceive and experience alterity, concentrating in particular on an analysis of the positions occupied by foreigners (chapter 1, "The Foreigner"), enemies (chapter 2, "The Enemy"), and whites (chapter 3, "The White Enemy") in this conceptual system.

In the book's second part, the native conceptions of otherness are re-examined, this time by analyzing a system composed of four myths that explore the three positions of otherness mentioned above, as well as the position of the affine/brother-in-law. Hence this part is divided into "The White Enemy" (chapter 4), "The Foreigner, the Dead" (chapter 5), "The Enemy" (chapter 6), and "The Brother-in-Law" (chapter 7). The partial overlapping of the chapter titles to parts I and II is designed to emphasize precisely the complementarity of these analyses, which evince a logical continuity between Wari' myths and historical narratives. The presentation and discussion of these myths is also intended to situate them within the wider context of the mythology of South American lowlands Indians, analyzed by Lévi-Strauss in the *Mythologiques*, particularly in the first volume, *The Raw and the Cooked* (Lévi-Strauss 1994 [1964]), and in one of the supplementary volumes, *The Story of Lynx* (Lévi-Strauss 1991). As mentioned earlier, the latter deals specifically with the productivity of the notion of alterity in Amerindian thought, closely examining the conceptions relating to whites.

The third part focuses on describing the various stages of the pacification process. Although the descriptions are based on the Wari' perspective of the encounters, chapter 8, "The Motives of the Whites," which opens this part of the book, presents the facts as described in the documents and narratives produced by the whites. This procedure is intended to help the reader situate the events narrated in the subsequent chapters within a wider historical context. Chapter 9, "The Widening River: Contact with the OroNao' of the Whites," examines the first peaceful contact between the whites and a Wari' subgroup that had been isolated from the rest for around thirty years by the

Pacaás Novos River. According to some people, this river was widened over-night by a torrential downpour; others claim that bank erosion caused by the increased use of motorboats was responsible. Chapter 10, " 'The Enemy Says He's OroNao' ': Contact with the OroWaram, OroWaramXijein, and OroMon," focuses on the second stage of pacification when the OroNao', who had already been pacified, accompanied the whites on the expedition to contact kin they had not seen for many years. Because they arrived along with the whites, they were taken for them, although they insisted, speaking in the Wari' language, that they were OroNao'. News of the encounter spread among the members of these subgroups in the form of the phrase that provides the title to this chapter, which sometimes varied slightly: "The whites are crazy. Now they say they are OroNao'." Chapter 11, "The Great Expedition: Contact with the OroNao', OroEo, and OroAt on the Negro and Ocaia Rivers," examines the last and largest of the pacification expeditions. This included the participation of national SPI officers (rather than regional officers, as in the previous cases), a Catholic priest, and various other whites recruited at the last minute in Guajará-Mirim. For reasons to be explained later, the missionaries of the New Tribes Mission, who had led all of the other expeditions, were absent.

In the conclusion I discuss how the categories of otherness analyzed during the course of the book are manifested today now that the Wari' have come to live next to the FUNAI posts, thereby becoming the coresidents of foreigners and enemies. There I aim to reply, albeit briefly, to a question posed insistently throughout the book (and to the Wari' by myself): Why did they decide to live alongside the whites? And why do they say that they themselves are becoming white?

PART I

OTHER BECOMING

CHAPTER 1

The Foreigner

The priest asked, "What tribe are you from?"
"My tribe is OroEo. My kin are OroEo."
—Mijain (1992)

The Wari' have no word for the group as a whole—what we would call a tribe or, more recently, an ethnic group. Pakaa-Nova was the name given to them by travelers exploring the area of Pacaás Novos River in the nineteenth and twentieth centuries. Wari' is used by the whites living with them: FUNAI agents, missionaries, and anthropologists. It is also used by members of the group to refer to themselves—or any "Indian"—when talking to whites. The name Wari' originates from the word *wari'*, "we," an inclusive first-person plural pronoun, which also means "human beings," "people."

The broadest ethnic unit defined by themselves is what I shall call a subgroup. There is no generic term for subgroup, only for "someone from another subgroup," *tatirim*, which I translate as foreigner. Each subgroup has a name: OroNao', OroNao' of the Whites, OroEo, OroAt, OroMon, OroWaram, and OroWaramXijein. Sometimes the Wari' refer to another two subgroups: the OroJowin and the OroKao'OroWaji. *Oro* is a collectivizing prefix translatable as "people" or "group." These subgroup names translate, in order, as "bat people," "bat people of the whites," "belch people," "bone people," "feces people," "spider monkey people," "other spider monkey people," "capuchin monkey people," and "unripe-eating people."

As Mijain reveals in the epigraph above, the Wari' use their concept of subgroup to translate our concept of tribe. This was how they identified themselves—insisting on the fact that they comprise distinct units—when they decided to approach the whites during the episodes of what the government agents called "pacification." This fact reveals the importance that the

Wari' attribute to these units, presenting themselves to outsiders as a set of groups rather than a single group, a level of reality that they know exists, but prefer not to emphasize.[1]

ORIGINS OF THE SUBGROUPS

No single discourse emerges when the Wari' are asked about the origin of the subgroups, yet a historical dimension is always present even when they turn to myth to explain their remote past. The core idea is that the subgroups did not originate simultaneously; rather, some were formed from others as the result of divisions and migrations.

The myth to which I (and the Wari') refer does not center on the origin of the subgroups; instead, the theme is developed as an appendix to just some of its versions (see chapter 6 for an analysis of the Nanananana myth). These versions recount that the different subgroups arose from couples formed by Wari' women, survivors of a deluge, and enemy men, the couples later spreading out across geographical space.

Rather than each subgroup deriving from one of these couples, as we might suppose, the subgroups are usually conceived to have emerged from each other gradually. This does not imply, though, that one of the subgroups gave rise to all the others. For the Wari', what matters is not the precise historical moment when a subgroup emerged as a physical entity (a set of people), but its genesis as a social unit determined from the outside. In other words, more important than knowing, for example, whether the OroNao' emerged from the OroEo or directly from the descendents of the marriages between the Wari' and their enemies, is knowing that they were recognized as a distinct unit by members of another group—a unit that only really came into existence at the moment of this recognition. It is this event that leads to a group acquiring a name, given by people from outside based on some feature peculiar to the group.

Thus, the OroNao' received their name—from another, unspecified Wari' subgroup—because the men stayed awake at night like bats, clutching their war clubs, ready to strike anyone who tried to have sex with their wives. The OroAt liked to eat bones. The OroEo belched after singing and speaking. According to some people, the OroJowin were likened to capuchin monkeys because their penises were always erect. The OroKao'OroWaji had sex with very young ("unripe") girls. The OroMon defecated near their houses and were also known as OroMin (*min'*: tapir) because, like tapirs, they abducted women.

The subgroups do not just come from the remote historical or mythical past, though. Some were created recently, such as the OroWaraXirim and the OroNao' of the Whites. The history of the OroWaraXirim is interesting and provides a good illustration of the emergence of the subgroups as a historical process founded on an externally recognized alterity. Until 1992 I had never heard of this subgroup. One day in Ribeirão village, a man who previously called himself OroMon told me he was actually OroWaraXirim. I asked him which subgroup this was, since I had never heard it mentioned, and he explained.

Everything began with his father, when he (my interlocutor) was still a child. Unlike the other OroMon, who changed their village site constantly in typical Wari' fashion, his father insisted on remaining at a particular locality with his family. Every year, people would go to his house to invite him to live with them elsewhere. He always refused. After a while, these people began to call them—the father and his family—OroWaraXirim (*wara* meaning "old," and *xirim* meaning "house"): the "old house people." I asked him whether the OroWaraXirim had become extinct with his father's death. He replied yes, to some extent, though the main factor in this disappearance was pacification, which had taken place during this interval and altered everything. In other words, the OroWaraXirim had lacked sufficient time to reproduce and constitute themselves as a group extending beyond the nuclear family. It was the aborted beginnings of a new subgroup. Most of the people I asked had never heard of the OroWaraXirim, a fact showing that the genesis of a subgroup is gradual, acquiring substance through its recognition by others over time.

The OroNao' of the Whites comprise a different case. At the end of the nineteenth century, some OroNao' families, as well as some OroEo, OroAt, and OroJowin, decided to live on the affluents of the left shore of the Pacaás Novos River, an area visited by the Wari' for hunting and fishing, but not previously used as an area to live. Some people claim that this relocation was prompted by the constant attacks by bats inflicted on the Wari' on the right shore. They wanted to escape these annoying—and sometimes fatal—bites, and so resolved to leave. After crossing, they initially continued to communicate with the Wari' still living on the right shore, facilitated by the fact the Pacaás Novos River was easy to traverse. Between the mid-1920s and the mid-1930s, though, the whites started to use this river intensely, effectively preventing the Wari' from crossing. Three decades passed before these Oro-Nao', who comprised the largest portion of the now isolated group, came into contact again with the Wari' from the other subgroups, who had continued to interact with each other. This was only possible thanks to the whites, who had previously prevented them from traversing the river. The first peaceful contact between the Wari' and the whites involved precisely these OroNao' from the left shore, and it was through them, who served as guides and interpreters during the pacification process, that the whites contacted the other Wari'. Or, more importantly from the Wari' point of view, as we shall see later, it was through the whites that these OroNao' were able to regain contact with the others. The Wari' name OroNao' of the Whites was given to them by the other Wari', who saw them arrive, after such a long time absent, in the company of the whites, as though white themselves. From their own point of view they are simply OroNao'.

If new subgroups can emerge through historical circumstances, then clearly others may disappear. This was the case of the OroJowin and Oro-Kao'OroWaji subgroups. Once distinct units, today they number a handful of people, who either identify themselves with one of these groups, or claim to be OroMon, OroNao', or OroWaramXijein. The OroJowin lived on the upper courses of the Laje, Ribeirão, Mutumparaná, and Formoso rivers in a mountainous region. Some people suggest they are the descendents of the enemies who married the Wari' in the Nanananana myth and that they lived in caves. The OroJowin dwindled in number until just a dozen adults remained; these joined the OroNao' and the OroMon. At first I thought that this extermination had been caused by the whites, but the Wari' rejected this idea. Some said that the OroJowin had simply died out without reproducing. Others claimed they were killed by OroNao' sorcery. The demise of the OroKao'OroWaji, who lived next to the OroJowin, is explained in similar fashion. I am unsure when these subgroups effectively vanished, nor am I sure that the whites had no involvement in their disappearance. What matters, though, is that the Wari' conceive the extinction and emergence of subgroups in the same way: as something that happens in the course of events.[2]

Other myths not directly concerned with the origins of subgroups touch on this topic implicitly, providing an insight into how the Wari' comprehend this process of internal differentiation. One of them is the Oropixi' myth describing the origin of the whites (see chapter 4). As this myth shows, the foreigner is above all a kinsperson and a coinhabitant (coinciding categories, as we shall see) who fell out with the group and moved away. The close relations of everyday commensality and living together are replaced by relations of ritual exchange—festivals—as an essential element in the relationship between subgroups. The foreigner is a pre-enemy. The process of internal differentiation, or "foreignization," forms part of the process of "enemization," which may occur when the rupture is more radical, involving the total cessation of exchanges of festivals and women. Nonetheless, this process is still reversible; in other words, people who become enemies can be reincorporated if they resume exchange relations.

Consequently, one of the key features of the subgroup is precisely its historical determination, a unit circumscribed in time and dependent on the relations sustained with other similar units. The subgroups are not ephemeral, though: the genealogies show that people situated three generations above present-day adults were already classified as OroNao', OroEo, and so on, revealing the persistence of these subgroups over time.

OCCUPATION OF SPACE: NAMED AREAS (*XITOT*)

In geographical terms, each subgroup was constituted by a set of local groups of varied composition, each occupying a named swidden area, or *xitot*. The local groups circulated through these areas, remaining in a location for one to five years. A set of named areas located in the same region formed a subgroup's territory. Before turning to this wider territory, it is worth examining the minor units, the named areas, and how they were occupied.

From the earliest recalled times to pacification, the Wari' have lived on Amazonian terra firme, usually in villages located close to small creeks, far from the big rivers. They never traveled by water, sticking exclusively to forest trails. Village sites were chosen according to their suitability for maize swiddens, their main crop.

Xitot is the Wari' name for swidden. It means not only the cultivated land but also any potential sites within the forest where maize can be planted. The Wari' do not conceive these areas as part of the forest, called *mi* or *nahwarak*, but as something separate and to a certain extent opposed to it. A swidden area is identified primarily through its vegetation. The most typical *xitot* species are, for the Wari', the aricuri palm (*torot*, in Wari': *Cocos* sp.); the pupunha palm (*temem': Guilielma speciosa*); the *to* tree, possibly the calabash tree (*Crescentia cujete*—Bignoniaceae); the *nain* palm (*Astrocaryum* sp.); the

karapakan (*Ficus* sp.); and the *pija* and *aro* trees, which I was unable to identify. Another feature of *xitot* is the fertility of the usually dark colored soil.

All the *xitot* are named, even those left unoccupied for one or two generations. As a result, adult men, particularly elders, possess a mental map of the
traditional territory based on the localization of each of these *xitot*, some
of them cleared and planted in the past by themselves. Others are known
because their parents and grandparents lived there. Some sites closer to the
current villages are occupied for seasonal periods when families clear, burn,
and plant the swiddens (September and October) and later during harvesting. They are also used as a base to gather Brazil nuts from nearby areas during January and February.

Living at the same location was more common, the Wari' say, before the
influx of metal axes. Prior to the latter, they would clear the swiddens earlier
in the year when it was still raining. The swiddens were smaller and only the
lower vegetation was cleared, along with the branches of taller trees. Fire was
used to clear the rest. Some people would use the same site two years running in order to avoid the work involved in clearing the swidden. Old maize
stalks and weeds were cleared before burning.

After metal axes began to be obtained during raids on white settlements
in the 1920s, agricultural work became much easier. Changing *xitot* each year,
which implied building a new village, became more common. Once the swidden site had been chosen, the group of people who were set to live there—
not necessarily the same as the previous village—began felling, which today
takes place in the dry months of July and August. Before this work started,
though, they constructed temporary shelters, basically a covering of patauá
palm leaves (*Oenocarpus bataua*), which all of the village's future inhabitants
would use to sleep. When the old swidden was close enough, a wide path was
sometimes cleared between the two locations to facilitate the use of maize
still stored in the former village. Usually, though, the maize had already been
used up by this point in the yearly cycle, leaving only a stock for planting.
Sometimes even this maize was exhausted, meaning seeds had to be sought
from neighboring villages.

Each married man cleared his own swidden (which still happens today)
adjacent to those of the other village inhabitants. Young bachelors living
in the men's house sometimes also cleared their own swidden, planted by
their mothers and unmarried sisters. This practice was more frequent among
young men already set to marry and who had to ply their parents-in-law with

1. Planting maize. Rio Negro–Ocaia, 1987.

presents, including game and maize-based foods produced by their mothers and sisters. Once the swiddens were cleared, the Wari' spent a while in the forest fishing and hunting, waiting for the right time to burn the cleared areas, just before the start of the rains (fig. 1).

After burning the swiddens, they would wait some days for the rain to soften the ground for planting, an activity traditionally undertaken by women only (see Conklin 1989, 66). When the maize had sprouted, reaching around 10 centimeters, the Wari' moved away: people explained that if the maize was seen while growing, it would die before producing any cobs. The verb used to express this movement is *pixi'*, meaning "to relocate." The period spent away from the swidden is called *ka pixi' wa*, "relocating."

All the inhabitants of the new village left. Some people preferred to return to the former swidden site until it was time to return to the new site. However, this was not common practice since the stored maize had usually already been consumed, leaving nothing to eat. In general, the Wari' took off into the forest where different local groups could meet up and stay together until returning to their respective villages. They trekked through the forest until discovering a site where they could live temporarily. This often meant visiting distant areas of their territory, regions where they did not usually produce swiddens. Here they constructed proper houses rather than temporary shelters.

In the forest, the Wari' essentially lived off game and wild foods. Estimating from the maize cycle, they must have remained in the forest for about three months, the time needed for the first maize ("green maize") to ripen after planting.

The ripening of wild fruits such as *ara hotowa, korowan, ajiwan,* and *towa* (Portuguese: *caucho; Castilloa ulei.* Moraceae) was a sign that the maize cobs were ready to be eaten and that the interdiction on seeing the maize was over. "We should have looked at our maize by now! We've been eating Brazil nuts for too long," someone would exclaim. On their return, about half a day's trek from the village, two or more bachelors would tell the group to wait while they went to look at the maize. They spied from a distance on the path leading to the swiddens, avoiding getting too close. If the cobs were ripe, they would make a basket from leaves and collect a cob from each swidden to show to its owner.

Once back at the spot where the rest of the group was waiting, the men would say: "Your maize is ready! There's lots!" The sample cobs were roasted and eaten at the camp. The next day, everyone set off to the village. On arrival, the first thing they did was bathe. People say that the smell of sweat can cause the seeds to die. After bathing, the women would pick up their baskets and go to the swiddens to collect the maize. They made a big fire and immediately roasted a number of cobs to offer to the men. They stamped on the still very soft kernels and prepared maize drink, which would be sweet and "white as milk."

As I stated earlier, the swidden, *xitot,* is opposed to the forest, *nahwarak* or *mi'.* This single term designates not only a site where maize can be planted but also the mature swidden. But although swidden and forest houses are both called *xirim* (roof)—a term designating a single house and the set of houses in opposition to the surrounding area—the true houses are considered to be the swidden "roofs" storing the maize.[3] When asked: "Is that his house?", the reply may be simply: "That's where his maize is kept."

In mapping geographic space, the Wari' name only rivers and swiddens. Consequently, although villages have always been located next to a swidden, the site as a whole is called *xitot* rather than *xirim.* This implies the idea that houses are temporary, shifting locations, but *xitot* are permanent and always ready to be occupied some day. They are why people move around: the starting and ending point. The rest of their territory, for the Wari', is composed of paths, woods, forest, and mountain. While people can list the names of the swiddens where they lived, frequently citing the name of everyone who lived there, they seldom recall the exact places where villages were built while "fleeing from the maize," and much less the names of the people who lived in them.

In my view, the emphasis on the periods spent in the *xitot* is related to the symbolic importance of maize for the Wari'. More than a staple food, maize defines being human. Only human beings—*wari'*—know how to grow the crop and produce maize-based foods and drinks. For the Wari', there is a clear incompatibility between maize and animality. Indeed, shamans repel the animals that accompany them by sitting amid the smoke of burning maize. The swidden villages can be conceived, therefore, as the dwelling places par excellence for it is in them that the Wari' are fully human. If so, the time spent in the forest primarily implies a time spent wandering through the limits of humanity, a counterpoint that serves in constructing life in the *xitot* as a moment when sociability is exercised to the full.

COMPOSITION OF THE LOCAL GROUPS

My information on the composition of the groups that occupied the swidden villages is based on nineteen life stories, collected from people from the various subgroups (with the exception of the OroNao' of the Whites). The age of these informants varied between forty and eighty, meaning that the groups considered here are those that formed from around the 1920s onward. Hence, the material has a fairly precise time span, preventing us from making any conclusive inferences about village composition in earlier periods. The Wari' say that their villages were larger in ancestral times, but not too large, since they disliked living in crowds of people, unlike ourselves. In the 1950s, at the height of their persecution by whites, they were forced to live on the run, especially the subgroups located in more exposed regions, such as the OroNao' of the right bank, who took refuge in OroAt and OroEo territories. In the 1960s, the Wari' as a whole began to abandon the traditional villages to live near the houses of the pacification agents: the SPI (later FUNAI) employees and the missionaries.

The number of houses in a swidden village varied considerably. Some had just two houses, others up to nine. Along with these houses, *xirim*, inhabited by nuclear families, every village had a men's house, *kaxa'*, where young bachelors slept, married men met for informal talks, killers withdrew during reclusion, and festival guests slept. According to Dom Roberto Gomes de Arruda, who was active in the pacification of the Wari' on the Negro and Ocaia rivers, most of the houses were arranged in a single line, parallel to the shore of the nearest creek. Xi Kam Araji, a former OroNao' village that had been abandoned after a massacre some fifty years ago, had contained, according to the Wari' who accompanied me there in July 2007, four houses and a *kaxa'* arranged around a central clearing.

The typical house had a single pitched roof thatched with palm leaves, including assai (*Euterpe* sp.), which rose from close to the ground to a height of around 10 meters (figs. 2 and 3). Underneath, located parallel to the roof's lowest point, 1 meter above the ground, was a platform made from stilt palm (*Socratea exorrhiza*) about 12 meters long and 1.5 meters wide, running the entire length of the house. The lateral edges of the platform were lined with tree trunks: while sleeping, people would rest their heads on the trunk nearest to the lower part of the roof, using it like a pillow, with the

2. Wari' and whites in front of a precontact style Wari' house (in the back). Probably Ribeirão during the first half of the 1960s. (Photo by Geraldo Mendonça da Silva)

3. Contemporary house style. View of Rio Negro–Ocaia village, 2001.

back of their knees draped over another. Since this trunk formed one of the
platform's edges, they slept with their legs hanging over the ground below
(except when sleeping in fetal position). In the family houses, the platform
was covered by mats woven by the women. In the men's house, occupants
slept directly on top of the stilt palm bark. Another, smaller platform was
built under the roofs of the family houses to store maize in a cylindrical pile,
reaching some 4 meters in height.[4]

The composition of these local groups varied—the number of inhabitants oscillating from ten to fifty people—and generally centered on a group
of male or female siblings, meaning the pattern was not classifiable as either
virilocal or uxorilocal. Typically the group was formed by a group of brothers
married to a group of sisters, along with kin from both sides and their own
spouses. As polygyny was frequent, especially sororal polygyny, the nuclear
families occupying the different houses often comprised a man and his two
or three wives, plus their children. Although the Wari' say that a man takes
his wife to live in the same village as his kin—usually when the marriage is
consolidated—the frequency of men living with their parents-in-law is just
as high as that of men living with their own parents. The point is that, as we
have seen, the constitution of the local group varied almost on a year-by-year

basis, meaning that various types of residential patterns were experimented. In all events, the central nucleus of these clusters, which tended to be maintained over time, was the group of siblings.

The data on the localization of swiddens and rivers comes from the life histories of people born after 1910. This being the case, I presume that most of the swiddens, as well as the rivers mentioned, are places known to them personally. Although some people may have cited the names of swiddens they had never seen, it was clearly easier for them to recall those that they had actually visited, essentially those sites inhabited by the Wari' between 1920 and 1960 when pacification occurred.

I should also point out that the bulk of my field research was conducted with inhabitants of the Rio Negro–Ocaia village, most of whom are from the OroNao', OroEo, and OroAt subgroups. Consequently, I have much more information on swiddens and rivers situated in the areas formerly occupied by these subgroups. My data on the OroMon, OroWaram, and OroWaram-Xijein territories is reasonably complete, but I know almost nothing about the region occupied by the OroNao' of the Whites, on the affluents of the left bank of the Pacaás Novos River. Based on particular life histories—namely, the most complete from the nineteen I collected—I was able to infer the period when particular swiddens were occupied. I am reluctant to specify periods of less than a decade given the imprecise nature of the data.

The Wari' locate past swiddens along the entire course of the Laje, Ouro Preto, Santo André, Da Gruta, Negro, and Ocaia rivers, as well as the left bank of the upper Ribeirão River and the headwaters of the Mutumparaná and Formoso rivers. On the left shore of the Pacaás Novos, they occupied the Dois Irmãos and Novo rivers, along with the sources of some of the affluents of the right bank of the Mamoré River.

I was able to record fairly clearly defined territories for each subgroup (map 3). The swiddens located on the affluents of the left shore of the Ouro Preto River, and both shores of the Santo André and Da Gruta rivers, were occupied by local groups, mostly OroNao', who also occupied swiddens along the Komi Wawan River, a right bank affluent of the Negro.[5] The OroAt occupied both shores of the Ocaia River and some swiddens on the right shore of the Negro River above its confluence with the Ocaia. The OroEo lived mainly on the left shore of the upper course of the Ocaia and on the right

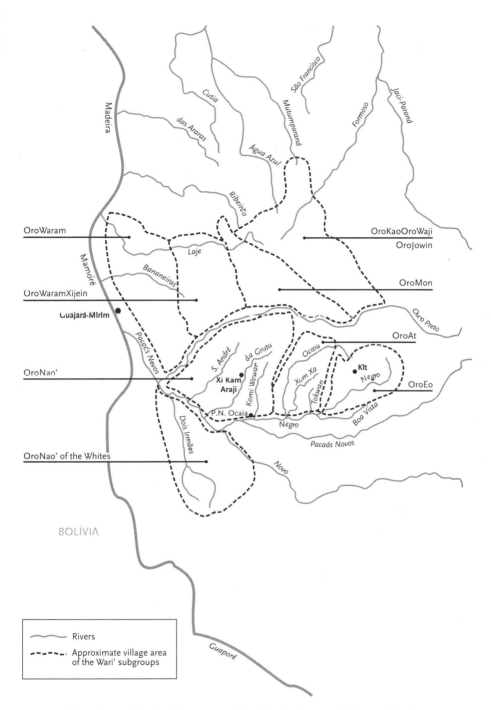

OroWaram

OroWaramXijein

Guajará-Mirim

OroNao'

OroNao' of the Whites

OroKaoOroWaji
OroJowin

OroMon

OroAt

OroEo

Madeira

Mamoré

Cutia

das Araras

São Francisco

Mutumparaná

Formoso

Jaci-Paraná

Agua Azul

Ribeirão

Laje

Bananeiras

Pacaás Novos

Dois Irmãos

S. André

da Gruta

Komi Wawun

Xum Xa

Ocaia

Tokwan

Xi Kam
Araji

P.N. Ocaia

Klt
Negro

Negro

Boa Vista

Pacaás Novos

Ouro Preto

Novo

BOLÍVIA

Guaporé

⌇ Rivers

▪ ▪ ▪ Approximate village area
of the Wari' subgroups

Map 3. Approximate village areas of the Wari' subgroups before pacification.

shore of the upper Negro. According to the oldest OroEo woman, in a more distant past they also lived on the left shore of the upper Negro, which was corroborated by the fact that they named the affluents located there. The OroNao' of the Whites occupied the affluents of the Dois Irmãos and Novo rivers on the left shore of the Pacaás Novos. As mentioned earlier, the latter river was traversed at the end of the nineteenth century by people from the OroNao' subgroup, as well as some people from the OroEo, OroAt, and OroJowin subgroups, who together formed the group later known as the OroNao' of the Whites.

The Laje River was mainly occupied along its left shore affluents. On the lower course affluents lived the OroWaram. The middle course affluents, especially the Tok Wi River, were home to the OroWaramXijein, while the upper course affluents were occupied by the OroMon. The OroJowin lived in the mountain uplands on the upper courses of the Laje, Ribeirão, Mutumparaná, and Formoso rivers. The swiddens of the OroKaoOroWaji were situated near those of the OroJowin, perhaps slightly further downriver. The OroKaoOroWaji also lived at swidden sites traditionally occupied by the OroWaramXijein. The swiddens on the right shore of the Ouro Preto were occupied by the OroWaram on the lower course, by the OroWaramXijein and OroKaoOroWaji on the middle course, and by the OroMon and OroJowin on the upper course (for a detailed map see Vilaça 2006).

One pattern that becomes clear is that the swiddens are mostly located on the shores of small rivers and creeks. Less than 10 percent of the 233 swiddens cited by my informants are found by the shores of the main rivers. This fact may have a natural explanation. Conklin (1989, 42) suggests that most of the patches of dark earth, *terra preta*, suited to the cultivation of maize are located near smaller rivers and tend to be much more scarce on the shores of the Pacaás Novos or other wide rivers. I lack the data to corroborate Conklin's findings. My interlocutors never expressed this association: whenever I asked them why they had not lived near larger rivers, they replied that they had actually lived near them, listing the names of some of the swiddens situated in such areas. At the same time, they recognized that most of their swiddens were located by smaller rivers.

Given that the whites invaded Wari' territory along the large rivers toward their affluents and headwaters, the location of swiddens on smaller river courses may well result too from this process of nonindigenous occupation. However, this does not invalidate Conklin's pedological argument, since even when they occupied the lower course of rivers such as the Ouro Preto, the Wari' chose to live almost exclusively on the smaller affluents rather than along the main river. The wave of nonindigenous occupation pushed the Wari' from the lower course affluents to those on the upper courses of these larger rivers. This upriver movement can also be understood as a relocation from the lowlands to the mountainous uplands: "The whites climbed the rivers, pushing the Wari' toward the mountains (serra)," people claimed. Indeed, the headwaters of many of these bigger rivers are located in the Serra dos Pacaás Novos, a continuation of the Serra dos Parecis.

My impression from listening to the Wari', though, is that living on smaller rivers was a choice rather than a natural or historical imposition. Living in such areas is highlighted by the Wari' themselves as a culturally distinctive trait, since they say: "We are Wari', we live in the forest; you are whites [wijam], you live by the water,"[6] while the idea of living along a large river— where, in fact, many live today—seems to provoke a certain aversion. Even if this is related to historical factors, I think, though, that their avoidance of larger rivers is rooted primarily in other kinds of cultural factors. The dead live underwater and, as we shall see, Wari' mythic discourse suggests that excessive water is related to the possibility of confusing the worlds of the living and the dead. Hence, as I discuss later, although connected to historical variants, the classification of whites as beings who occupy large bodies of water is also associated with mythic and/or cosmological dimensions.

When discussing these historical migrations from the river mouths to the upland headwaters under pressure from the whites, the Wari' also refer to a much earlier movement in the opposite direction: from the mountains to the lower river courses. A number of people stated that the Wari' originally came from OroEo territory, on the upper course of the Negro River. From there, they migrated along the courses of the Ocaia, Santo André, Da Gruta, Ouro Preto, and Laje rivers. Leaving the headwaters, they moved downriver, occupying the affluents of the middle and lower courses of these rivers.

An important piece of evidence corroborates this hypothesized migration from the upland river sources to the lowlands. The stone used by the Wari' to make their axes came from a single locality: the swidden named Kit, located at the upper course of the Negro River at the right shore,[7] traditionally occupied by the OroEo. Until they began to raid the whites for metal axes, people from all the subgroups had to travel to Kit to obtain both the axe stones and the resin used to glue the blade to the handle, derived from a tree said to have grown only in this region.

As a whole, this data suggests two large-scale movements in opposite directions: an older migration from the uplands to the middle and lower courses of the rivers, and a more recent migration following the invasion of the whites, moving back toward the mountains. However, while the second movement is verified by concrete data, the first is extremely difficult to verify historically. Hence the remote origin of the Wari' remains obscure.

During the first rubber boom at the end of the nineteenth century, two important rivers crossing the Wari' territory were subject to intense navigation and occupation by rubber tappers, which meant traversing them became highly problematic for the Wari': the Pacaás Novos and the Ouro Preto. According to the Wari', the Pacaás Novos River was completely "closed" sometime between the mid-1920s and the start of the 1930s, when the OroNao', OroEo, OroAt, and OroJowin, who lived on the left shore, became isolated from their kin on the right shore.

I infer these dates from various cases recounted by the Wari'. According to the late Jimon Pan Tokwe, who would be about eighty-five years old now, the isolation of the group on the left shore occurred in the generation of his maternal grandmother, OroWao Towirain, who remained on the right shore, while her sister became isolated on the left. Manim, who would also now be around eighty-five years old, told me that his father had been born in Kit. Still a young man, his father had crossed to the left shore of the Pacaás Novos to take part in a festival and ended up marrying an OroNao' woman from this region. The whites arrived and he never returned. Manim was born there and only met his OroEo kin following pacification. He added that his maternal grandmother had been born among the OroNao' on the right shore, having crossed to the left shore when his mother was already a young woman. The paternal grandfather of Tem We, a sixty-year-old man, managed to cross from the left shore to OroWaram territory in search of bamboo to make arrows. But it was the last time he was able to traverse the river; on returning to the left shore he was unable to leave there again.

While they were unable to use the Pacaás Novos River, the Wari' continued to cross the Ouro Preto, albeit taking a lot of precautions such as avoiding the lower course and the light of day. Only men and unmarried women who did not need to carry children usually risked traversing the river. Consequently, the visits between the subgroups from the different shores became more infrequent and they ceased performing the *huroroin'* festivals, where the presence of adult women is indispensable. The last of these festivals among the OroMon and the OroNao' probably took place between 1905 and 1910.

Seen from a broad perspective, each subgroup occupied a particular territory, a geographically defined unit, though one without fixed boundaries. However, closer examination of the territories revealed that the frontiers between the subgroups were evidently more fluid. At a narrower level, this mixture resulted from the marriages between members of different subgroups. An OroNao' woman, for example, could go to live in an OroEo or OroWaram territory with her foreign husband, or OroWaram men, married to OroNao' women, could live in OroNao' territory. Isolated foreigners were absorbed by the local subgroup. However, when a group of foreign men decided to live in a village located in the territory of another subgroup, this village became the territory of their original subgroup.

This is what happened to the group of Jimon Pan Tokwe, an OroWaram man who lived at the Rio Negro–Ocaia village. Jimon and his two brothers were sons of an OroWaram father and an OroNao' mother. They lost their mother in childhood and went to live with their maternal kin. Later their father went to fetch them and they returned to OroWaram territory. As adults, the brothers themselves married OroNao' women and went to live with their wives' kin. They lived at various swidden sites traditionally occupied by the OroNao' and formed the nucleus of these local groups. The Wari' are unanimous in stating that since these swiddens were inhabited "by OroWaram," the sites were "OroWaram territory" (*makarakon orowaram*). Here we can note a peculiarity in the relation between subgroups and space: instead of the territory defining the subgroup, it is the subgroup to which the inhabitants belong that defines the territory.

However, while such cases happened, they failed to annul the association of each subgroup as a whole with a specific territory. The Wari' emphasize this point, going as far as to assert that "in the distant past" marriages between members of different subgroups were extremely rare. For example, the OroEo lived among the OroEo alone, in villages situated in a region inhabited by them over a long period of time. Indeed, the subgroup's relation to physical space is so marked that, in the Wari' language, the antonym of foreigner (*tatirim*), the member of another subgroup, is coinhabitant (*win ma'*).

The differentiation of physical space seems to have been insufficient to determine a subgroup, comprising merely the substrate for other more marked forms of differentiation. Put succinctly, people who move away become different. This applies both to individuals—as we shall see, someone who decides to live in another subgroup is eventually incorporated by it—and to groups: members of different subgroups speak with another accent (or even display differences in dialect), possess other dietary habits, sing differently, cry for their dead in another way, and so on.

SUBGROUP AFFILIATION

In principle, a person is a member of just one subgroup from birth to death. According to my interlocutors, a child's subgroup is the same as his or her father's: "The person belongs to the subgroup of the one who generated him or her" (and, for the Wari', it is the father who generates the child). However, the genealogies reveal various cases of matrifiliation,[8] associated with situations where the mixed subgroup couple decided to live with the woman's parents and kin. We can conclude, then, that the children of exogamic couples belong to the subgroup of either the mother or the father, depending on the residence pattern. In other words, if an OroEo man marries an OroNao' woman and opts to live with her parents, accompanying them as they change swidden locations, rather than taking her to live with his own, the couple's children will belong to the mother's subgroup.

Contrary to what Meireles (1986, 199) and Conklin (2001, 28) suggest, this does not imply the existence of a rule stipulating that a person's subgroup affiliation is determined by his or her place of birth.[9] Both the genealogies of people living at the Rio Negro–Ocaia village and the explicit Wari' discourse on this theme negate the existence of any such rule. In my view, inferring any such norm projects an alien notion of belonging onto Wari' concepts of territory and physical space. A person's identity is not given by the place where he or she was born, but by the relations established over the course of his or her life. An OroNao' is someone who lives with other Oro-Nao', eats and sleeps with them, and speaks in the same way. Paletó's father, for example, was born among the OroAt, the son of an OroAt father and an OroNao' mother. He married an OroNao' woman, repeating his father's type of marriage (the repetition of alliances between two families—groups of people related genealogically—is a common pattern among the Wari'). He subsequently went to live with the OroNao', his kin via his mother's side, rather than affines. Various people close to him said he became OroNao': his accent was no longer OroAt and, indeed, by the end of his life, he also called himself OroNao'.

But although people claim that a person's subgroup is the same for his or her entire life[10]—which in fact it may be, depending on the point of view

adopted—there is a desire to exploit these exogamic marriages as a potential source of indetermination. Hence, the Wari' leave open the subgroup
affiliation of anyone with parents from different subgroups, merely stating
that such a person is, for example, the daughter of an OroEo man and an
OroNao' woman, avoiding any determination of his or her affiliation. (This
does not mean, however, that the person in question will not readily state
the subgroup to which he or she belongs). It is as though people anticipate
the possibility of the person switching his or her affiliation one day, as happened with Paletó's father, who went to look for a spouse among his mother's OroNao' kin, thereby opting to become one of them eventually. For the
Wari', exogamic marriages are more problematic, doomed to failure because
of the numerous incompatibilities between the spouses and their families.
However, these marriages are the starting point not only for relations between subgroups (which would otherwise remain mutual enemies) but also
for something beyond this relationship: a mixture, the blurring of the limits
between them.

This kind of mixture is never emphasized when the issue is the subgroup
as a whole and the existence of these distinct units. As I remarked earlier,
Wari' discourse emphasizes the spatial and social distance separating the
subgroups. Older people say that marriages with foreigners were infrequent
in the past: the OroEo lived with the OroEo, the OroNao' with the OroNao',
and so on. They interrelated through festivals in which guests and hosts ritualized their differences and mutual hostilities. This radical separation is not
found in the genealogies, although they do reveal a high degree of subgroup
endogamy (see Vilaça 1992, 316–52 and 2006, 554–77). Not only did marriages between subgroups take place, but the visits between kin from foreign
subgroups were very often the motive for festivals. Exogamy was something
dangerous but absolutely necessary to make these units a concrete reality. It
seems to me, therefore, that the Wari' emphasis on the distinction between
subgroups is primarily an affirmation of their existence vis-à-vis an interlocutor from outside, a way of affirming that the Wari' must be conceived as
a set of distinct groups that interrelate. This is precisely what they did at the
time of pacification.

The contemporary situation provides an excellent illustration of the type
of relation established by the Wari' between physical space and the subgroup
as a unit. The subgroups from the time of pacification continue to exist.
The Wari' name these as the OroEo, OroAt, OroNao'—the OroNao' of the
Whites, taken to be a distinct group from an external perspective, consider

themselves simply OroNao' (see note 2)—OroWaram, OroMon, and Oro-WaramXijein (when pressed, some also say they are OroJowin and OroKao-OroWaji). The majority of the OroEo, OroAt, and OroNao' live in the Rio Negro–Ocaia village, located on the border of the territory formerly occupied by the OroNao' and close to the land of the OroAt and the OroEo. The OroNao' of the Whites continue to live on the left shore of the Pacaás Novos River, mainly at the Santo André and Tanajura villages. Most of the Oro-Waram live in Lage village, close to the territory once occupied by the Oro-WaramXijein. Many of the OroMon live in Ribeirão village, a region that the Wari' occupied sporadically when they hunted or "fled from the maize," but without any swidden sites. Some OroWaramXijein live with the OroWaram in Lage, and others with the OroMon in Ribeirão. When someone from outside, a foreigner, refers to Lage village, for example, he or she says that it is the land of the OroWaram (*makarakon orowaram*). "I'm going to dance in the OroWaram land," the Wari' say when they are heading to Lage for a festival. The Rio Negro–Ocaia village is "OroNao' land" (since OroNao's comprise most of its inhabitants), while Ribeirão, which was not occupied by the Wari' prior to pacification, is "OroMon land."

The social changes occurring with pacification, including the greater mixture of subgroups, reaffirm the idea that the subgroup determines the territory rather than the other way round. Living together produces an identity emphasized from the outside, despite being undone from the inside. The OroWaramXijein, for example, were to a certain extent supplanted by the OroWaram at Lage village, and by the OroMon at Ribeirão. Neither village is associated with this subgroup. However, the absence of any rule associating the subgroup with the territory of birth also seems to be indicated by the fact that, although no OroWaramXijein land exists, various people born at these current villages continue to be classified as members of this subgroup through either paternal or maternal affiliation. Likewise, many of those born at the Rio Negro–Ocaia village are OroEo and OroAt despite the fact that the village is said to be "OroNao' land."

A new variable to the issue of subgroup affiliation was introduced by the inclusion of indigenous people as voters and recipients of rural pensions at the end of the 1980s. This meant the need for identity documents, voter ID cards, bank accounts and cards, and so on. Each individual's subgroup is written on his or her identity card as a surname, fixing the name for at least the document's period of validity. A missionary from the New Tribes Mission—who, according to the Wari', was responsible for registering most of the recipients—decided that subgroup affiliation should be determined via the person's paternal grandfather. Although this imposition undoubtedly bears some relation to Wari' criteria, it provoked significant distortions by ignoring the historical processes that produced classifications diverging from the general rule. An example is Paletó—the son of an OroAt father and an OroNao' mother—who always identified himself as OroNao', along with his own children. After the registration made by the missionary, fixed "indelibly" in the documents, Paletó and his children were considered OroAt, with the exception of the eldest, Abrão, a teacher who refused to be registered in this form and kept his OroNao' identity.

This is not just a question of formal bureaucracy since the new identity is also accepted by the Wari'. Paletó frequently referred to his subgroup as OroAt and even told me that I too, as his daughter, am OroAt. In other contexts, though, he claimed to be OroNao' and joked ironically about the missionary's mistake. The Wari' once again found a creative way of exploiting a transformation imposed from outside, combining it with the value attributed by themselves to double subgroup identity. The future consequences of this error cannot be ignored, though, especially if we take into account the growing importance of these documents in Wari' life, not only for the older people receiving state pensions but also the increasing numbers of teachers and indigenous healthcare workers who receive salaries.

COINHABITANCE AND CONSANGUINITY

We can begin with the process of producing consanguinity. In the Wari' theory of conception, men are responsible for making the baby, formed from continual injections of semen. The verb to generate (*waraxi*) can only be conjugated with a male subject. If a woman with various sexual partners becomes pregnant, all of them are said to have generated the child, although normally only one of them is eventually considered a father: the one who decides to assume paternity. The involvement of women in conception is an open question. According to Conklin's research (2001, 116), the women contribute with blood, which forms the baby's blood, while the semen forms the body properly speaking. As I have discussed on other occasions (1992; 2002a, 352), my interlocutors were somewhat vague on this topic. When asked what forms the baby, the immediate reply was "the man's semen." However, if the question was reformulated, that is, when asked whether the woman's blood also constituted the baby's body, people seemed to entertain the possibility of female blood being involved. What is certain is that the Wari' are not overly concerned with the physiological aspects of conception. As Paletó once told me, "We just didn't think about this."[11]

Whatever the conception theory, though, mother and child are consubstantial from the beginning due to the physical intimacy from before birth. Consubstantiality and physical proximity are indissociable for the Wari'. People who live together become physically similar, if they were not so already. Body substances pass directly from one individual to another through contact—especially the intimate contact on the platforms during the night. Additionally, though, people who live together also share daily experiences and memories (which also constitute the body, as we shall see later) and, above all, eat together. For the Wari', food is central to defining identity. People who eat together (or consume the same type of food) become similar; analogously, the strongest form of establishing difference is through predation: those who eat each other are different, or constitute themselves as such through this act (see Vilaça 1992, 1998, 2000a). The Wari' often refer to the type of diet to differentiate themselves from other Indians, the whites, and animal species: they eat maize, larvae, and so forth; the whites eat rice, salt, and sugar; the jaguar eats raw meat; the peccary eats certain fruits. Likewise, when a shaman transforms from one animal to another, they say he stopped eating one kind of food and began to follow the other animal's diet.

There is a considerable distance between the Wari' concept of consubstantiality and our own (Euro-American) biological concept of genetic inheritance. Paletó frequently insists that our kinship relation of father and daughter is not fictitious; by living together for some time, I became his true daughter. Conversely, as I discuss later, consubstantial kin who become spatially and socially distant cease to be included in the group of close consanguines in diverse contexts, and may even become enemies, as occurs in the Oropixi' myth on the origin of whites.

What we can observe is a gradation of kinship according to physical proximity. Generally speaking, those who live together form the closest kin, while those who live further apart are more distant kin. Consequently, the Wari' today tend to classify all the inhabitants of the same village by consanguine kin terms,[12] performing highly complicated genealogical calculations to arrive at the desired result. This does not imply that genealogical kin living further away are classified as nonkin; the latter, when it occurs, is an extreme case, arising from complete and long-term distancing. Moreover, everything depends on context: when visiting the village of another subgroup, for instance, emphasis may be given precisely to the close kinship relations with people living there who have not been seen for a long time.

The idea of coinhabitance is expressed by the concept of *win ma'*, where *win* means "same," and *ma'* is the verb "to exist." These two words form a single composite noun, always accompanied by a subject pronoun. People say: *win ma' ne* (my "same existent"), *win ma' nixi* (our [inclusive] "same existent") and so on. *Win ma'* also means "that which is alongside, physically close." The prototypical *win ma'* is a same-sex sibling, partly because siblings are constituted from the same paternal and maternal substances, but mostly because they sleep and eat together, as well as being the most frequent companions in day-to-day activities.

However, a person may refer to various sets of *win ma'*, depending on the type of grouping he or she wishes to emphasize, whether shrinking to the sibling group or expanding to encompass the rest of the nuclear family, inhabitants of the same village, members of a subgroup, or the Wari' as a whole. In general, when someone is said to be *win ma'*, he or she is automatically assumed to be consanguine kin. Indeed, the term kin, *nari*, was frequently given to me as a synonym of *win ma'*. In practice, when someone is designated as *win ma'*, people attempt to trace a genealogical connection that will enable him or her to be classified as consanguine kin. When a calculation based on ascendant generations is unfeasible due to the absence of real genealogical relations, the problem can be resolved in two forms: either a term is used that can be applied to the established relationship, without any genealogical basis, as in the case of my relation with Paletó, or a teknonym is used, basing the calculation on descendent generations, since someone who comes to live in a new village frequently establishes alliance relations with the local inhabitants (with the exception of whites). Thus, for example, following marriage and the birth of children, a person may become "my grandson's grandmother," "my son's aunt," and so forth.[13]

Frequently the subgroup emerges as a kind of wider limit—one to be emphasized—of the *win ma'* category. Thus while coinhabitance may be conceived as a gradient and hence a relative category that depends on a person's point of view and interests, the boundary of the subgroup forms a kind of ideal limit. In fact, the Wari' use the term *win ma'* as the opposite of *tatirim*, meaning a member of another subgroup, a term I have translated here as foreigner. One woman once said to me, "If they're not our coinhabitants [*win ma' nixi*], they're other people [*xukun wari'*], they're foreigners [*tatirim*]." Once again, although these boundaries are traversable in some contexts, there is a clear ideological interest in maintaining the subgroups as distinct units.

Furthermore, if the coinhabitant is by definition consanguine kin, then the foreigner is nonkin. When working on the Wari' genealogies, my informants would always reply impatiently whenever I asked them whether someone from the same subgroup was their kinsperson (read: consanguine kin). They would say, for example, "He's OroAt, he's not a foreigner. He's my kin, my true kin!" They justified the exclusion of someone from their circle of kin in the same way: she's not a coinhabitant, she's a foreigner. They claim they are unable to trace a kinship relation with the person in question. However, this kind of assertion is rarely made in front of a foreigner. People do precisely the opposite: they try to trace any relationship justifying the use of a kin term. I observed this practice when I accompanied an OroNao' man, his OroMon wife, and their family to Lage village, where a number of the woman's kin lived. Not only did the man address all the Lage inhabitants by kin terms, I even heard him tell another man that their children (all of whom called themselves OroNao') were actually OroMon, adding that they were clearly physically very different from the people of the Rio Negro–Ocaia village where they all were living at that moment. In fact, this stemmed less from a desire to please the foreigners than to tame any latent hostility. The man, finding himself on foreign soil and surrounded by nonkin, in actuality his affines, sought to minimize the possibility of a fight erupting.

THE FOREIGNER AS AFFINE

The Wari' marry foreigners, despite claiming that they dislike doing so. They explain this aversion by pointing out that a foreign son-in-law or brother-in-law will take the daughter or sister away one day, adding that his strange customs mean that he will never be a good affine. He is likely to hit his wife, or, if the foreigner is a woman, she will be unfaithful to her husband and fail to look after him properly. The distance characterizing the initial relation quickly transforms into anger and a desire for revenge. While clashes between affines are inevitable, they can be more easily avoided when the people in question are relatively close, coinhabitants or kin.[14] When the affines are foreigners, the conflict explodes more quickly. Any outbreak of hostility becomes uncontainable and the reprisals more alarming.

From this point of view, the typical affine is a foreigner since only he (or she) acts as an affine rather than a kinsperson. In other words, the foreigner, because of his difference, the spatial and social distance that defines him, forms the ideal substrate for the alterity that defines affinal relations. In everyday life, the Wari' strive to transform affinity into consanguinity. Effective affines address each other by name or by consanguine kin terms, cooperate with each other, and share food in a process that gradually leads to the much desired consubstantiality. If the affine is a foreigner, though, any complication or lapse (especially extramarital affairs and physical aggression) is immediately attributed to his or her status as a foreigner, highlighting the fact that attempts to consubstantialize others are not always successful.

During conflicts, the group of coinhabitants, who previously emphasized their relations of consubstantiality, divide into groupings split along subgroup lines. Enraged, the affines attack those who treated their kin badly. Cases of adultery may lead to war club fights in which the two groups—the offending and offended parties—attempt to strike each other on the head without killing.[15] This does not mean that fights between affines from the same subgroup do not exist. They also occur. However, when the affines are foreigners, the conflict is attributed to this fact. Moreover, the conflict is inevitably more serious and mediation more difficult. The foreign spouse may decide to return to his or her own kin. Hearing about the incident may provoke such anger in the latter group that they embark on a major war club fight. Or worse: they may decide to exact lethal revenge through sorcery or poisoning. Many deaths among the Wari' are attributed to sorcery, the end result of conflicts between affines. And the sorcerers are always foreigners.

Killings also occurred on a large scale in the past, invariably between two allied subgroups. This collective poisoning involves placing a special mixture of substances under the roof of the victims' house. After a while, all of them become feverish and quickly die, unless someone discovers the poison and halts the process.

There are also cases of death caused by physical attacks. Paletó told me that in the past a woman killed her husband and their son. The former was killed by hanging with the help of her lover. After this episode, the woman fled with their son to the top of a cliff and threw him over. The dead man's kin, puzzled by the family's absence, eventually forced the lover to reveal the murder. They headed toward the cliff, armed with bows and arrows, shouting war cries: "We're going to shoot! We're going to kill enemies!" Arriving at the scene, they shot the woman and forced the lover to do the same under threat of death. As she was not a real enemy but a Wari' (who acted as an enemy), they could not openly take back parts of the corpse to eat at home. So they did so in secret. They took back a piece of the woman's belly, relished for its excess fat. They roasted it in the middle of the night so her kin would not suspect that she had been murdered. But the smell of Wari' flesh is unmistakable, and they were quickly forced to extinguish the fire. The odor emitted during the roasting, however, was lethal to the transgressors. A Wari' person cannot be killed like animal game or an enemy. Internal conflicts must be resolved with the war club, or secretly using sorcery and poisoning. Wari' are not enemies, people insist. But what these episodes demonstrate is that disrupting this fragile internal equilibrium between aggression and cooperation is always possible. The foreigner is not easy to consubstantialize and can become an enemy. Indeed, this is the only possible genesis of enemies: from the interior of Wari' society itself.

The association between foreigner and affine will become clearer in the analysis of the festivals held between the subgroups.

THE FESTIVALS

The festivals are the legitimate place for manifesting the rivalry between subgroups. There are three main types of festival: the *tamara*, the *huroroin'*, and the *hwitop'*. I shall not provide a detailed description of these festivals (see Vilaça 1992); however, some background information is necessary for the reader to be able to follow some of the conclusions reached below.[16]

All of the festivals have as a basic structure the relationship between a group of hosts and a group of guests (uninvited, in the case of the *tamara* festival) who are mutual foreigners—or act as such. The guests arrive animalized (in their appearance or actions) and are "punished" either with mocking remarks or with an excess of drink.

Tamara

The *tamara* festival is usually held in the dry season, after the swiddens have been burned and before planting (September–October). According to some people, it may also take place in the rainy season when soft maize has already ripened (December–January).

As a baseline for my description, I shall take the *tamara* festivals performed before pacification, a period when the subgroups still lived in relatively well-defined territories. Various festivals of this kind took place in the 1980s and 1990s when I was carrying out my field research. The hosts and

guests at these events were inhabitants of different villages who each classified the other group as foreigners.

The catalyst for a festival was someone announcing, "Let's dance and see
our kin!" The explicit motive was the desire to see kin living in foreign lands.
A *tamara* was also organized as a way of visiting foreigners and asking them
for things that were needed, such as stone axe blades—requested from the
OroEo, who lived in the only area where these stones existed—or maize
for planting when no seeds had been stocked. Little else was solicited from
others since there is no kind of specialization in the production of material
goods. The requests for goods—bows, pans, annatto dye—at the end of festivals were more a form of indemnity for mistreatment than part of a ritual
exchange of goods.

The visitors arrived unexpectedly from the forest, painted in red annatto
with black genipap designs evoking animals (jaguars and snakes). They also
carried the *towa*, a pottery drum covered in strips of rubber (fig. 4).

While still at some distance from the host village, they whistled to warn
its inhabitants of their arrival and then began dancing in a line and singing
music composed by men. *Tamara*, the name for these songs, was translated
by one man as "people's gossip": they refer to extramarital relations, failure
to share food, stolen items, mishaps during day-to-day activities, and so on.
The melody was always the same, sung in a thin, high-pitched voice by both
men and women. The drum was passed from hand to hand.

The group of visitors comprised men of all ages and young women, most
of them unmarried or married with no children as yet. These women were
accompanied by their husbands, brothers, or fathers and danced next to
them during the festival.

Visitors generally came from a single subgroup. Sometimes people from
more than one subgroup were involved: for example, when the OroEo went
to dance in a particular OroNao' village, they would often be accompanied
by people from the OroAt subgroup. The latter decided to accompany them
either because they were already living among the OroEo, or because the
OroEo had passed through an OroAt village on the way to the OroNao' and
invited its inhabitants. In each case, though, all the visitors were foreigners.
If one of the guests belonged to the same subgroup as the hosts, he or she
would behave like a member of the visiting subgroup—that is, as a foreigner
to his or her kin.

Tamara festivals not only occurred between neighboring subgroups, such

4. A'ain covers the pottery base with rubber strips.
Rio Negro–Ocaia, 1986.

5. *Tamara*. Hosts feeding the guests (holding the drum) in the forest.
Santo André, 1986.

as the OroNao', OroEo, and OroAt. However, those held between more
distant subgroups, separated by a river such as the Ouro Preto, could only
take place in the dry season when the river could be waded or swum across
(since the Wari' did not build canoes). Additionally, as these larger rivers
became more intensely occupied by whites, crossing them was too dangerous for women to attempt. As a result, these *tamara* groups were generally
composed solely of men.

When the visitors reached the forest close to the host village and whistled
to the local inhabitants, the latter immediately realized it was a *tamara* and
rushed to meet their visitors in the forest, yelling, laughing, and taking whatever they had available to offer them to drink. The visitors sang and danced
while the hosts scolded them for not knowing how to sing properly, or for
bringing a dancer with deformed legs, and so on. The guests withstood this
abuse without any response, their heads lowered, singing and dancing without pause. The hosts returned to their houses to prepare more maize beer[17]
and to search for food. The visitors remained in the forest for two days, receiving visits and food from the hosts, and ensuring that a group was always
kept dancing (fig. 5).

Late in the afternoon on the second day, the visitors finally prepared to enter the host village: they covered their bodies with fresh paint and put on more adornments. This was the culmination of the festival when they danced and sang all night and tried to perform as well as possible, maintaining a passive indifference to their hosts' verbal provocations (figs. 6, 7, and 8). The latter, for their part, offered even more drink, especially to the drummer entering the village. This young man or adult was forced to drink until he vomited. The hosts also intensified their mocking provocations, going as far as to cross-dress in order to confuse the singers.

At dawn, the roles were inverted: the visitors stopped singing, and the hosts took the *towa* drum and started singing and dancing, mocked by the visitors who claimed to be exacting revenge. This was soon over, however. By now visibly exhausted, the visitors were eager to leave. Before departing, though, they asked their hosts for everyday objects. The visiting men would usually ask the other men for bows, arrows, arrow sharpeners, and even axe blades when the festivals were hosted by the OroEo. The visiting women would ask the other women for baskets and annatto dye.

The *tamara* festival can also involve other kinds of guests and hosts. When the dead wish to come to earth to see their kin, they take the form of white-lipped peccaries and emerge from the depths of the waters, painted and carrying the *towa* drum. The only people to see them are shamans, who interact with them by assuming the role of hosts. The peccaries are treated as foreigners by the living, represented by the shamans, and at the end offer themselves as hunt game to the Wari'. What is of special interest to us here is that the Wari' held another type of festival where the guests—men only—said they were peccaries and indeed arrived acting just like the animals. The host women ran up to them and covered their bodies with ashes and clay. The host men then arrived, shouting, "Let's kill peccaries!" This involved a symbolic killing in which the male guests were forced to drink a lot of maize drink and vomit, in similar fashion to the offering of maize beer. According to the Wari', this type of rite could take place between foreigners or between people from the same subgroup, who treated each other as foreigners.

Huroroin'

Huroroin' is the most complex festival of the three since it involves gender differentiations within both the guest and host groups. Until the early 1900s, the festival was held between all the different subgroups. The OroNao', for

6. *Tamara.* Guests dancing during the night at a village house.
Santo André, 1986.

7. *Tamara.* Guests dancing. The man playing the drum looks straight at
the instrument, while the others look at the ground. Santo André, 1986.

8. *Tamara.* Hosts offering maize drink and food to the guests.
Santo André, 1986.

example, would invite both the OroEo and the OroMon. After crossing the Ouro Preto River became complicated, these festivals, which depended on the presence of invited women, were suspended between those subgroups separated by the river. The *huroroin'* festivals were then held between the OroMon, OroWaram, OroWaramXijein, OroKaoOroWaji, and OroJowin, on one side, and the OroNao', OroAt, and OroEo, on the other (some people locate the OroJowin in the latter group). I have never witnessed a *huroroin'* festival, and my description here is based on accounts of festivals that took place before pacification, plus two festivals held in 1986.

Preparations for the *huroroin'* festival began as soon as the maize was fully ripened, sometime in January or February. Unlike the *tamara* festival where it was dispensable, sour (fermented) maize beer formed an essential ingredient of the *huroroin'* festival. It was prepared by the female hosts months ahead and left to ferment. During the festival, it was offered by the male hosts (and sometimes by the women too) to the invited men. The man who had first conceived the idea of the festival led the preparations and was called the "owner of the tree trunk" in which the beer was stored.

After the tree was hollowed out and impermeabilized and the beer was already being brewed, a group of men traveled to the villages of another subgroup (or subgroups) to issue the invitation. The owner of the trunk arrived decorated with red macaw tail feathers inserted in a small basket hung over his back from his head by a liana strap. All the men played bamboo flutes, announcing their arrival and the purpose of the visit. In the village, they sat in the men's house and were castigated for the treatment they would inflict on their future guests. They were forced to drink all kinds of "rubbish": water mixed with bits of termite nest, mud, bitter fruits, raw maize, ashes. They vomited and drank more. Those offering this drink said, "We're filling you with fake maize beer because you're going to fill our brothers with beer afterward." They then went on to the next village.

After the invitation, the guests began to count the full moons to calculate when the maize beer would be ready. For some interlocutors, three moons should elapse, for others, four. Consequently the actual festival took place at the end of the rainy season, around April or May, the period when the last two *huroroin'* were held in 1986.

When the guests arrived in the host village, the trough (trunk), stuck perpendicularly into the ground, was ideally full of beer already well fermented. The men arrived playing various types of bamboo flutes, including a very

9. *Huroroin'*. Flutes and log drums.
(Archive of the Guajará-Mirim Prelacy)

long one with a Brazil nut pod on its end, called *huroroin'*. The male hosts
greeted them, playing log drums in pairs (fig. 9). The female guests brought
a small rubber drum, *orowin*—like a miniature of the *towa* drum played in
the *tamara* festival—and remained in the forest for two days, sitting on the
ground, singing the female musical pieces called *ijain je e*. The theme of this
ancestral music is things of the forest (the singing of birds, and so forth).
However, the refrain of all of the pieces—*ijain je e* (be excited) leads me to
suspect a sexual connotation, given that the women interacted predominantly
with their male hosts who penetrated them symbolically with their drum
sticks.

The invited men entered and left the village a number of times. They arrived screened by a barrier of leaves, like animals in the forest, and behaved
wildly, destroying parts of the houses, killing domestic animals, simulating
sexual acts with their hosts' wives, and exclaiming aloud that they would
"eat" these women.

They were punished by the hosts, who forced them to drink large quantities of beer, requiring them to vomit in order to drink more. Afterward they
left the village for the forest to meet their wives. A while later, they returned
and repeated the same actions. These endless rounds of drinking and vomit-

ing eventually caused them to fall into an unconscious state, *itam*, described as a kind of death. The hosts claimed to have killed them, just like animal prey; indeed, I once heard them refer to a well-known drinker as "that man who has already died and revived various times" (see Albert 1985 for a similar case among the Yanomami).

While these events were happening in the village, in the forest the invited women sang ceaselessly (in turns) and were harassed by their male hosts. These women did not drink maize beer; instead, they were frequently offered raw food—which they then cooked—or already prepared food by the host women. In contrast, the invited men ate absolutely nothing, otherwise, the Wari' say, they would be unable to vomit, meaning they would be unable to drink more and more beer.

At the end of the third day, the invited women entered the village, sat down, and continued singing the entire night. The host men continued pouring pots of maize beer into the mouths of their guests until the last drop of beer was consumed. The following morning, the last day of the festival, the host men danced in front of their female guests—an energetic dance in which they beat the ground with percussion instruments made from bamboo and maize seeds. The allusion to sexual intercourse is clear.

By this point, the invited men were lying unconscious or exhausted and were doused with warm water by their male hosts, abruptly awakening them. As in the *tamara* ritual, the guests asked their hosts for objects as they left: bows, arrows, baskets, and such.

Hwitop'

The *hwitop'* festival was held between neighboring villages, generally those from the same subgroup or nearby subgroups. As in the two previous festivals, the guests and hosts act like mutual foreigners. Judging from the Wari' accounts, *hwitop'* was a kind of intimate festival, held between people who knew each other well. For example, the Rio Negro–Ocaia village twice divided into two groups: one half acted as hosts, preparing and offering the drink, while the other formed the invited group of drinkers. Although kin, the guests and hosts behaved as though they were foreigners, imitating a relationship marked by distance and latent hostility. Indeed, they even make this explicit: "We're like foreigners to ourselves," one man told me when I asked how this festival between two halves of the Rio Negro–Ocaia village could have happened.

10. *Hwitop'*. A trough with *tarawan* (*patauá*) fruits in which the drink
will be made. Rio Negro–Ocaia, 1993.

Like *huroroin'*, the *hwitop'* festival is held in the rainy season, though it
is not dependent on maize since the drink can be made from fruits such as
patauá palm or from honey. I saw two of these festivals: the first was in April
1987 in Tanajura village, held in celebration of Indian Day; the second was
held in the Rio Negro–Ocaia village in December 1993. The latter is the basis
for the following description of *hwitop'*.

When I arrived at the Rio Negro–Ocaia village in November 1993, I knew
that the local inhabitants had invited the residents of Santo André village
(predominantly OroNao' of the Whites) to a *hwitop'* festival. The drink
prepared was made from *tarawan* (Portuguese: *patauá*; it was cooked and
squeezed to extract the juice) and stored in containers made from wooden
laths (fig. 10). Throughout this process, the men played the log drums in
pairs.

The guests—men and women alike—arrived in a line, playing transverse
and end-blown bamboo flutes of various sizes. There is no singing in the festival. According to the Wari', the flutes' sounds imitate birds and frogs.[18] They
did not bring the pottery and rubber drum, probably because they had neither the time nor the means to make it. The hosts—men, older boys, and un

11. *Hwitop'*. Hosts offer fruit drink to the guests. Rio Negro–Ocaia, 1993.

married girls—ran up to them with pots filled with drink, which was poured into their mouths. At the festival in 1987, the hosts offered live chickens for their guests to slaughter. The latter behaved like animals (jaguars, some people said), pretending to bite the birds, but ended up wringing their necks or clubbing them to death. The executors were then punished with larger doses of sour maize beer.

The hosts offered the drink to the guests in a highly provocative tone, clearly affirming that the guests were paying for the harm caused (for having inebriated the hosts on another occasion or caused small material damage) and making fun of everything they did (fig. 11). Those who had drunk large amounts vomited so they could consume even more drink, prompting the hosts to laugh loudly. When a girl began to vomit, the lad who was giving her drink shouted, "I killed her, I killed her!" Eventually, just four men were still able to drink.

There are a number of significant points here. It is apparent to everyone that the guests are there to suffer. For anyone watching this festival, the impression is that of a massacre. Not that the guests complain or show they are suffering. On the contrary, they appear to submit cheerfully to this ritual of mocking, vomiting, and provocation without response, except in another festival in which they assume the role of hosts. Neither do the hosts act without a worry for the state of their guests. They are concerned, but behind the scenes, so to speak. One or other will ask whether it is time to stop giving drink to a particular person, but never their kin. My surprise at the Rio Negro–Ocaia festival was seeing men and women pour pots and pots of drink into the mouths of their real siblings pitilessly. At no moment did they call them by kin terms and indeed they seemed to be most assiduous in the task of making them drunk and causing them to vomit. At the end of the rite, the musical instruments are left for the hosts to play, as in the other types of festival. But in contrast to *huroroin'* and *tamara*, the guests do not request objects for personal use from their hosts.

I wish, now, to demonstrate two points. First, I wish to emphasize the way in which predation emerges as the central theme of the festivals, with the guests comprising the prey of the hosts. Second, I intend to show that the relationship between guests and hosts—that is, the ritual relation between foreigners—is conceived as an affinal relation.

A myth is told of a man who failed to use the proper culinary procedures to cook a game animal and as a result all of the animals disappeared. People left anxiously in search of them, eventually discovering that they were all living under the water. They decided that the best way to attract them would be to invite them to drink maize beer in a *huroroin'* festival. The animals came up to the surface, were made drunk on beer, and fell unconscious. The Wari' killed them and since then have never gone without their prey.

At the *huroroin'* and *hwitop'* festivals, the guests are not just transformed into prey animals at the end; they arrive as animals. The body paintings imitate jaguars and snakes (also found in the *tamara* festival) and they act as unsocialized beings. The drink offered to them is a punishment for these acts, the revenge of those supposedly being assaulted. And this drink kills. "I killed my prey!" the host proclaims. The drink is the weapon used to kill a foreigner by causing him to fall unconscious. Moreover, as an antifood that provokes vomiting rather than satiation of hunger, the maize beer turns whoever offers the drink into an eater and the one who ingests it into food. Offering an antifood is a logical equivalent of eating, and what one eats is necessarily dead (see Vilaça 1992).

The guest/prey association is less obvious in the *tamara* festival, though this does not mean it is absent. First, the tone of the festival is identical: the guests are humiliated but passively accept their treatment. In addition, there are clear parallels between the maize beer offered in the other festivals and the food offered to visitors in a *tamara* festival. The latter guests have to swallow food stuffed into their mouths, whether or not they want it or their mouths are still full. Even so, the visitors of a *tamara* festival continually complain of hunger. Although not vomited like the beer, this food is also an antifood. As well as being offered in a subjugating way, it fails to satiate the guest's hunger, even in large quantities, just like something that is eaten and then vomited. Moreover, although the drink offered in the *tamara* festival is unfermented, it is given as though it were: the guests must consume the maize drink in excess, especially the man who enters the village with the drum on the last day.[19]

The identification of the *tamara* guests with prey is not only made evident in the kind of food involved. As I remarked earlier, *tamara* is also the festival held between the living and the dead, the latter in the form of peccaries. After the festival, the peccaries offer themselves up as prey, the game most appreciated by the Wari'. The festival briefly described above in which the visiting men arrive as peccaries who are then killed by their hosts bears an obvious relation to this ritual between the living and the dead.

Before turning to my second point, which concerns the classification of foreigners as affines, I wish to stress another aspect that singularizes the *tamara* festival. The visitors do not provide immediate motives for being punished, as the guests do in the other festivals. They simply arrive and sing. They neither enter the village of their hosts, nor seduce their women, nor destroy anything. The punishment seems to be for a previous transgression and, moreover, is clearly attenuated when compared to the explicit "murder" occurring in the *huroroin'* and *hwitop'* festivals. Why this difference? Conklin (1989, 148–49) suggests that *huroroin'* and *hwitop'* are not held between spatially and hence socially distant subgroups, precisely because they involve this symbolic killing by fermented drink. Only close allies, she writes, have sufficient trust in each other to take part in this type of rite. The *tamara* is (also) held between distant subgroups not because the women are dispensable in this festival, but because it does not involve the consumption of maize beer, meaning the guests are exposed to less risk.

We should note, though, that before crossing the Ouro Preto River became virtually impossible, the distance between the OroMon and OroNao' on one shore and the OroNao' and OroEo on the other was virtually the same. Likewise, if we accept the possibility that the subgroup territories were even closer to each other before the whites invaded the region, this idea of distant and proximate subgroups becomes even less viable. According to my interlocutors, *hurøroin'* also used to be held between these now separated subgroups, the last such festival having occurred at the start of the twentieth century at an OroNao' swidden village.

However, spatial distancing did indeed occur and some subgroups did become more isolated than others. The *tamara* was maintained between distant and "more foreign" subgroups possibly because it involves less direct aggressions on people who may be more dangerous because they are more distantly related, as Conklin suggests. In fact, it is precisely for this reason that they do not need to commit any transgression for them to merit punishment: the distance and difference that they represent as true foreigners (*iri tatirim*) is already sufficient reason.[20]

Let's turn now to the second point: the foreigners establishing this kind of predatory relationship are affines in the rite. Earlier I remarked that the Wari' oppose *win ma'*, used as a synonym for kin, and *tatirim*, designating a member of another subgroup. The foreigner is by definition nonkin. However, since all Wari' conceive of each other at a wider level as consanguine kin, the foreigners must be the most distant consanguines. As I mentioned, the Wari' terminology for consanguinal kin excludes affinal positions—there is no prescriptive affinity, in other words—a feature found in Crow-type terminological systems in general. I also remarked that the Wari' look to avoid marrying close genealogical kin. From a sociological perspective, though, the opposite occurs, when we consider that the *win ma'* with whom the Wari' ideally seek to marry are considered closer (or more consubstantial) kin due to the physical proximity that enables conviviality, mutual cooperation, and food sharing. Despite the apparent contradiction in claiming that foreigners are the prototypical affines, the fact that when these foreigners become real affines they are the most difficult to make consubstantial would seem to justify this assertion. In this sense, they are the only ones who can be truly classified as affines. Put otherwise, we are dealing here with a concept of affinity dissociated from the effective relation of alliance.[21] Let us see how this appears in the rites.

Conklin and Meireles define these events as alliance festivals. For Conklin (1989, 148–49; 2001, 44–45), this alliance does not have the restricted sense of matrimonial alliance, but a wider connotation of cooperation and friendship. For Meireles (1986, 251, 262), though, the meaning of alliance is related to marriage. These festivals were, she argues, the place where marriages were negotiated. I agree partially with Conklin's claim and disagree with Meireles's idea. The festivals provide the occasion for establishing rela-

tions between foreigners in their own terms; that is, in the form of a ritualized and domesticated antagonism. The outcome is not peace and friendship, as though the aggressions prompted a catharsis, but only the certainty
of a relationship—of the existence of an encompassing unit constituted by
the set of subgroups. In summary, the foreigners are Wari' (wari') and not
enemies, a condition that would happen—and indeed does happen—when
the exchange of festivals and women is broken. In this sense, marriages between subgroups are essential to enabling the possibility of a relation, serv-
ing as a catalyst for approximation and the domestication of rivalries. It is
as if the actual experience of affinity with foreigners were necessary for this
to be rejected and for them to be considered prototypical affines, precisely
the kind of people with whom alliance should not be concretized. Meireles's
claim, however, makes little sense. The Wari' are unanimous in asserting that
marriages were not negotiated in these festivals; indeed, not even love affairs
were initiated. Young women felt enormously ashamed of the foreigners, except where they were not real foreigners but win ma'—members of the same
subgroup or genealogically close kin—living among the foreigners.

In the tamara, huroroin', and hwitop' festivals, what is ritualized is not
alliance. The sexual insinuations between guests and hosts of the opposite
sex are present in the rites, especially in huroroin'. However, these do not involve alliance proposals, but illicit and predatory sexual relations. The men's
targets are not unmarried women but the wives of men from the opposing
group. It is as though the men were proposing an impossible alliance, almost
an abduction of the women, implying it is these women who are desired,
not affines. Stealing women is the way of possessing them without having
to provide the prestations that define affinity. In the festivals, the foreigners
clearly propose sex alone rather than marriage, and sexual relations in general are independent of affinal relations. In fact, it is precisely because of this
negation of affinity that they are affines—because they are bad affines, affines
who do not act as consanguine kin.

During a tamara festival at Tanajura village, I heard the young male hosts
call the male guests who were dancing in the village "cunhados" (brothers-
in-law), directly in Portuguese. This was the only time I witnessed such an
incident. After overhearing this, I asked older people whether the use of affinal vocatives for festival guests was common in the past or even today. All
of them told me yes: the men were called "taking brothers-in-law" (nem) and
"giving brothers-in-law" (namori), a practice rarely observed in everyday
life when the Wari' attempt to mask actual affinity by calling everyone by a

kin term or by their proper names.[22] I was also struck by the fact that close
consanguine kin—real siblings in the case of the *hwitop'* festival at the Rio
Negro–Ocaia village—did not use consanguine vocatives among themselves
during the ritual. Usually when a sister offers maize beer to her brother, for
example, she says, "Here is your beer, younger/older brother!" Asking one
of the elders about the use of affinal terms in the festivals, he told me that
"brother," "father," and other vocatives are used by women when they offer
sweet maize drink to their real cognates in everyday life. During the rite, in
contrast, sour maize beer is offered to brothers-in-law.

When I talked to the Wari' about pacification, I was surprised to discover
that festivals were still frequently being held just before the establishment
of peaceful contact with the whites—a period when they were being heavily pursued and often forced to move village after armed raids or in order
to evade such attacks. Numerous festival guests were caught in foreign villages when the pacification teams arrived. Even with all the confusion of the
postpacification period and the epidemics that ensued, the festivals were
resumed as soon as possible. During this period, the Wari' presented themselves to the whites not as a single group but as a set of subgroups.

I do not intend to examine the periods before and after pacification in
detail here. What we can once again note, though, is the importance attributed by the Wari' to their internal differentiation into subgroups and the
central role played by the festivals in structuring these units. The foreigner
is the embodiment of alterity—an otherness that people wish to maintain
"inside" without fully incorporating it. And indeed the subgroups remain
today, surviving the many recent changes. The groups are now more mixed,
but the Wari' found a way of transposing the concept of territory to the villages built around the FUNAI posts: each of these villages was identified with
the subgroup to which most of its inhabitants belonged. Furthermore, in the
underwater world of the dead, these former territories are still well defined
and occupied by the subgroups associated with them.

In the world of the dead, each subgroup exists as a differentiated unit,
something that can no longer be fully achieved today in the world of the living. There below the water the dead hold *huroroin'* festivals. This is the only
type of festival performed under the water, which again demonstrates the
conclusion we reached: *huroroin'* is the most complex festival, symbolizing
the essence of the relation between foreigners.

To conclude this chapter, I wish to relate the question of the subgroups to
an observation made by Paletó. This remark followed his comment, cited in

the introduction, that the Wari' had failed to accept the call of the first whites. Had they done so, he affirmed, the Wari' today would be whites and would know how to build airplanes. Hearing this, I asked Paletó what seemed to me the obvious question: "But don't you like being Wari'?" His reply was completely unexpected: "But we are only Wari' because you whites said so. Before that, we didn't know." The implications of this surprising response are many. One of them relates, I think, to the question of the Wari' social units. When the whites encountered them, they made themselves known as a set of subgroups rather than a single ethnic group. Not that the latter unit was nonexistent: as we have seen, the relations between the subgroups were so important precisely because they provided a means of making this unit a reality. At the start, the whites treated them as members of different subgroups, as the first reports produced by the Indian Protection Service (SPI) reveal: in the space allocated for the name of the tribe, the SPI employees wrote Oro-Nao', OroEo, and so on. A little while later, though, the name "Pacaas Novos" had already appeared in these reports. I have no idea what happened in this short interval, but perhaps Paletó's observation reveals that, for the Wari', it was the whites who made the idea of a single unit supplant that of the multiple subgroups. This may have been so not only because whites substituted the names of the subgroups with the term "Pacaas Novos" in their reports, but primarily because pacification led to a previously unknown mixture of subgroups in the same locality, as well as their need, perhaps, to emphasize a shared identity in the face of the many catastrophes and transformations that followed pacification.

Interestingly, this emphasis on themselves as a single unit did not occur immediately on encountering the white enemies, as a form of marking the difference with them more clearly. In my view, the Wari' did not do so precisely because they were not interested in this difference, but rather in similarity and the possibility of incorporation. As a set of subgroups, aware that the foreigner is the place of movement, enabling people to enter and leave Wari' society, they were perhaps telling the whites that they could become one more of them, another Wari' subgroup. As we shall see, the OroNao' of the Whites, the first subgroup to approach the whites peacefully, desired foreigners, other people for themselves. By making them Pakaa-Nova—or Wari'—the whites curtailed the possibility for them to experience their own historical becoming, related to a conception of society as something in a constant process of transformation.

CHAPTER 2

The Enemy

The Wari' use the word *wijam*, enemy, to refer to any Indian from another ethnic group and to whites. Two Wari' myths describe the origin of enemies. The first of these—analyzed later—concerns Oropixi', a man punished by his older brother after having sexual relations with the latter's wife. Oropixi', furious with his brother, went to live far away, taking all the water with him. This caused the Wari' enormous suffering. The older brother went after Oropixi' and offered his wife, persuading him to return with the water.

In some versions, Oropixi' remains with his kin and the myth ends. In others, he returns to the great river where he settled during his exile, taking all those wishing to accompany him. At first, the two separate groups interact with each other as foreigners from different subgroups, exchanging festivals and visiting in turn. Time passed and those who had stayed were astonished by the clothing and other novelties found among those who had moved away (Oropixi' means precisely "people who moved away": *oro*, collectivizing prefix; *pixi'*, to move to live elsewhere). In some versions, perceiving this difference provokes the change in the relationship: either the two populations lose touch completely or they start warring. Sometimes the war seems to be provoked or initiated by the Wari'; in other versions, those who left are the first to attack. At first arrows are used, later replaced by clumsy firearms making a lot of noise but failing to propel the lead shot. Later still, the guns become identical to those used today. The Oropixi' people had turned into whites.

The other myth is about a stingy old man. The conflict began when he refused to distribute a tapir he had killed to his relatives, flouting Wari' custom. A boy, his grandson, was hiding one day and heard people complaining that his grandfather was selfish. He went to tell him. Irate, the man took the tapir meat and hurled it rudely at the complainers. Some people from his house had returned to their original village. So the old man told those with whom he lived to chop down the trunk of a tree called *horokip* to be filled with maize beer. This species of tree is used as a recipient in the *hwitop'* festival, usually held between people who are close, frequently from the same subgroup. The others declined the invitation and the old man threw away the maize beer. He cut down another *horokip* and again the guests failed to appear. So he ordered a huge trunk to be cut down, the kind used in the *huroroin'* festivals held between different subgroups. This time some people accepted the invitation, despite suspecting they might be killed. Fearful, one of the guests hid and waited to see what would happen. When the guests fell unconscious from drinking all the maize beer, the grandfather took them to lie down in the men's house, as customary during festivals. There he killed them one by one, extracting their forearm bones to use as sticks for the log drums played by the hosts in the *huroroin'* and *hwitop'* festivals. Horrified, the man in hiding managed to escape and tell his people what had happened. In revenge, the latter attacked the old man's village with arrows; the villagers shot back, but the assailants escaped injury by using animal skins as armor. Narrating the myth, Awo Xohwara concluded, "Those who died and their kin are Wari' [*wari'*]. The kin of the old man who refused to give the tapir meat became enemies [*wijam*]." Listening to this narrative, Paletó added, "This is the myth of the enemies [*wijam*] who stayed in the forest, and Oropixi' is one of the enemies [*wijam*] who stayed by the water." In both cases, we can observe a gradual transformation of Wari' into enemies: from kin to foreigner, from foreigner to enemy.

THE INDIAN ENEMIES

The Wari' say they have always been warriors. Before the whites arrived, their most frequent enemies were the OroAoAo, OroMawin, OroTarakom, and OroWin.[1] It is difficult to know for sure who these Indians were because the informants mix their names in their accounts and are inconsistent about where these enemies lived. Apparently, the OroAoAo are the people known in the literature as the Uru-Eu-Wau-Wau (Tupi-Kawahiv), who lived—and continue to live—on the headwaters of the Pacaás Novos (and in an area to the southeast of this river). The OroAoAo mostly warred with the OroEo and the OroAt, Wari' subgroups who occupied an area close to their own.

Like the Wari', the OroWin speak a Txapakuran language and also inhabited the headwaters of the Pacaás Novos. Almost exterminated by an assault organized by rubber bosses, the surviving OroWin lived in rubber-tapper settlements for a while before being transferred to the Rio Negro–Ocaia village in 1980. There they remained along with the Wari' until September 1991, when they were taken to a new village (São Luís), close to the area they occupied before contact.[2]

The OroTarakom are the Karipuna (Tupi-Kawahiv), who, the Wari' say, lived near the headwaters of the Jaci-Paraná River. They warred especially with the OroMon and OroWaramXijein on the affluents of the Laje and used to trek through this region.

I am unable to identify the OroMawin. While some informants say this group lived near the headwaters of the Laje River and fought with the Oro-Mon and OroWaramXijein, others claim they inhabited the sources of the Pacaás Novos and were enemies of the OroEo and OroAt. But this lack of precision, due primarily to a disinterest in clearly differentiating their enemies, is not limited to the OroMawin. The same enemy group may often be called OroAoAo, OroWin, or OroMawin, even within the same account. Likewise, the OroTarakom are sometimes called the OroMawin. Nonetheless, some differences are always discernible: the accounts never describe the OroTarakom at war with the OroEo and the OroAt, while the OroAoAo and OroWin are never said to have been at war with the OroMon.

Other enemies mentioned by the Wari', albeit less frequently, are the OroTaopa, OroPana, OroWaxik, OroMawo, OroTukuWao, and OroToxik.[3] Identifying them, or even determining whether they were real or mythic enemies, proved impossible. Many Wari' myths tell of peoples who are human, despite their animal appearances. This applies to the OroMawo (*mawo* is a species of hawk), the OroMaĥo (*maho* means vulture), and others. Nor is it only in myths that animals are enemies who shoot and kill the Wari'. As I discuss later in the chapter, many of the Wari' game animals possess spirit, making them humans and enemies.

WAR HISTORIES

As far as I know, the Wari' had no peaceful contacts with any ethnic group. But this may not have always been the case given that the European invasion of the Americas led to the disappearance of innumerable native peoples and forced many of the survivors into isolation for the first time. The only episode implying peaceful relations with other Indians is a myth telling how the Wari' only hunted and ate lizards, convinced they were eating peccaries, spider monkeys, pacas, and so on (their contemporary prey). In contrast, the latter animals were seen as spotted jaguars, meaning they never killed them for food. In one version, a man from the OroAoAo enemy group enables them to perceive that what they were eating were in fact lizards, and what they thought were jaguars were actually the animals they should have been killing and eating all along. Thereafter, they recognized animals properly and ate the appropriate game.

We can note the peculiarity of this apparently peaceful relation with the enemy: in effect, the Wari' incorporated the enemy's point of view, just as the shamans do with the animals with which they interact—and just as the Wari' themselves have done with the white enemies ever since pacification. I return to this point later.

This kind of collaboration with enemies—or an enemy—is limited to this specific mythical episode. Until pacification there was never any truce with non-Wari' people. Hence what this discourse makes explicit is not the disappearance over time of ancient allies or trade partners, but the vanishing of enemies. Forced to flee from the whites and isolated or even exterminated by them, their former enemies became scarce from the start of the twentieth century onward as the whites became the most frequently encountered enemies and the only enemies with whom the Wari' could actually war.

Nonetheless, the scarcity of indigenous enemies affected the Wari' subgroups in distinct ways. The OroEo—and, some people say, the OroAt—neighbors of the OroAoAo and the OroWin (or OroMawin), apparently fought intensely with enemies until at least 1915. Wem Parawan, an OroEo woman who would be eighty-five years old today,[4] was born in Pan Toropain, OroNao' territory, because the OroEo were fleeing their enemies at the time. This surprised me, since I assumed she was referring to the whites, who, against all historical evidence, must have penetrated the Wari' territory via the river headwaters, since that was the only way they could have threatened the OroEo before the OroNao', who lived further downriver. Paletó explained that Wem Parawan was not referring to the white enemies, but to the OroMawin. Orowao Toko Jai, an OroAt man of about eighty, confirmed this fact on another occasion, saying that his grandfather had told him that the OroAt had lived in OroNao' territory for a while, when running from the OroMawin.

I have records of some of these confrontations. Wem Parawan told me that a man she called grandfather had killed an OroMawin. They took his head and ate the brains. Her mother was one of the people who ate him. The skull—with the jaw bones bound with vines—was painted with annatto and used as a bird cage. I estimate that this episode happened at the start of the 1900s. Wem Parawan added that the OroAoAo had always attacked them and that a man named Orowao Mumum, also her grandfather, had died "prey to the OroAoAo" (*watamakon OroAoAo*). This must have been around 1910.

According to Wem Parawan, after this event, an OroNao' man called Mamxun Mete, who was trekking in the mountain uplands, shot an Oro-Mawin man and returned to his companions to ask them to help him carry back pieces of the dead enemy's body, which they subsequently roasted and ate. This man's daughter was near her father at the time of the attack and be-haved like a killer on her return: she drank maize beer and lay down, but in her own house rather than in the men's house as male killers do. She fattened and aroused envy in the other women, who fantasized: were she a man, we'd have sex with her to fatten too. The enemy's spirit-blood, responsible for the fattening process, had entered her via her father's sweat.

We also have Paletó's account of an expedition to attack the OroMawin involving his father, who was invited to join the OroEo war party while he was living among the OroNao'. This episode, richly described in my inter-views, seems to have happened around 1915. I explore the event in detail later in order to illustrate Wari' warfare practices.

I obtained few accounts on the war between the Wari' OroMon and OroWaramXijein (and perhaps OroWaram) subgroups and the enemy Oro-Tarakom/Karipuna. Perhaps this was because I was unable to talk to many people from these subgroups. But since the Wari' enjoy talking about war, it is more likely that this paucity reflects the absence of conflicts. Given that we know the whites arrived in the territory of these subgroups at the start of the 1900s, the war with the Karipuna may have ended well before the conflicts between the OroEo/OroAt and the OroAoAo/OroWin/OroMawin. But a late confrontation did occur. An OroWaramXijein man, accompanied by other Indians, one of them OroMon, killed a Karipuna man (whom he calls OroTarakom in Wari', and Karipó in Portuguese) around 1950. I heard him describing this feat proudly: apparently it had been a long time since he had killed an Indian.

While the above subgroups were nearly always at war, the OroNao', living in the center of the Wari' territory, spent a period without enemies when the other Indians had effectively disappeared and the whites had yet to approach. This must have occurred between 1900 and 1920. Paletó said that his father, who was born OroAt but later decided to live among the OroNao', had found it difficult to become a killer due to the lack of enemies. The first enemy he killed was OroMawin, in the episode cited above, at the invitation of the OroEo. But not all of the OroNao' had the chance to become killers before the whites invaded: "Then the whites arrived. They came by water and traveled upriver. It had been a long time since our ancients had killed. They no longer wore their hair long and parted down the middle [like killers]. They cut their hair like women do. Big men, who already had children. There were no enemies to shoot. They had nothing to do. Only when the true enemy arrived [*iri wijam*—whites][5] and they shot them were they able to part their hair down the middle" (Paletó 1992).

From this point of view, the arrival of whites was providential. The men were anxious to become killers and, at least in terms of warfare practice, drew no difference between indigenous enemies and whites, calling both of them *wijam*, enemy. The difference resided in the fact that the whites possessed objects that the Wari' quickly came to covet and steal, and in the peaceful intentions displayed by the whites during the initial contacts. I return to this question later. For now let us examine how Wari' warfare was conducted.

PREPARING FOR WAR

A man would decide to kill enemies to avenge the death of a relative, or simply to become a killer and thus beautiful, fat, and long-haired. Killing an enemy also made the killer's wife more beautiful, fattening her with his semen, impregnated with the enemy's spirit-blood. His decision made, he would either invite his coinhabitants or travel to join up with men from other subgroups. The invitation could be made in various ways: "Let's kill the enemy,[6] let's do to him what he's done to our kin!" Or, "Let's make war! Let's get fat!" Or even, "Let's make war! Let's fatten our women!"

Those taking part in a war expedition made themselves new bows and arrows, reducing the danger of the bows snapping during the attack. *Mapat* arrows were employed, fitted with the same sharp bamboo tip used to kill large animals such as tapirs (fig. 12).

Sometimes collective hunting trips were undertaken before the departure. The killed prey were handed to the women with the exclamation, "Burn the enemy!" After being roasted or boiled by the women, the meat was eaten

12. Hwerein Pe e' prepares a new bow using a peccary jaw as a file.
Rio Negro–Ocaia, 1987. (Photo by Beto Barcellos)

by everyone. Jubilant, they danced and sang male music (*tamara*) before departing.

This is what happened when the OroEo invited Paletó's father to attack the OroMawin.

> My father had never shot an enemy. It was only after his first child, the father of Tem Arakat [a recently deceased woman, who would now be about sixty years old], that the OroEo arrived. [They] knew how to kill every kind of true enemy [*iri wijam*].[7] It was they, the ancients of the OroEo, who killed the OroMawin. So the OroEo arrived, a long time ago, and said, "Let's kill the enemy, my son!" He was the only one here who had short hair. "The killer [*napiri*]. The killer is arriving!" the OroEo said. "Our son is arriving; he's a killer. He's Wao the killer. Wao the killer is arriving. The OroNao' is arriving. Our son is arriving. He's Wao the killer, Wao Em' the killer." They called him Wao the killer although your grandfather [referring to me, since Paletó classifies me as a daughter] had never killed an enemy. Wao the killer. . . . "I'm going to carry the fire" [Paletó's father said]. "Stay here" [his hosts said]. He stayed. "I'm going to fetch my fire" [Paletó's father said]. And so they danced and danced. He put down his fire. At night, they [other OroNao'] appeared. They danced all night. When dawn came, they said, "Let's go to the enemy, my son, let's go!" "Okay" [Paletó's father said]. (Paletó 1992)

On arriving at the OroEo village, from where they would depart for the land of the enemy, the OroNao', now accompanied by various OroAt men invited en route, danced and sang again. The OroEo welcomed them as foreigners (Wari' from other subgroups) arriving for a festival. Here the future killer is already called *napiri*, as are all the warriors who return home after killing at least one enemy.

THE RITUAL FIRE

The ritual fire carried by the expedition leader consisted of a bundle of stalks (*muruhut*) from the aricuri palm (*torot*—*Cocos* sp.)—or, according to some people, from the babassu palm (*towaxi'*—*Orbignia martiana*). It was tied with lianas and decorated with annatto and babassu oil. The liana used to tie the bundle was shaped into a handle by which the bundle was hung over the shoulder of the fire owner (*waximain xe*).

Until his return, this man was called simply "Fire" (*Xe*) and followed a series of restrictions. He had to treat the ritual bundle with extreme care, like a child; indeed, according to a man he called it "my child." While trekking toward the enemies, he had to carry the bundle on the same shoulder, making the task painful and exhausting. The torches were unlit, except for one held in Fire's hand. As this began to fade, he lit another torch. The fire was used to cook the game killed on the expedition, eaten with toasted maize flour prepared by the women before the men departed. Sometimes, when the journey home was too long, parts of the victims' bodies were roasted to prevent them from rotting.

The bundle of torches could not be deposited directly on the ground. When the men stopped to rest or sleep, it was "laid" on a leaf next to Fire. The latter could not speak loudly and ideally said nothing. Under no circumstances could he become dirty. He could not hunt or handle the killed game; when he was about to sit down, his companions rushed to fetch a leaf for him as a rough mat to sit on. Nor could he touch food directly. Instead, he had to use sticks to skewer the meat. He also used twigs to scratch himself.

As we shall see later, these restrictions also apply to those who have just killed an enemy, though the Wari' themselves explain the practices differently. When asked why Fire cannot become dirty, people replied that he could not come into contact with water. Likewise, the bundle of torches could not be placed on the ground lest it become dirty, as though it were an extension of Fire's body. Were he to become dirty, he would feel the need to wash and torrential rain would fall on the Wari', knocking over trees that would kill the war party.

When they neared the enemies, the fire owner deposited the bundle on the ground and was the first to shoot an arrow. The other expedition members then fired their own arrows, even if the first had been sufficient to kill, though this was seldom the case.[8] All of those shooting arrows became killers too, but releasing the first arrow made a difference: some people said the killed enemy was called the "prey" of the man who had shot first, although everyone could take parts of the dead body back home. One man said that the enemy's spirit-blood only really penetrated the first warrior to shoot, and "entered the others just a little bit," especially if they had shot the enemy when he or she was already dead.

On this expedition, other warriors appear to have wanted to shoot first, telling Paletó's inexperienced father to stay behind at the moment of the attack: " 'Keep back,' they [the Wari'] said to me [Paletó's father]. They told him [Paletó's father] to retreat. He sat down. Another man then said: 'No! If you retreat, the others will shoot [the enemy] and not you. They're going to shoot in your place. You've already carried the heavy fire for them!' " (Paletó 1992).

After the attack, the fire owner used to give a lit torch to each warrior so he could survive alone in the forest, should the raiding party need to disperse as it fled. According to other informants, and to another of Paletó's own accounts, the fire was distributed as soon as the enemies were encountered and before any arrows were shot.

The restrictions on the fire owner continued, at least those prohibiting contact with water. He could only bathe when he arrived home: a storm would still break out over the village, but there the falling trees would pose no threat since the Wari' houses were built in clearings.

It is intriguing that the danger posed by being careless with fire was linked to an excess of water rather than an excess or absence of fire (such as a forest blaze or the extinguishing of the fire) as might be expected. I return to this point later in my analysis of various Wari' myths, including the myth describing the origin of fire. This system of myths turns on the theme of water, either in excess, as in the flood myth, or absent, as in the Oropixi' myth on the origin of whites. In the fire origin myth, fire is confronted with water several times and extinguished. Humans only succeed in obtaining fire definitively when they eventually manage to separate it from water.

THE ATTACK STRATEGY

The main Wari' war strategy was the ambush. The warriors hid near the enemy village and waited for their victims to approach. The Wari' avoided attacking large groups of people and I never heard them mention direct raids on enemy houses, for example. They had no interest in a confrontation or war in which both sides were simultaneously active. What interested them was killing enemies and just one was enough given that everyone shot him or her. Whenever possible, they killed more than one enemy and took the bodies (head, arms, and legs) to be eaten by people back in the villages. Anticipating the enemy's desire for revenge, the war party would flee quickly. The objective of the expeditions was to kill enemies rather than capture them. The Wari' never mentioned abducting an enemy, though this does not mean the idea was never considered. In some versions of the myth describing the time when the Wari' ate only lizards (see above), the man who teaches them to recognize their real prey is the son of enemies killed by the Wari', brought back to live with them. Another myth contains this idea in reverse: a Wari' girl called Piro was caught by Indian enemies and lived among them until she had become an adult, married, and had children. Advised of their whereabouts by a bird, Piro fled back to her own people. Arriving home, she taught the Wari' everything she had learned among the enemies: cooking maize pudding in water (previously only ever roasted), chewing maize beer to make it sweeter and less thick, and singing the appropriate words during funerals.

Paletó's account of his father's raid on the enemies illustrates the Wari' attack strategy perfectly:

[Enemy] women were sitting weaving tucumã [*wao'*] palm fiber. They were laughing. Some men approached and they all walked off. They looked [to the Wari'] like true people, covered in annatto dye, like Wari' from another subgroup. . . . The oldest turned round [to look at the women] and laughed. The women looked back. They pushed each other: "Walk!" . . . They walked. . . . "Then I remembered I was supposed to shoot" [said Paletó's father]. "Shoot the enemy, son," they said to him. This is what they told me [Paletó observed]. "The enemy is after us, older brother!" [the enemy exclaimed]. The youngest ran back. They struck him from behind in the shoulder blade, but he escaped. The largest fell dead. They filled him with arrows. "The enemy is after us, older brother!" [the enemy exclaimed]. "We shot and shot. The women fled into the forest. We continued to shoot. The oldest man died. A man, presumably the women's jealous husband, was sitting where they had been weaving the fiber. When he saw the other man fall, he shouted, 'The enemy hit the lad!' " "The enemy is after the lads!" He [an enemy] cut down a tree branch and waved it to protect himself from the Wari' arrows. "The enemy is after the lads, let's escape!" [the Wari' said]. "Flee the enemy, son," they said to me [Paletó's father]. We ran into the forest. One of them pursued us alone. (Paletó 1992)

A narrative describing a confrontation decades later shows the same strategy in use. At the start of the 1950s, a group of OroMon and OroWaramXijein men encountered a small Karipuna group in the forest. They shot a woman and ran off, fearing pursuit. Here I transcribe part of the account given by a

OroWaramXijein man (which I collected in 1992), who was the first to shoot an arrow.

> We were living in the forest [during the period of the rainy season spent away from the maize swidden]. We walked far and found them [the Kari-puna] on a creek. . . . The river's name was Naxi, near the sources of the Laje. They were cutting down a tree. We hid and waited. When the sun began to set: "Let's go to them!" We headed off toward them. The women were crushing maize. As dusk approached, the women appeared. "Ta ton!" [sound of an arrow]. I shot her [one of the women]. [The warriors] pulled back their bows and shot. She fell in the water. . . . We ran away from where she had fallen, finding the path back home. "Let's go!" We ran and ran until nightfall. We slept until daybreak. "Let's go!" We continued until we arrived where our women were waiting.

This strategy was also used when attacking the whites. Below I transcribe part of an account collected in 1993, describing an attack on the outskirts of Guajará-Mirim in 1960. An OroWaram man, whose family had been extermi-nated by whites, left with other warriors on a revenge attack as soon as he fin-ished mourning. They lay in waiting by the road connecting Guajará-Mirim to Porto Velho until a lone man came past, unarmed. He shot him. Later he learned that the victim was the former police chief of Guajará-Mirim.

> The road to Porto Velho was not very big. . . . The houses in Guajará were visible in the far distance. There were many trees. The tractor had cleared the road. Many wild banana trees. It was thick forest. We lay in wait for the enemy. Then some whites came walking along the road, two of them. We were afraid of their guns and stayed still. Then a jeep came. We only saw their heads because the windows were closed. "Why are whites so strange? Why do they stay inside that thing?" the warriors said. "We want to shoot them!" A truck came, blowing its horn. "Their strange thing is coming. It looks like a train!" It was filled with whites. Had a white man not appeared walking alone, we would have shot at the truck. We thought that we would catch a white disease and become crippled if we shot the vehicle. Our ancients had shot one in the past: by nightfall, they were crippled. They couldn't walk. The truck had gone, taking them to work. Then the police chief came. He had left his house, which was about as far away as my present house is from the river [about 100 meters]. . . . He came alone. They had shot whites on bicycles before. I fired an arrow.

It's impossible to hit someone on a bike. He was using spectacles, clothing, and shoes. There was a big tree that the tractor had left intact. We
hid there. He came quickly: when he looked behind, we struck him in the
armpit. He fell to the ground. The Wari' shot more arrows at him. I shot
first. "Ai, ai, ai." They don't groan uiu, uiu, uiu [an aspirated sound: the way
the Wari' groan]. The bike rode on by itself. Hearing his cries, other whites
began to arrive. The Wari' were hidden, waiting to shoot more. "Tou, tou"
[sound of gun shots]. The other whites' guns could be heard. We fled. The
man we had shot was already dead. We didn't know he was their chief. The
SPI staff told us later. (OroWaram man 1993)

Although in this and many similar episodes the Wari' were forced to flee
from the guns, the whites were easier prey than their indigenous enemies
as they tended not to retaliate immediately. This, they say, was because
the whites lived in isolated nuclear families (probably referring to the rubber tappers, their most frequent victims). Even so, the Wari' were always
extremely careful to avoid any chance of reprisal. They never attacked the
houses themselves and when they decided to enter a house to steal tools,
they always made sure it was unoccupied. When attacking, they waited for
moments such as a man leaving his house to wash in the river or, as in the
episode with the police chief, someone walking alone along a track or road.
They often avoided attacking men, waiting for the husband to leave for work
before attacking the wife and children left at home.[9] This allowed the victims
to be cut up more easily and carried back to be roasted and eaten.

I obtained just a few accounts of attacks on Indians, but significantly
the victim was devoured in only one of them. This involved the above-
mentioned confrontation between the OroEo and the OroMawin at the
start of the 1900s when the victim's head was taken by the Wari' warriors
and his brains were eaten in the village. In other clashes, the Wari' apparently had no time to cut up the victim's body as they were forced to flee.

The pattern of conflicts with whites altered radically from the 1940s onward when large waves of rubber tappers and explorers penetrated the Wari'
territory. The Wari' then began to flee from the invaders, no longer isolated
rubber tappers grabbing their shotguns in response to a Wari' attack, but organized groups raiding their villages before dawn, killing everyone in their
path, especially those still asleep. One man declared, "The whites killed us.
It was like they were eating us, as though the Wari' were their *karawa* [prey,

food]." Most of these massacres seem to have taken place between the mid-1950s and the beginning of the 1960s when the Wari' were pacified.

Orowao Xain, an OroWaramXijein man, said that when he was a young man (the late 1950s), the whites came up the Ouro Preto River and killed a couple and their child in Tokon Pipin, an OroWaram village: "The whites killed three of their prey [*watamakon wijam*] in Tokon Pipin." They then headed to Tokon Jam, an OroWaramXijein village. They arrived early in the morning when everyone was asleep. First they shot the oldest brother of Orowao Xain, who was asleep in the first house on the path. Woken by the gunshot, the villagers ran away: those who succeeded in escaping abandoned the village and headed toward the headwaters of the Laje, an OroMon area. They took the bodies of their dead kin to be eaten there.

In the mid-1950s, Pan Kamerem, an OroWaramXijein man, was living in Tain Werem, another OroWaramXijein village located on the Tok Wi River. The whites arrived in Tain Wakaram, a nearby village where his younger brother Nowi lived. They attacked before dawn with machine guns, whose sound Pan Kamerem heard from his settlement. His sister Toko Pi'am was killed. In this episode the Wari' had time to roast and eat their dead kin before fleeing to the OroMon territory.

Jamain Tamanain, an OroAt man, recounted how the whites set fire to any abandoned villages and swiddens. This was the case of Tamajain, a village located on the Komikon Tarama River, an affluent of the Ocaia. Its OroEo inhabitants had managed to flee after a warning from the OroNao' that the whites were approaching.

The OroNao' on the left bank of the Pacaás Novos River also suffered attacks. After one raid in which many were killed, they left on a revenge expedition. According to Jamain Xok Ta, a number of men headed toward the Mamoré River and killed a Bolivian woman. They took her head, which was later eaten in Kaxima.

Events tended to follow the same pattern: the Wari' were attacked, generally by surprise, and they fled. Whenever possible, they carried their dead with them to provide an adequate funeral. When the whites remained at the locale, though, they had to wait for the latter to leave before returning to fetch the corpses, which, though already putrefying, were roasted and partially eaten. Later they would undertake a revenge expedition against the whites in general.

Paletó lost his entire family in a massacre that took place, I estimate, some-time between 1954 and 1959, in Xi Kam Araji, an OroNao' village situated on the Da Gruta River (We Turu).[10] Many others were also killed. The massacre occurred soon after a festival. Some villagers were in the river, bathing to "clean the dirt from the maize beer." This was the case of Paletó, his wife, and his two children.

> I'd gone to bathe, taking the maize beer path [used by guests to enter the village] to the river. My late daughter, To'o Em, had already finished bathing when the enemy killed her. "Let's go, Father. I'm cold." "No. Let's bathe a while longer." "Let's go, Father. I want to catch some sun." "Come on!" "Okay. Will you carry me, Father?" "No, I don't want to. Your mother can. I'll carry your younger brother," I said. "Okay." Her mother carried the girl. She walked ahead. "Let's go," I said to her. They went.
>
> We were still at some distance from the houses when we heard a shot. . . . They were shooting lying down. They struck one of the house posts. They [the Wari'] thought the post had split by itself. They shot again. The shot hit your dead father, Wao Em' [Paletó's younger brother, whom I would call Father were he alive]. "Run from the enemy!" they screamed. They started to flee. Manim, who was building a house, came down from the roof. I heard shots. They seemed to be shooting from be-hind me. I wanted to run. They hit the arm of Tem Arakat's dead mother [referring to his wife] and she stopped. I was still running when I saw the enemy. They were already there. [Noise of gunshots.] It must have been a machine gun for them to have killed so many of us. Your older brother fell wailing, Tem We fell wailing, her older brother too, those who stayed in the house. Orowao Kukui, the daughter of the old woman Topa', was behind the house and collapsed. Further on, the wife of Hwerein Pe e' fell and those of his children who were with her.
>
> Your grandfather [Paletó's father] ran along the path to the river. There were no enemies. He stopped and shouted to the enemy: "You killed all my grandchildren, wretched enemy! . . . These are my grandchildren you killed, wretched enemy!" The enemy saw him. He was some distance away. He shouted, turning to face the enemy. He [the enemy] shot him in the chest. "Ei, Ei!" He died. They shot at me on the path too. One of them chased me. A bullet hit my daughter's leg here. Her foot fractured at

this point. She became separated from her mother: "Father, Father, it's the enemy, Father! Mother, it's the enemy!" [she shouted]. I sat down, hiding in the forest. The enemy arrived. They pointed their guns at her [Paletó's daughter], wanting to kill her. As they pointed, her mother approached: "I'm going to get my daughter, who is crying." She was crazy. She didn't see the enemy. Covering her eyes with her arm, she crawled over to her daughter and lay beside her. The enemy remained quiet, waiting for the mother to arrive so they could kill them both. They tried to hit their heads. She had a bit of life left. She ran away from her daughter.

That's why I dislike the enemy who killed my father. We weren't going to shoot the enemy. We just fled. We were scared of them. We fled to OroEo land. We ran and ran until arriving there. "Let's return to cut up the dead!" The enemy was still there. By the time they left, the dead were already rotten. The vultures had eaten my daughter: "Look at her foot!" [someone showed Paletó the girl's partially eaten foot]. My father too. The vultures had eaten his buttocks. And sucked out his eyes. Everyone, the vultures had eaten everyone. They lit a fire to roast the rotten remains . . . and ate them, although they were very rotten. Rotten, very rotten. Many maggots. They washed and ate them without another thought. That's how the enemy killed us. (Paletó 1992)

Afraid the whites might return, they cut up the dead and transported them in baskets for roasting in a nearby village, Pin Karam. Later they were taken to be eaten in another village, Takat Jowin, located on the upper Komi Wawan River. Paletó's younger brother, Xiemain, who was five years old at the time, managed to escape despite being struck by lead shot in several places. He spent days wandering lost and alone in the forest, walking along the Wari' tracks but encountering nobody. He was only found, sitting on a path, when the Xi Kam Araji villagers returned to gather the remains of the dead.

Some months after narrating this episode, Paletó told me that these enemies were not actually whites (hence I have maintained the word "enemy" in translating the term *wijam*), but Makurap Indians sent by the whites. He cited each of the killers' names, one of whom took part in the pacification of the Wari' some years later. It was because they were Indians rather than whites that they took so long to leave, Paletó said: they were waiting near the dead for more people to kill. Had they been whites, they would have left soon after.[11]

In this episode, retaliation was directed against the whites, in part since the Makurap themselves were living among the latter. The kin of the victims, filled with rage once their mourning was completed—a period when they cry much of the time, eat almost nothing, and lack the energy to make war—organized various expeditions to kill whites, many of them successful.

Reports of the SPI mention various massacres of the Wari'. In 1952, Francisco Meireles informed the agency's director that the rubber boss José Pereira da Silva had sent Raimundo Bezerra and another fifteen men to destroy a Wari' maloca near the rubber-tapper settlement on the upper Ouro Preto: "It was the same maloca where we had left gifts during the expedition to find Father Mauro. They killed twenty Indians and blinded the children. This is the fourth massacre suffered by the 'Pacáas Novos' in the last two years." In 1955, the rubber boss Manussakis, who ran various seringais on the Ouro Preto River, sent men to attack malocas. Various Indians were killed and a victim's ear was taken. In 1960, a massacre was perpetrated in the region of the Ouro Preto River and, in January 1961, armed whites in the Iata farm colony region apparently raided Wari' villages.

Dom Roberto Gomes de Arruda, the former bishop of Guajará-Mirim, who died in 2003, recounted these massacres in an interview:

> These intensified more, perhaps, during the period when rubber was being extracted because the bosses sent their employees into the forests to work, but naturally they wanted the product back. And this meant imposing peace and respect on the Indians. So they organized armed groups to "clear" the area, as they put it. And this clearing involved destroying all the villages, killing everyone they found. . . .
>
> With machine guns, they really did use machine guns. Afterward, they entered the village, liquidating the remaining women and children. I also heard an account given by an OroNao' man whose wife had died in these attacks. . . . The terrible thing was that he saw the moment when a white man grabbed a relatively small child from the mother's arms, and as he held one of the child's legs, another man held the other, and with a machete they sliced the child straight down the middle. Then they stabbed the mother clean through with a machete and left them both for dead. (Dom Roberto 1993)

As I stated, the Wari' tried to exact revenge whenever possible. Records of whites being killed by the Wari'—found in official SPI reports, as well as local and national newspapers—are not rare. The deaths were never on a large

scale like the massacres inflicted on the Wari', but the Brazilian public was
horrified by the often mutilated bodies found pierced with dozens of arrows
(all of the warriors shot the corpse). The SPI's reports from 1957 mention
constant Wari' attacks on the Major Amarante post (today the Ribeirão village) and along the Madeira–Mamoré railroad. A man was also reportedly
killed at the 9 kilometer point on the railroad between Guajará-Mirim and
Iata, his belly sliced open and one arm missing. A news report from June
1960 also tells of the death of the former Guajará-Mirim police chief, Odacil
Pires Almeida. The report states that both of his legs had been amputated. If
this is the victim killed by the OroWaram man cited earlier, this contradicts
the latter's observation that the body was left intact because the warriors
were forced to flee from the gunfire.

The press, armed with photos displaying limbless corpses, published spurious texts depicting the Wari' as torturers of living people—precisely what
the whites did to the Wari'—and ravenous for human flesh.[12] The report cited
below was published under the headline: "Pacáas-Novos kill whites out of
hate and hunger in Rondônia."

> This anthropophagic scene occurred in December last year, some two
> kilometers from the center of Guajará-Mirim town, on the border with
> Bolivia; yet only now has news of it been published in the press. . . .
>   The small victim of the Pacáas-Novos was called Antônio. The boy was
> alone at home while his parents worked the fields a short distance away. . . .
> It was around midday when . . . he ran toward the plantation, but was hit
> by a well-aimed arrow before crossing a nearby stream.
>   Still alive, as was discovered later, the Indians took their victim to a
> clearing in the forest and cut him into pieces. The yells of the Indians
> during the pre-dismemberment ritual attracted the attention not only of
> Antônio's parents, but other plantation workers too.
>   As the group approached, the Indians abandoned their victim, taking
> the legs, which were never found. The local inhabitants, well aware of the
> habits of the Pacáas-Novos, have no doubts that the attackers feasted on
> the amputated limbs in another forest clearing and were only prevented
> from devouring the whole body by their discovery. (*O Jornal*, July 23,
> 1963)

Two photographs accompanied the report. One of them shows the dead
boy, without legs, under the caption: "Here, in all its cruelty, is proof that
the Pacáas-Novos practice anthropophagy. The body of Antônio, without

his legs, taken by the savages." The other photo shows three Wari' men aiming arrows in the air, taken after almost all of the Wari' had been pacified (a process undertaken between 1961 and 1962, before the report's publication). The caption to the second photo reads: "The Pacáas-Novos have not abandoned their arrows and are true masters of hunting. But from time to time they shoot a civilized person, just for fun or to improve their aim."

THE ARRIVAL OF THE WARRIORS AND RECLUSION

Whenever possible—that is, when not forced to run—the warriors cut up the body of their *dead* victims (contrary to the report's claim, they never sliced up their enemies—or even animal prey—while still alive) to take certain parts with them. They cut off the head, the arms at the shoulder or elbow, and the legs at the thigh or the knee. These parts were taken back home, transported just like animal prey: slung over the back, tied with a vine wrapped around the warrior's forehead. The trunk was usually left intact. Sometimes they also took the genitalia, especially those of men so that the women could see the enemy's penis. But in contrast to the head, arms, and legs, which were roasted and eaten, the genitalia were thrown into the forest or river after being admired.

When the warriors came from different villages, each one could take a piece of the enemy home. The body was distributed exactly like animal meat: the owner of the prey—the first to strike the enemy with an arrow—always kept the largest part and the head.

While those returning from a war expedition were always greeted euphorically by the people waiting at home, the welcome was even more effusive when they brought back bits of the enemy. The enemy was generally transported raw and roasted on a grill by the women in the village. However, when the journey back was long, the warriors themselves—barred from eating—sometimes roasted the flesh in the forest to prevent it from rotting. The flesh of an enemy, just like animal meat, could not be eaten or roasted once it had begun to rot.[13]

Close to home, the warriors whistled or blew their flutes. Everyone ran to meet them, shouting, "Did you shoot the enemy?" "I shot him," each warrior replied. This was greeted with elated cries. They handed the enemy's flesh to the women, saying, "Roast my prey" (*Xain je watama*). According to Orowam, mothers would jokingly offer to breastfeed any sons who had killed. Afterward, the killers—only called as such (*napiri*) while the reclusion lasted—went directly to the men's house and sat down. There they discussed the expedition and were washed by the women, covering themselves afterward with annatto and babassu palm oil.

Parents would tell their children to shoot the remains of the enemy's body, even after it was grilled. This was typically the first sight Wari' children—and women—had of the enemy: body parts. Many people told me this when I asked, "What was it like the first time you saw an enemy?" Because of the age of the informants, the responses below all refer to white enemies.

> I saw the arms and the head. Only the men saw him alive. (To'o, Sagarana village, 1993)
>
> My other father, Maxun Kohot, cut off the upper section of a woman's trunk and took it for the women to see. I was astonished; I thought they walked on all fours, but no, she was beautiful, she had breasts. (Piwan, Sagarana village, 1993)
>
> It was a body the ancients had chopped up. Just arms and legs. I was a child. (Orowao Xain, Lage village, 1994)
>
> It was the head. I was surprised: "It's like a Wari' head!" The skin smelled of clothes. (Orowao Powa, Ribeirão village, 1994)
>
> Maxun Horok chopped up an enemy and took the hands to the village. That was when we saw his body. (Tokohwet, Rio Negro–Ocaia village, 1993)

When the enemy's body was still raw on arrival, the women roasted and ate it along with the men (generally older men) who had stayed behind in the village. They ate the brains and the meat from the arms and legs. To eat the brains, they made a hole in the skull and removed the mass with their fingers. The meat was torn into strips and eaten by hand, or eaten directly off the bone, just like animal meat, and was accompanied by maize cake or flour.

There was no singing, dancing, or beer drinking. It was essentially a lavish meal, with one difference: the enemy's flesh was eaten in anger. Paletó added that eating the enemy's flesh angrily distinguished this meal from the funerary feast where the flesh of a dead Wari' was eaten with sadness and delicacy, the small strips of meat placed on a mat and eaten by anyone who was not consanguine kin of the deceased, using chopsticks to raise the bits of flesh to their mouth slowly. Furthermore, Paletó explained, Wari' flesh has a different

13. Boys on a *xijat* hammock. Santo André, 2003.

flavor: enemy flesh tastes like spider monkey. According to another Wari' man, the taste is more like tapir, due to its high fat content.

As I mentioned earlier, the skull could be discarded or decorated and used as a bird cage. The limb bones were not employed in any way.

On arriving back home, and after being bathed by the women, the killers made large assai fiber hammocks capable of holding two or more warriors; the hammocks were lined with mats woven by the women (fig. 13). They also made a small bamboo flute with a tucumã coconut mouthpiece, used to request unfermented maize drink, their main food during reclusion. They also wove a small mat of tucumã straw, decorated with red macaw tail feathers. Holding this under the arm, they performed an individual dance, proudly celebrating their feat.

The killers were excluded from devouring the enemy because their bodies had been penetrated by the victim's spirit-blood, making killer and victim consubstantial. Eating the enemy would provoke their own deaths, replicating the effect of eating one's own consanguine kin.[14] Here I have used the expression spirit-blood (also used by Conklin 2001, 33) since the Wari' alternate freely between the two terms when referring to the part of the enemy that penetrated the killer. According to my informants, either the enemy's spirit (*jamikon wijam*), the enemy's blood (*kikon wijam*), or the enemy's spirit-blood (*jamikikon wijam*) penetrated the killer's body. This spirit-blood could not be lost and indeed the main objective of the restrictions imposed on the killers during reclusion was to avoid release of the enemy's spirit-blood.[15]

The killer had to avoid speaking to prevent the enemy's spirit from escaping via his mouth. He refrained from walking to avoid the risk of cutting himself and losing the enemy's blood. All of his movements had to be very slow. The killers could not have sex. Were they to, the enemy's blood, transformed into semen,[16] would pass to the woman, who alone would fatten. Consequently, during reclusion the men's house was sometimes circled by a barrier of palm leaves through which the women handed the killers pots of maize beer. The killers avoided looking at the women so they would not be tempted to have sex: an erection would be enough for them to lose the enemy's spirit-blood.

Inside the body, the enemy's spirit-blood induced the killer's fattening, the main objective of warfare and reclusion. The killers fattened so much that the fat seeped out from around their eyes. The limbs of boys who had accompanied their fathers on the expedition were stretched daily by their mothers to speed growth, whether they had shot the victim or not. People say that at least some of the enemy's spirit-blood had penetrated their bodies.

The presence of this spirit-blood, however, was insufficient to fatten the killers by itself. They also had to drink large amounts of unfermented maize drink. This was prepared unceasingly by the women and requested from them day and night by the men playing the small tucumã palm flute. The consumption of maize drink was so high that they even drank it warm, something never contemplated in everyday circumstances. At the end of reclusion, which lasted around a month (see Vilaça 1992, 107), the women were exhausted from the work. Indeed, sometimes they were the ones to end the reclusion, arguing that the killers were fat enough and could resume walking about and hunting.

Other restrictions were not directly linked to preventing loss of the enemy's spirit-blood but to preserving the killers' physical integrity: eating slow animals or those that sleep during the day would make them lazy, while animals with a lot of blood, including some fish, could cause their abdomens to swell from an excess of blood. And like the fire owner, killers had to avoid becoming dirty and therefore could not handle food directly, using twigs instead. Here, though, the problem is not an incompatibility with water: the killers could be bathed without risk of provoking violent storms. Indeed, killers took pride in their bodies, desiring to look beautiful. They also had to avoid scratching themselves directly with their own fingernails or else they would grow white hairs (a sign of rapid aging). Their nails could only be cut at the end of reclusion and their hair, having grown over the period, was left long, a characteristic so important for killers that a man would invite another to war by saying, "Let's kill enemies! Your hair must have grown by now!"

The exogenous blood present in the bodies of the killers was eminently positive, an excess of blood potentialized by the maize beer that fattened the killers, augmenting their vigor and productive capacity. However, the latent threats to their bodies' physical integrity, the risk of precocious aging, and the fact that the killers continually covered themselves in a thick layer of annatto dye—a known neutralizer of blood—indicates that something potentially dangerous was contained in this blood. Or more precisely, the traces of the enemy within the killers' bodies. Reclusion was primarily a period for processing the dead enemy, who was eventually "physiologically" eliminated in order to be socially incorporated, like a birth after pregnancy.[17] At the end of reclusion, the killers' bodies were painted with the blood of game (generally collared peccary) and they went to bathe. This blood is likened to a soap that washed off whatever remained of the enemy's blood. From then on, the enemy's spirit remained close to its killers and became their child, eating their food.[18] At the death of a killer, the spirit of the enemy accompanied him to the world of the dead and indeed these dead enemies were the only non-Wari' to form part of this world. Similarly, the Wari' killed by enemies became part of the enemies' group, acquiring a body like theirs and accompanying them wherever they went.

In summary, the presence of the enemy's spirit-blood inside the killers represented a danger to the latter. But as a container of the dead enemy, did the Wari' killers pose a danger to society as a whole? Was there a kind of "ritual fusion" (Viveiros de Castro 1996b; 2002, 265–94) between killers and victims, making the former a threat to the group, just like the killers among the Tupian Araweté and Parakanã (Fausto 2001)? The Wari' do not make this threat explicit, although Conklin (1989, 237) does note that killers should keep away from their young children because the enemy's spirit could make them sick.

I also heard of one case—told to me as an illustration of how the enemy's spirit ate with the killer—where the killer had not been properly fed by the women and went hungry. One day, the killer's younger sister was inexplicably shoved into a pot of boiling maize beer and died. They concluded that, starving, the enemy's spirit had taken revenge by killing the girl. My informants stressed, though, that it was not the killer, her brother, who pushed her—the implication being that the enemy's spirit had acted alone.

This differs considerably from the Araweté, for instance, who suggest a "fusion" between the killer and enemy, expressed in sudden outbreaks of violence: "As soon as he kills his enemy, the killer's weapons must be abandoned; the spirit of the deceased, filled with a desire for revenge, provokes a homicidal fury in him, capable of turning the killer against his own [fellows]. When it arrives over the killer, the enemy's spirit transforms him into an enemy for us,' the Araweté told me" (Viveiros de Castro 2002, 279).

Although this description bears no similarity to the actions of the Wari' killer, it does match what happens to the shaman: as we shall see later, the latter is clearly an enemy in the midst of his own group. The Wari' seem to take to an extreme the difference (in the context of an underlying similarity) between killer and shaman formulated by Viveiros de Castro in relation to the Araweté (2002, 282): the killer is a "being unto himself," while the shaman is a "being for the group." The killer's group does not appropriate any kind of symbolic wealth from the dead enemy: no songs, names, or emblems.[19] Neither does it appropriate any of the enemy's "negative" attributes: his anger, a thirst for vengeance—in sum, an enemy position. Everything appears limited to a transfer of substances, an operation confined to the level of individual physiology, culminating with the enemy spirit's transformation into a (parthenogenetic) child of the killer.

However, while the dead enemy is not a direct source of symbolic wealth, he or she does enable the elaboration of the figure of the killer, without which, as Viveiros de Castro (2002, 282) writes of the Araweté, masculinity would be unthinkable. In this sense, the enemy's death enables a differentiation within Wari' society: the distinction between men and women. The Wari' express this idea clearly. A man who failed to hit the enemy with his arrow was called a woman, as Maxun Kworain discovered when he repeatedly failed to hit the missionaries trying to attract the Wari' at the end of the 1950s. When the Wari' passed through a period without enemies to attack, people said that the men were "like women," using short hair and bangs.

But the dead enemy not only defines a male term or position: the war victim is also an essential medium of gender relations.[20] The dialogues between warriors and women found in Wari' war narratives suggest that men killed enemies for women. To illustrate this point, I turn to the dialogue between Paletó's father and a woman whom he classifies as we (either an older sister or his father's real or classificatory sister). The excerpt is a fairly formal dialogue in which the correct forms of speech are being taught to Paletó's inexperienced father before his first war expedition (the raid on the OroMawin cited earlier).

> A woman who was a *we* to him arrived and said, "You arrived then, killer?" "Yes, I arrived." "Aren't you afraid of the enemy, killer?" "I'm not afraid, *we.*" "Be brave when confronting the enemy!" My father sang *tamara* [male music]. . . . "Be brave, killer. Shoot the enemy, killer! Talk to your *we.*" "I'm going to shoot the enemy, *we!*" "Cut him up for me, killer." "Bring his flesh to your *we*" [they all said to Paletó's father]. (Paletó 1992)

This account implies, I think, that men killed enemies at least in part to please women. The war narratives reveal that women desired the enemy's flesh as a present, highlighting the fundamental role played by women in warfare, since it was their desire that led to enemies being killed.

According to men, women desired this flesh because they mistakenly believed that were they to eat it they would fatten like the killers without having to wait for the sperm injected into them by their husbands at the end of reclusion. But this did not happen and, as Paletó explained, "women must wait for the semen (of the killer)," which is the sure way of fattening. During reclusion, women approached the killers and provoked them: "Have sex with me. Look how I'm making lots of maize drink for you." Paletó recounted that the women spread semen over their bodies, downed maize drink, and copied the killers' food taboos.

Interestingly, though, the role of women as eaters of enemy flesh only becomes explicit in the war narratives. All of the women whom the men identified as eaters of enemies vehemently denied having done so.[21]

But what does it mean to be fat? Fat people are more vigorous, more active. For men, this means greater aptitude in performing their activities, such as filling the bellies of women with hunt game and children. The Wari' have a specific verb for being pregnant, *nam'*, but people often say that a pregnant women has a full belly, *ma'am*, like someone with a stomach full of food. Through warfare, men are able to actualize this capacity—not only by immediately satiating women's hunger with enemy meat, but making them fat with their semen, just as in pregnancy.

Animal meat and enemy meat—or an enemy that transforms into meat/ fat—mediate the relations between men and women, differentiating them. Women mediate the relations between men, enabling another differentiation within Wari' society, the opposition between affines and consanguines.

Women also mediate between the Wari' and enemies: given by the former to the latter, they attenuate the difference between the two groups, transforming enemies into Wari' affines. This suggests not only a potential equivalence between women and enemies/game, but also an equivalence between enemies and affines in the form of the relation between "taking brothers-in-law" (*nem*) and "giving brothers-in-law" (*namori*), a theme explored in chapter 7.

As for the equivalence between women and prey, the Wari' conceive of sex, particularly illicit sex, as predation in both its hunting and warfare varieties. A special verb exists for having sex, *wan*, which only admits a male subject. But the sexual act, especially outside of marriage, can also be verbalized as to eat, kill game, or shoot an enemy, where the man invariably figures as the subject of the action. A man asking another whether he had sex may use a number of equivalent expressions: "Did you have sex with her?" (*Wan mam?*); "Did you eat her?" (*Kao' mam?*); "Did you kill game?" (*Pa' main karawa?*); "Did you shoot the enemy?" (*Huru mon wijam?*).[22]

The equivalence between enemies and affines can be seen from two angles. The first involves social incorporation, as the Nanananana myth analyzed in chapter 6 makes clear: offering women to enemies transforms them into Wari'. The second involves incorporation through predation. According to some informants, the term *napiri*, killer, can also be used to designate pubertal girls who are ready to consummate their marriages: in other words, the husbands to whom they have been promised since childhood can fetch them and take them back to their houses or villages. Pursuing this comparison, we could say that the killer is like a woman given by the Wari' to the enemies, making them into "taking brothers-in-law," incorporating the prey to be devoured into society. From both perspectives the enemy enters Wari' society as a "taking brother-in-law"—alive in the myth, and dead in the warfare association between killers and women (for more on this idea, see Vilaça 1992). In symmetrical fashion, "excorporation"—the transformation of a Wari' into an enemy—involves the medium of affinity, as the myth on the origin of the whites, analyzed later, makes clear. In this process, a consanguine is turned into a foreigner before becoming an enemy—and, as we have seen, the foreigner is the prototypical affine.

Hence we find various forms of predation that connect sex, warfare, and hunting. Men prey on women as if they were enemies and animals, making the relation between affines a relation mediated by predation; men prey on their affines—because by killing an enemy they are "affinizing" him and also because they directly eat their real affines in funerary cannibalism, and symbolically kill their prototypical affines in the rites analyzed in the previous chapter; and men prey on enemies and animals to satisfy women. We can conclude that predation—characterized as devouring the other—is the primary means of relating two different terms, establishing or modifying these terms through the act itself. Predation may therefore be direct, where one term of a pair eats the other, or indirect, involving a third term, the prey, which passes from one term to the other as the medium of the relation. As Viveiros de Castro writes in an article on Araweté warfare:

> As we find recurrently in the regional ethnology, the general schema of every difference is cannibal predation, of which affinity is merely a specific codification, albeit a privileged one. At the risk of falling into allegorical excess, I would venture to say that, in the cosmologies in question, the generic attributive proposition is a cannibal proposition. The prototype of the predicative relation between subject and object is predation and incorporation: between affines, between men and women, between humans and animals, between humans and spirits, and, naturally, between enemies. (Viveiros de Castro 2002, 165)

As we shall see, however, while predation involves an objectification of the victim that is essential to defining the subject/human position occupied by the predators, ideally Wari' men, the victim is only constituted as such when it is human, or has the potential to become human—like the animal prey that can prey upon the Wari' (which I discuss later). In the words of Viveiros de Castro on the Wari':

> Predation here is not the mere appropriation of an inert and naturalized Other by a Subject that contains within itself the values of humanity and agency; it is inevitably and immediately a *social relation*. Speaking of cannibalism, in the Amerindian world, means speaking of a relation between socially determined subjects. Here predation is not production, but communication, exchange, combat. And this is why predatory relations are essentially reversible and reciprocal: what one eats will eat in the future, and who eats will be eaten. (Viveiros de Castro 1992b, xiv)

One point remains to be explored: namely, the association between warfare and the fermented beverages commonly found among Amerindian groups: for example, the Tupinambá beer ritual held at the moment of ingesting the flesh of the enemy, or the Juruna beer festival in which warfare emerges as one of the main topics of conversation (Lima 1995, 391; 2005, 252–73). Among the Wari', warfare also emerges as a theme in the festivals involving the consumption of maize beer. However, warfare is not a topic of conversation in these festivals: here we are dealing with symbolized rather than verbalized warfare. Fermented drink—or nonfermented drink offered like a fermented drink, in the *tamara*, for example—is a weapon that kills affines and foreigners, but not enemies. This association also surfaces in the Wari' description of a person's death. The spirit of the deceased heads toward the underwater world of the dead where it is offered maize beer by one of the inhabitants. If the spirit accepts the drink, its body dies on the surface; if the beer is refused, the spirit returns to the world of the living and the body is cured.

Although offering maize beer is equivalent to warfare, the drink consumed in the warfare ritual is unfermented. However, the difference between the two types of drink resides merely in the time elapsed between production and consumption: the fermented drink, consumed exclusively in festivals, must be fabricated several days before being drunk, while the drink ingested by the killers is consumed as soon as it is ready (cooked), often while still warm. The latter can therefore be located on the opposite extreme of an imaginary scale of fermentation. This unfermented maize drink, preferred to water to quench thirst in daily life, is usually allowed to cool before being consumed. The drink made for the killers is not an antifood like maize beer, but an aliment that produces blood, which in turn is responsible—when combined with the enemy's blood—for an augmentation in the killer's body through fattening, producing vitality. The only similarity here is the quantity of drink ingested, which is considerable. Even so, the killers drink a lot because they wish to and continually ask for more rather than being forced to drink. Moreover, this drink must be kept inside the killer's body and not forcefully expelled, as happens in the beer festivals.

The Wari' description of the world of the dead, where everyone becomes young and beautiful, performing their ideal roles, shows that the relation between producing and consuming sweet maize drink typifies cross-sex gender relations as a relation between husband and wife. On arriving in the world of the dead, by drinking large quantities of maize beer, vomiting, fainting, and regaining consciousness, a man transforms into a *napiri* (killer) and enters reclusion, playing his tucumã palm flute and drinking lots of unfermented maize drink. A woman, likewise after drinking maize beer, vomiting, and coming round again, devotes herself to making the unfermented drink for the killer (see the Hwijin myth below).[23]

But Wari' descriptions of the world of the dead indicate that those wives do not make the maize beer. This function belongs to the wife of an underwater being called Towira Towira (*towira* meaning "testicle") due to his enormous gonads. Although associated with the dead as an inhabitant of their world, he represents on his own the role of the foreigner in a festival held to inebriate his guests, the spirits of the dead. Like Wari' festival hosts, he pesters the female guests to have sex with him. As I suggested earlier in relation to the arrival of the dead above ground in the form of white-lipped peccaries for a *tamara* festival, the relationship between the dead and the living involves the same kind of affinity dissociated from alliance thematized in festivals.

Hence women do not prepare maize beer for their husbands; instead, they feed them with sweet maize drink, both during homicide reclusion and in everyday life. They prepare sour maize beer for those who have no wish to marry them, since they desire them sexually rather than maritally. While unfermented drink is related to alliance, fermented drink is related to the absence of alliance, or even its negation, and hence to warfare too. As Viveiros de Castro proposes for Amerindian peoples in general: "As a product practically and symbolically marked by femininity, drinks can help us elucidate the nature of gender relations in Amazonian societies. There, the symbolic division of work between the sexes associates women with horticulture and men with hunting and warfare: but the true correlate of male cinegetic and warfare activity is not the simple female production of plant foods, but the production of fermented drinks" (Viveiros de Castro 1992b, xvi–xvii)

Here we can establish a correlation. What differentiates the preparation of fermented drink from the unfermented variety is simply the passage of time involved in fermentation. If unfermented maize drink symbolizes alliance—that is, the relation between affines rather than sex—while maize beer symbolizes the negation of alliance and the affirmation of predatory sex, then we can conclude that the difference between alliance and its negation likewise merely involves the passage of time. Alliance takes place in order to be negated. Nobody ever remains satisfied with the wife he receives and because of this discontent and the danger it arouses, affines are turned into consanguines. Alliance can easily be transformed into its negation, like the two types of maize drink, sweet and sour, with which each are associated.

Indeed, the Wari' call maize beer "furious," as if the froth of the beer was a metonym of the fury existing between these foreigners, the affines with whom alliance is absent because it would never work.

PREY AS ENEMIES AND ENEMIES AS PREY

Other Indians and whites are not the only enemies. As I mentioned earlier, some animals, including the main Wari' game, are conceived to be humans, *wari'* ("us" in the plural inclusive, "human being," "people"), since they are attributed with a spirit, *jam-*, and can shoot and kill the Wari', whom they perceive as enemies or prey. Given that *jam-* is primarily manifested as another body, or a body perceived as different from another perspective, I shall provide a brief explanation of the Wari' concept of the body.

The Wari' term that can be translated as body is *kwere-*, which, like *jam-*, is always accompanied by a possessive suffix. Not only human beings possess *kwere-*, and it is not limited to our definition of living beings: stones, water, and even the wind have *kwere-* too. In addition, while one of the meanings for *kwere-* is flesh, bodily substance, evident in the expression "to eat the *kwere-* of a game animal," the term *kwere-* primarily reflects a specific mode of action, a way of being. Someone may be said to be quick-tempered because his or her *kwere-* is that way, just as an animal species feeds on one fruit rather than another due to its *kwere-*. The Wari' explanation for why white-lipped peccaries wander in bands is *"je kwerein mijak"* ("the peccary's body is like that"). Similarly, the wind blows strongly because the wind's *kwere-* is that way, and the rain's specific *kwere-* means that it soaks everything as it passes. In sum *kwere-* designates "a set of affections or ways of being" (Viveiros de Castro 1996a, 128; 1998a, 478) rather than a physical substrate.[24]

Although everything has a body, only humans, including indigenous enemies and whites, various mammals (such as the jaguar, white-lipped peccary, tapir, and capuchin monkey), various birds, all bees, snakes, and some plants, possess *jam-*.[25] Unlike many other Amazonian peoples, the Wari' do not link *jam-* with any vital principle. There are living beings without *jam-*, such as the spider monkey (see Vilaça 1992). In some ways, no living being acting in an ordinary manner has *jam-*. *Jam-*, for the Wari', implies the capacity to *jamu*, to transform, especially in the sense of extraordinary action. Thus when they say that a particular animal *jamu*-ed, they mean it acted like a human, shooting and killing a Wari' (perceived by the Wari' as the victim's sickening and death). Likewise, the shaman *jamu*-s when interacting with his animal partners, perceiving each other as similars.[26] *Jamu* is therefore a capacity to change affection, to adopt other habits, and thereby be perceived as a similar by other types of beings.[27]

The human beings (*wari'*) endowed with *jam-* display typically human behavior: they make houses, have families, sleep on mats, eat cooked foods, and so on. The difference between these beings resides, therefore, not in a specific "culture," but in their bodies, as Viveiros de Castro observes in his analysis of Amerindian perspectivism (see also Lima 1995, 1996, 2005; Descola 2005, 196–202). According to Viveiros de Castro, for many Amerindian peoples "the world is inhabited by different sorts of subjects or persons, human and non-human, which apprehend reality from distinct points of view" (1998a, 469) related to their bodies. This is not a case of multicultural relativism, which supposes "a diversity of subjective and partial representations, each striving to grasp an external and unified nature, which remains perfectly indifferent to those representations. Amerindian thought proposes the opposite: a representational or phenomenological unity . . . indifferently applied to a radically objective diversity. One single 'culture,' multiple 'natures'" (Viveiros de Castro 1998a, 478).

Instead of multiculturalism, therefore, Amerindians conceive of a multinaturalism (477). Hence, the jaguar—which sees itself as human, *wari'*—drinks maize beer like the Wari'. However, while the Wari' see their own maize beer as a drink made from maize, the jaguar's maize beer is blood, just as the tapir's maize beer is the mud found on the shores of rivers. The Wari' know that the jaguar kills its prey with its body and teeth, and that it eats its kill raw. But for the jaguar, or better, from the jaguar's point of view (which the shaman alone can share), it shoots its prey like a Wari' kills a game animal or enemy, takes it home, and hands it to its wife, who cooks the meat using fire. For the Wari', one of the main defining factors of corporal specificity (whether of the individual or the species) is diet. They say: we are Wari', we eat larvae, we drink maize beer, and so on; the white-lipped peccary eats fruits; the jaguar eats raw flesh. Later on we shall see that when a shaman wants to change species, he starts to accompany the animals of the new species and eat their food. However, while the diet produces identity, since eating the same food forms similar bodies, sharing food is also a strong indicator of a prior identity and those who eat together affirm their similarity (see Vilaça 1998, 2000a).

The Wari' spirit's relationship to the body is simultaneously symmetric and asymmetric. As a capacity for bodily transformation, the relation between body and spirit is equivalent to the relation between one and many, making it asymmetric. However, as this capacity is always actualized in the form of another body, which is the person seen from another perspective (see Lima 2002), the spirit also has a symmetric relation to the body. It is precisely this symmetric relation that seems to be implied in the association made by the Wari' between spirit, shadows, reflections, and the traces left by the body—all equally called *jam-*. This association is not confined to the Wari' (indeed, it is prevalent in Amazonia: see Viveiros de Castro 1986, 514 on the Araweté; and Lima 1995, 139–40 on the Juruna). The obvious relation between the shadow and the body, the former comprising a projection of the body on another surface, seems to suggest that the spirit or soul is actualized as a body in another world, very often conceived as a world in negative, precisely like that of the shadows. For example, people say that it is night in the world of the spirits when it is day in the world of the living, suggesting that the clear/dark contrast involved in the perception of the body and its shadow may also be pertinent to understanding the body/soul-spirit relation. This takes us to Viveiros de Castro's suggestion (2000a; also see 2001 and 2002) that the relation between body and soul is analogous to the relation between form and background, as explored in Gestalt studies. Viveiros de Castro (2000a, 2001) argues that this switch of perspective is central to Amazonian thought, evoking Guss's analysis of Yekuana basketry (1989) in which the background/form alteration, as a light/dark contrast, is heavily explored; this is an insight that can be extended to many other textile patterns and body paintings in Amazonia.

Although only some beings—those that consider themselves human—are endowed with this potential for transformation, inanimate beings and artifacts are also often subject to perspectival alterations. In the case of the Wari', this seems to be related to the indigenous comprehension of knowledge as a process of continual subjectification. Viveiros de Castro (1998b) points out that knowledge in Amazonia is the symmetrical opposite of our scientific knowledge, which takes knowledge to be dependent on a maximal and continuous objectification, where subjects need to be transformed into molecules in order to be understood.[28]

In Amazonia, then, humanity may be attributed to everything, at least when seen in an informed way. In other words, the most powerful shamans would be capable of subjectifying the entire universe, finding human agency in all things or their immediate surroundings. And it is in this agency that their interest resides: a rock only becomes an object of attention when perceived by someone as a spirit, or as a tool or object imbued with some kind of human agency.

Confirming this tendency to leave the process of subjectification an open issue, the Wari' shamans, as I mentioned earlier, do not fully agree on which animals possess or lack *jam-*. Wari' mythic accounts also suggest that the spirit is not a fixed ontological attribute, but a capacity linked to specific relational contexts: some objects had spirit but lost it through some kind of accident or mishap. People say, for example (as Paletó did when he came face to face with a mechanical digger in Rio de Janeiro), that the baskets fabricated by women once walked on their own, carrying the heavy loads of maize in jumps along the forest tracks. One day, a woman walking with others in front of a group of animated baskets turned round and, astonished by the ridiculous way in which the baskets moved, burst into laughter. Offended, the baskets decided never to act in this extraordinary form again. The Wari' explain this by saying that the basket's *jam-* ended.

Let us return to the question of the predation of the Wari' by animals. Perceiving themselves as humans (*wari'*), beings with spirit see the Wari' as prey, *karawa* ("animal," "food")—in other words, precisely how they themselves are perceived by the Wari'. They may therefore prey on the latter, shooting them and transforming them into members of their own species.[29] Hence, Wari' who die from symbolic or real animal attacks acquire an animal body and become part of the aggressor species. According to some shamans, this is indeed the animals' ultimate aim: they desire people for themselves, they want to make kin (see Vilaça 2002a, 2009). And the mode of incorporating different beings into one's own species is predation. Sometimes this predation is conceived as a hunting trip in which the animals see the Wari' as animal prey (*karawa*). At other times, it is a war: the animals perceive the Wari' as enemies (*wijam*) and attack them. Here too the victim becomes a member of the aggressor species, since a war victim is destined to become consubstantial with his or her killer, a member of the latter's group. This transformation becomes clear in the case of those Wari' killed by enemies: as I already mentioned, they acquire bodies identical to those of the enemy—in the case of whites, a white body, with clothing—and end up living with the enemy as part of the latter's population.[30]

It should be stressed here that the Wari' tend to conflate rather than differentiate warfare and hunting. When they hunt and eat their favorite prey, they are immediately subject to a reprisal, a counterpredation, which is

14. A'ain Xit carries his prey, a spider monkey, Rio Negro–Ocaia, 1987.
(Photo by Beto Barcellos)

equally defined as hunting or warfare. Several times I heard shamans claim
that they had appealed to animals coming to kill the Wari' to look carefully
and observe that the Wari' were not enemies (*wijam*), but *wari'*, their kin (as,
from a certain perspective, all Wari' are kin to each other). Enemy (*wijam*)
and prey (*karawa*) are thus equivalent positions involving the same type of
relation: both are shot and eaten. This equivalence explains why the Wari'
almost always included detailed accounts of hunting in their narratives of
war expeditions. It is as though the war began earlier with the warriors proving their ability by killing the forest animals. In the hunt, the Wari' already
start to identify themselves as human beings distinct from all other beings by
occupying the predator position. This process culminates with warfare when
beings ontologically indistinct from the Wari' become their prey, occupying
their proper place and ensuring the Wari' the humanity associated with the
active position in the predatory relationship (figs. 14 and 15).

The identity between enemy and prey is often made clearly explicit by
children. I heard a little girl of about four years old exclaiming as she saw
some cattle: *Wijam*! *Wijam*! Everyone laughed uproariously, but her grandparents, who classified me as a daughter, were clearly embarrassed by her
stark revelation of how the Wari' conceive the *wijam*, a category to which I

15. Peccary hunting. Rio Negro–Ocaia, 1987.

belong. The term *wijam* is used to refer to me wherever I am unknown. And until recently, even those who know me well only used my name in my presence; when I was absent, I was simply *wijam*. An example of this occurred at the Rio Negro–Ocaia village, where I had already worked for several months. As I approached the house of friends, the small daughter exclaimed, "*Wijam* is arriving!" Her mother, ashamed that I had overheard, admonished her, "If she was a *karawa*, she'd be walking on all fours!"

Accounts of the first sightings of whites are also revealing. The conceptual relation between enemy and animal prey is so strong that people said they were shocked on seeing the human aspect of the enemy. What enabled this humanity to be perceived, though, was not usually the view of a living enemy or a whole body. Instead, the Wari' perceived this new enemy as human when they received whites as prey: that is, when they saw the parts of their bodies cut up to be roasted and eaten. As I discussed earlier, the first sightings of whites were almost always those of body parts. Toji's account illustrates this perfectly: "At first we thought it was a creature. You know, some kind of animal. But no. When we saw the body of the white we even felt sorry for him, for the pieces that they brought back for us. Part of the arm. . . . The elders had killed them, but we had never seen them. Until finally one day we did, and we felt sorry for them. We thought it was some kind of creature wandering around" (Toji 1992).

On the one hand, the identity between *wijam* and *karawa*—enemy and animal—stems from their common difference from the Wari', who occupy the position of humans: the only humans, *wari'*. This equivalence emerges in the context of predation. Ideally, the Wari' are those who prey on other beings and this is what distinguishes them as human—*wari'*—and defines the enemies and animals, both equally prey, as nonhuman. On the other hand, what enables the relation between them and the Wari' is precisely their potential humanity, their capacity to act as humans. In this sense, legitimate prey are those beings capable of being predators and, for this reason, the animals preferred by the Wari' as prey are precisely those that can avenge their predation. These animals and enemies can occupy the position of predators: they are capable of attacking, killing, and eating the Wari' and at these moments are human, *wari'* (making the Wari' nonhuman—*wijam* or *karawa*). The Wari' take the subjectification of war victims (see Viveiros de Castro 2002, 286 and Fausto 2007b) to an extreme, extending it to the animals they choose to eat.

It is important to note, though, that when the Wari' talk about enemies and game in the context of predation, they emphasize their animal features rather than their human ones. They stress that the beings they kill and eat are not people, in contrast to other groups, such as the Tupinambá, who strove to humanize their prisoners of war, future victims of cannibalism, by socializing them (see Viveiros de Castro 1992a, 45). The Tupinambá transformed these captives into real brothers-in-law, offering them women to marry; at the moment of execution, the prisoners were adorned as members of the group and a dialogue unfolded in which the equivalence between executor and victim came to the fore: I am you tomorrow, said the victim. As I mentioned earlier, the Wari' do not usually employ the female gender when speaking of enemies, even enemy women, since the female gender only exists for human beings. In order to refer to a woman from an enemy group, they say "female enemy," not "enemy wife" just as one speaks of a "female animal."

But though animals and enemies are equivalent as prey (and potential predators), the Wari' can differentiate between them. The humanness of enemy bodies is undeniable. Only enemies are ontologically identified with the Wari'; only they can be incorporated socially by becoming coinhabitants, commensals, and affines. While the animals can act as *wari'*, they can never become Wari'.[31]

From a broader perspective, however, humanity is a potential inherent to every type of being endowed with spirit. This potential is realized as a position in the act of predation: the predators are *wari'* and the prey are *wijam* or *karawa*. The actions of Wari' shamans and warriors aim to assure the Wari' the place of humanity, the position of *wari'*.

SHAMANS

The shaman (*ko tuku ninim*) is "the one who sees," a special being, simultaneously human and animal. Everything begins with a serious illness in which an animal attacks the future shaman, trying to turn him into its companion, a member of its species. The spirit of the sick person arrives at the house of the animals and can already see them as human—that is, he can adopt the animal's point of view. He is bathed with lukewarm water and receives a girl from his hosts who is set to be his future wife when, at death, he becomes definitively animal. The future shaman also receives magical annatto and babassu oil, which he stores in his body and which characterize him as a member of the captor species, endowing him with special vision and the power to cure.

From then on, this man (examples of female shamans are rare: see Vilaça 2002a) starts to be perceived by the animals as human, someone similar, and can appear to the Wari' as an animal. The shaman is said to have *jamu*-ed: in other words, by means of his spirit, he has transformed and acquired another body. Depending on the animal he is "accompanying" (always an animal species with spirit), the Wari' say of the shaman's spirit: "It went to the white-lipped peccaries" (*Mao na jami mijak*), or "It's with the tapirs" (*Peho' non min*). What defines him as a member of a particular species is primarily living with the animals of the species and sharing their diet, meaning that a shaman can "swap" species if he starts to accompany other animals.[32]

What characterizes the shaman, therefore, is the capacity to maintain social relations with different human groups simultaneously—a capacity realized as a double body, since this body is perceived distinctly by each of these sets: a human body visible to the Wari', which relates to them normally as a member of their society; and an animal body (from the Wari' perspective), which he and his animal companions perceive as human. This animal body relates to them as a member of their society, itself just like Wari' society. In the words of the shaman Orowam: "I'm a jaguar. I'm a true jaguar. I eat animals. When people are sick, I go to see them and they get better. Sick people have things in their heart. They cool down [get well, without fever]. I have babassu oil and annatto. I go into the forest, journey far, see other people. I see whites, everyone. I'm a true jaguar, not a fake one" (Orowam 1995). Or, as Orowam said some years earlier in 1987: "The jaguar is my true kin. My true body is jaguar. There's pelt on my true body."

The animals, and the shamans among them, adopt the visual perspective of human beings, *wari'*, seeing the Wari' as animals or enemies. Hence they prey on them. Just like Wari' men on war expeditions, these animal spirits may arrive in a group, brought by the wind, shouting, "Let's shoot enemies!" (The shamans who arrive in this way are generally members of other subgroups, foreigners.) The local shamans can see them and attempt to establish a dialogue, preventing the Wari' from being hit by these arrows and falling sick. They try to alter the animal spirits' vision: "Look carefully, they aren't animals, they're *wari'*! They're your kin!" The animals then recognize the Wari' as equals and retreat. If someone becomes ill, the shaman works to prevent the victim from transforming into an animal, removing all of the residues left by the attacking animal from his or her body and trying to rescue the person's spirit from among the animals, actually a body that is already (to the shaman's eyes) turning into an animal body. This transformation may be completed, leading to the death of the Wari' body, or the uncured victim may continue to live, thus becoming a shaman.

As a result, the shaman's presence within the group has two aspects, one positive, as a curer of diseases, and the other negative, as a being who can become an enemy at any moment, attacking his kin and even causing deaths. Here, though, he acts unintentionally, almost through a "technical failure": his vision becomes erratic and he starts to see his own people as enemies or animal prey. It is as though his different bodies—or his different perspectives—become mixed, meaning that he, as a Wari', adopts the animal's point of view. This applies not only to foreign shamans coming from other Wari' subgroups; the local shamans, classified by kin terms as is customary among coinhabitants, are also prone to such outbreaks, reminiscent, as I mentioned earlier, of those of killers among some Tupian groups during their period of reclusion. I myself once saw the shaman Orowam, who lived with the spotted jaguars, prepare to attack the people around him, including myself and his classificatory grandson. He rubbed his eyes and roared. Realizing what was happening, his grandson talked to him, reminding him that those present were his kin (kindly including myself in this group). Among the Wari', therefore, it is the shaman rather than the killer who sees from the enemy's point of view—as though the evident humanness of human enemies, whether indigenous or white, makes them insufficiently Other, *karawa*, to represent an alterity capable of being continually controlled and domesticated, continually because, in contrast to the Tupi killers, the outbreaks of shamans do not cease after a certain lapse of time: instead, they occur throughout the shaman's life, or while he remains a shaman (since he can cease to be one).

The outcome is akin to a set of mirrors in which the images are reflected to infinity: the shaman becomes an animal and as an animal he adopts the perspective of human beings, *wari'*, and starts to see the Wari' as *karawa*, nonhumans. In this sense, the shaman, unlike the Wari' killer, provides Wari' society as a whole with the experience of another (enemy) point of view: from being *wari'* they come to see themselves as prey, *karawa*, since they know this is how the shaman now sees them. A double inversion occurs: a man separates from the group, turning into an animal and adopting a human point of view, so that the rest of the group, remaining human, can adopt the animal point of view. Although this operation does not correspond to the figure of the Wari' killer, it does display clear parallels with the relation between the Tupinambá killer (who did not eat his victim) and devourers of the dead enemy. As the famous phrase of Cunhambebe to Hans Staden reveals, uttered while he was chewing on a human leg, "I'm a jaguar. It's tasty" (Staden 1974, 132).[33]

Clearly, though, this experimentation of another position is not exclusive to the shaman, who merely embodies this transposition. The fact that any prey and any enemy can see themselves as *wari'* reveals how the Wari' recognize their own potential as prey. Once again, a child provides a clear insight into the complexity of this ever latent inversion, the capacity to see oneself with the eyes of the enemy. A man was telling me the flood myth (Nanana-nana) one day in the company of his small son. At a particular point in the action, an unknown people, called "enemy" (*wijam*) by the narrator from the outset, perceive the Wari' approaching and exclaim, "The enemy [*wijam*] is arriving!" The child corrected his father, saying that these people would actually have said the Wari' (*wari'*) were arriving. The father then explained to him that, for these people, the Wari' really were *wijam*.

If the animals are potentially human, the Wari' are potentially prey. This means that humanity is not something inherent but a position that has to be won continually. Ultimately, this sophisticated logic of two-way predation offers a profound reflection on the human condition. The Wari' experience life as constantly unstable (see Vilaça 2005), risking themselves by living forever on the boundary between the human and the nonhuman, as though the inability to know what it is to be *karawa* would mean being unable to experience what it is to be really human.

CHAPTER 3

The White Enemy

"Nowi,[1] do you remember the first time you saw a white-bodied enemy?"

"When I was a child, about so high [three to four years old], they tried to capture us on the Ribeirão. The white man caught me but I escaped. . . . Ah, he brought many tools, hammocks, mosquito nets, clothes. . . . Many tools. The white man said to us, 'Stay here, clear a swidden; the medicines will arrive later.' And he went away, saying, 'I'm going to fetch more things.' Our late relatives fled. It seems he was good. Had we answered his call, we'd have been living with the whites for a long time now."

"Jimon,[2] what was it like the first time you saw a white-bodied enemy?"

"When we were boys, our father came to fetch us. We crossed back over the river [from OroNao' territory, where Jimon was living, to OroWaram territory, where his father lived and Jimon had been born]. They cut down a tree trunk. The women crushed maize. The container was filled. The elders said, 'Our trunk is full of maize beer!' They made a rubber drum [in preparation for a festival]. We danced in a line. . . . We were still dancing when the white man arrived. They [the Wari'] exclaimed, 'Wari'! Wari'!' and then asked, 'What kind of Wari' are these? Are they OroNao'? If they are OroNao', A'ain Towa would have recognized them when he saw them.' 'I didn't recognize them. They look like enemies' [A'ain Towa said]. They told the whites to drink some maize beer. They were hesitant, 'Should I drink it?' [said the white man]. Only the man was standing. The woman remained seated. They told them to drink the maize beer. 'I don't want to,' she said. She got down from the house platform where she had been sitting. 'This is the enemy!' [said the Wari']. 'Go and get the machete,' they ordered him. The white man went. His wife stayed and then she left too. He came back. He was carrying a strange object, like those things the young people make [necklaces]. They appeared because of the drum [the whites located them from the sound of the drum played during the festival]. 'Let's kill them, let's kill them!' [the whites thought]. But they later desisted. I saw him. He was good to the Wari'. Their clothing was torn and you could see the woman's genitalia. The wife had cut the husband's hair. The Wari' fled into the forest. The whites didn't know how to speak the Wari' language. So they didn't understand anything. The Wari' fled. . . . I fled too. The white man took my father to fetch clothing and he came back with a machete in each hand. He called to them to come back [the whites also came back with machetes and shouted for the Wari' to return]: 'Here's the machete!' The late Hwara Waraki arrived. 'Get his machete, my son!' [Hwara Waraki said to Jimon's father]. 'Be cautious! The white man is going to kill you!' [the Wari' said]. They got lots. The white man hugged our late relative. They [the Wari'] said to themselves: 'Take him along the path.' They were going to shoot him. . . . The woman fetched clothes [to give to the Wari']. They didn't want them. They wanted to kill them. They were ready. Maxun Taparape shot the first arrow, my grandfather. It struck her husband's arm. He ducked his head as the arrows flew by. Many arrows. They were ready to shoot the woman. They hit her body many times, all of them, all the men. Her husband ran off. She remained. The elders stood up and went to look at the corpse. They had shot her in the neck and she had fallen close to the house. They shouted happily. They heard shots from afar. . . . They took away the corpse and ate it. They spread the news to the OroWaram, OroWaramXijein, and OroMon: 'We killed a white-bodied enemy!' 'Let's go there! Let's see it!' [the others said]. They took everything: machetes, knives, harmonicas. The whites had already gone. Just their things remained. The woman was still lying on the ground. 'Let's take the white man's things.' They cut up the corpse. People from the other villages shouted, 'They've killed an enemy!' They ate her. The killers gave the white woman's flesh to everyone to take away. My father took the head, roasted it, and shredded the meat. He kept the skull. This was the first time I saw the white-bodied enemy [*wijam kwere towa*]."

"Hwerein Pe e',[3] could you tell me about the first time you saw a white-bodied enemy?"

"My father invited me to go on a war expedition when I was still very small. I took a bow and arrows. We killed a white-lipped peccary and ate it. The following day we continued. 'What does the enemy look like, Father?' I thought it was like a collared peccary, walking on all fours. 'It's a person [wari'] [said the father]. The Wari' killed them for no reason.' We walked far and eventually found his path. 'Is he a foreigner [a member of another Wari' subgroup], Father?' 'No, he's an enemy' [his father replied]. He [the white man] whistled. 'I don't know, he looks like Wari'! Did he spread white clay on his body, Father?' 'No, he wears clothes.' I thought it was white clay. One spread white clay and the other spread something dark. 'No, he's the enemy' [the father said]. He went to bathe and took off his clothes. Trousers. 'Why are you going to shoot a foreigner?' [asked Hwerein Pe e']. 'Be quiet!' They yelled [the whites] as the arrows hit them. He fired [a gun]. We fled. I thought it was an animal, but he moaned from the arrow. 'Why do you shoot foreign Wari'?' [Hwerein Pe e' asked]. 'He's an enemy!' [the father insisted]."

"And you, Watakao,[4] what was it like the first time you saw a white-bodied enemy?"

"My father left on a war expedition. We children stayed behind. Xijan [who would be about seventy years old today] was very small. They went as far as the Pacaás Novos River. The river was low. The white man was tapping rubber. They [the Wari'] sat down. He walked in their direction, striking the pans to see whether they had rubber sap. 'He's coming.' Xijan ran. They shot the white man with several arrows. He fell in the water. He groaned from the blood that gushed from him. Had the Wari' not detested the whites so much . . . They called to your father, Xijan: 'Shoot his buttocks, nephew, shoot his buttocks!' And Xijan, still a child, shot the buttocks of the white man. He was already dead. They cut off his head, one arm, the other arm . . . and left the rest lying on the ground. It was just one man. [The killers returned to the village.] Hwerein shouted [from afar]: 'We killed an enemy!' And we children said: 'Let's shoot the enemy!' We looked. 'Wari'!' It was just like the foot of a Wari', the arm of a Wari'. They passed me my arrow: 'Shoot along with your father' [they told Watakao]. I shot his arm with my arrow. My father said, 'Roast our prey, my son.'"

The Wari' refer to the whites as enemies—*wijam*—in the same way they refer to other indigenous peoples with whom they warred. This produces a certain difficulty in translating the texts, meaning that I sometimes translate *wijam* as enemy, and other times as white(s). I have opted to use the term white whenever I was sure that the Wari' wanted to differentiate them from enemies in general. In other cases, when the intention was to mark the enemy nature of the whites, deliberately avoiding any differentiation, I translate the word simply as enemy. In all cases, whenever the term white appears in the text, the term used in the Wari' language was *wijam*.

Sometimes they refer to whites as "white-bodied enemy" (*wijam kwere towa*); other times, they differentiate whites as *iri wijam* (where *iri* means "true") in contrast to those simply called *wijam*, the members of other ethnic groups. In such cases, I place the Wari' terms in brackets next to the translated terms. When they speak in Portuguese, they call whites "civilizados," following regional usage, and call Indians in general, including themselves, "caboclos."

The myth of the origin of the whites explains that they, like all of their other enemies, originated from Wari' society and are distinguished from those "enemies that stayed in the forest" by their possession of manufactured goods, particularly firearms. In other words, the whites stand out especially because of their war arsenal, making them dangerous enemies. But they were not so at first. According to the myth, the whites gradually created or acquired these goods, though they always desired war. The Wari' add that at first the whites were peaceful and well intentioned: it was they with their resolutely warlike behavior who stirred the whites' anger with unprovoked attacks, forcing them to become enemies.

THE FIRST SIGHTINGS OF THE WHITES

At first, Paletó said, "The white man liked us, but we didn't like him." A'ain Towa Tok, an OroWaram woman who would be about ninety today, mentioned the same episode related by Jimon Pan Tokwe and transcribed above. She was four years old when an attempt was apparently made to contact the Wari' of the OroWaram subgroup. The Wari' consider this to be the first attempt at pacification, similar to those made in the 1960s. Doubtless due to her very young age at the time, A'ain Towa Tok said that everything she knew about the episode came from her father.

> "She didn't look white. She was like the Wari'. Her body looked like ours. We were drinking maize beer and the white man called [unintelligible sounds]. The Wari' shouted, 'Enemy! Flee from the enemy.' We fled. It

was just a man and his wife. The man shouted, 'Don't flee from us! [*ta jein mahu me*]. Her father sent us to search for people. Her name is To'o, To'o Tarakam.' To'o was his wife. The white man was friendly . . . but it made no difference. They killed the woman, his wife, and the man returned alone. They killed her with arrows. They ate To'o Tarakam. That's what my father told me: they roasted To'o Tarakam over the fire and ate her, the white man's wife. They ate her in Hu Pije [name of the village].''

"Did the white man pursue you all with a gun?" I asked.

"No, he didn't. He seemed a bit foolish. He was an ancient white man, from a very long time ago. They shot the white man who was friendly to the Wari'." (A'ain Towa Tok 1994)

Paletó said that after the attack on the woman, the whites began to use guns, a fact also mentioned by Jimon. Barnabé, an OroWaramXijein man, added to his version of the event: "They were Oropixi's people," referring to the Oropixi' myth on the origin of whites.

On another occasion, Paletó said, "The white man came just to capture us. He didn't kill, he didn't know how to kill. He wasn't angry with us. He just wanted to have sex with the women. The white man liked vagina. All the whites on the Pacaás Novos River. We called them sex makers. We didn't call them enemies of the Pacaás Novos River, but sex makers. . . . We shot them, which is what made them angry" (Paletó 1992).

According to Jimon Pan Tokwe, "the whites were friendly before the Wari' started to shoot them on the Pacaás Novos River. The Wari' women had sex with them and returned laden with machetes."[5] Various accounts exist of women and children who were taken away only to return a few days later carrying many presents. Paletó tells of an episode on the Komi Wawan River, an affluent of the right shore of the Negro River, involving his maternal grandmother, Jap. The whites arrived eager for sex. After having sex with some women, they told the latter to follow them. Their relatives wept, imagining that they had been killed. The next day, these women returned bringing lots of machetes and news of what happened: "We ate manioc; we ate turtle. They had sex with us."

The Wari' add that the whites were also inoffensive due to a technological deficiency: they lacked firearms when they first arrived. When the Wari' attacked, they tried to repel them with arrows but their aim was extremely poor. After a while, they started to use guns loaded only with gunpowder.

According to Nawakan, an OroWaramXijein man, they sometimes lacked even gunpowder and imitated shots by slapping their thighs.

> Our father said that the guns had no lead. They just exploded. They lacked lead shot, apparently. So Awo Xohwara shot him with an arrow. The whites said: "Let's kill the Wari', let's do the same as they've done to us." They came and opened fire on the village. That was in Kaxima, close to Pin Karam [both names of villages]. They killed Topa Eo and another woman. A boy the size of Main's son survived. He was left on the ground crying. The whites knifed the boy because they [the Wari'] had killed their companions. He was the son of our mother's true brother. They hurled the child in the air to fall on the knife. He had no teeth yet, he didn't know how to walk. They stamped on his brains with their shoes. The white man was very angry. It was then that the whites became angry. . . . They used to be friendly. They only recently started shooting us.[6] (Paletó 1995)

Some people simply said they had no idea where the guns had come from: "We don't know how they obtained guns. One day we encountered the whites and they already had firearms" (Nawakan). Others, when asked to explain the origin of these weapons, often had surprising responses. Paletó said that firearms had been created and brought by the Americans.

> The whites didn't have guns yet. They just shot the ground with arrows. Then those who knew about firearms arrived, the Americans. Your distant ancestors. The people here didn't know [about guns]. The whites from Guajará had no knowledge of firearms. Only the Americans knew. The guns arrived so they could kill game. . . . When the whites didn't know how to make guns, they went away to learn. But the guns made here aren't as good; the good ones are made far away. That's where all your things come from. The people from Guajará had nothing. It was the Americans who came by motor boat; everything came from there. (Paletó 1993)

The accounts of people's first sightings of whites suggest that, for the Wari', as we shall see in the pacification episodes, the peaceful approach of enemies—or toward enemies—must have been motivated by the desire to reconstitute a group that for some reason had been exterminated, as happens to the Wari' in the Nanananana myth, where Wari' society is reconstituted after a flood (see chapter 6). The whites were looking for people, as the husband of the woman shot and eaten by the OroWaram explained.

They and those of their kin who arrived later would be incorporated as a new subgroup, hence the association of this couple with foreigners. However, the Wari' were interested in enemies rather than foreigners, precisely the opposite of what happened during pacification of the OroNao' of the Whites, who, isolated for many years, wished to incorporate the benevolent whites as foreigners, "people for themselves." During this earlier period, the Wari' desired enemies and war, and urgently so, since the men were finding it difficult to become warriors given the protracted absence of Indian enemies. Read in this light, the emphasis on the whites' peaceful intentions and technological shortcomings implies, I think, their inability to act as predators, leaving just one alternative: to animalize them and thus turn them into legitimate war victims, prey to be killed and eaten. Contrasting with this passivity, the Wari' accounts emphasize their own bellicosity and their position as humans in the predatory relation.

A problem exists, though. According to historical data,[7] the Wari' had been located by the whites since the beginning of the nineteenth century. If they had been so eager for enemies, why had they not attacked these first whites, rather than avoid contact with them altogether? Two answers are possible. Probably the Indians seen by these explorers were not the Wari': according to my interlocutors, the first whites were seen only one or two generations ago. This takes us back no earlier than the end of the nineteenth century and the start of the twentieth, precisely when rubber tappers began to invade the region occupied by the Wari'. Manim, an OroEo man, who would be about eighty-five today, declared, "There were no whites in the time of the ancient ones. They arrived recently, coming from Guajará. They went in search of rubber in the forest."

However, it is also possible that the Wari' really were seen by travelers at the start of the nineteenth century, but avoided them after perceiving their strangeness—an aspect they tend to downplay when discussing the first whites. During this earlier period, the Wari' were probably not after new enemies since indigenous enemies were still available for warfare.[8]

From what the Wari' say, the only nonindigenous items to seduce them initially were metal tools: axes, knives, and machetes. They seem to have organized expeditions to steal these goods from the houses of rubber tappers from the start of the twentieth century onward. They took the tools and left everything else: clothes, mosquito nets, hammocks, and food. Until pacification, the Wari' found white food virtually inedible, especially sugar and salt. During raids, they would taste the foods but spit them out immediately.

Sometimes they became ill, but only later associated these diseases with contacts with whites. They also had no interest in guns and ammunition; sometimes they set fire to the rubber tappers' houses and were startled by the exploding gunpowder. Possessing these goods apparently had no bearing on how whites were initially classified: they were simply enemies who owned strange things. According to an OroNao' man of around seventy years: "We saw sugar and said, 'This is white men's bad stuff.' Salt too. . . . We just wanted axes and machetes to clear the swiddens. That's what we liked. . . . Once we took hammocks, blankets, mosquito nets, clothing. We wore their trousers. At night we made a clearing, suspended the hammocks and mosquito nets, and slept. The following day we threw everything away" (OroNao' man 1993).

CALCULATING DATES

Taking the Wari' claim that they were immediately interested in metal tools as a lead, I tried to calculate the dates for contacts with whites based on when people acquired the first metal instruments.[9] First, it should be observed that none of my interlocutors, even the oldest, has ever used a stone axe. Even so, they can describe in detail the method of manufacture learned from their fathers, many of whom had used the tool. As I mentioned earlier, the stone used, called *kit* or *xixe*, is only found at the Kit swidden site at the right shore of the upper course of the Negro River, an area traditionally inhabited by the OroEo.

Jimon Pan Tokwe, a now deceased OroWaram man who would be around eighty-five today, recounted that only his paternal grandfather, Orowao Pin Kan (also OroWaram), had used stone axes as an adult. He was still strong enough to clear a swidden when the whites arrived and he began to use stolen metal axes. Jimon's father had never used a stone axe. Assuming a twenty-year period between the generations of the two men, we can calculate, therefore, that the OroWaram obtained metal axes in the first decade of the twentieth century. According to Paletó (OroNao'), the OroWaram were the first to obtain metal axes because their territory was the first to be invaded by whites. This makes sense given that the OroWaram were living the furthest downriver, their swiddens being located on the affluents of the lower Laje, which flows into the Mamoré almost where the latter joins the Madeira.

Other data corroborate the idea that the OroWaram were the first Wari' to encounter the whites. According to Paletó, the OroNao' became aware of

white people's diseases (or at least what they later identified as such) when
the OroWaram went to dance with them after killing and eating a white man.
Paletó's maternal grandmother, Jap Korojim, fell sick. The first attempt at
peaceful contact with the Wari' also involved the OroWaram. As mentioned
above, those responsible for the attempt remain unknown. Extrapolating
from the age of my informants, all small children at the time, this attempt
must have occurred between 1910 and 1915.

Paletó told me how his father learned about metal axes:

> My father heard the OroWaram say there was a type of enemy with an axe
> that really ate [wood]. "It's not like the OroEo axe [made from stone], it's
> angry." "Let's see this enemy," they said to my father. "Okay." He went with
> the OroWaram. They arrived at the white man's house and found axes.
> They took them. On their way back they found honey in a tucumã palm
> tree [which is hard-wooded]. "Fetch your axe," the OroWaram told my
> father. "No, it will break it." So they explained, "It's very strong; it cuts
> tucumã, patauá." The OroWaram chopped down the tree to show my fa-
> ther. When he returned to the OroNao', my father said, "I captured an
> enemy's axe." They liked it and wanted one too. They didn't want the
> OroEo stone axe anymore. . . . While just my father had one, when sum-
> mer arrived, everyone asked for it: "Give me it, give me it!" They went to
> the whites and took more. My father showed it to the OroEo: "We took
> the white men's axes! They're different from the axes we have to glue." So
> they went to the whites and took more. They didn't want that stone one
> anymore. Had it been any good . . . We would use it a few times and the
> blade would fall out. Then we had to glue it again. (Paletó 1993)

The account also indicates that the OroNao' obtained metal axes after the
OroWaram (via the latter) and before the OroEo, understandable consider-
ing that the OroEo lived in areas much less accessible to the whites. Tokohwet, an OroEo woman of around sixty, claimed that her paternal grandfather
used metal axes stolen from the invaders. Jamain Tamanain, an OroAt man
nearly seventy years old, said that his paternal grandfather had used stone
axes, but not his father. The OroEo and OroAt may have obtained these
tools soon after the OroNao'. However, Orowam, an OroAt man of about
eighty, recalled that when he was a young boy, he saw his father using a stone
axe to clear a swidden. Only later did they go to Guajará to steal metal axes
and immediately abandoned the stone ones. However, either Orowam erred
in his calculations—since 1929 is very late for the OroAt to still be without

metal axes—or not everyone obtained axes at the same time, which seems plausible.

Although some people could replace their stone axes with metal ones immediately, others had to wait longer to own or even borrow the tool—since there were too few for everyone to use—and had to continue using the inefficient stone axe. Oroiram, a man from the OroNao' of the Whites who is around eighty-five years old, told me that his father crossed to the right shore of the Pacaás Novos and journeyed to Kit to get axe-heads from the OroEo, although by then the Wari' were already undertaking expeditions to steal metal tools. Hence the Pacaás Novos River was not yet "closed" when the Wari' discovered metal.

According to Nawakan, an OroWaramXijein man of about eighty, the first man from his subgroup to possess a metal axe was Wem Kakami, the father of Wao Xain, a woman of around seventy. Soon after, everyone went to fetch these axes and abandoned stone ones. According to Harein, an OroMon man, his father, Pa' Tokwe, who would be around ninety today, used a stone axe even as an adult. His mother-in-law, To'o Xiri, also OroMon and who would also be nearly ninety today, said that her husband had cleared swiddens with a stone axe.

This information suggests that the OroWaramXijein and OroMon only acquired metal tools much later, around 1920. This seems fairly unlikely, at least in the case of the OroWaramXijein, who lived close to the OroWaram and had frequent contacts with them. The situation was different with the OroMon and especially the OroJowin, a subgroup to which Harein's father belonged. The OroMon lived much further upriver on the Laje headwaters, while the Wari' say that the OroJowin lived "on the rocks themselves" in the uplands. Possibly it was more difficult for them to find white houses to raid.

Along with these descriptions of acquiring metal tools, people mention abductions and attempts at contact. The first contact attempt, already mentioned several times, was with the OroWaram sometime between 1910 and 1915. People mention only a white couple, apparently naked (one man even told me the woman was menstruating), carrying industrial goods to offer to the Wari'. The latter were already familiar with metal tools, and indeed asked the couple for them.

Another episode, the earliest case of abduction I was told about, took place in OroEo land, though the exact whereabouts is unknown. Wem Parawan, who would be around eighty-five today, said that her mother, Piro, had been captured while pregnant with her. Some white men had knocked her to the ground. They also took Hatem Xao' OroAt, the paternal grand-mother of Ki'moi, who today lives at Santo André village, and a woman called Moroxin We, along with her small child. Wem Parawan's mother told her that they were taken as far as the right shore of the Ouro Preto River, the land of the OroWaram, OroWaramXijein, and OroMon. Although Wem Parawan did not tell me herself, the men apparently had sexual relations with her mother since a number of people joked that she was the daughter of the whites, one or more of them having helped form the baby's body with their semen. I have no idea how these women escaped or returned to their people. The episode probably occurred around 1915.

Official documents concerning the Wari' include the record of an abduc-tion in 1910, predating the above: this probably occurred in OroWaram ter-ritory since it was carried out by workers on the railroad running close to the borders of this subgroup's territory. Various Wari' children were captured and taken to Porto Velho to be exhibited. I have no information from the Wari' referring explicitly to this episode.

One of the oldest abductions among the OroWaram involved a man called Maxun Taparape. This must have occurred around 1925. According to Jimon Pan Tokwe, the capture took place in Tokon Wijam, an OroWaram swidden situated on the left shore of the lower Laje River.

> "The whites took my sister's son, Maxun Taparape. I was already a child of about six. He was very little. They pursued us by day. They killed his older brother, Mon. The younger brother ran off but the white man caught him. When Maxun returned, he was already a man. . . . Today he lives with his younger sister, Orowao Pin Kan. He turned completely white. He married a white woman and had children. People told me, "Your mother's brother is alive!"
>
> "Could he write?" I asked.
>
> "He's white! [laughing]. Were he Wari' . . ."
>
> "Does he really look like a white man? Even his face?" I asked.
>
> "Only his face is recognizable. He doesn't know my language anymore."
> (Jimon Pan Tokwe 1993)

I had the chance to meet Maxun for the first time in July 2003, in the house where he lives with two adult daughters, on the Limão River close to Lage village. Maxun, who appears to be over eighty years old, was married to a Brazilian woman, Edna, who had died just a few months earlier. He was apparently unable to understand the Wari' language, even when Paletó and

To'o Xak Wa, who were accompanying me, spoke to him. We talked in Portuguese and I reproduce here an excerpt from his account.

The *civilizados* attacked at about two in the afternoon. They attacked, killing my brother Mon. My father grabbed my sister and ran along the path toward my mother on the creek, carrying the girl on his back. I tried to run but was unable and fell. I was small. And so the whites got me. They killed my brother first. I was so sorry. Even today I remember my brother [at this moment Maxun starts to cry and interrupts the account]. They didn't kill my father or my sister. They ran toward the creek. My mother had gone to wash something in the river. Then they caught me. I made a lot of gestures, pleading with them not to kill me. It seems they felt sorry for me; they picked me up and took me. They then picked up the macaw and took it to eat when night fell. I slept. Actually, I didn't sleep, I spent the night thinking of escape, but it was impossible, you know, because I was afraid. The next day we left to reach the canoe. . . . There were some tame Indians who had been on the raid too. But they were from another tribe . . . from upriver, from the Guaporé. From there we arrived at the seringal and house of Manuel Higino. He was a rubber boss. They left me there. Later Mr. Meireles [Francisco Meireles], who worked for the SPI at the time, went to fetch me and brought me to the mouth of the Ribeirão [river]. I lived there for a few days. Not a few days, actually, more than four years. . . . Living with the people who Mr. Meireles, Francisco, had found for me. People there from the Guaporé. . . . Other *civilizados* and a few already tamed Indians. . . . They took me to Porto Velho to see if they could arrange for me to go to school. I spent almost two months there, but nothing was worked out. (Maxun 2003)

Paletó remarked that when Maxun was spotted by his brother-in-law at a barracks in Guajará-Mirim soon after the pacification episode, he failed to recognize anyone. He also added that the episode of abduction had happened in Na Tao village:

My father told me, "The whites took away my [classificatory] son and killed his brother." . . . They didn't know where the whites had taken him. Perhaps they had killed and eaten him. They thought the whites ate Wari' perhaps. We finally saw him when we arrived with the whites. The Maxun from the past. Maybe he had gone to war [against the Wari', he suggests ironically]. Maybe he joined his coinhabitants [the whites] when they went to war. Like the Makurap. But this didn't happen just recently! He was completely white! (Paletó 2003)

Another abduction took place in OroNao' territory at a swidden site called Panawin, located on an affluent of the right shore of the upper Da Gruta River (We Turu). Women and children were taken. According to Paletó, who was about five years old at the time, and his brother Paulo, the person responsible for this persecution was the SPI officer Francisco Meireles, who tried to make peaceful contact with the Wari'. Paletó recounted:

Chico Meireles pursued us there. They caught Mo'am, my mother's sister. We didn't live together. We had to walk far to get to our house, about the distance from here to the post [around 2 kilometers]. Tem Arakat's grandmother, who was also abducted, was making maize beer. The whites appeared. . . . It seemed like they were painted with genipap. As soon as her mother began to run, they captured her. "The enemy caught me, children! Run away!" They fled. They caught my mother's sister, Mo'am Min, too. They caught Paulo's mother, who was unmarried still. They also captured Mo'am's mother, the Mo'am who lives here. They caught Mijain Iro, the youngest brother of Hwerein Pe e'. He was a small child. They took him. My father followed them. He followed a long way until eventually deciding to turn back. The Wari' cried. The whites later told the women to return, which they did. Their trek was long and, deep in the forest, one of them died from a white men's disease. Mo'am's mother carried on and reached home. She brought her grandson, Mijain Iro. On arriving, Mo'am's mother said, "Your mother, your older sister died of an illness. I left axes and machetes next to her." "Let's roast her!" everyone said. They walked all the way there. The corpse was still lying on the ground. They roasted the body at the spot and then took the meat home to eat. The cough got us. Our eyes hurt. I don't know how we survived. We removed tree bark, made remedies and medicated ourselves without much idea of what we were treating. We dripped all kinds of things in our eyes. We medicated ourselves a lot and somehow survived. Only two people died from sickness in the forest. (Paletó 1993)

Paulo, Paletó's younger half-brother on his father's side, explained that Mo'am Min was the mother of Wan e' (who would be over ninety today were he alive). She had been taken by the whites and failed to return as her foot had started to hurt on the way back. She had to turn back to the whites. She never returned to the Wari'. Her son, Wao Em', was very small and was raised by his older sister, Paulo's mother. Who did return was Tokohwet Memem. She brought many presents, machetes, matches. Only the grandmother of Tem Arakat (a woman of nearly sixty, recently deceased, who lived at the Rio Negro–Ocaia village) died on the way back.

Based on the age of the informants, I estimate that the episode must have occurred around 1930.

None of the people describing these abductions emphasized the violent aspect of the episodes, even when the cruelty is clearly present (see Gow 2001 for similar behavior among the Piro). Reflecting on these events, the Wari' say that the whites only wanted to capture them, just as they would do later during pacification. Hwerein Pe e', when I asked him why the women captured in Panawin had received so many presents and whether the whites had been trying to seduce them to have sex, replied that they had given them presents simply because they liked the Wari'. Another account by Paletó of the same episode helps explain this point: the Wari' men followed the captured women, but the whites set off fireworks and forced them to retreat, thinking they were gunshots. They returned later to look for the dead, but found none. They wept for them anyway. They slept a few nights, and Mo'am's mother came back. She had a cough, flu. She said that when she wanted to return, the whites let her leave and gave her the presents, saying, "Here's a machete and an axe for your husband to use." Arriving home, she said, "I returned from where the whites were. They liked me." The Wari' were elated with the presents and exclaimed, "Let's kill the whites!"

This "distillation" made by the Wari' in thinking back over these events is intriguing, especially their insistence that the whites were initially friendly. As I suggested, the emphasis on the whites' passivity seems to be a way of disqualifying them as predators, and thus qualifying the Wari' themselves as human. Insisting on the "friendliness" of whites, despite all the evidence to the contrary, may also be a foil to later experiences when the Wari' were massacred by the whites, who invaded villages armed with rifles and machine guns and killed many, many people. As I noted in the introduction, the Wari' perhaps perceive a radical, qualitative change, where for us there is only a quantitative change, an exacerbation of a violence intent that was always present.

Paletó recalls various other cases of abduction. His father told him that Tem Hwijin, an OroNao' man, had been taken by whites from the I Pa' Wijam swidden, on the left shore of the middle Da Gruta River (We Turu).

Paletó's maternal grandmother, Jap Korojim, had also been captured, along with Wan e' (mentioned above) who was very small at the time. The whites cut his hair and ordered them all to work. The Wari' took their chance to escape when the whites left to harvest Brazil nuts, leaving them alone with the cook. Saying they needed to go to the forest to defecate, they ran off. They arrived at the Komi Wawan River, a right-shore affluent of the Negro River. Arriving home, they reported that the whites ate caiman tail, and that they themselves had eaten turtle, a prohibited food among the Wari'. They failed to bring any metal tools when they fled. Tem Hwijin stayed among the whites, alleging that his maternal grandmother, responsible for raising him, did not feed him properly and complained whenever he ate a little more than usual. He said he would grow up among the whites and would return later to kill the Wari'. This is probably what happened. People suspect he was one of the whites who killed his maternal grandmother since one of the killers looked very much like him.

This episode must have occurred around the same time as the capture in Panawin, perhaps a little earlier, since Jap Korojim died soon after Mo'am's mother returned to Panawin, ill with white disease.

The most interesting aspect here is the attribution of cruelty to a Wari' rather than the whites. This idea appears in other accounts, examined later, which blame the later massacres on the OroNao' of the Whites, unseen for many years. It is as if warfare only makes sense for the Wari' when waged between people who share the same worldview. The true enemy—or better, the meaningful enemy—is Wari', or someone who once was Wari', just as we find in the myths on the origin of enemies discussed earlier.

Other captures were reported. The mother's brother of Zaqueu, an Oro-Mon man about fifty-five years old today, was taken along with many other Wari' on the headwaters of the Ribeirão River. Zaqueu's mother was still un-married, which suggests that the event occurred around 1950. They took the captives to where the Ribeirão village is located today. From there they took them on the train to Porto Velho. Afterward the whites brought them back. Tem Wito, an OroMon man, and a white man fell from the train and died. The Wari' were transported with their arms tied to prevent them escaping. Arriving back, the whites untied them and told them to settle there on the mouth of the Ribeirão River. The Wari' fled.

There was also the episode involving Nowi, an OroWaramXijein man of about seventy, described by himself as the first time he saw whites (an excerpt from his account appears at the start of this chapter). Nowi said he was then about twelve years old, meaning the event probably took place around 1945. The Wari' were camped near the headwaters of the Ribeirão River during the rainy season, waiting for the maize to grow in their swiddens. The whites arrived by day in large numbers. The men ran off and, apart from a single adult man, only the women and children encountered the invaders. Nowi took a radio and one of the whites—"who liked me a lot"—picked Nowi off the ground, the same way that a Wari' father picks up his child. The Wari' joke today that this white man was Nowi's father. The whites sat on the stilt palm platform inside the house and talked. The Wari' understood nothing. The whites gave many presents: knives, hammocks, mosquito nets. They left saying they would fetch more presents and the Wari' took the chance to escape. The whites returned and yelled for them to come back. Receiving no response, they became angry and shot, perhaps in the air since they could not see anyone. They carried away all the presents they had brought. Nowi said that the expedition leader had been Francisco Meireles, since the latter himself had later claimed to have been present. Pan Kamerem, Nowi's older brother, claimed that the whites began to hang metal instruments on the path after this encounter. There was a house built by whites where the Ribeirão post is today. They also hung tools near the headwaters of the Ribeirão River where there was another house occupied by whites. The Wari' took the tools they found hanging, but did not encounter the whites.

In another episode, a man called Mijain Karamain attempted to shoot a white man, but was hit in the shoulder by a bullet. The white man took him to Porto Velho, where he lived for many years. He became white. The Wari' thought he had died. One day the white man became angry and hit him: he ran away, returning to the Wari' carrying a knife. When he arrived home, his hair was cut short and he had difficulty speaking their language. But his kin immediately recognized him. This man may have been the same one shot and taken to Porto Velho cited above.

Paletó told me that Francisco Meireles attempted twice more to contact the OroNao' after the episode in Panawin when the women were captured. Paletó was already married to his first wife and had children, but his current wife, To'o Xak Wa, now about sixty years old, was still a girl. Francisco Meireles flew over Tokon Torowakan, situated on the left bank of the middle Santo André River (Mana To). The airplane did not land; the whites launched fireworks and the Wari' shot back arrows. Since the daughter of Paletó's wife from her first marriage had already been born, and this woman would be about sixty today if alive, this episode must have occurred around 1940: "We had just finished burning the swidden when it arrived. We shouted. The airplane kept circling. 'Let's kill the enemy!' they said. My father was making a house. The swidden was very large. When the airplane approached, we shot our arrows. It flew down as though it was going to crash to earth. We shot. The wind took our arrows. We shot many arrows and it flew away" (Paletó 1993).

Another time, when Paletó was already married to To'o Xak Wa, an airplane flew over Pin Karam, a swidden located on an affluent of the left bank of the middle Da Gruta River (We Turu). The airplane threw out something like powdered fruit drink, and Xijam Pixam fired so many arrows that he made it fly away.

It is impossible to say for sure whether some of these contact attempts were conducted by the SPI, or whether all of them were carried out by settlers or railroad workers, either simply curious or interested in living in peaceful proximity to the Indians. There are no records of direct, face-to-face contacts with the Wari' until 1956 at the earliest. Apparently the SPI arrived in the region in the 1930s, when the Doutor Tanajura post was founded on the shores of the Pacaás Novos. However, by 1939 this post had already been transferred to the Guaporé River, prompted in part by the Wari' raids. The post only returned to its original location in 1956, the same year as the first peaceful approximation of the Wari'. In 1940 the Major Amarante post was founded on the Ribeirão River, and in 1945 the Tenente Lira post on the Laje River. Consequently, any contact attempts prior to 1930 are unlikely to have been made by the SPI, and the attempts attributed by the Wari' to the SPI officer Francisco Meireles, going by my estimates, all occurred after 1930. Although the whites did act ambiguously, always employing some degree of violence and making attempts at peaceful contact seem like abductions, the Wari' also appear to have little interest in differentiating the behavior of whites during these initial contacts, ignoring the violence and emphasizing the friendly intentions of these enemies.

I wish to conclude this section by summarizing what I have been able to infer concerning the dates of these first invasions and encounters. The Wari' accounts of acquiring metal tools and of initial conflicts suggest that the first whites were not seen before the start of the twentieth century—or at least, it is only from this time that the Wari' differentiate these enemies as whites. This shows that the rubber tappers, who had arrived in Amazonia at the end of the 1870s, took a while to enter Wari' territory, corroborating the fact that the Wari' avoided living by large rivers.

The first subgroup to have encountered the whites was apparently the OroWaram, who obtained metal tools at the start of the twentieth century. Likewise, they were the most affected by the construction of the Madeira–Mamoré railroad, began in 1905 and concluded in 1911. The OroWaram were also the first to succumb to the new diseases and indeed transmitted them to the other subgroups. They were also the first to be approached in an attempt at peaceful contact, sometime between 1910 and 1915.

But the whites evidently spread very quickly across the region, arriving in the territory occupied by the OroEo on the upper Negro River by 1915, as testified by the abduction of various women around this time. According to Orowao Toko Jai, an OroAt man of about eighty, his grandfather—who must have been an adult around 1910—told him that during this period the whites invaded as far as the Kit swidden of the OroEo on the right shore of the upper the Negro River. The OroNao', who suffered most from this occupation, had to relocate to swidden sites customarily used by the OroEo. After a time, the whites retreated and the OroNao' returned to their own swiddens. Paletó rejected the idea that the invasion was this intense, arguing that had it been, his father would not have reached adulthood (around 1915, I estimate) without being a killer and would have obtained metal tools much sooner. According to him, the OroNao' only took refuge in OroEo territory sometime later when he himself was already an adult (not prior to the end of the 1940s, therefore). However, on another occasion, Paletó stated that before he was born, the whites had already occupied the Ouro Preto River, forcing the OroNao' who lived there to move their villages to the Santo André and Da Gruta rivers. Later, frightened by the Wari' attacks, the whites pulled back and the OroNao' reoccupied their former swiddens.

Analyzing this information, I am immediately struck by the dates relating to the fluctuation in international interest in Amazonian rubber. After 1911 and the success of the Malaysian plantations, there was a sudden drop in extraction and many rubber tappers returned to their home Brazilian states. Perhaps, therefore, there was an intense incursion into Wari' territory followed by a vacating of the region, which the Wari' attribute to their own military prowess.

Still in the 1920s and 1930s, various captures and apparent contact attempts were made, revealing a clear intensification of the nonindigenous presence in the Wari' region. So although many rubber tappers moved away, others remained and continued to penetrate further into Wari' territory, no longer in big waves as during the rubber boom, but in slower and deeper form, reaching remoter areas in smaller numbers.

At the start of the 1940s, interest in Amazonian rubber surged once more and an unparalleled number of migrants arrived. It was during this period that the conflict between the Wari' and the whites intensified and the first village massacres took place. The Wari' were forced to recognize both the ferocity of the whites—which they had tried hard to ignore—and their military superiority. The narratives relating to this warfare were examined in chapter 2.

SIMPLY ENEMIES

The Wari' accounts of the first whites are remarkable not only because of their insistence on attributing peaceful intentions to them but also because of the lack of surprise concerning these very different looking beings. The peculiarity of the Wari' view becomes much clearer when we contrast it with the response of other native peoples to the first whites, where their strangeness led to their association with returning gods, spirits, and mythic heroes. This occurred, for example, when the Tupinambá came face to face with Europeans (Viveiros de Castro 1992a, 30); the Aztecs, Mayans, and Incas with the Spanish (Wachtel 1971, 42); the Hawaiians with Captain Cook (Sahlins 1981, 7); and some peoples from Papua New Guinea with the arrival of the first non-natives (Schieffelin and Crittenden 1991b, 3).

As I pointed out in the introduction, the fact that Europeans were associated with gods does not mean that the natives were unable to perceive the singularity of these events. They were not confusing "myth" and "history." Instead, the difference resides in their relationship with their gods and spirits (see Sahlins 1995, 6–7): in contrast to Western most widespread theologies, the gods are not ontologically distinct and there is no impassable frontier between them and humans; indeed, the gods were frequently humanized.

In this sense, the Wari' perception was not markedly different: whether humans, animals, or gods, the whites could be killed and eaten. Indeed the Wari' universe is not peopled by gods, but by enemies and humanized animals—beings with whom the Wari' relate within what we usually call their cosmology. It is as though everything were merely a question of naming: humans and animals here; gods, spirits, and heroes there.

It could perhaps be argued that the encounters mentioned above were all spectacular, even cinematic, which may have led to whites being classified as entities with superhuman powers or qualities. Schieffelin and Crittenden argue that we need to differentiate between encounters with individuals and encounters between groups of people. When a single stranger arrives among a people who have never seen anyone like him, he is considered an anomaly rather than a representative of a different culture or a different world. In Papua New Guinea, the authors continue, first contact always took place with large organized expeditions, which bring along their "own cultural context" (Schieffelin and Crittenden 1991b, 3).

This is an interesting point. In terms of Amazonian ethnology, it can be questioned somewhat, though, by citing the case of groups such as the Yanomami whose first contacts with whites were just as unspectacular as those of the Wari'—with harvesters of forest produce, foreign explorers, or agents sent by the federal government—but who nonetheless perceived the invaders as very strange beings.

> The apprehension, or fear, experienced by the Yanomami in response to this irruption of whites in their territory was connected to a hesitation in classifying them ontologically between two categories of inhumanity. The inhumanity manifest in their repulsive appearance and their unknown origin, their inarticulate language, the fact that they entered Yanomami territory from downriver, and the paleness and baldness of some of them made people think, based on the rumors of indirect contact, of ghosts who had fled from the "back of the sky." . . . Informants recall that this was the first interpretation to pass through their parents' minds. But the strange features of these creatures, such as their horrible pilosity, their trekking through dense forest, the lack of toes on their feet [shoes], their capacity to leave their own skin easily [clothing] and their extraordinary possessions suggested the possibility that these were malevolent spirits . . . coming from the remote depths of the Yanomami forests. (Albert 1992, 166)

The Yanomami case is particularly illustrative not only because of the rich detail in describing whites but also their historical proximity to the Wari':[10] skins that come off, feet without toes, hairy bodies (the latter is always highlighted by the Wari' when differentiating the whites). Why do the Wari' speak as though they were not in the least surprised? We cannot know what the first Wari' to encounter the whites actually saw. But this matters less: what really interests us is how this moment is reconstructed. In contrast to the Ya-nomami, the "parents" of my informants expressed no feeling of surprise, no difference that could not be situated within the domain of human-to-human relations or between humans and potentially human animals.[11] The point to stress, though, is that the Wari' were keen for war and eager to become killers—and this war is waged with enemies, not spirits.

An encounter between some Wari' villagers and a Catholic priest in 1950 is reminiscent of the first encounters between the Wari' and whites, although the episode occurred when they were already involved in actual war, rather than the potential war desired (by the Wari') in earlier times. I refer to a di-sastrous attempt at pacification conducted by this priest, who ventured alone into Wari' territory at the moment when the tension between the Indians and whites was at its highest.

According to a contemporary report published by the magazine *O Cru-zeiro*, in August 1950 the Benedictine priest Mauro Wirth, who was fifty-two years old, asked the bishop of Guajará-Mirim, Dom Rey, for permission to venture into the territory of the Pakaa-Nova, "to save the pagan Indians, shepherding them into the Lord's flock." Dom Rey tried to dissuade him, insisting that the Pakaa-Nova were remote and wild Indians: "Do you know, brother, that death awaits you among the Pacaas Novos Indians? Are you aware that only a miracle will save you from being pierced by the arrows of the Pacaas Novos?" But Father Mauro was undaunted and eventually re-ceived the bishop's authorization.

He left on November 2, 1950, "taking some presents for the Indians and the paraphernalia required to perform a religious service. He traveled up the Ouro Preto River in a boat belonging to the rubber boss Manuel Manus-sakis, accompanied by four woodsmen. Eight days later he reached the last civilized point and then, after a religious ceremony held for the rubber tappers and Indians, he made his way to the malocas of the Pacaas Novos" (*O Cruzeiro* [illegible date]).

It seems that the woodsmen accompanied him only as far as "a maloca that had been destroyed some time ago by white men." From this point on, Father Mauro journeyed alone. According to the magazine, nine months went by without news of the priest. On August 9 the following year an expedition led by the SPI officer Francisco Meireles and another eleven men set off to search for signs of the priest. Twenty-one days later the expedition reached the maloca visited by Father Mauro. It was abandoned, "the Indians had left behind even their weapons." After scouring the area, one of the woodsmen found two combs, recognized by one of the men who had accompanied the priest as presents the latter had taken for the Indians. After a whole day of searching they finally found a scrap of cassock tangled in a vine by the shores of a stream.

In an interview for *O Cruzeiro* magazine, Francisco Meireles speculates wildly over the murder of the priest, surmising that the Indians had taken him to be a powerful sorcerer and killed him with their arrows and clubs, offering up his life to their gods. Afterward, they had eaten him to absorb his powers. They had then abandoned the maloca, believing the place to have been bewitched by the priest.

I asked the Wari' directly about the episode, which seemingly occurred in OroWaram territory. This explains why the OroNao' knew nothing about the event, as Paletó assured me. According to an OroWaram man and his OroWaramXijein wife, both about sixty years old today, the priest came via the Ouro Preto River, arriving at the Pan Orop swidden site located on the Tok Wi River, a left-bank affluent of the lower Laje. It was the rainy season. He used long clothing down to his feet (a cassock) and wore glasses; he did not think straight.[12] He was not very old, but he was big. "He was a very happy and friendly man." On seeing him approach, the Wari' fled. He arrived at the village and found it empty. He sat down on a house platform, drank some sweet maize drink, and called for them to appear. He was carrying paper ("tree bark") and a pencil ("charcoal"), which he used to write (*xirao'*: to make designs, as in body paintings). Some men, including an OroWaram man, who has since passed away, and my interlocutor's father, shot him with arrows. He walked to the river wailing and fell in. They removed him from the water, threw away his clothing, and roasted and ate him in the Xat Araji swidden village, also located on the Tok Wi River. The interlocutor said that his mother was one of those who ate the priest. Fearing reprisals, the inhabitants abandoned the Pan Orop swidden. After pacification, the whites said to them, "You killed your father," referring to the priest.

Two OroWaramXijein men claimed, however, that the priest had not been eaten. Shot, he had fled and fallen in the river. The Wari' had abandoned the corpse there, believing that the priest's companions would come to rescue him and shoot them. One of them claimed to have seen some of the priest's mortal remains. The other man concluded, "The men remained hidden in the forest a long time, watching the priest, and then decided: 'Let's shoot him. This enemy might kill our women.'" Intriguingly, this man added that the men who had led the priest to the village were OroNao' of the Whites, the same who eleven years later, during pacification, returned to the region accompanied by the whites.

Given that the accounts match closely in terms of the names of the killers and the place where the episode occurred, it is perhaps somewhat surprising to find a lack of agreement concerning an apparently crucial detail: did the Wari' eat the priest or not? I suggest that for the Wari' this fact is not particularly important to the episode as a whole, hence the variation. As we saw in chapter 2, whether the enemy was eaten or not was secondary: what matters is that the person is killed. Killing already constituted the victim as prey, and eating the body was a kind of redundancy, a luxury to be indulged when possible. From what they say, the Wari' never risked their own lives to eat an enemy, despite risking themselves to kill. The determining factor in the war complex and in making men into killers was the enemy's death, not his or her ingestion.

This episode is fascinating since we have versions from both sides involved of an event that strongly evokes Wari' recollections of their first encounters with whites. On one side we have an idealistic priest of European origin, filled with ideas of "the good savage." Sure of the fascination exerted by Western manufactured goods and of divine protection, he dispensed with the woodsmen who had accompanied him and entered the village unarmed, carrying only presents, certain that he would be enthusiastically welcomed by the Indians. On the same side we also find an SPI employee, experienced in contacting remote Indians, equally imbued with fantasies concerning the primitive mind, who fed the press with ideas of sorcery, sacrifices to the gods, and the absorption of powers through cannibalism. And on the other side, we have the Wari': What did they see? Simply an enemy who entered their houses alone and unarmed. The objects he brought and his strange appearance neither intimidated them nor especially attracted them. They killed an enemy who made himself easy prey and became killers, and thus humans by becoming predators. At issue for the Wari' was their relation to humanity, the desire to assure for themselves an intrinsically unstable position that always has to be won. And so the Wari' killed the priest, a white man like those they had encountered before the warfare started, just as, at the start of the twentieth century, the OroWaram killed the wife of the white man who had arrived in their midst full of presents.

PART II

IN MYTH

CHAPTER 4

The White Enemy

Oropixi' is the Wari' myth describing the origin of the white man. Oropixi', the hero's name, can be translated as "the people who moved away" (*oro*: collectivizing prefix; *pixi'*: "to relocate"). I should note from the outset that not all versions of Oropixi'—in all, I collected twenty-four, provided by various narrators from each subgroup—associate him with whites. Below I present the complete version given by an OroMon man, about seventy years old, which was recorded in October 1992 in the Wari' language. I chose this example since it includes the main episodes found in the other versions and is explicitly announced as an origin myth of the whites.

> As a baby, Oropixi' cried inconsolably. One day his mother asked his older brother's wife to hold him. She cradled him in her arms and walked off. As they passed behind the older brother's house, Oropixi' turned into a man and had sex with her. Afterward he turned into a baby again, slept, and the woman returned him to his mother: "Here's Oropixi'; he's sleeping." He then suckled on his mother's breast. Every time he cried, his mother asked this woman to hold him as only she could calm him down: "Hold your husband's young brother." She carried the baby to his older brother's house. In the manioc swidden, Oropixi' had sex with her. Oropixi' cried whenever he wanted sex.
>
> A parrot was in the manioc swidden. Oropixi' went there and had sex with his older brother's wife. The parrot saw them and squawked: "Oropixi' is having sex with the wife of his older brother [*aji'*]! Here he is, having sex behind the house!" His older brother went to check and, finding Oropixi' still on top of his wife, yelled at him: "I was worried about you. I thought you were a child." Oropixi' fled and returned to his mother's house at night. The older brother said to his mother, "Your son is weird." He found the little mat on which Oropixi' as a baby slept and burned it. Their mother

sobbed, saying he should have just disliked his younger brother [and not burned his belongings]. Oropixi's older brother fell silent.

Oropixi' stayed in hiding. One day he told his father to chop down tree trunks to store water: "I'm going to take all the water away." He planned to take the water found in vines and other plants too. The father said, "That can't be true!" Even so he prepared the trunks, dug holes in the ground, set them upright inside the fence he built around the house, and filled the trunks with water. He covered them with lids made from mats. Oropixi' asked, "Are they full, Father?" "Yes," he replied. Oropixi' warned, "A storm is going to take the water away." As they were sleeping at night, a strong wind blew and took the water away.[1]

Early the next morning, the parents sent their children to bathe. Instead of the river, they found Brazil nut trees. Menstruating women and others who had just given birth went to wash away the blood and found there was no water. The children returned and told their parents, "All of the water is gone." The adults did not believe them: "Let's see for ourselves." They went to where the river had been but there was no water. It was forest, filled with Brazil nut trees and many other types of large tree.

Oropixi's parents had no sympathy for the son who had yelled at his younger brother. They refused him any water: "You should have liked your younger brother." The older brother listened silently. A long time passed. One day the older brother sent his children to ask their grandmother for maize drink. She gave some to them and to Oropixi's older brother too. Their anger had passed. After drinking he spoke seriously to his father: "I want to discover where my younger brother went, Father. I'm going to look for him." His father scolded him: "You should have just disliked him; you shouldn't have messed with his belongings. That's why he ran off." "I'm going after him," the brother said. So his mother showed him the direction Oropixi' had taken. They filled various baskets of maize for the journey.

They walked and walked, finally stopping to sleep. They walked and walked and stopped to sleep. Then the maize ran out and they returned: "I didn't find my younger brother, Father." His father said, "Your younger brother told me: keep on going and going. At the place where I arrived the water makes a boiling sound." So they prepared white and red maize flour.[2] When everything was ready, they set off again. He took his wives with him: the wife who had sex with Oropixi' and another who already had children. They walked and walked. The older brother decided to climb a tall tree to listen; he heard the sound of a large body of water far away. The maize flour ran out and they returned: "I heard my younger brother, Father. I reached a place where you can hear the sound of my younger brother's water." "That's what your younger brother told me: the place where I'm going makes a boiling sound." So he asked his mother to make more maize flour. They set off on their journey once more.

They arrived at the shore of a very large river. It was extremely large. The older brother and his wives covered themselves with annatto, ready to meet Oropixi'. They saw many houses, but Oropixi' lived alone. He had a maize swidden, a manioc swidden, and perhaps a banana plantation too. He had also planted some cotton.[3] Oropixi' was bathing; hearing them arrive, he set off to meet them. They met on the path. Oropixi' was warming himself in the sun. Turning round, he looked at the people who had arrived and failed to recognize them. They saw each other and said nothing. They sat silently on the stools he had made. After a long time staring at each other, they decided to speak. The younger brother said, "You came?" "I came."[4] "I went away because none of you liked me," said Oropixi'. "Why did you run away from our mother?" the older brother asked. And they talked and talked. "Stay until your feet get better," Oropixi' said. So they stayed until his feet had rested.

"I'm going away with our children. Your wife will stay," the older brother said. "No, you can take her back," said Oropixi'. "No, she can stay and you can marry her," the older brother insisted. So Oropixi' said, "Take her back. Don't stop on the way. After a while, I'll arrive too. Tell our father to reinforce the house posts. Reinforce your house posts too. A gale is coming." The other Wari' knew nothing about the coming gale.

The older brother arrived at his father's house. A very strong wind blew up, smashing everyone else's house. It was his water. Oropixi' had sent the wind. Only the houses of his father and older brother were left standing. Oropixi' arrived and lay down next to his mother. The next day, everyone saw Oropixi': "He returned!" The people bathed in the rain and collected the water in pans. "He's the owner of the water. That's why the water arrived when he came back," they remarked. Early in the morning he sent his brother's children to bathe. There was water finally.

After a while he suggested to his father that they leave together. They journeyed to the place where Oropixi' had stayed. He married his older brother's former wife. Later, his older brother went to live with them.

Many other people went there too. Some preferred to stay behind. All of Oropixi's kin went. They turned into whites [*wijam*]. That's why the whites appeared. They used to be Wari'. Oropixi', who took away the water, and the other Wari' who accompanied him turned into whites. It was our ancestors who transformed into whites.

The two groups exchanged festivals. One time the Wari' went there and on arriving at the end of the trail discovered a very wide path and returned. They saw that the members of Oropixi's group were wearing clothes. They used shorts, the clothing of the ancestors of the whites. They had turned into whites. "Let's shoot the enemies," the Wari' said. So they fired arrows at them. Oropixi's people no longer had bows and arrows. They had guns but fired them to no effect since they lacked any bullets. They only acquired lead recently. Later the Wari' went to dance again and the others already had lots of clothing. There were now many of them and it was impossible to recognize anyone. People like them began to appear on every river. They ceased being kin to the Wari'. The festivals ceased. "You turned into whites! Let's go away!" And so the Wari' forgot about them.

This ending, in which Oropixi' returns to the large river with his kin and gave origin to a strange people, who gradually differentiate themselves from the Wari'—making the narrative a myth on the origin of whites—is typical of the OroWaram, OroMon, and OroWaramXijein versions. Here I transcribe the ending to another OroMon version: "Oropixi' returned [to the large river] and took various people with him. At first one group would go to dance in the other's village. One time, they went to dance where Oropixi's people lived and found them wearing clothes. They did not like the Wari' anymore. They had turned into whites. They invented clothing: shorts, shirts. After a time, the whites invented firearms and shot at them."

Below I transcribe the finale to two OroWaram versions:

Everyone agreed to dance with those living on the main body of the river. They made a rubber drum and went to dance there. The people from the river also came to dance in the house of those who stayed. They danced a number of times, until one day the Wari' visited those living on the large river only to discover that the latter had turned into whites. They extracted rubber and wore clothes. They shot arrows at each other. And so they ceased exchanging festivals.

When the dry season arrived, Oropixi' invited his father to go away with him. His father agreed. His older brother, other siblings, and the rest of his kin went too. He took nobody else. Oropixi' finally married the woman and everyone went to live on the large river. People went to visit Oropixi's family until eventually they disliked each other and became mutual enemies. People stopped visiting because, they said, the others had turned into whites: "Don't go near them anymore. They turned into whites. Look how they live close to the large river!"

And this is the ending to an OroWaramXijein version:

They became whites and began to acquire beautiful things. Those left behind resolved to visit the whites, but they had already gone to the other shore of the large river. They [the Wari'] were unable to cross. They went there all the time to spy the other shore, until an old man told them to search for the whites in the forest. They discovered their path, but the whites received them [the Wari'] with gunfire. And so they waged war against each other. The whites are Oropixi's kin. They know how to row large canoes. The Wari' regularly went to see the whites because they wanted metal tools. The whites lived on the other shore of the large river. The Wari' war expeditions became frequent.

The OroAt and OroEo versions make no association between Oropixi' and the whites and present an interesting variation: when he brings the water back, he brings too much, causing an overabundance of water similar to the large river where he has been living. A boy goes to bathe and is eaten by a caiman. They ask Oropixi' to put an end to this excess of water and he complies. He remains with his kin permanently. In the versions told by the OroNao' of the Rio Negro–Ocaia village and the OroNao' of the Whites, only in the middle of the myth do some narrators allude to the fact that Oropixi' is white, at the moment when his brother goes to meet him and discovers that, though solitary, he lives in a place full of houses, reached by a very wide path. In the finale, he brings back the water and remains with his own people, as Wari'.

Here, though, an interesting point can be highlighted. According to most of the OroAt, OroEo, and OroNao' versions (as well as an OroMon version), the brother, on first arriving at the great river, surprises Oropixi' when he is having sex with a caiman. In one of these versions, the narrator says that Oropixi' called the caiman his "wife," and in another, Oropixi's brother, when his children tell him that they have seen Oropixi' having sex with a caiman, replies, "Yes, he does that. He's not a true person [wari']."

The OroNao' of the Whites also situate the origin of whites in the Nana-nanana myth, which tells of the reconstitution of Wari' society after it was destroyed by a flood. The OroEo and OroAt do not narrate any myth on the origin of the whites; it is probably significant that they lived in remoter regions and were thus the last to contact these enemies. Conversely, the subgroups that most elaborated the Oropixi' myth as a narrative on the origin of whites were those living near the area traversed by the Madeira–Mamoré railroad and who therefore first came across these enemies in their territory. The OroMon comprise an exception since, despite living relatively far from the railroad, they narrate the myth in a similar way to the OroWaram and OroWaramXijein. This can be explained, I think, by the once intense levels of contact between these three subgroups, forming a dense network of intermarriages and ritual exchanges.

While keeping in mind that the Oropixi' myth is not always about the origin of whites, we can note that the endings to the above myths provide a clear conception of the process of constituting white people. The whites are Wari' who moved away to occupy a kind of geographic region usually avoided: a large river. Whites are also the ones who substitute (or induce the substitution of) the exchange of festivals with the exchange of arrows and, later, substitute arrows with gunfire. The Wari' make it clear—and not just in the myth—that whites are enemies[5] and that rather than constituting a particular type or species of being, the enemy is the outcome of a relation. Rather than being ontologically distinct from the Wari', enemies are Wari' who pursued (or who were subject to) a process of "enemization," materialized in two forms: one geographic, involving spatial distancing; the other social, involving a rupture in the exchange of festivals and women. This is a reversible process: enemies can become Wari' once more by inverting the movement, shifting from warfare to exchange and moving closer spatially. This becomes clear in the OroNao' versions: Oropixi' is only associated with the whites in the middle of the myth. After he receives his brother's wife and returns to their village, he becomes Wari' once again and no more mention is made of him being white.

While the myth endings highlight the importance of exchanging festivals in maintaining the bond between the groups, there is apparently little emphasis on the exchange of women. However, at the start of the myth, it is the initial refusal to cede a woman that leads to an increasing distance between the two sides involved in the conflict. This refusal causes a unity—a pair of brothers—to split into two poles: first, foreigners and coinhabitants, then

Wari' and enemies, and finally Wari' and whites. Starting out from a minimal difference between two brothers (who end up on "the same side"), a maximal difference is produced between Wari' and enemies, and, later Wari' and whites, passing through a mediating difference between coinhabitants and foreigners.[6]

These kinds of successive bifurcations from an initial unity are a constant theme in the mythology of the Americas and form the substrate of *The Story of Lynx*, in which Lévi-Strauss (1991) examines the productivity of the notion of difference in Amerindian thought. In this book, Lévi-Strauss also analyzes the way in which New World peoples conceptualized the arrival of Europeans in their world, beginning with the observation that the myths on the origin of whites—particularly the Tupian myths—form part of a system of myths that focus on the successive production of pairs of opposites in constant disequilibrium. The differentiation between whites and Indians is thus part of a wider set of bipartitions and must be analyzed as such: "What, then, is the underlying inspiration to these myths? . . . They represent the progressive organization of the world and society in the form of a series of bipartitions, but without a true equality ever emerging between the parts resulting at each stage. . . . The smooth functioning of the system depends on this dynamic disequilibrium without which it would be continually at risk of collapsing into a state of inertia" (Lévi-Strauss 1991, 90).

Agreeing with Métraux's conclusion (1946, 95) that we cannot simply explain the remarkable similarity between the origin myths on whites of various tribes as direct loans, Lévi-Strauss argues that the similarity is based on something prior to them, namely the dualist organization of Amerindian thought:

> If the Amerindian origin myths rest on the framework I have been trying to reveal, the problem posed by Métraux is explained. The myths, I would say, order beings and things through a series of bipartitions. Ideally twins at each stage, the parts always prove to be unequal. Now, no disequilibrium could appear stronger to the Indians than that between the whites and themselves. But they possess a dichotomous model that enables this opposition and its after-effects to be transposed en bloc into a system of thought where their place was, in some sense, reserved. (Lévi-Strauss 1991, 91–92)

A blank space for the whites was reserved in thought systems based on a dichotomous principle that at each stage requires that the terms split into two; such that the creation of the Indians by the demiurge makes it automatically necessary that he created the non-Indians too. (292)

The myths on the origin of whites are merely part of a broader system of myths distributed throughout the Americas. Lévi-Strauss analyzes the importance of twins in this dualist mythology, noting that this derives from the internal difference that they harbor. Amerindian twins, conceived as a unity containing a seed of division from the outset, prove ideal for representing the duality contained within any apparent unity. Lévi-Strauss compares Amerindian twins, whose initial difference increases over their lifetime, with twins in Indo-European thought where the emphasis is on suppressing any original difference. He concludes that "twins occupy an eminent place in Amerindian mythology. However, this is no more than an appearance, since the reason for their importance, and for the role that the myths reserve for them, is due precisely to the fact that they are not twins" (92). Lévi-Strauss adds, "Amerindian thought therefore attributes symmetry with a negative or even malefic value" (305).

But twinhood is not restricted to its embodied form, as we conceive it. In the chapter "The Fateful Sentence," Lévi-Strauss shows that the Gê myth on the origin of whites (Auké) can be read as an almost perfect inversion of the Tupinambá myth—Maíra Monan—describing the creation of the world and of social difference (81). What makes the inclusion of Auké in this system of dualism-based myths even more evident is the presence of the "fateful sentence" proffered by the mother while the child is still in her womb: "If you're a boy, I'll kill you; if you're a girl, I'll raise you" (83). For Lévi-Strauss, this sentence has a precise meaning: "A being still to be born, or already born but not yet seen, has a merely virtual existence which leaves its sex indeterminate. It possesses a double nature; only by coming into actual existence will this ambiguity dissipate. A twin to itself, so to speak, it needs to be born or to appear to acquire an individuality" (87).

Oropixi' presents various similarities with Auké and hence with the complex of myths described in *The Story of Lynx*. Here I summarize a Canela version of the Auké myth presented by Roberto DaMatta (1970, 83–85). The plot is as follows: A child still in the womb talks to its mother and announces the day of its birth. When the mother begins to feel delivery pains, she utters the "fateful sentence": "If you're a boy, I'll kill you; if you're a girl, I'll raise you." A boy is born and she buries him alive. Her own mother, the boy's maternal grandmother, decides to raise him. Auké pressures his mother and she consents to raise him. Auké grows rapidly and has the gift to transform into any animal: when bathing, he becomes a fish, and in the swidden, a jaguar, frightening his kin. His maternal uncle decides to kill him, but Auké survives. On the second attempt, Auké imprisons his uncle on steep cliffs for days, almost starving him to death. The uncle tries again and, after hitting Auké, burns his body. Everyone abandons the village. After a while, Auké's mother asks for his ashes to be fetched. When they arrive at the abandoned village, they discover that Auké has transformed into the white man: he has a house, servants, cattle. He tells them to summon his mother to come to live with him.

According to Lévi-Strauss (1991, 81), who bases his account on the versions compiled by Johannes Wilbert, Auké invited the villagers to share the bounty of the whites. Depending on the version, they either refuse Auké's offer or gradually become "civilized" in his company.

The relation between the Auké and Oropixi' myths is clear: in both, the hero is a magical baby capable of controlling his own growth. Auké is burned on a grill by his maternal uncle; Oropixi's belongings are burned by his older brother, terminologically equivalent to the maternal uncle (aji'). Among the Wari', a baby's belongings are only burned when the child dies, and this is done after roasting the body, which allows us to conclude that the older brother treated Oropixi' as dead; that is, as a body roasted on a grill, a fate identical to that of Auké. Oropixi' abandoned his kin and left his older brother to starve indirectly from the lack of water;[7] Auké was abandoned by his kin, though not before making his maternal uncle starve by imprisoning him on cliffs. Isolated, Oropixi' is transformed into a white man, having previously returned the water and ended the hunger. Isolated, Auké is transformed into a white man after freeing his maternal uncle from starvation on the cliffs. Oropixi' and Auké invite their kin to live with them, sharing goods that only they possess. Both the Oropixi' and Auké myths include versions where the Indians either accept or refuse the offered goods. In the Auké myth, these versions present different endings; in the Oropixi' myth, a division occurs within the group—part of the population is transformed into whites, while the other part remains Indian. The two sides begin to war, the mode chosen by the Wari' to deal with the whites (in contrast to the Canadian Cree, who have a myth similar to that of Oropixi', but who entered into a peaceful relationship with the whites: see Lévi-Strauss 1976a, 261–74).

As I mentioned above, in analyzing the system of myths related to the story of Lynx, Lévi-Strauss concludes that dualist thinking employs the

idea of twins as a metaphor to express the idea of division being found everywhere, even in a supposed unity. Auké is part of this system of myths,
and twins are present in the "fateful sentence." If Oropixi' also forms part of
this system, then we are prompted to consider the question of twinhood in
Oropixi', or indeed the question of dualism among the Wari'. In contrast to
most Amerindian groups, the Wari' valorize the birth of twins and strive to
raise both infants, especially when male twins are born.[8] We can even suggest that twins are conceptualized as a pair of siblings whose birth interval is
simply much smaller than usual, the firstborn being referred to as the older
brother (*aji'*) of the secondborn. There are no myths concerning twins,
though several include a pair of brothers in their plot.[9] Hence it seems that,
for the Wari', the paradigm of dual unity is not the pair of twins, but the pair
of brothers. What does this unity involve and why are the marked siblings
male rather than female?

Same-sex siblings, the Wari' say, are identical because they were originally composed of the same substances, were gestated in the same place
(their mother's womb), and/or have lived in daily physical contact from a
young age, making them constant companions in all of their activities. Kinship terminology differentiates between older brother (*aji'*) and younger
brother (*xa'*), and between older sister (*we*) and younger sister (*xa'*). The
older brother is terminologically identified with the mother's brother, whose
children are considered to be a generation below ego, a feature typical to
Crow-type systems. The older sister is identified with the father's sister,
though this identification is partial since the father's sister's children are not
identified with the older sister's children. However, the more important difference is found in matrimonial practice. Until pacification, a man could
marry two or more women, frequently sisters, but there were no cases of
adelphic polyandry. A brother calls the wives of the other brother "our wives,"
but can only marry them after his brother's death. A woman also calls her
sister's husband "our husband," but marriage to him can take place while her
sister is alive.

Hence, while one sister is a perfect equivalent of another even matrimonially, the same does not apply to male siblings. As in the myths with twins
analyzed in *The Story of Lynx*, a preexisting difference—masked by an affinal terminology that makes them husbands of the same woman—is made
explicit: one brother cannot be equivalent to another matrimonially, except
in death. In the Oropixi' myth, the nonidentity between brothers is sharply
revealed when having sex with a brother's wife (equivalent to occupying the

brother's place or wishing to be his twin) results in exposing or exacerbating their initial difference.[10] Since taking the other brother's wife is to consider him dead, Oropixi' symbolically murders his older brother. This in turn is punished by another symbolic murder, the one most heavily marked by the myth: burning a baby's things is effectively to consider the infant dead.[11] Following this symbolic death—equivalent to the impossibility of twinhood, a feature of the dualism-inspired Amerindian myths—Oropixi' goes far away and becomes white. The tension is situated in the pair of brothers, representatives—like the twins of other Amerindian myths—of a unity that contains the seed of division.

The Wari' conceive of matrimony as an exchange of women. Normally it is the woman's family—her parents and brothers—who offer her to the husband. However, when a man is close to death, he may act like a consanguine of his wife by offering her to his brother (indeed the Wari' often say that spouses eventually possess a single body, implying the idea of consubstantiality). The same act is made by Oropixi's brother, on meeting him at the large river, and the brother of Hwijin—the hero of another myth—when already dead, as we shall see later. This implies that brothers are consanguines in whom one can locate a germ of affinity.[12] And for the Wari', affinity means alterity, a relation of latent hostility and tension. The typical affine is a foreigner, a member of another subgroup. It is into a foreigner that Oropixi' turns himself before becoming white. Analyzing the different versions of the myth and the ethnographic evidence, the foreigner clearly emerges as the locus of movement: someone who can be incorporated as a coinhabitant, or turned into an enemy.

CHAPTER 5

The Foreigner, the Dead

The idea of a pair of brothers as the starting point for the separation between coinhabitants and foreigners—the basis of a process of "enemization"—becomes more clearly evident in the Hwijin myth. While in the OroNao' versions the initial conflict is between two brothers who vie over a woman, in the OroEo and OroAt versions the myth begins with a ritual confrontation between coinhabitants and foreigners (a maize beer festival). The correlations between Oropixi' and Hwijin are multiple: indeed one informant even mixed up the myths when I asked him to narrate Oropixi'. Intriguingly, the name of the protagonist in one of the myths, Hwijin, is used as a descriptive term for the protagonist in the other. Hwijin means "whiner," a perfect description of Oropixi's behavior at the start of his myth, while the true Hwijin's conduct bears no correlation to his name. Here I present a version told to me in Wari' by Paletó, an OroNao' man, in January 1993. It was chosen from sixteen versions collected from the different subgroups (two other versions can be found in Vilaça 1992, 255–60; and Conklin 2001, 247–51).

> Hwijin had sex with his older brother's wife. The older brother shouted at him. They didn't hit each other. Perhaps the older brother did strike his wife.
>
> Hwijin fled. He went to stay with another brother, also older than himself, in another village. Hwijin arrived and said, "I've arrived, older brother. Our older brother shouted at me, older brother." "Really? He's like that. Our older brother is very hot tempered. Stay here." So he stayed, on the other side of the great river. The brother with whose wife Hwijin had sex continued living on the opposite shore.
>
> He stayed there many years and planted swiddens. After a very, very long time, they still hadn't met. So the older brother [with whose wife Hwijin had had sex] told his wives, "Crush maize for my younger brother."

They agreed and set about crushing the maize. The wife at the center of the fight with his brother also helped prepare the maize beer, along with his other wife. When the beer was ready, he told his sons, "Boys, go and tell your father:[1] Come and drink maize beer." "Okay. Let's go!" the older brother's sons said. They arrived at the village of Hwijin's older brother, the one who liked him. Hwijin was at home. They had built a bridge over the river. They announced, "Our father is inviting you to drink beer, Father." "No, I don't wish to," Hwijin said. So the older brother with whom Hwijin lived said, "Go and drink beer with our older brother. You can come back here after drinking everything." "Can I? Okay then," said Hwijin.

He painted himself with genipap and the older brother said [to the boys who had delivered the invitation], "You can go." Hwijin painted himself with annatto too. He spoke to the older brother with whom he lived: "Older brother, I'm going to drink our older brother's maize beer." "Go right away, drink all the beer. If you lie down, sleep and come back tomorrow." "No, I'll come back straight away, older brother." "Okay then, go now." So they went. They arrived at the bridge and crossed the river.

They continued. It was not far and they soon arrived. The older brother looked behind him and said, "My younger brother arrived!" Perhaps he was slightly angry still, ready to strike his younger brother over the head. He climbed onto the stilt palm platform in the men's house and asked, "You came?" "I came," Hwijin said.

Hwijin was afraid. They were afraid of each other. He saw the woman with whom he had had sex. The older brother said to his wives, "Fetch beer to fill my younger brother." "Okay," they replied. They filled a big pan of beer and he gave it to Hwijin. "Drink." So he drank. They fetched more beer and gave it to him. And more and more. Then the owner of the wife said, "I was just angry with you. I didn't hit you over the head because of what you did with my wife. I'm merely filling you with beer." Hwijin said nothing. The pans were emptied one by one. Hwijin was dizzy. The beer had caught him. He looked like he would pass out. He drank and drank and became very full. He vomited repeatedly and lay down when he had finished.

After a short while, though, he became scared of his older brother and said, "I'm going, older brother. My older brother told me to return quickly rather than sleep here." "Okay, go then. That's why I filled you with maize beer, since I didn't hit you over our wife."[2] "Really?" "Yes. You can leave." The older brother then told his sons, "Accompany your father. Follow him and come back." "Okay, we'll go with our father!" They walked and walked and once far away they said, "We're heading back, Father." "Okay, return then." Hwijin continued onward. Arriving at the bridge over the river, he climbed onto it. He walked across but when he was in the middle he looked down. His dizziness returned and he fell into the water. Except that he fell onto the roof of a house. It wasn't water, it was a village. He fell, puncturing a hole in the roof of the house and falling onto the men's house of the spirits, the damned Orotapan. There were various Wari' there, the water Orotapan, the water fish perhaps. The Orotapan ate him. They ate all of him; his body vanished. Just a little blood remained. Then Hwijin's former [dead] kin arrived, who liked him; they quickly took his blood and remade his body. He became a person again, revived. He went to the men's house [under the water] and sat down.

Ever since Hwijin had drowned the sun had vanished and it rained constantly. Not hard rain, just drizzle. By night it was very dark, by day it was windy. People wondered what had happened to the day. No explanation existed. One day they [the water people] told Hwijin to leave. "Okay," he said, and he walked off. The water spirits played log drums.[3] "I'm going right away," Hwijin said. He walked through the spirit village, listening to the drums. As he was climbing through the hole he had made when he arrived, his ears already on the outside, the sound of the drum turned ugly, like the sound of thunder. So he returned to the water to hear the drum [with its beautiful sound]. He stayed there. He wanted to tell people [on the surface] to listen to the spirit drum. He would tell them he had dived into the water.

So that's what he did, coming and going, until finally he left for good. He took a vine and wrapped it round his head.[4] The older brother with whom he lived said, "My younger brother returned." Turning to Hwijin he asked, "Did you drink our older brother's beer?" "Yes, I did," Hwijin replied in a faint voice, almost inaudible. He couldn't speak clearly. He asked, "Light a fire, older brother; I'm very cold." The Orotapan had eaten his throat. He sounded hoarse, like when we have flu. "Did you drink our older brother's beer?" "Yes," he replied weakly. He warmed himself by the fire and slept. The next day, very early at first light, he got up and warmed himself a little more. Then he returned to the river and dived under. He arrived back at the Orotapan village. Once more the [sunny] day ended. He told his older brother, "Older brother, the Orotapan ate me. I drank beer and as I was coming back, I fell in the water." The older brother said, "You can go there, but when you come back you should drink the true beer our wives make." And Hwijin replied, "I can't older brother. I like them a lot." He liked the underwater Orotapan very much.

Early in the afternoon he returned [to the surface]. He slept deeply and when dawn arrived he went again. Nobody could stand any more rain. It rained too much. He came back. The next day, he went again. His older brother's wives made maize drink and served it to him. They asked, "Where did Hwijin go?" "He went that way. Perhaps he went to defecate." They waited and waited, but there was no sign of him. They drank all the maize beer. When he returned, they offered him a new batch of beer: "Here's the beer, Hwijin." He spoke in a groan and drank. The next day he left again.

So his older brother, his true older brother [who was not angry with him], said, "Why is he returning there [to the water] so often? The village must be good. I'm going to look." His older brother was crazy. "I'm going to look. If it's no good, I'll come back." His wives thought he was joking, spouting nonsense to the children. He then fashioned a bamboo blade and stored it. He went to the forest, chopped down some trees for a grill, and bound them. He cut some firewood. He prepared some leaf containers to roast his liver. He lit the fire and cut a branch to roast his liver on. He fetched water so they could rinse off his blood after they had chopped him up. Everything was ready. He asked for a mat so they could shred his flesh on it. When the grill was ready, he took an old mat—not a true mat because the corpse is cut up on an old mat. He then spoke to his children. Perhaps he spoke to his wives too. He said, "I'm going to see my younger brother. I'm going to him. If it's a bad village, I'll probably return." "He'll return," they said. He then sat down and said, "Chop me up and eat me quickly." He took out the blade he had made and plunged it into his throat. Blood gushed out. They then sliced his body into pieces. They roasted his liver. His fire was already alight so they placed the pieces of body on the grill. They took the old mat and shredded the meat on it.

His spirit set off to meet Hwijin, who was singing music and enjoying himself. His older brother blew a flute. The Orotapan and Hwijin stopped what they were doing. Hwijin looked behind and exclaimed, "Hey! Who's died?" They looked and saw the image of the smoke. His body was wrapped in smoke. It was the image of the smoke from roasting his body.[5] "Who died?" Hwijin asked. So he returned to the surface, running. He arrived and heard the funeral song. The Wari' yelled to him, "Your older brother killed himself. There were some days you went to see your

Orotapan, other days you stayed with your older brother. You stayed a short while and the next day were off again. Your older brother killed himself. Look at your older brother who was eaten." Hwijin sat down and began to wail and sing the funeral song. Then he returned to the water with the idea of calling his older brother back. He dived under.

Hwijin asked the spirits whether they had seen his older brother. They replied, "Yes, we saw your older brother. He's right there, he left already." He went to another house and asked, "Have you seen my older brother?" "Yes, he's just departed." He saw the trail of vomit left by his brother. "Your brother drank maize beer and went." He walked to another house: "Have you seen my older brother?" "There he is, look," they said pointing in the direction he had taken. "He left just now, you can see his back." So he went to the next house: "Have you seen my older brother?" "There he is. Your older brother shot an enemy." He already had a hammock woven from assai fiber. He had pounded the fiber and made the hammock. And he blew a tucumā bamboo flute.[6] He went across to his older brother, who asked, "You arrived?" Hwijin replied, "Is this where you are, older brother?" "I thought this village was bad," his brother replied. He had no wish to return to his children. He wanted to stay. The spirits' village is a good place. The older brother continued: "I thought it was bad here and told our children that I'd be back after a while." Hwijin cried and asked, "Let's go, older brother!" And he replied, "I can't go." So Hwijin said, "I'm going right away, older brother." "Okay, go."

Hwijin went and came back another day. His older brother said to him, "Ask our wife to fetch my ball of cotton. I stored it in the roof." Hwijin agreed and returned home. He wept on arriving. After calming down, he went to his older brother's wives and asked, "Where's the cotton my older brother told me about?" And he added, "My older brother won't be able to come back." This was when his wives really sobbed. "Where's the cotton my older brother mentioned?" "He stored it up there some time ago, I saw him," said one of his wives, who had no children yet. "Fetch it," Hwijin said to her. She agreed. When she stuck her hand in the thatch to search for the cotton, she was bitten by a spider. She yelled, "A spider bit me!" Hwijin told her, "Be careful, or you'll be accompanying me!" She was going to die. She screamed, "I'm going to die, I'm going to die!" And she died. They wept. Hwijin cried a little and soon left; he wanted to arrive quickly to have sex with her. He dived under the water, but she had already gone. He wanted to have sex with her on the path. On arriving, Hwijin asked, "Have you seen my older brother's wife?" "She just passed by. She's over there, look!" Hwijin ran and reached another house. She had vomited beer right there. He asked, "And my older brother's wife?" "She's right over there. She just left. Run!" He ran. At another house: "Have you seen my older brother's wife?" "She's right over there. She left just now!" She had already reached her husband's house. "Have you seen my older brother's wife?" "Here's your older brother's wife. She's the one crushing maize for the maize drink." She was indeed already crushing the maize. "Here's our wife; she's crushing maize." "Here's your older brother's wife," all the spirits said. Hwijin cried. His older brother soothed him and suggested he go. Hwijin agreed. The older brother said to him, "Ask our wife about the resin."

Hwijin left and arrived home. He cried profusely. They had already eaten all of the corpse. He said to the wife [of his brother] who already had children, "Where's my older brother's resin kept?" "I've no idea. Only he knows." Hwijin went to her and said, "My older brother asked me to fetch his resin." But the woman was cautious: "He stored it here. You fetch it. You already acted wrongly before! I don't want to fetch it." Hwijin replied, "We didn't act wrongly. There was a spider and it bit the dead woman." The other young wife said, "I don't want to. Get it yourself, it's stored right there." Hwijin insisted, "Fetch it for me, fetch it." So the wife who had children said to the younger one, "Do what he's asking." She agreed. "It's stored here [in the roof]." When she stuck her hand in to get it, a scorpion stung her. She screamed, "A scorpion stung me!" It was a large scorpion. Hwijin arrived and asked what had happened. "A scorpion stung me!" Hwijin said, "Be careful, or you'll be accompanying me." And she yelled, "I'm going to die, I'm going to die!" Her kin wept. She died. Hwijin cried a little and rushed to the water to have sex with her. On arriving, he asked, "Where's my older brother's wife?" "She already passed by." She had already left. "Where's my older brother's wife?" "She's already gone." He went to the next house and asked the same. "Look, she's right over there." He ran quickly and reached another house: "And my older brother's wife?" "She just left. Look at her vomit." There was a trail of vomit on the ground. At the next house: "Where's my older brother's wife?" "She's there. Your older brother's wives are over there. They're crushing maize." Hwijin wept profusely. When he had calmed down, his older brother told him to return: "When you return, marry the mother of our children. Lie with her, my younger brother. Don't come back here; stay there." Hwijin agreed. He returned and had sex with the wife who already had children.

The rain continued to fall. Everyone told him: "Go there, Hwijin!"
"Okay. Wait a bit." And he entered the water. They sang. They sang for
Hwijin. Hwijin also sang. First Hwijin sang, then Orotapan. Then Hwijin
again, then Orotapan.[7] Hwijin returned [to the surface]. "So what happened, Hwijin?" "No luck." He returned [to the water] several other times
and when he arrived [on the surface] said, "Be patient, trust me." Hwijin
talked with the animals. He was weird. He talked with the giant armadillo [*Priodontes giganteus*]: "Go to Wem Paron,[8] giant armadillo. Go and
scratch him, perhaps the clay pan [the base of the rubber drum played
in festivals] will break. And then the rain will end and we'll finally have
some sunshine." The giant armadillo found Wem Paron and scratched
him. When he scratched him, he stumbled a bit, but quickly recomposed
himself. He continued to dance in a line[9] and sing. [Sound of drum being played.] They danced and danced. Then a seven-banded armadillo
[*Dasypus septemcinctus*] came and Hwijin said, "Go to Wem Paron, seven-
banded armadillo. Scratch his leg." The seven-banded armadillo also dived
under the water. Wem Paron wobbled slightly but continued dancing in a
line. No animal worked. The seven-banded armadillo returned: "No luck."
Hwijin thought deeply and found the six-banded armadillo [*Euphractus
sexcintus*].[10] He said, "Go to Orotapan, six-banded armadillo. Scratch his
leg. He's the one who always calls the others: 'Come and sing *tamara*, let's
have fun!' Scratch Wem Paron, the spirit of the great white-lipped peccary." The six-banded armadillo found and scratched him. Wem Paron
sang. He looked down and wobbled. The six-banded armadillo scratched
heavily and caught his thighs, making him stumble and hurl the drum to
the ground. Wem Paron yelled, "It was Hwijin, it was Hwijin!" He hurled
the pan [the drum base] away and the sun reappeared. Wem Paron spoke,
"You want me because I'm a large prey animal."

Hwijin returned [to the surface] and they asked him, "Did it work?"
"Yes," he replied. Hwijin decided to return to the water. He went to Wem
Paron, who said to his sons, "Go with your father, boys! Go and ask for
Brazil nut cake.[11] Fetch some annatto." Hwijin summoned Orotapan's
children: "Let's go!" They walked and walked. Hwijin joked. Having almost arrived, Hwijin said to them, "Quick, boys. You're not true people!"
"Okay." So they transformed into small fish called *oropara*. Hwijin picked
up a leaf and wrapped them in it. He took a length of vine and tied the
bundle. They walked and walked. Arriving in the village, Hwijin stored

them on a high beam in the men's house. Hwijin sat down. "Did it work, Hwijin?" they asked him. "Yes, finally," he replied.

Hwijin said, "Don't look at their children. You could only look if they were true people." "Okay," the men replied. "Sure," all the women replied. The women returned to their houses. In the men's house, Hwijin took down Orotapan's children and unwrapped the leaves, and they appeared in human form. Hwijin offered them some beer. He returned, fetched more beer, and served them. They vomited. The spirits vomited beer. Hwijin eventually said, "Okay, you can go. Walk quickly!" He picked up their leaf and wrapped them up again. Holding the bundle, he walked back. In the middle of the water, he opened the leaf packet and they jumped out: "We're going, Father!" They dived. Hwijin returned home and said, "Their children have gone. Wait for the peccaries." So they waited.

Next day, Hwijin sent the women to fetch Brazil nuts to make cakes: "Run and fetch the nuts!" They cut down Brazil nuts, crushed them, and made the cakes. Once ready, the women stored them. Hwijin then said, "Make beer!" They produced many pans of beer. The village was full of beer. Early in the afternoon, Hwijin spoke: "Their pets are coming." Great potoo [Nyctibius grandis], ko pu [possibly Pulsatrix koeniswaldiana, tawny browed owl], xoxori [apparently Otus choliba, tropical screech owl], spectacled owl [Pulsatrix perspicillata]. The great potoo arrived at night. The bird perched on the platform in one of the houses. Hwijin said, "Don't speak to their animals." The tawny browed owl arrived. "Say nothing to them," Hwijin warned. It hovered a while and flew off. All the other owls flew away too.

Dawn came and Hwijin said, "Wait. They said they would come. Sharpen your arrows." They sharpened them. Soon they heard the noise of the peccaries in the water. They came along the path from the port. The peccaries seemed to emerge from below the water. People shouted, "They're arriving!" Hwijin said, "Say nothing. Wait for them to surface." The peccaries emerged from the river. They arrived. The one leading the group wasn't particularly big. The largest was right in the middle. Hwijin warned, "Don't speak to them, don't speak to them." They entered the village and ate the Brazil nut cakes placed there [the narrator mimics peccary noises]. They ate all the cakes. They knocked over the beer pans. The beer spilled across the ground and they lapped it up. Hwijin said to the Wari', "Wait, wait." They were many tiny peccaries, but one of them was enormous, the size of an elephant.[12] It was Wem Paron. His wife was also very big. Hwijin said, "That's Wem Paron!" The Wari' yelled, "Who's going to kill him?" And Hwijin added, "And that's his wife!" The Wari' said, "It has to be someone who knows how to kill tapirs. Here nobody kills tapirs." "Who knows how to kill tapirs? Someone who knows how to kill big prey!" So someone said, "I'll kill it. Big prey don't escape from me." Hwijin told them to wait. The peccaries were drinking beer.

They went to the planted annatto bushes and snapped off some branches. Back in the men's house, Hwijin said, "Kill Wem Paron!" So they shot him. Wem Paron squealed and fell. They also shot his wife. All the Wari' were there. The peccaries didn't flee; they were all packed into one house. The Wari' shot them. "Kill the adolescent one! Kill the little one that's crying!" So the Wari' killed them. They also killed the Wari' spirits [the dead]. They killed the spirit of Hwijin's older brother who had killed himself. They killed the spirits of their kin. They killed the recently deceased son of a woman whose head was still shaven [in mourning]. They had eaten him [the corpse] and the next day he returned [as a peccary] and the Wari' killed him.[13] The peccaries then went away. On reaching the water, they dived under.

Hwijin told them to pile up the dead peccaries. "Okay!" the men said. They placed a number of mats together and dumped the peccaries on top. They laid Wem Paron down. "That's Wem Paron?" "Yes. This isn't the spirit of a person, its Orotapan. He's the one who made the rain and sang the music." They also set down his wife. They rounded up all the dead peccaries. There were many. "And this one, Hwijin? Is it a person?" Hwijin knew by looking: "This is an acará [*Hypselacara temporalis,* a *Cichlidae* fish]. Note how small his neck is. It's a very fat peccary. This is an acará." "And this one, Hwijin?" "This is golden trahira fish [*Hoplerythrinus unitaeniatus*]." "What about this, Hwijin?" "That's a characin [probably *Acestrorhynchus* sp., pike characin]. Look how the neck of this peccary is large." "It's true! What's this one, Hwijin?" "This is red wolf fish [*Erythrinus erythrinus*]. Look how the neck on this one isn't big." "What's this one, Hwijin?" "This is *iriwi* [unclassified fish]. He identified all the fish.[14] The people asked him, "And this one, Hwijin?" "Our grandfather, who died some time ago in another village." "This is our grandfather!" they exclaimed. All of them laughed; he had been long dead. "And this one, Hwijin?" "Our older brother, whom we ate there." "Ah! That one from a long time ago?" "What about this one, Hwijin?" "The father of her children, from a long time ago, whom we ate." "And this one, Hwijin?" "That's our older sister, who died there." He named all the dead. "And this one, Hwijin?" "It's our older brother, the children's father, who died just recently." His wife cried, the one Hwijin had married. "And this one, Hwijin?" "It's the son of that woman over there, who died." "And this one, Hwijin?" "That's her daughter." These were the children of the woman who had been stung by a scorpion.[15] "What about this one, Hwijin?" "It's that woman's son." She was still not speaking fully [she was in mourning], she whispered only. They asked again, "And this one, Hwijin?" "It's her son, that woman's." And the woman began to cry and sing the funeral song. Hwijin said, "It's just a peccary, it's not a person." And she cried and cried. Hwijin spoke, "Wait, I'm going to wipe off their annatto." He took a leaf and wiped the peccaries. He said, "Look at their annatto!" When he had finished, he also removed the bird feathers from their heads.[16] He removed and showed everything: "Look at their plumes!" Then he said, "Cut and eat them!" So they did.[17]

The wife of Hwijin's older brother was pregnant. People commented, "Hwijin's wife is pregnant!" "Really?" Her belly grew. The baby appeared to be moving. Then she started to feel pains. When she gave birth, it wasn't a person, it was an *oropara* [soapfish, *Rypticus* sp.]. "Throw it in the water!" So they threw her child in the water. He had sex with her again. She became pregnant again. "Maybe this time it will be a true child!" The day of the birth arrived: "It's hurting." It was born: "It's coming!" A soapfish. "He's strange. He doesn't make children properly." They threw it in the river too. They said to the woman, "Poison him. He doesn't know how to make children properly!" "Okay," she said. When the water level fell [in the dry season], they went to catch fish. They saw the soapfish, caught them, and Hwijin's wife rolled the fish in leaves and roasted them. When they were ready, she called to him, "Hwijin, here's your fish. Eat them!" "Okay, give me them." So he ate his children. He went inside, lay down, and asked, "Where's the maize drink?" He drank and lay down. He began to groan: "Argh! My belly hurts!" And the diarrhea started. "I'm going to die!" And he died. She poisoned him with his own children.[18] He died, Hwijin was finished. This is what the ancient ones said. What a long story!

The two versions given to me by the OroNao' of the Whites are practically identical to the above (OroNao') version, except that one of them locates the brother's suicide at the end of the myth. The OroAt and OroEo versions show significant differences and I summarize the plot here.

A *huroroin'* festival takes place between two subgroups. Hwijin, one of the guests, falls unconscious from drinking so much beer and vomiting. The hosts bathe him. Hwijin stays in the foreign village longer than his co-inhabitants and returns home alone. On the way, a little dizzy still, he slips off a bridge and falls into the water. The underwater people call him a foreigner (member of another subgroup) and ply him with beer. Hwijin tries to leave, but returns various times to hear the sound of the log drums better. He finally manages to return home, but soon returns to the water. His older brother complains that Hwijin rejects his wives' maize drink, offered by his children, kills himself, and asks to be roasted and eaten immediately. Underwater, Hwijin sees his brother's spirit enveloped in smoke but fails to recognize him. On the surface, he learns of his brother's death and rushes to the water in search of him, but discovers only the trail of vomit from the beer drunk by his brother. Hwijin finds his brother, who asks him to fetch some objects from his wives. The latter are bitten by poisonous creatures, die, and go to join him. Hwijin marries the surviving wife. A shaman tells the people to fence off the houses because the Orotapan are going to rise to the surface to eat everyone. They arrive, spilling the beer. In the houses they ask whether anyone is there: everyone remains quiet, except for one woman, who replies, "We didn't flee because you're not enemies." The Orotapan burn down the houses and eat almost everyone. It continues to rain. The survivors fill a trough with beer for a *huroroin'* and the Orotapan come to dance. Hwijin asks the armadillos to scratch the feet of Wem Paron, but only the six-banded armadillo manages to knock over the drum.

The OroWaram and OroMon versions (I lack an OroWaramXijein version) are a mixture of the OroNao' and OroAt/OroEo versions: During a festival involving two subgroups, Hwijin falls unconscious from too much beer and vomiting; he is bathed, returns later than his kin, slips on a bridge, falls into the subaquatic world, and is eaten by the spirits of fish or by jaguars (one version does not mention being devoured). Hwijin is remade by those who ate him and returns home. He warns the Wari' that his sister's pet will arrive after coming from the water. It is a parrot (the same species that denounces Oropixi') and the Wari' should not kill it. Hwijin sees things differently and eats dung beetles, saying they are crabs; he eats snakes, saying they are fish. The parrot arrives and the Wari' shoot it. Hwijin shows everyone that the parrot was using festival adornments, proving its humanity. Hwijin warns them that the Orotapan will now come to the surface to eat the Wari', but they should not flee, since this would only ensure they are pursued and eaten. The Orotapan come to the surface (in human form), playing a rubber drum (as during a *tamara* festival). A musical duel with Hwijin ensues. Wind and rain follow. Hwijin sends an armadillo to scratch Man Paran's foot (the same Wem Paron), who lets the drum fall and break. The Orotapan return to the water without eating the Wari' and the rains end.

The main theme of Hwijin is the relation between the living and the inhabitants of the underwater world, related to the Wari' dead. The myth, effectively the main basis of Wari' eschatological discourse, states that when someone arrives in the subaquatic world (like Hwijin's brother and the hero himself), he or she must drink beer in excess. Comparing the different versions, this is equivalent to being devoured.[19] After vomiting and falling unconscious, the person is bathed or, when eaten, remade from a small leftover.[20] Hwijin, having never truly died, has a special fate, allowing him to return to the terrestrial world and become a shaman-like person, transiting freely between the two worlds. As a shaman, Hwijin adopts the animal's point of view: he can see peccaries as people (the dead) and, as in the OroWaram and OroMon versions, sees the foods he eats (radically different from what the Wari' consume) as though they were Wari' foods.[21] Hwijin's older brother's fate directly associates the possibility of access to the underwater world with death followed by consumption of the body.

In this episode, the myth clearly shows that one of the specific functions of funerary cannibalism is to enable the spirit's journey to the world of the dead. While the body is roasted on the grill, the spirit travels to its final home under the water, enveloped in the image of the smoke from the terrestrial grill. But, having died properly, the brother cannot return to the surface, a fate that also befalls Hwijin when he finally dies at the end of the myth (Oro-Nao' version). In the world of the dead, the men become the best that men can be: killers of enemies. Women (Hwijin's brother's wives) become sweet maize drink makers, the drink given to these killers during reclusion. The myth also states that when the inhabitants of the subaquatic world, including the dead, want to return to the surface, they do so in the form of peccaries, which can be killed and eaten by the living. The relationship between the living and these water beings is always mediated by festivals: those arriving underwater are treated as guests for a festival (OroAt, OroEo, OroMon, and OroWaram versions); when the Orotapan arrive on the surface, whether to offer themselves as food (OroNao' version) or to devour the Wari' (OroAt, OroEo, OroMon, and OroWaram versions), they always act like guests at a festival, playing rubber drums, drinking or spilling beer. The relation between the living and the dead emerges as an equivalent to that between subgroup members (coinhabitants) and foreigners, likewise equivalent to the relation between consanguines and affines.

In table 1, I list the main correlations between Oropixi' and Hwijin.

In the two myths, the conflict begins with a younger brother having sex with his older brother's wife. The betrayed brothers punish the infractor by killing him: Oropixi's brother burns his belongings, an action only ever taken after the deceased's body has been roasted; Hwijin's brother offers him beer in excess, the way in which festival guests are symbolically killed and eaten by their hosts. As I remarked earlier, this correlation between devouring and offering beer becomes evident when we compare the different versions of Hwijin: either he is devoured underwater or he is invited to a festival, drinking beer in excess. The outcome of the punishment inflicted to the protagonists is their dislocation to water. Oropixi' purposefully travels to the shores of the great river inhabited by the whites; Hwijin carelessly falls into the water, the dwelling place of the dead.

The Wari' explain that living on the shores of the great rivers is a defining characteristic of the whites. Whenever I asked them why Oropixi' was a myth on the origin of whites, people replied that the whites had first arrived via the river mouths: hence, the whites live near the large rivers, while the Wari' live in the forest. I cite verbatim some phrases: "Those who are whites went to the Mamoré [river]; those who are Wari' stayed." "We Wari' live in the headwaters; we don't know how to live along the main course of the river. You whites live on the middle of the river." "Oropixi' must be an ancestor of the whites because he lives next to the great river."[22]

The Wari' call themselves forest dwellers and were effectively this until pacification. They made their villages and swiddens on terra firme and are unskilled in river navigation. Fishing was limited to small fish and the main techniques were weir fishing and *timbó* (vine) poisoning. Although providing an important protein substrate to their diet, eating fish and other aquatic animals was always marked by prohibitions, since water beings possess spirit and may, therefore, cause illnesses. During my field research, when the Wari' had already been living for more than twenty years by the shores of rivers—some of them voluminous such as the Pacaás Novos—I overheard shamans warning children not to play in the water because the latter was actually the village of the dead and other subaquatic beings, who are always trying to attract the living to join them.

Table 1. Oropixi' and Hwijin

OROPIXI'	HWIJIN
Has sex with older brother's wife.	Has sex with older brother's wife. / Foreigner in *huroroin'* festival.
Older brother punishes him by burning his belongings.	Older brother punishes him by offering beer in excess. / Hosts of the festival give him beer in excess.
Oropixi' leaves for the shore of the great river, provoking a brief storm,* transforming the river beds into bare earth and leaving the Wari' thirsty and hungry.	Hwijin falls in the river, provoking constant drizzle. He is devoured by water carnivores and remade. / He is a foreigner in an underwater *huroroin'* festival, receiving beer in excess.
Older brother journeys toward the water to meet him.	Older brother (other) dives into the water to meet him (killing himself).
Older brother discovers that Oropixi' lives in a village with humanized caimans.	Older brother discovers that Hwijin visits a village inhabited by the dead and humanized animals.
Older brother offers Oropixi' a wife.	Older brother offers Hwijin a wife.
Oropixi' returns to join his kin.	Hwijin returns to join his kin.
Oropixi' arrives at the village bringing wind and rain. The water returns to the river beds and the hunger ends.	The subaquatic beings ascend to the village, bringing rain. They are beaten in a musical duel, the drum breaks, or they are killed and eaten. / They eat the Wari'.
Oropixi' returns definitively to the shore of the great river, becoming white.	Hwijin (killed by the wife who makes him eat his children) returns definitively to the underwater world, becoming dead.

* As I remarked in a note in chapter 4, some versions of the Oropixi' myth explicitly state that a storm occurred, though in the reference version this is only mentioned by Oropixi'.

The relation between the great river shore and the bottom of the river, the dwelling places of Oropixi' and Hwijin, respectively, is of considerable interest since it allows us to hypothesize an equivalence between whites and the dead. From the outset, Oropixi' is effectively a dead person, at least for the brother who burned his belongings, and for other villagers. One version of the myth describes how a woman asks Oropixi's mother for a little water to wash away the blood of her newborn child, telling Oropixi's mother that she will call her son Oropixi'. The hero's mother refuses to give the water, saying that her son, Oropixi', is not dead; his name could only be given to babies were he so. Moreover, he is not a dead person because even his brother knows that he is alive and indeed leaves in search of him.

Something similar happens to Hwijin: on falling into the water, he becomes a kind of living-dead person, transiting between both worlds. He is not really dead, unlike his older brother who committed suicide and can no longer return to the surface. Both Oropixi' and Hwijin can be said to be altering, transforming into an Other: Oropixi' gradually becomes an enemy, the fact that he lives with caimans, as if they were humans, revealing that he is starting to acquire a different point of view from the Wari'. Hwijin gradually becomes a dead person, or a white-lipped peccary—the form taken by the dead on the surface—and adopts the viewpoint of these people: he sees the dead as *wari'*, which is how the dead and the peccaries see themselves. In this sense, both heroes are shamans who experience two points of view and possess two bodies, so to speak. Dead, enemies-whites, and animals with spirit are equivalent to Others, subjects who see the world with other eyes and who think of themselves as *wari'*.

What are the other implications of this relation between shore and river bottom? Living on the shore of a large river means living near an excess of water, that is, an excessively saturated or wet locality, just like living within or at the bottom of any river. While this association is clearly possible, it obscures another one strongly emphasized by the Wari' and which comprises the key to the myth's action. Before leaving to live on the shore of the great river, Oropixi' takes all of the water of the rivers away. And what is the consequence of drying a river if not to merge the bottom with the shore? As one version states: "The river bed turned into forest, Brazil nut tree forest. Once the river had gone, it became no more than a path." The river, where the dead live, becomes forest, where the Wari' live. The cataclysm caused by Oropixi' involved the merging of these two worlds: earth and water, living and dead. It is as if the thirst and hunger of the Wari' after the event was a hunger for difference: a discontinuity in urgent need of being reestablished. And this is why Oropixi's brother left, determined to ask him to return with the water and fill up the rivers again. This is also what Hwijin's older brother did by killing himself, since he could no longer stand his brother's transiting between these two worlds, which resulted in a constant drizzle, a phenomenon revealing the presence of the subaquatic world to the living.

The Wari' possess no genesis myth or cosmogony. For them, everything that exists in the world always existed. But conceiving that the creation of an inhabitable world requires establishing discontinuities, some people, extrapolating from the Christian discourse on genesis, drew an association between God and Oropixi': "Perhaps it was God who ordered the waters to spread everywhere, and that's why there are so many river branches. That's what the Americans [missionaries] tell us," one man told me as he narrated Oropixi'. This association can be extended further if we consider that the Christian God, for the Wari', is the creator and master of a hell whose horror derives from the mixture between the process suffered by the corpse on the surface (putrescence, roasting, devouring) and the spirit's journey to the world of the dead. Earth and water mix, the worlds of the living and the dead combine (see Vilaça 1996a, 1997, 1999a).

This allows us to pursue a more specific reading of Lévi-Strauss's observation (1991, 305) cited earlier that Amerindian thought attributes a malign value to symmetry. In the Wari' case, it is as if the twins that cannot be identical are the terrestrial and aquatic worlds, or, more broadly, all the different worlds: those of the dead, the Wari', the animals, and the enemies. The difference between beings is essential, and this, for the Wari', depends on the existence of various worlds and multiple perspectives.[23]

This also takes us back to the relation between Amerindian twins and the pair of Wari' brothers, allowing us to clear up a problem. Why, if the tendency of twins-brothers is to become increasingly separated, do the Wari' pair end up united at the end of the Oropixi' myth (his brother becoming white like the hero)? The climax to Oropixi' is actually the middle of the myth when the two brothers are separated: the first in an excess of earth and a dearth of water, the second in an excess of water and a dearth of earth, as one informant said: "The river was so wide that the trees on the other shore were invisible." This is the moment when most of the versions associate Oropixi' with the whites. It is as though when the Wari' say that whites are those who live next to the great river, and locate their origin in the Oropixi' myth, they are conceiving the great river as the myth conceives it: as an outcome of the rivers completely drying up. Hence, whites are above all those who—in the middle of the myth—brought together the shores and bottoms of the rivers. This seems to be precisely what an OroNao' man meant when he added the following to his version of the myth: "[People said,] 'Don't be angry with Oropixi', or else he'll leave again, taking the water with him.'" Oropixi's difference resided in his power, and his power was the capacity to take the water away, provoking a thirst for difference.

It is also as though the "original" ending to the myth was the episode common to all the versions: this foreigner, enemy, white, is reincorporated into Wari' society after receiving a wife and returning to his village. The return to the water is seen to result from Oropixi's return, as though he were the water. The incorporation of this white person into society reestablishes the cosmological order. This suggests, therefore, that the ending to the Oro-Waram, OroMon, and OroWaramXijein versions (where Oropixi' returns to the great river and is separated forever from the Wari') is something beyond the myth, a kind of excess, a supplementary or historical elaboration apropos the whites. It is as if the gradual transformation of Oropixi' into a white person is related to the Wari''s growing perception that whites are an atypical enemy, one that cannot be absorbed by society.

A problem remains: why are the OroAt and OroEo versions, which contain the water stealing episode, not described as myths on the origin of whites? We could surmise that these subgroups, due to their isolation, had no interest or time to think about the origin of whites, which is possible given that they were less directly affected by colonization until recently. Alternatively, we could discover something more in these versions, an element differentiating them from the others. As I mentioned above, the only significant difference is the mode in which the water returns: in excess, which to a certain extent annuls the difference between Oropixi' and the others, as if he had transformed them all into whites. The OroEo and OroAt versions of the Hwijin myth also display a kind of attenuation of the action: instead of "eating" his brother's wife (as mentioned earlier, the Wari' verb to eat may also designate the sexual act), Hwijin is invited to a festival whose main themes are the symbolic predation of women, killing, and the devouring of affines. Likewise, once in the water world, instead of really being eaten by the Orotapan, Hwijin is once again invited to a festival. In the OroAt and OroEo versions, the devouring is shifted to the finale, when the Orotapan ascend to the surface and eat the Wari'. Instead of an inhabitant from the surface who falls into the water and is eaten, we have water beings who come to the surface to eat. Comparing the OroAt and OroEo versions of Hwijin with those told by the OroWaram, OroMon, and OroWaramXijein, which begin in the same way with a festival instead of sex with the brother's wife, we can see that the latter differ in terms of the underwater episode: Hwijin is devoured by the subaquatic beings (making these "strong versions" of the myth). In the finale to these versions, moreover, the devouring is not concretized: the water beings ascend to the surface with the aim of eating the Wari', but the latter manage to escape. It is as though the fact that human beings are devoured by the subaquatic beings at the start of the myth means that this eventuality does not need to recur at the end—or as though the final act of devouring were merely an attenuation of the first.

CHAPTER 6

The Enemy

In *The Story of Lynx*, Lévi-Strauss (1991) shows that the creation of whites typically coincides with the creation of the Indians, a consequence of the dualist organization of Amerindian thought, which leads to a successive doubling of terms. This applies to the Tupinambá genesis analyzed by Lévi-Strauss himself, as well as various other Amerindian myths concerning the origin of whites. Among the Wari' (and Gê groups, among others), though, we appear to find an intriguing anomaly: the origin of whites is not simultaneously a myth about the origin of native society.

A specific myth describes the latter event, the flood myth, which here I call Nanananana.[1] Rather than comprising a genesis myth as such, it describes the reconstitution of society after its destruction by water. What is interesting is that, in some versions, the myth also tells of the origin of whites, revealing strong structural affinities with the Oropixi' myth, to the point of one informant beginning his version of Oropixi' with the flood. The analysis of this new myth also helps elucidate some episodes of Oropixi' that have so far remained obscure.

Here I present the version of an OroWaram man, who spent most of his life among the OroNao'. Were he alive still, he would be about eighty-five. The myth was recorded in Wari' language in December 1993, having been selected from a total of thirty versions.

> This is what the ancient ones told about the spirit of the rain. A very long ago time, it rained heavily for days on end. Eventually the spirit of the rain arrived. It appeared like an old woman, their maternal grandmother, the mother of the women. She brought a very old basket. The women said, "Our mother arrived!" She was just like the mother of the women. The rain had transformed [into a person]. "You came, Mother?" "Yes. The fire of your older brothers went out. They have nothing to eat," said the old

woman faintly.[2] "Really?" replied the daughter, stirring maize beer over the fire. The old woman sat down next to the fire and warmed her hands. She warmed them a long time and said, "I'm going. Give me fire to take to your older brothers [mother's brother, elder brother] and mothers [mother's sisters]. They're dying there." She said they wanted the fire to roast their food and eat. A lie. She probably had fire. The rain had transformed [into a person]. "We'll go with you, maternal grandmother. We feel sorry for you in this rain." "Stay, stay. I'll go alone." She said this because the spirit of the rain was not human. She took the fire. "Take an old mat, maternal grandmother." She took an old mat to shield herself from the rain. "If only the old woman wasn't so cold," people remarked. She picked up her stick and hobbled away.

As she left, the rain started to fall heavily. The water began to seep into the houses. The fish swam into the houses and people began to kill them. Nanananana was wiser: "Let's flee. There's a chance we'll drown here, children. Let's go to the house next to our maize swidden. The water will kill us," he said to his daughters. He and his daughters went, but their husbands stayed. "Go with your father. We'll stay here to kill fish so you can roast them for us," they said to their wives. At night they roasted fish and ate. They were sleeping when the ancestors drowned.

The next day, the father [Nanananana] said, "Let's go to see the village where our grandchildren's fathers live." The water had flooded the swiddens. Only the house posts were visible. "Our grandchildren's fathers drowned, nanananana." They could hear the sound of women grinding maize on stone, coming from under the water, as though people were still alive in the village. "Let's get them!" Nanananana cut down some tree branches, bound them together, and went to the village: "I feel sorry for my daughters, nanananana." The single girls [those underwater] said, "Okay. Let's go with our older brother." They climbed the makeshift ladder, climbing, climbing. Their hands emerged. When their heads broke the surface, they slipped and turned into river dolphins. Nanananana said to the boys, "Boys, have pity for us. We were left all alone." "Okay. Let's meet our older brother [referring to Nanananana]." So those who had been asleep in the men's house[3] began to climb the ladder. When their arms broke the water surface, they slipped and became otters [*Lutra platensis*]. "I'm going to fetch the red macaw!" The macaw climbed up the ladder but slipped and turned into a hoatzin [*Opisthocomus hoazin*, a riverine bird]. "I'm going to fetch the trumpeter bird [*Psophia sp.*]." And it turned into a type of heron. "Have pity for the children, Mother" [who was under the water], he said. "Okay," she replied. The old woman agreed. She climbed the ladder, slipped, and turned into a caiman. "I'm going to fetch the war club [said Nanananana]." But it [the club] fell in the water and turned into electric eel [*Electrophorus electricus*]. "I'm going to fetch that bit of pan for us to eat [maize] flour [said Nanananana]." It fell in the water too and became stingray.

They returned to their new village. After a time he said, "Let's look for people [*wari'*], nanananana." He went into the forest with his daughters and found a swidden made by another people [*xukun wari'*]. He saw fruits, papayas. He told his daughters, "I found people [*wari'*]. Let's get them so we can eat fruit too." "Okay," said the women. "Don't be afraid of them," he said. "Okay," the women replied. The father sat down near the fruits. He waited until the women [of the other people] appeared. They came to eat fruit. They were daughters of another people. Their father had stayed in the rocks [uplands]. "Cut down [the fruit] for me, older sister," one of these women said. They were eating the fruits when Nanananana appeared. They shouted. "You don't need to shout on my account. Our grandchildren's fathers drowned, nanananana." He grabbed one woman's arm: "We won't kill you. Our grandchildren's fathers drowned, nanananana." "Really?" He told them everything and asked, "Do you have older brothers, on your mother's side?" "Yes we do. Our older brothers live over there." "Run and tell them!" "Okay," the women replied. They left. Later their younger and older brothers arrived. "You came?" they asked [Nanananana]. "I came, nanananana. Our grandchildren's fathers drowned." "Really!" "Marry my daughters," he said. So the rock people became married men.

The father of these men, who lived inside the rocks, wanted to emerge. His sons had already emerged. He said, "I want to see your wives, my sons." He rubbed his body with a leaf to become slippery, but he couldn't squeeze through the hole in the rocks. He was very corpulent. Their mother too: "I'm going to see my sons' wives!" She tried to get out, but couldn't squeeze through the hole. She couldn't leave. The newly married young men had children. When the latter were older, they took them to see their grandparents. They made many swiddens, first close to their parents' house, but as they procreated and became many, they had to clear swiddens ever further away. Perhaps their father had died. They spread further and further and their children cleared new swiddens.

This can be considered an OroNao' version of the myth. I should note, however, that some OroNao' versions make no mention of uplands or caverns. The surviving family meets this "other people," marry them, and have children. The OroWaram, OroMon, and OroWaramXijein versions present some important differences, summarized here.

It began to rain relentlessly. The old maternal grandmother arrived (her motive unexplained). She left while it was still raining and the earth began to soften. The water rose up to the houses from the path to the port and began to gush from the ground. The Wari' went about killing the fish, while Nanananana fled with his wife and daughters to the maize house. People, animals, and objects transformed into aquatic animals (no attempt to save them is mentioned). The surviving family decided to look for people elsewhere. Nanananana met the people in the rocks, who, despite their human appearance, had tails (in the OroMon versions, these are the OroJowin, the "capuchin monkey people," the name of the Wari' subgroup that once occupied the headwaters in the uplands region). Nanananana offered his daughters in marriage. The children were born tailless or their tails were cut soon after birth. The father and mother of the rock inhabitants were unable to leave, remaining stuck inside. They curse those outside, saying that nobody would grow anymore and parents would stay the same height as their children.

Two OroWaram versions and an OroMon version call the uplands inhabitants OroXina, "people of the sun." The story is narrated as follows.

After the flood and the transformation of people and animals into water beings, Nanananana's family left in search of people. The OroXina arrived along a wide path. They were men (apparently two) having sex with a section of carved trunk. They welcomed the Nanananana family, calling them *tatirim* (foreigners, members of another subgroup), and soon called Nanananana "older brother." These OroXina were red deer and sometimes offered their animal bodies as a present to the girls' mother, whom they called "mother-in-law." They convinced their future wives' younger brother to allow himself to be killed, saying that, like them, he would revive. The boy died, transforming into a little brown brocket deer (*Mazama rondoni*), but failed to revive. Enraged, the couple decided to leave with their daughters, who were still children. As they departed, the girls looked back at the OroXina and grew magically.

From this point on the two OroWaram versions diverge. One (identical to the OroMon version) continues the account of the Sun and Moon, brothers who took these young women as spouses and were killed by their father-in-law after their wives had become pregnant. The earth remained in darkness until the children of Sun and Moon were born. On reaching boyhood, they disguised themselves and had sex with the mother. Subsequently punished, they end up killing her. In another version, Nanananana, his wife, and their daughters meet tailed people who live in the rocks. He offers his daughters in marriage and the children are born without tails. When no food is left inside the cavern, they move to the lowlands to plant swiddens. The parents are unable to get out of the cavern and curse their children's families: nobody will grow anymore and parents will remain the same height as their children. Notably, this version begins with the episode of the flood from the biblical Genesis.

The OroAt versions are very similar to the OroNao' versions, apart from a few details: the old woman goes to the village to ask for her hair to be cut, not for fire; the myth emphasizes that with the excess of rain, water began to seep from the ground in the village. Nanananana escaped with his wife and daughters not to a maize swidden but to a place where no rain was falling. Of the three OroAt versions I collected—I lack any OroEo version—two end at the moment when Nanananana decided to leave in search of people. Only one version mentions his encounter with enemies (*wijam*) who marry his daughters. These *wijam* would be the OroEo who inhabited the uplands.

The three versions of the OroNao' of the Whites are distinguished by their particular ending and other minor differences. Like the OroWaram, OroMon, and OroWaramXijein versions, the maternal grandmother does not explain the reason for her visit, nor is there any mention of an attempt to save those who drowned and transformed into aquatic animals. As in the OroNao' versions, the people met later live in the uplands, but they lack tails. They marry, reproduce, and spread far and wide. The parents remain struck in the rocks, but do not curse anyone. This is one of the endings:

> The father said, "Shoot the OroKarakat[4] to make them retreat. They'll want the women and you must take revenge." The father added, "When you approach the swidden, the OroKarakat will shoot you and you should do the same. The OroKarakat are bad." They agreed and left. In the middle of the forest, close to their future swidden, many OroKarakat appeared, firing arrows. The Wari' ran, shouting, "Flee from the enemy!" The OroKarakat retreated. The Wari' arrived at the swidden and felled the trees. They had children. They then decided to search for the OroKarakat. "Let's make war on the enemy!" On locating them, they encountered an old man

roasting a caiman. They [the Wari'] didn't eat caiman. They returned saying that the OroKarakat ate caiman. They went again and this time they saw them using cotton bands on their arms. Again they visited the enemies to shoot them and take revenge, only now to find them wearing white people's clothes. These were the people who turned into whites.

In the second version told by the OroNao' of the Whites, the OroKarakat are not whites but other types of enemies: Makurap, Canoé, OroWin, Oro-AoAo. In the third version, the father stuck in the rocks curses those who had left, causing them to war among themselves; the different subgroups began to shoot each other as well enemies. Just one OroNao' version (from seven in total) associates this myth with the origin of whites. It tells that the couples reproduced and spread along the Mamoré River, Rio de Janeiro, and eventually everywhere: "Perhaps this is why the whites came into existence."

Of the thirty versions I collected of the myth, only three of them—one OroWaram and two OroMon—constitute an origin myth of the Wari' subgroups. Here I transcribe the ending to one of these three versions, the same OroWaram version cited above, beginning with the biblical flood and containing part of the Sun and Moon myth in the middle:

The OroMon's ancestors fashioned arrows with tips made from pupunha palm and kept biting them. The OroWaram's ancestors chewed maize cobs, explaining why we have soft teeth. They spread outward. The Oro-Nao's ancestors found their way here [the narrator today lives among the OroNao']. The Wari' have existed ever since then. Our ancestors [those of the OroWaram] crossed the Ouro Preto river to search for bamboo. Other Wari' stayed on this shore. The OroWaram's ancestors ate unripe fruits like spider monkeys. The OroMon's ancestors were called OroTakat. Our name has always been the same, OroWaram. The OroTakat went to dance among the OroWaram and drink maize beer. They soon went to defecate. One after the other. They finished drinking beer and immediately went to defecate. Later the OroWaram went to their village and as they arrived saw that they defecated close to their houses. From then on they called them OroMon [*mon*: shit]. The OroWaramXijein [*xijein*: other] lived in the middle. It was like Santo André [village]. It was though we here [at the Rio Negro–Ocaia village] were OroMon and the OroWaram lived in Tanajura [village]. They lived midway on the path. The OroMon passed by and told them to live elsewhere, not on the path to the OroWaram. They replied, "We are OroWaram." So the others called them OroWaramXijein.

This is what some said to the others. I don't know about the OroNao'. They must know.

Despite so many variations, the myth always describes the reconstitution of Wari' society from women who survive the flood and marry men from an enemy group.[5] As in Oropixi', "enmity" clearly emerges as a reversible relation, where the incorporation of these strange beings (such as Oropixi' or the rock men) is achieved by giving women. Nanananana knows that his daughters are a powerful weapon in this encounter. This idea becomes even clearer in an OroNao' version: "When the *wijam* saw them, they said, 'We'll kill you!' But he [Nanananana] said, 'Don't kill me! I have daughters!'" Here we should note the incorporation involved: by marrying the enemies, the Wari' make them Wari' (clearly illustrated by the children born without tails or whose tails are cut off).[6]

The status of these enemies is always ambiguous, as if the narrators were unsure who should be considered the enemy (*wijam*) in this encounter: the Wari' or the strange beings, since everything depends on the viewpoint adopted. Either the strange beings become frightened in the encounter, or Nanananana. In some versions, the narrator says that Nanananana encountered *wari'*, in others, *xukun wari'* (*xukun*: other); and in others still, *wijam*. One narrator called them "*wari', iri wijam*" (*iri*: true; *iri wijam* being how the Wari' frequently refer to Indian enemies) and another "*wari', wijam, wari'.*" The intervention made by the child listening to his father narrate this myth, cited in chapter 2, demonstrates clearly that, for the Wari', the enemy is not a specific type of being, but a position, the pole of a reversible relation, and that they can see themselves from this perspective. In this episode, the child was surprised to hear his father refer to the Wari' as *wijam*, obliging him to explain that being Wari' (*wari'*) or *wijam* depends on one's point of view.

The parallels between Nanananana and Oropixi' are clear (table 2).

As a being that controls water, Oropixi' is associated with the simulacrum of the maternal grandmother, the "spirit of the rain." Both provoke heavy rains, but the consequences appear to be diametrically opposite: inundation and drought. However, bearing in mind my earlier conclusion concerning the ultimate meaning of a river drying up, we can note that the actions of Oropixi' and the old woman produce the same outcome: a merging of land and water. In the Nanananana myth, the river invades the village, making the earth disappear. In the Oropixi' myth, the village effectively invades the river, causing the water to vanish.

Table 2. Nanananana and Oropixi'

NANANANANA	OROPIXI'
Maternal grandmother ("spirit of the rain") provokes storm.	Oropixi' provokes storm.
Rain brings excess water.	Rain takes the water away.
River waters invade the village, transforming it into a wide river.	River transforms into bare earth.
People staying behind become associated with water as riverine animals. People leaving remain on dry land.	People staying behind remain on dry land. Person leaving, Oropixi', is associated with water, living with caimans (riverine animals).
Wari' family departs in search of *wari'-wijam*.	Wari' family departs in search of Oropixi' (who is *wari'-wijam*).
Wari'-wijam found in the uplands (rocks, caverns).	*Wari'-wijam* found on the shore of a wide river that sounds like boiling water.
The Wari' offer women (daughters) in marriage.	The Wari' offer a woman (wife) in marriage.
Wari'-wijam transform into Wari'.	A *Wari'-wijam* transforms into Wari'.
Version of the OroNao' of the Whites: internal rupture. Consanguines become foreigners, start to make war with each other, and become whites.	Version of the OroMon, OroWaram, and OroWaramXijein: Oropixi' leaves again, turns into a foreigner, enemy, and white.

The association between Oropixi' and the maternal grandmother in the myth openings extends beyond the outcome of their acts. In the flood myth, a maternal grandmother becomes a caiman (Nanananana's mother, when the hero tries to save her), while Oropixi' becomes closely related to caimans, having sexual relations with them or living among the humanized form of these animals. The caiman, a predator associated with large rivers, lives between land and water, as though its habitat objectified the mixture of worlds resulting from the action of the old woman (water) and Oropixi (land).

The relation between these two figures can be extended even further if we turn to the Wari' version of the biblical flood. In Genesis, God is the author of the rain, just like the old maternal grandmother in the Wari' myth. As we saw, Oropixi' is associated with the Christian God through his capacity to create order, restoring the separation of domains, but also through his power to provoke disorder and horror by mixing environments and worlds.

In the second part of the myth, there is a clear association between Oropixi' and the enemies. This helps explain the fact that, in many versions of Oropixi', his dwelling place on the shores of the great river is associated with the sound of boiling water. This sound is not typical to even a voluminous river, but it is the sound of the upland waterfalls, an area frequented by the Wari' and inhabited by them in the past, as well as being the territory occupied by enemies in the Nanananana myth. Mouth and source become equivalent, producing in the juxtaposition of the two myths what each of them produces separately: the mixture of land and water, since if the source and mouth were brought together, the river would not exist: it would be transformed into land, as in the Oropixi' myth.

Other details from these two myths that seem incomprehensible start to make sense when read in conjunction. Oropixi' is a baby filled with semen and sexual desire and, as a number of versions explain, cries from a lack of sexual relief: "He cried because he wanted to have sex." "After having sex, he became calm and stopped crying." "When he became full of semen, he cried again." "He cried because of his semen." In the OroWaram, OroWaramXijein, and OroMon versions of Oropixi', he becomes white at the end. The versions of Nanananana recounted by these same subgroups explicitly associate the rock people with capuchin monkeys (*Cebus* sp.), or relate the latter to the OroJowin (*oro*: collectivizing prefix; *jowin*: capuchin monkey), a Wari' subgroup today practically extinct, which once occupied the upland headwater region. The contemporary OroJowin were perhaps called by this name precisely because they used to live in the uplands, like the *wari'-wijam* people called OroJowin in the myth. But why capuchin monkeys? The association between these animals and caverns is strange given that they typically inhabit the canopies of trees, nonexistent in rocky regions with their scrublike vegetation. Unless, that is, we consider the comment of an OroMon informant ("they know how to have an erection, capuchin monkeys") and the Portuguese name for *Cebus* sp.: *macaco-prego*, "nail monkey," so-called because its penis, always erect with a flattened gland, resembles a nail. Like Oropixi', the capuchin monkeys are beings with excess libido, a characteristic the Wari' also attribute to the hyper-reproductive whites. In the Nanananana myth, the enemy people are identified primarily as reproductive men, that is, producers of semen like Oropixi', while the Wari' family relates to these enemies through women, Nanananana's daughters.

A small detail, present in the finale to some versions of Nanananana, begins to make sense when it emerges inverted in Oropixi'. The parents who remained stuck in the rocks curse the families that left: "You'll never grow and adults will remain the same height as their children." This phrase can be related to Oropixi's fate when forced to flee from his brother's anger and unable to return to being a baby. In other words, Oropixi', as a child, is condemned to remain the same height as his parents.

Notably the OroAt and OroEo versions of the flood myth show the same dilution observable in their versions of Oropixi' and Hwijin. The myth sometimes ends when Nanananana decides to leave in search of people, completely omitting the episode of encountering enemies.

The exceptional ending to the OroNao' of the Whites' version of the Nanananana myth seems to be related to the equally exceptional ending to the OroWaram, OroMon, and OroWaramXijein versions of Oropixi'. After the incorporation of the enemies, a new rupture occurs. The rupture in Nanananana is prompted by the theft of women, the same motive provoking the first departure of Oropixi'. The resulting groups war with each other and separate spatially, giving rise to the whites. As in Oropixi', this atypical ending to the versions told by the OroNao' of the Whites seems to be the result of an a posteriori historical adaptation. But why would one subgroup choose the Nanananana myth for this adaptation, while other subgroups chose the Oropixi' myth? The solution to this problem involves another issue, mentioned above, concerning a specificity of the Wari' myths (and those of other groups, including Gê peoples) when compared to those analyzed in *The Story of Lynx*: the origin of whites is not directly connected to the origin of Indians. This problem does not arise as such if we consider the inclusion of the episode of the origin of whites in the flood myth, since the latter myth effectively describes the origin of indigenous society. Everything seems to be explained when we take into account the structural similarity between the two myths. The Wari' oscillation concerning the localization of the whites appears to result from a perception of the relationship between Oropixi' and Nanananana as myths whose theme is the rupture of discontinuity, the mixture of worlds.

However, discovering that the Nanananana and Oropixi' myths are closely related does not mean that the Wari' specificity does not exist. In contrast to the Amerindian myths analyzed by Lévi-Strauss (1991), these genesis myths provide a less obvious link between the origin of the Wari' and the origin of whites, or enemies in general. However, Paletó's observation, cited in chapter 1, that the Wari' only knew they were Wari' because of the whites reveals the existence of the same dichotomy regulating Amerindian genesis myths, but in the reverse direction. Instead of the creation of Indians by the demiurge leading logically to the creation of non-Indians (Lévi-Strauss 1991, 292), it was the emergence of whites that gave concrete reality to the Wari' as a singular ethnic group: first, because it turned a set of subgroups into a single group; and second, because by promoting a mixture of different domains, they provoked something akin to a flattening of perspectives, inducing a sudden reduction of the *wari'* position to the Wari' people. It is a reduction that, as we have seen, the Wari' knew how to overcome, although it has recently been reinforced by the reading of the Bible—specifically Genesis—by believers, in which the *wari'* and *karawa* positions are fixed as categories in the act of divine creation.

CHAPTER 7

The Brother-in-Law

We began our analysis of Wari' mythology with a myth in which a wife-taking man took away all the water from the Wari'. We now finish with a myth apparently the inverse of Oropixi': the story of a wife-taking man who took away fire from the Wari'. This myth, referred to here as Pinom, is the Wari' origin myth of fire and funerary cannibalism and, in some versions, a myth too about the origin of death.

Here I present Paletó's version (OroNao'), recorded in Wari' in January 1993 and chosen from twenty-two versions—collected from representatives of different subgroups—because of its wealth of detail.[1]

> The spotted jaguar [*kopakao', Panthera onca*] had become a person. She was magic. She was the spirit of the jaguar who lived in the village. She had grandsons, who were the only ones to hunt for her. The houses of the real people were located a little apart from her own. "Let's search for game for the damned old woman!" They killed opossum [*waxik, Didelphis marsupialis*], sloth [*xomin, Choloepus didactylus*], and collared anteater [*pik, Tamandua tetradactyla*]. She didn't eat the good game. The owner of the game was going to bring her some. "Here's the game, maternal grandmother." "Okay. Fetch some maize flour to eat with your game. Fetch fire as well to roast your game." She ate raw meat with the true maize flour, the red flour.[2] She swallowed the head of the game and, satiated, lay down on her mat and slept. The next day she ate more.
>
> Then the dry season arrived and the river fell. "Let's catch fish," the women said. I don't know, they should have taken fire. None of those who had gone fishing had taken fire. Apparently it had gone out, who knows why. They should have taken fire to roast the fish. I don't know why only the old woman had a lit fire. The women asked, "Did you find strange fish for the old woman?" "Yes." There was *iriwi* [unidentified], wolf characin

[*wam, Erythrinus erythrinus,* Erythrinidae], bacu [*kaji karora,* Doradidae].
She only ate strange fish: threespot leporinus [*pokorop, Leporinus friderici,*
Anostomidae], trahira [*xikin, Hoplias malabaricus,* Erythrinidae]. When
all the women had caught strange fish, they returned home. Once there,
they said, "If only we had fire." Only children fetch fire from others, not
adults. "Go and take the fish to the damned old woman, Daughter. Fetch
her fire." "Okay," the small girl said. "Here's her wolf characin, tied up with
liana." She walked off. The old woman looked behind: "Maternal grandmother, here's your wolf characin." "I'll get it. Put it here. Fetch firewood.
Fetch one that's burning too." And she took one that was burning and another that wasn't. The child came back: "Here it is, mother." So the mother
lit the fire. Another child arrived: "Fetch fire from the old woman." Another fire was already alight. If only the women had then fetched fire
from each other. But they didn't. They all went to the old woman's house.
"Here's the fish, old woman." "Leave it here." They just left the fish and she
ate it. Another child came, and another. All the women who had caught
fish did the same. One woman said to her daughter, "Go and steal fire off
the old woman, Daughter." The old woman was eating fish. The daughter clambered onto the old woman's stilt palm platform and took the fire.
The old woman carried on eating her fish. The girl returned and was already some distance when the old woman turned around and pounced.
"The jaguar ate my daughter!" She bit her neck. She ate her raw. She was
a strange person, the jaguar. She threw the rest away, eating just the neck.
They wanted to kill her, but were afraid and she was left alive.

The people were trekking through the forest and saw the liana. It looked
just like real land, a ladder. Pinom [*cipó-escada,* "ladder-vine," *Bauhinia* sp.,
Leguminosae-Caesalpiniacea]. It had steps. It climbed through the clouds
and descended to the ground. "Do you think this liana is resistant? We can
climb it and leave the old woman behind." One person climbed up. He
climbed and climbed. It seemed like he was walking on land. He saw the
leaves of the trees. The liana grows upward at a slant. The person reached
the clouds. He saw the root of the liana. He walked high above. It was true
earth. "It's good there. Let's go there."

"Hunt game for your damned maternal grandmother," everyone said
to her grandsons. "Okay" [one man said]. They went searching and found
fruit. It wasn't *jamain, pija,* or *parara* [fruit trees typically used by the Wari'
to hide in wait for birds]. Its name was *ho pawin,* a large fruit, similar to

jamain. This is what the ancient ones used as a lure. They found the fruit and made a platform. At night they returned: "Maternal grandmother?" "What do you want?" "We are going to wait near the *ho pawin* to kill birds." "Okay. Where is it?" "Over there." Early next morning they went, saying to her, "Follow us, maternal grandmother!" "Okay." They set off. They arrived and sat waiting. They killed a toucan and left it there. The old woman arrived. Many birds were already lying on the ground. She picked them up and ate them. Then the surucuá arrived [*Trogonurus surrucura*]. The boys said to him, "When she comes to get you, fly away, Grandfather. Take her to another river, far away, this damned old woman who eats children." Then the arrow struck him. When she stooped to pick him up, he flew away. The boys yelled, "Did you get him, maternal grandmother?" "No, no I didn't." He flew into the distance. "Did you get him, maternal grandmother?" "No, no I didn't." She was already far away [in a barely audible voice]. "Did you get him, maternal grandmother?" "No, no I didn't." Finally they asked and there was no reply. "She's gone. Let's go down!" The people had already left, the village was empty. Early morning, when they had led the damned old woman away, the others had climbed up. Other old women stayed on the ground as well, it seems. [One of the boys said,] "Let's roast this bird, younger brother." They roasted and ate it. They drank maize drink. "Let's go!" They picked up their bows and arrows, and began to climb. The older brother went first, the younger one following behind. They climbed and climbed. They passed the highest trees and rocks. They climbed and climbed and climbed. High, high above, they saw the cloud they were going to enter nearby but suddenly felt the liana shake; they looked down and saw she was coming. "She's coming, older brother." "Let her. Let's leave her there." Had she been a true person, she would have climbed slowly. But she was an animal and climbed very quickly. "She's coming, older brother." "Let's get going." When they reached the cloud he said, "She's coming, older brother. I'm tired." "Why? Don't be tired!" "I'll turn into a *kut kut pixao* [unidentified woodpecker species], older brother." This bird looks like *wito* with speckled wings. "I'll fly to the roof of our grandfather's house, older brother!" "Don't say that. Don't do that." She was very close. "I'll come back, older brother. I'll turn into a *kut kut pixao.*" [Bird sounds.] He flew off to the village. The boy was no longer. The older brother continued climbing and reached the cloud. Everyone was already there, all the animals, Pinom. "You came?" "I came."

So they said, "You, *iriwi* [fish species]?" "It's no use, I've no teeth." "And you, wolf characin [*wam*]?" "If only my teeth [were] hard." "And you, characin [*omiji*, probably Ctenoluciidae or Characidae]?" "My teeth are soft." "What about you, trahira [*xikin*]?" "My teeth are soft." "And you, jatuarana fish [*tohojan*, Caracidae]?" "My bite is soft." Pinom spoke, apparently, "Bite, bite [the liana]!" He spoke to all the fish. "And you, acará [*takao*]?" "I've no teeth." "What about you, pike cichlid [*tomin, Crenicichla johanna*]?" "My bite is soft." They looked back and saw her. They talked and talked, stood on the edge of the cloud. The liana was nearby. Then they spoke to piranha [*pita, Serrasalmus* sp., Serrasalmidae]. The old woman was about to place her hands on the cloud edge. "What about you, piranha?" "Okay." She was climbing and climbing, reaching the edge of the cloud. So the piranha cut the liana. She fell, the liana twisting round her. A fire was lit on the ground below. Perhaps the younger brother who had turned into *kut kut pixao* had lit it. We also wonder who lit this fire if everyone had climbed up to the clouds. Who knows? The fire was big and burning fiercely. Her intestines started to burst: *kawa kawa* emerged [a red snake that doesn't bite people]. Perhaps the *kut kut pixao* boy told those in the cloud that a *kawa kawa* snake had appeared. *Juju, majowin,* and all the other types of snake emerged: *ara tao, torototo, tonain, oropita* [the last two poisonous], *wan nomon, ara mete, naja, majowao, ara taparain pana, irao, ara xinain at, papa wajo* [the last three poisonous]. All the jaguar kinds started to emerge too: ocelot [*Felis* sp.]. This is why jaguars and snakes exist today. And for this reason [the other jaguars] call the ocelot older brother, because he was the first jaguar to emerge from her belly. And all the small kinds of jaguar: *ororoin*, tayra [*Eira* sp.]. And also *orotapan* [wood fox],[3] every kind of animal. And the true jaguars too: *iri mamop, tain hu, hoho, mijak ko mixem.* Every kind of jaguar. That's what happened to the old woman's intestines. And that's the end of what I told you before.

Now I'll tell you about the damned wood-quails [*Odontophorus* sp.] and the rest of what our ancient ones recounted. They stayed up above. Perhaps there was maize up there. [I asked whether there was fire up above and the narrator replied:] Yes, there was. Had the spider monkeys descended with the fire, the Wari' would have eaten roasted abiu fruit [*kahwip*, Sapotaceae]. But they didn't.

They stayed up above until they grew bored. "Let's look for fruit!" They looked down toward the earth and saw that the abiu was still green. So they returned to their house [above]. "Let's go and see the fruit." Now the fruits were already ripening. They then decided what types of animals to mimic. "What shall we do?" "Let's turn into animals." Someone said, "I'll become a tamarin; its tail is short." He fetched just one leafstalk from a patauá palm, some *naran* [a type of resin], and molded a tail. Squirrel monkey [*koxeo, Saimiri sciureus*] also molded a tail from resin and leaped away while making monkey noises. He spread genipap around his mouth, which explains its dark color. He then took a type of annatto, *pijam*, which is yellowish rather than the usual red, making himself yellow-colored. Capuchin monkey took some true resin and made a black tail, just like the spider monkey's. The capuchin is small and the tail was very big. Spider monkey made a small tail, like the capuchin's, and imitated his sounds. So spider monkey said, "I'll take capuchin monkey's tail! If only he were big, but only his tail is big. I'll swap tails with him." He went and pulled out his tail, sticking his tail on the capuchin. The capuchin monkey said, "You only got my tail. You'll be hit [by arrows] and you'll stay in the branches." "And you too. People will kill your children. Your wives will flee from them, but they'll be killed just like yourselves." Capuchin monkey walks along the ground with its offspring on its back, allowing people to shoot them. Spider monkey never descends to the ground. Not so capuchin monkey: the male descends and men kill it. Likewise the female, who goes off to eat fruit, leaving her small offspring behind in the forest and letting people kill them. This was the spider monkey's curse. The capuchin young don't follow their mother. "They'll kill your children. You'll leave your children behind and they'll be killed." Then their anger subsided. "Show us what you do with it!" "And you spider monkeys, show us what you do with your tail!" And the spider monkeys wrapped their tails round the branches. Some people turned into tapirs, others into giant armadillos [*Priodontes giganteus*]. Their wives turned into capuchin monkeys, spider monkeys, squirrel monkeys, and tapirs: the same animals as their husbands. Yellow-spotted river turtle too, a strange animal. I don't know how they modeled the shell, maybe from wood. He crawled off. He eats fungus. "Okay?" "Yes, fine."

Many people then sat on the cloud's edge, looking down at the fruit below. Perhaps it was Pinom, the leader, who asked everyone, "Who's going [first] to call the others? You, spider monkey?" "No. I'm heavy. If I jump down, all the fruits will fall from the tree and you'll no longer be able to see which ones are ripe." "What about you, capuchin monkey?" "We're hungry. If we go first, we'll eat all the fruit." "And you, *tapan* [a tamarin, probably]?" "If I were bigger." "And you, tapir?" "If I go first, I'll break off the tree branch and you won't see the fruit anymore." "And you, giant armadillo?" "You true people who eat fruit should go. I eat earthworms." "And you, giant anteater [*Myrmecophaga tridactyla*]?" "No, I don't eat fruit, I slurp ants. I don't know how to eat fruit," he told everyone.

[I asked whether Pinom too had transformed into an animal; the narrator replied,] They didn't tell us this. We only know that once on the ground he went to kill the wood-quails [*Odontophorus* sp.]. Perhaps he had transformed into a jaguar.

He spoke to all of them. He hadn't yet spoken to the squirrel monkey [*koxeo*]. "Will you go first, squirrel monkey?" "Okay, I'll go first." He went to the cloud's edge and cried, "Xeo, xeo, xeo." His mother-in-law came and told him to carry his small wife: "Take your small wife. My daughter wants to eat fruit."[4] That's why it's the male squirrel monkey who carries the offspring. "Pass her to me. She'll eat fruit." The mother-in-law said, "Don't look down because you could become dizzy and fall. Here, take her." He ran to the cloud's edge and then came back. He ran to the edge again and this time jumped. He fell spinning through the air, landing right on top of the tree. As he was small, only a few fruits fell to the earth. "Xeo, xeo, xeo. Eat the fruit," he said to his small wife. "Okay," she replied. He carried her to another tree and returned to the fruit tree. He snapped off a twig, skewered a fruit with the tip, climbed to the top of the tree, and whistled. There he shook the fruit on the twig. So the spider monkey jumped down without having to be asked. He took his wife. They landed below and turned into people. They sat down. Capuchin monkey and squirrel monkey also descended. They ate fruits and descended to earth. There they turned into people. All the animals turned into people. All the animals that didn't eat fruit climbed down. Tapir descended and ate some very green abiu fruit. He quickly turned into a person and stood up. Yellow-spotted river turtle came crashing down through the branches until hitting the ground. He too stood up. They gathered many abiu fruits. "If only we had fire. Did you bring any?"

[I asked whether abiu can be eaten raw and the narrator replied,] We eat it roasted. Only animals eat it raw. Eaten raw it causes itching and mouth sores. You don't roast it lightly. You let the skin burn thoroughly and then clean away the blackened part.

"Did you bring fire?" "No." "And the boys?" "They haven't come down yet." "Perhaps they'll bring it. Let's wait for them." The boys were in a fruit tree high above. "What bird shall we transform into?" "I don't know, maybe into a curassow [*Mita* sp.]." They tried it out but didn't like the curassow's eyes, which seemed to water continually. They experimented with other birds like tinamou [*Crypturellus* sp.]. Then they tried out wood-quail [*Odontophorus* sp.] "What about wood-quail?" "Okay." The older brother stayed in one place and the younger brother in the other. They whistled to each other [bird sounds]. They ate the bits of maize left on the grinding stone [while they were still up above]. And the others said, "What about us? Let's turn into *totororo*." They imitated the bird's sounds. This bird has a red chest and a crest on its head like spot-winged wood-quail's. "Let's fetch fire," they said to each other. "Fetch the fire," they said to spot-winged wood-quail. "Okay. I'll take a licuri palm leafstalk [*Cocos* sp.]." He lit the leafstalk. *Totororo* took a leafstalk from *maxiwat* palm. *Totororo* took fire as well: "Let's go!" They carried on ahead. The people waiting below were concerned: "They should have arrived by now!" "Who knows. Let's wait." The wood-quail cried, "Hey, they're arriving, they're arriving!" They descended to the abiu tree, landing on the same tree on which the others had come down. They ate. All of them descended. "They're coming!" They weren't satiated with the leftover fruits though. People asked, "Boys, bring fire! We want to roast the abiu." [Bird sounds.] When the people shouted, they jumped away. If they hadn't shouted, they would have eaten until full. Then they would have gone over to the people and given them fire. But they went away.

Pinom stood up and began to whistle, imitating bird sounds: "I'll kill them!" This is where Pinom, who killed the wood-quails, enters the scene. He went and shot them. He opened one up, took out the fire, and swallowed it. He took another, opened it, and swallowed the fire. He tore open a *totororo*, opened it, and swallowed the fire. He returned. "Did you kill the wood-quails?" "No. They jumped away and flew off. I didn't kill them." This was when he became selfish about the fire. "And the fire?" "Let's stay here." So they stayed in that swidden. They cleared the swidden pointlessly, since they had no fire to burn it. Pinom also cleared a swidden. His wife planted maize. People said, "Pinom has maize." When it had ripened, they asked, "Give us some maize, Pinom." "I don't have any." "Where does the fire you use to cook come from?" Pinom didn't reply. He gave neither the maize nor the fire. People killed game and said to each other, "If only we had fire for the game." They left the game lying in the sun, turning it over and over until the meat rotted. When the river level fell, they went weir fishing [ko]. They caught the fish and left them to dry under the sun. They rotted. They saw Pinom roasting Brazil nuts: "Give us fire!" But he refused. Finally they became annoyed: "Let's watch him!" "Okay!" [a man said]. So the man, who was weird, went. He walked a little and stopped, a little more and stopped, so that Pinom would not notice he was being followed and avoid lighting the fire. Pinom carefully checked that nobody was watching. He climbed a tree, snapped off some Brazil nuts, made a leaf container [ja, impermeable], and went to fetch water. He collected a lot of water, which he left around the fire. He gathered some old branches, took some smaller ones, and climbed up the pile of firewood. On top he defecated the fire. The fire blazed and burned the Brazil nut husks. The embers popped, sending sparks flying everywhere. He stamped them out. The weird man was still there observing everything. He said to the fire, "Jump over here, my grandfather." The embers were flying everywhere. Pinom stamped out [the embers], but failed to put out one of them. The weird man, who was a *torain* toad, swallowed [the ember]. "It was you, it was you! You all took my fire!" shouted Pinom. The man leaped into the water and escaped. He turned into a person. He carried the fire in his hands. Pinom was so enraged he even forgot about his Brazil nuts; he left them on the fire. He made a weir, threw out the water, and began to catch fish. He caught a wolf characin and ripped open its belly but found nothing. He did the same with *iriwi*. Nothing. He ripped open all the toads in the water and found nothing. He became angry. He ran off and saw leaves burning along the path. The man who had taken the fire was burning the bush on the path. His [Pinom's] wife was fuming: "Why did you steal your brother-in-law's [*nem*, sister's husband] fire? He would have refused, but eventually he would have let you have it." "If only your husband wasn't strange!" they said to her. He then arrived and went over to his wife: "The damned boys took my fire. When they die, they'll be roasted, they'll face the fire." After a while he said to his wife, "Let's go to them!" "Okay!" They went to the village where all the people lived: "Why did you steal my fire?" "You're strange." "You stole it. When your children die, they'll be roasted and eaten. When you die, you'll be roasted and eaten too." And the people replied, "The same will happen to you. When you die, you'll be roasted on the fire and eaten." After a time, their anger faded.

Only his wife continued [selfish]. The people made a swidden and went to their older sister [Pinom's wife] to ask for maize: "Give us maize!" "Okay, okay!" The maize was already roasting over the fire. She said, "Plant it!" But the maize didn't sprout. The people went to ask again and she gave them very old maize, which didn't sprout either. They called her: "Urin, Urin." "Who'll take the maize?" "That one over there will go, so we can plant our swiddens right away." "Okay." He went and turned into pavonine quetzal [*Pharomachrus pavoninus*]. She picked off the maize grains and set them aside. He said to the maize, "Jump over to me, Grandfather." The maize jumped and he swallowed it. She became angry: "I'd have refused you the maize, but I'd have eventually let you have it. You stole it!" "You're very damned." "When you die, they'll cook maize cake to eat with your roasted flesh." Later their anger subsided. This is what the ancient ones said.

The OroAt (two) and OroEo (two) versions make no mention of the exchange of game meat with the old maternal grandmother jaguar. From the start of the myth, the relationship with the old woman is limited to women and their daughters. As in the other versions of the myth, the single women take the fish to the old woman, an eater of raw foods. But in contrast to all of the other versions, there is no mention of her making maize flour (which presumes the use of fire) to accompany the meat. The liana-ladder descends from above, and both OroAt versions state that this ladder is the penis of a man called Pinom (the name of the liana). In the versions of the OroNao' and the OroNao' of the Whites, the sky is initially explicitly inhabited by fish, named one by one. However, in the OroAt and OroEo versions (as well as those of the OroWaram, OroWaramXijein, and OroMon), the population of fish in the sky is less marked, suggested only by the detail of the piranha being responsible for cutting the liana. The narrator of our reference version merely remarks in passing that some old women remained on the earth rather than climbing the liana with the others. An OroAt version (and the OroWaram, OroWaramXijein, and OroMon versions) expounds on this episode, telling that the old women on the ground—fearful of the jaguars and snakes that emerged after the jaguar-woman burst over the fire—transformed into nine-banded armadillos (*pikot, Dasypus novemcinctus*) and tunneled into the ground. As in the OroNao' versions, hunger is not explicitly cited as the reason for descending to the earth. While narrating the more complete OroAt version, the informant stated that the people in the sky even cleared swiddens. I asked him whether there had been any meat to eat in the sky. He replied that there were birds, which suggests the idea that the sky is simply the space above where the birds live. He was unable to explain why they came down to eat fruit. The OroEo version states that the descent was prompted by the desire to eat abiu fruit. No other differences exist in relation to the reference version. Pinom's wife also refuses to give maize, which is stolen by a woodpecker. A detail from the more complete OroAt version is particularly interesting: Pinom, angered that his fire has been stolen, grabs a war club to strike the Wari'. None of these versions specify the kinship relation between Pinom and those from whom he hid the fire. An OroEo version gives special emphasis to death in Pinom's final words: "When your children die, you'll break all the maize that the dead person planted. You'll roast him. And you'll die."

The versions collected from the OroWaram (four), OroWaramXijein (four), and OroMon (five) are also fairly consistent with the reference version. The jaguar-woman eats raw game accompanied by maize flour, which presumes her use of fire. As in the reference version, people try unsuccessfully to kill her. Emphasis is given to the episode of the old women who remain on the ground below. Two versions tell that when scorpions and snakes crawled out of the jaguar, the old women killed them; however, when the other jaguars started to emerge, the startled old women transformed into nine-banded armadillos (*pikot*) and buried themselves underground. The sky is not explicitly inhabited by fish, but the figure who cuts the liana is a man called Pipita, the name for piranha in the dialect of these subgroups. This man is in the sky spinning cotton when the two brothers who tricked the old woman arrive. They call him grandfather. One version names him as the "liana owner" and another as Pinom (that is, the liana itself). Several of these versions associate him with the Christian God.

Another specific point concerns the descent of the animals from the sky. Although some versions cite hunger as the explicit motive for descending, in others this reason is only implied by their desire to eat fruit and the appetite of those who arrive at the tree. But here not all of them become human again; some refuse and remain animals. This refusal to humanize themselves is attributed to a fight between spouses: husbands who did not like their wives, or wives who had been ill-treated by their husbands, reject the appeals from their spouses to turn back into humans. An OroWaram version specifies that those who remained as animals were spider monkeys: they stayed up above, eating fruit. One of the OroMon versions merely states that those who remained as animals stayed in the trees. Here we reencounter the idea that the upper world is simply the canopy formed by the tops of the trees. Nonetheless, another three OroMon versions and an OroWaram version mention animals that descend; a white-lipped peccary wife and another of an unidentified species are immediately shot as prey by their husbands. This OroWaram version describes the episode as the origin of Wari' prey. As in the reference version, the Wari' try unsuccessfully to cook their food by leaving it under the sun: the food perishes before it can cook. In three versions Pinom is defined as the older brother (*aji'*) of the people to whom he denies fire. In an OroWaramXijein version he is called *wira*, the term used for a foreigner with whom kinship ties cannot be traced (see note 13 to chapter 1). Only one version mentions the recovery of maize by a bird. Neither was the origin of death spontaneously cited. However, when I asked the two narrators whether people died before this confrontation with Pinom, the reply was immediate: it was after this event that they began to die.

The two versions given by the OroNao' of the Whites are very similar to those of the OroNao'—that is, the reference version, another version from the same narrator, and a third, fairly incomplete version. The jaguar-woman eats raw meat with maize flour; the fish are summoned one by one to cut the liana, but only the piranha accepts the task; the hunger of those in the sky is emphasized; and one of the narrators explained to me that they could not descend from the sky because the liana was cut. The attempts to cook food under the sun fail and the food rots. A specific detail differentiates one of these versions: the figure who steals the fire from Pinom is a shaman. Recovery of the maize is not mentioned. As for the origin of death, one of the informants replied affirmatively to my question: before, nobody died.

FIRE AND WATER

We can now try to relate Pinom to the other myths analyzed here. I draw attention to a detail common to Pinom and the Gê myths (M7 to M12) on the origin of fire analyzed by Lévi-Strauss in *The Raw and the Cooked* (1994): the figure who initially possesses fire is the jaguar. In contrast to these myths, though, in which humans are unaware of the use of fire until the hero's encounter with the jaguar, Pinom is a myth about the struggle to recover fire, which humans not only knew but also needed to prepare their food. Here the human/jaguar opposition, marked among the Gê as nonusers/users of fire, appears in attenuated form: both need fire, although the jaguar uses it merely to prepare maize flour, which she ingests as an accompaniment to raw meat.[5] In the second part of the myth, in which the brother or brother-in-law, Pinom, steals the fire for himself, this opposition seems to intensify: on the one side, the man who has fire; on the other, the remaining people who now cannot obtain it even through exchange. However both parties know of fire and need it.

In the first part of the myth, the problem seems to revolve around keeping the fire alight. The Wari' have fire, but they cannot maintain it. Paletó, the narrator of our reference version, remarks on this fact during his narration. The jaguar-woman was not the only one to have fire or to master the technique of producing it. What she seemed to have mastered was the technique of keeping it alight. Here I emphasize an essential point, already observed in passing earlier (see note 2 of chapter 6): the Wari' claim they have never known how to make fire. A log or palm stalks must always be kept alight in the villages or houses, protected from the constant threat of rain.

The ephemerality of fire in the Pinom myth could be seen as a way of emphasizing the inability to produce it, in contrast to the jaguar's capacity. Judging by Wari' discourse, though, the technique does not seem to be an issue. Every time I asked them how they acquired fire, they replied either that they took it from someone—and ended up narrating the Pinom myth—or that this was not a problem since they never let the fire expire. This was always a big Wari' concern: choosing the right wood, one capable of remaining alight for days, and tending the fire constantly. Hearing them speak, it seems that it was inconceivable that someone, apart from the whites with their matches and lighters, could produce fire. They laughed incredulously when I tried to explain to them the friction technique using sticks. This is somewhat strange since they very probably had contact with groups that made fire. They warred with the Karipuna and Uru-Eu-Wau-Wau (Tupi groups), for example, and although warfare involves sudden attacks, it also requires a prior period of observing the enemies. There is little to add to this, except perhaps that denying any knowledge of the technique for making fire may be related to how the Wari' live the question of humanness; it is as if they liked the possibility of losing fire and experiencing themselves as animals. The loss of fire also implies the need to establish relations with other people and other villages, or indeed with the jaguar, as in the myth.

The short duration of fire in the myth, at least when in human hands, may simply be a way of expressing its absence, as if each day were a new beginning: awakening fireless, it has to be fetched from the jaguar-woman. What is at issue is the relation between the humans and the jaguar, characterized as direct or indirect predation, while the jaguar imposed herself as a commensal.

Taken at face value, though, this explication leaves out something important in the myth concerning the relation between fire and water. Presuming that fire has to be obtained every day because it goes out, or because, as Paletó's observation implies, the Wari' were unable to keep it alight, the question is this: What extinguished the fire? For the Wari', what puts out fire is water. Although wind can have the same effect, I never heard anyone mention the need for special care in relation to the wind. For them, fire's basic incompatibility is with water. And it is this possibility of rain putting out fire that provides a link between Pinom and the other myths analyzed here: Oropixi', Hwijin, and Nanananana.

Before proceeding, however, a detail from the myth must be examined. All the versions state that the fish to be exchanged with the jaguar-woman are obtained through weir fishing, a practice undertaken by women. Though practiced all year round, use of this technique intensifies during the dry season, and the narrator of the reference version, in introducing the theme of weir fishing, clearly states that the dry season had arrived (for a description of weir fishing, see Conklin 1989, 58).

In contrast to the reference version, all of the other versions of Pinom mention only the weir fishing and not the dry season. If we combine this with the fact that weir fishing can be practiced at any time of year, the fishing technique may be included in the myth less to mark the season than to show that the jaguar-woman's relation was with women and their daughters.[6] Moreover, the Nanananana myth shows that this type of fishing may actually be associated with rain. The capture of fish when the water reaches the village is a kind of weir fishing (tapagem), given that the fish become trapped in pools and are easily captured by hand.

I continue to argue, therefore, that the Pinom myth suggests both an incompatibility and a complementarity between fire and water. First, this idea is present in other episodes of the myth, with a gradual attenuation of the opposition between these elements, culminating in a kind of solution. Other reasons for insisting on this question emerge when we situate Pinom within the set of myths analyzed here, as well as within the wider system explored by Lévi-Strauss in The Raw and the Cooked (1994). I shall examine the main points of this question.

In Pinom, fire is constantly confronted with water. At the outset of the myth, humans flee to the sky—in the Wari' language, simply called "above" (*pawin*)—a place of water since its inhabitants are fish. This water makes the fire taken to the sky effectively inactive, since it is not used for anything and its existence is only recalled when people find themselves on earth once again and, human once more, need fire as they cannot eat the abiu fruit raw. The first person to possess fire is Pinom, who swallows the element after extracting it from the wood-quails. All the versions emphasize the water collected by Pinom before lighting his fire and used to put out the embers that escape, thereby preventing other people from acquiring it. Together these episodes would seem to suggest that what prevents the Wari' from having fire is water. When the toad swallows the fire to take it back to everyone else, his journey is made underwater (the narrators typically imitate the sound of the toad diving into the water on fleeing). Hence fire eventually reaches the Wari' via water, as though to emphasize that the latter had been the impediment all along, overcome to such an extent that the fire managed to stay alight in the water. Like an inverted pot, fire inside and water outside, the toad's body allowed these incompatible elements to come together.

From the point when the Wari' descend from the sky in the second part of the myth, the inside of the body is the means chosen by everyone to transport and keep alight the fire. First the wood-quails descend with it from the sky; then Pinom tears open the birds and swallows the fire; finally, the toad swallows the ember to take it to the Wari'. We should note that, at the end of the myth, this fire, maintained inside the body of a living person, becomes the wrapping of a dead body. Carrying the fire inside himself, Pinom seems to rehearse the position of prey to which the Wari' will be condemned when dead, squatting on top of the firewood—where the meat to be roasted is placed—and lighting the fire as though defecating.

The owners of the fire are responsible for transforming the Wari' into prey, a central theme of the Pinom myth that develops over the course of the struggle to possess fire. At the start of the myth, when fire is negotiable but ephemeral, the Wari' are like animal prey to the jaguar-woman, but are eaten raw; in other words, their bodies have no contact with fire. Later in the sky, when the fire is inactive or extinguished, people transform into the preferred animal prey of the human Wari'. This transformation into prey becomes more explicit in the episode of the husbands and wives who refuse to turn into people again—a refusal to remain married that results in the wives being immediately preyed on by their spouses. However, their bodies were still not subjected to fire since, at this point, it was still in the sky. From then on, fire is kept alight inside living bodies until it finally reaches the Wari'—via the weird man who turns into a toad—who are then transformed into prey of one another after death. The definitive possession of fire coincides with the earlier moment when the body of the Wari' encounters fire and the latter becomes externalized. Some versions even state that Pinom is a myth about the origin of the Wari' prey animals, implying that the origin of Wari' prey is indissociable from the moment when the Wari' transform into prey of each other. Being able to eat, which includes possessing fire, implies turning into food (explaining the reversibility of the positions of *wari'*, people, and *karawa*, prey).

But let us return to the question of water in the Pinom myth. Turning to the wider system of myths analyzed by Lévi-Strauss in *The Raw and the Cooked*, we can note that the theme of the origin of fire may be present even in myths that only directly thematize wind and rain. This is the case of the Bororo reference myth (M1) which, Lévi-Strauss argues, is a myth on the origin of fire by proxy, since the hero's grandmother ends up as the only owner of fire because of the rain (Lévi-Strauss 1994, 136–37). Situating Pinom within this mythic system, it seems to be located halfway between the Gê myths (M7 to M12) and the Bororo myth. As among the Gê, the owner of fire is the jaguar, who provides the source for humans to obtain the element. However, in Pinom the humans already know of fire and use it, although it seems to be lost on a daily basis. In this sense Pinom is closer to the Bororo myth in which the sole owner and source of fire is a maternal grandmother. The reason for the loss of fire, not immediately evident in Pinom, becomes explicit in the Bororo myth: the rain (Lévi-Strauss 1994, 36). In turn, a detail present in the Wari' flood myth, Nanananana, provides another connection between Pinom and the Bororo myth. In Nanananana, the episode of the maternal grandmother, the sole owner of fire, appears in inverted form: the maternal grandmother is the only person not to have fire, which is extinguished by the rain.

We can conclude, therefore, that Pinom is not properly speaking a myth about the origin of fire, but about the clash between fire and water. While the jaguar and Pinom are owners of fire, they are also, like Oropixi' and the old maternal grandmother in Nanananana, masters of water, since they can control its action. Pinom is another myth about the relation between the

dry world of the living and the submersed world of the dead. This idea becomes even clearer insofar as Pinom is also a myth on the origin of funerary
cannibalism, showing that roasting the dead is a way of passing to the other
world. By meticulously balancing the contact between water and fire, collect-
ing water before lighting the fire so every ember can be extinguished, Pinom
enables the passage from earth to water—which he had already achieved as
a liana, linking the earth to a sky that, like water, is full of fish—by making
fire, which he removes from inside himself as part of his own body. Fire comprises an essential element in this passage by preparing the dead body for
consumption. The spirit becomes definitively an inhabitant of the waters the
moment when the corpse is ingested on earth.

MEN AND WOMEN

At the myth's outset, the owner of the fire is an old maternal grandmother,
who is actually a jaguar. Apart from the reference version in which fire is
swapped for game meat obtained by boys, the exchanges exclusively involve
the jaguar-woman and women, who give her fish to obtain fire. For the Wari',
fire is a female concern. Women control it to such an extent that I cannot recall ever seeing a man lighting a fire in the village. I once saw an old widower
who was unable to cook his raw fish because his granddaughter, absorbed
in conversation, ignored his pleas for her to light the fire. Only in the forest
when on hunting expeditions or war trips do men control and tend fire.

In the second part of the myth, after the Wari' descend from the sky, the
owner of fire is a man-liana-penis, the same figure who at the start enables
the communication between the earth and the aquatic sky. He is called a
wife-taking brother-in-law (*nem*) in the reference version and, indirectly, in
another version where it is suggested that he should have grabbed the war
club and struck those who had stolen the fire from him. As I mentioned earlier, this type of aggression is typical of the relation between affines, when
brothers and other members of the wife's kin attack the kin of the husband
who attacked her. We can also cite the war-club fights between two men vy-
ing over the same woman: the betrayed husband formally assaults the wife's
lover. In three other versions, Pinom is classified as an older brother in his
wife's irate discourse. The fact that he is called older brother is entirely com-
patible with his classification as a brother-in-law given the Wari' preference
for using consanguinal terms to refer to their affines. Pinom acts by taking
fire away from the Wari', the same action taken by Oropixi'—a brother who

acts as a wife-taker—in relation to water. As a wife-taking brother-in-law, Pinom more precisely occupies the place of the jaguar-woman, who, though a woman and elderly, acts like a brother-in-law by choosing as prey (eating being a metaphor for having sex) only single girls who went to fetch fire for their mothers.

The Wari' emerge, therefore, as women, or wife-givers, vis-à-vis these "brothers-in-law" (the jaguar-woman and Pinom), the owners or stealers of fire. Taking into account the evident analogy between women and fire—and here I recall the episode cited above in which Pinom thinks about attacking the fire thieves with a war club, exactly as one does with wife thieves—we can note an apparent desire among the Wari' to receive back the sisters or daughters stolen by these strange brothers-in-law, who cannot be punished directly. In the case of the jaguar, for example, the versions tell of failed attempts by the Wari' to kill her. Hence, the myth displays the same tension present in Wari' alliance relations, attitudes, and discourse analyzed in chapter 1.

In Pinom, the relation between different universes—represented as a relation between the living and the dead—is mediated by a man acting as a wife-taking brother-in-law. In Oropixi', it is the white man who controls this relation, provoking a mixture of worlds that he later agrees to separate. Oropixi' is also a man, or even a super-man, since he acts in response to an excess of libido. In Nanananana, the Wari' once again occupy the position of women when they enter into contact with alterity: the Wari' family surviving the flood, formed by a father and his marriageable daughters, meets capuchin monkey enemies, who are likewise characterized by their sexual potency, suggested by the constant erection of their penises. In Nanananana, an idea common to all of the myths analyzed here comes to the fore: the enemies are domesticated or subjugated by the Wari' by giving them women. Nanananana's reply to these strange beings, shouting that he should not be killed because he has daughters to give in marriage, is echoed in the other myths. Whites, the dead, enemies, and brothers-in-law, the Others par excellence, are turned into men by the Wari' so they can be incorporated. The male position of the enemies is evident not only in Nanananana but in the entire symbology of warfare and homicide: the killer, *napiri*, is like a woman given by the Wari' to the enemies (see Vilaça 1992, 103–5).

The dead are also clearly male in relation to the living. Various elements lead to this conclusion. When a dead person arrives in the subaquatic world, he or she is welcomed by a being with enormous testicles, called Towira

Towira (*towira* meaning testicle), which reminds us of Oropixi's exaggerated libido and the erect penis of Nanananana's monkey enemies. This being
offers the newly arrived person maize beer, but, according to one informant,
what he does is to have sexual relations with the women who arrive. Towira
Towira occupies the place of the dead, while those recently arrived in the
underwater world are the living, since they can refuse the beer and return
to earth. When the dead, already established inhabitants of the underwater
world, want to see their living kin, they ascend to the surface as the (predominantly male) guests of a *tamara* festival. Recalling the association made by
the Wari' between sex and eating, we can point to an episode from the Hwijin
myth in which the Orotapan, inhabitants of the waters, climb to the surface
to eat the living, or devour Hwijin when he falls in the water. A myth exclusive to the OroWaram, OroWaramXijein, and OroMon—similar to Hwijin
in various aspects—tells of beings that leave the water for the land, taking a
Wari' woman with them.

The funerary chant, performed throughout the funeral, also suggest the
same conclusion. As they weep for a dead person, men refer to him or her
in the same way as women. For instance, a man calls the dead person son
or daughter in the same way a woman refers to her child, not the way a man
would do. As we can see, the Wari' already become women in relation to the
corpse.[7]

THE ORIGIN OF MORTALITY

To finish, the question remains whether Pinom is a myth about the origin of
mortality. Perhaps it is more accurately a myth about the origin of the dead,
since the theme is the origin of fire, which allows the cooking of bodies and
their transition to the world of the dead. Moreover, if the dead are roasted
and cooking is a process of maturation, it makes sense that this maturation
causes the raw living to age and die. However, the evident correlations between Pinom and Oropixi' on the one hand, and the myths on the origin of
whites and the brief life, or the origin of mortality, on the other, suggest a
relation between Pinom and the origin of mortality. Various myths describing the origin of whites define the moment of separation between Indians
and whites as the result of a bad choice. Viveiros de Castro (1992a, 30–31 and
2000b) shows the clear relation between these myths and the myths on the
origin of mortality analyzed by Lévi-Strauss in *The Raw and the Cooked*: a

wrong choice, related to the bad use of the sense, such as hearing too much or too little, makes men mortal. As Viveiros de Castro (1992a) points out, the dramatic mortality rate following the arrival of the whites probably has a direct bearing on the fact that myths on the origin of whites have been elaborated in correlation with the mythic schema of the origin of mortality. The theme of the bad choice is not evident in Pinom, though we do find the theme of noise, which characterizes these myths: the girls cannot make a sound when they try to steal the old woman's fire or they would be eaten by her; in order to steal Pinom's fire, the toad has to wait in silence. Noise provoked the loss of fire and devoration. In Oropixi' too the theme of the bad choice present in other myths on the origin of whites appears to be absent, unless we consider the final choice of the Wari', who decided to remain where they were rather than accompany Oropixi' to the great river. The problem with this model, in the Wari' case, is that there is no obvious misuse of the senses, a central feature of the myths of the bad choice. However, the general association made by Viveiros de Castro (1992a and 2000b) on the basis of a set of South American myths allows us to at least suggest that the correlations I have highlighted between Oropixi' and Pinom stem, among other reasons, from the fact that the origin of whites and the origin of mortality are closely associated in indigenous thought.

WHITES, THE DEAD, ENEMIES, AND BROTHERS-IN-LAW

Our analysis of this set of Wari' myths has shown that the whites are conceived as enemies and that the enemy is related to the dead and the brother-in-law as well as the foreigner. But how can whites be brothers-in-law if the Wari' do not marry whites? Precisely for this reason, we could say. As I have already shown, brothers-in-law—and affines in general—are those with whom one avoids exchanging women, but with whom one is forced to live in relatively peaceful coexistence, as is visible in the relation with the foreigner.

Before pacification, the Wari' never lived with enemies, whether Indians or whites. Enemies were to be killed and eaten without any exchange of words or goods, much less women. The white enemies arrived and the Wari' began—partly out of choice, partly through coercion—to live with them on a daily basis, exchanging words and objects, though not women, as they did with Indians from other ethnic groups, who became coinhabitants and ended up being incorporated as Wari'. As we have seen, real affinity is

a primary means of incorporation since marriage involves intimate coexistence—and with it, the exchange of bodily substances and commensality—
and results in the consubstantiality of those living in spatial proximity. As a
result, they come to be treated as consanguines rather than affines. Whites,
aside from no longer being able to be killed and eaten, are also coinhabitants
with whom one should live in peace. So are they not brothers-in-law or enemies whom one can no longer engage in war, with whom one is forced to
live in peace? I return to this question in the conclusion.

PART III

WE WANT PEOPLE
FOR OURSELVES:
PACIFICATION

CHAPTER 8

The Motives of the Whites

THE FIRST PHASE OF THE INDIAN PROTECTION SERVICE (SPI) IN THE REGION

The conflict between Indians and whites in the Guajará-Mirim region worsened from the 1940s onward with the arrival of a new wave of rubber tappers. In 1945 the government of Getúlio Vargas established the Iata agricultural colony close to the mouth of the Laje River. In the 1950s, the region of the Laje and Ribeirão rivers was invaded by prospectors interested in the high-quality tinstone discovered in the Pacaás Novos mountain range.

An SPI microfilm document[1] records the founding of the Doutor Tanajura attraction post in the 1930s on the Pacaás Novos River at the mouth of the Ouro Preto. In 1939 Marshall Rondon ordered the transference of the post to the Guaporé River, the location of the present-day Ricardo Franco post. The motives given for the transfer were "diseases, scarcity of food and fish, and the ferocity of the Pacaás Novos." In 1956 "transport problems" saw the post return to a site close to the initial location on the left bank of the Pacaás Novos, where it is still found today.

In 1940 Francisco Meireles founded the Major Amarante post, close to the mouth of the Ribeirão River, at the 294-kilometer point of the Madeira–Mamoré railroad. Now called the Ribeirão post, it is still situated on the same river, though further upstream. The Tenente Lira post was created in 1945 on the shores of the Laje River, the present-day site of the Wari' settlement known as Lage Velho.[2] Two more posts were founded that year to attract the Wari', one of them on the banks of the Jaci-Paraná, the other on the Mutumparaná. Both, though, were soon abandoned.

The first Indians began to approach the Tenente Lira post as early as 1945. Reports from this period are unclear about the names of the groups that approached, simultaneously calling them "Pacaás Novos," "Araras," "Bocas Negras," and "Caripunas." Sometimes the same group is called by different names in the same document. Whatever the case, the Indians involved do not seem to have been the Wari', but isolated groups of Karipuna. After some years without incident, a report issued by this post, dated from 1950, records that Indians were venturing increasingly closer, attracted by the presents, but left only traces. In 1954 the approach of "Pacaás Novos" Indians is mentioned. They took the presents. In 1956 a letter reports that "wild Indians" appeared on a seringal path close to the post; they left a bow and two arrows as they ran away. In January 1960, a report signed by Juvêncio Ferreira Borges, the head of the Tenente Lira post, claimed that "the Indians" came as near as the clearing around the post twice that month "without attacking." However, in May of the same year, Juvêncio said he was attacked without injury by some "Pacaás Novos" Indians close to the post. He took the opportunity to request tools to "catechize them," claiming that these Indians lived in the post's vicinity. Fresh visits to the post were made in July and September 1960, and in October the post was attacked. These records dating from 1950 onward probably relate to the Wari', whose own accounts confirm their approaches in search of tools.[3]

All I was able to learn from the reports about the first approaches to the Major Amarante post was that it was frequented by Makurap and Karipuna Indians in the 1940s. There is no mention of the Wari' apart from a document stating that the post was attacked by these Indians in May 1957.

In all events, these "official" contacts—in which whites and Indians did not actually meet each other—involved members of the OroWaram, Oro-WaramXijein, and OroMon subgroups who lived in this region, the area most heavily invaded by the whites. No records exist of peaceful approaches by Indians to the Doutor Tanajura post in the 1930s, before its transference to the Guaporé River in 1939. This suggests that the SPI had no contact with either the OroNao'—located on both shores of the Pacaás Novos River—or the OroEo and OroAt, who lived in a more remote area, until the 1950s.

As we saw in chapter 3, the Wari' claim that Francisco Meireles, an SPI officer who held various senior positions in the organization, was responsible for a number of pacification attempts, some of them involving the capture of women. Some of these attempts occurred between 1930 and 1940. The SPI documents do not allow us to identify these events and, if they happened, it is more likely that the agents had no idea that the "Pacaás Novos" were involved since all official records of attempts to contact these Indians postdate

1940. As for Francisco Meireles, I doubt he participated in the first expeditions attributed to him, much less in those involving captures. I presume that the Wari' deduced some time after pacification that these contact attempts were undertaken by him, since although he took no part in these contact teams, he often visited newly contacted Indians, making explicit that he was one of the SPI heads.

THE ARRIVAL OF THE NEW TRIBES MISSION (NTM)

The New Tribes Mission, founded in 1942 in the United States, defines itself as "a non-denominational agency that sends missionaries from the fundamentalist tradition to spread the gospel and establish churches among uncontacted tribal peoples. It works in linguistics, literacy teaching and Bible translation" (*Mission Handbook*, cited in R. Fernandes 1980, 134). The mission's activities are sustained by donations from believers, prompted by the reports and letters from missionaries in the field, which tell of their work, diagnose the stage in which the Indians find themselves in the process of conversion, and also ask for prayers and financial help to enable their missionary work.

The first expedition made by its missionaries was to Bolivia the year the NTM was founded. Guajará-Mirim, a Brazilian town on the border with Bolivia, was therefore probably one of the entry points for this mission in Brazil (fig. 16). Between 1946 and 1948, the first missionary in Brazil, Virgílio Sharp, built a house in Guajará-Mirim that served as the mission's local office. The institution acquired official status in Brazil in 1953 when it was registered as the Missão Novas Tribos do Brasil (Gallois and Grupioni 1999, 85).

The first group of missionaries arrived in Guajará-Mirim in 1950 and according to Royal Taylor—a member of this group who worked in the pacification of the Wari'—he and the son of Joe Moreno explored the Guaporé River the same year in search of "a tribe." Others arriving with him traveled to the region known as Boca do Acre, "where there had been rumors of Indians." In Taylor's words, "All of us came to make contact with tribes and help them to know Christ" (Taylor, interviewed by myself in January 1994). On this trip, Royal met the Moré Indians, a Txapakura group living in the Guaporé River basin in Bolivia, close to the border with Brazil. At this time, the Moré were already living under the protection of the Bolivian government and had probably been "contacted" too much to interest the missionaries. Whatever the case, the latter returned to the Moré later, around 1957, for a

16. The town of Guajará-Mirim, 2005.

brief linguistic study that would help them in the contacts with the Wari', by then already under way.

The subsequent expeditions of the NTM missionaries in Guajará-Mirim explored an area to the town's northeast, in the region of the Ribeirão, Mutumparaná, and Jaci-Paraná rivers, accompanying SPI officers. Their aim was to contact the Indians attacking the seringais (rubber extraction sites) found there. A letter signed by Francisco Meireles, then the head of the Ninth Regional Inspectorate (RI) of the SPI, dated October 1, 1951, states, "Given the complaints of Indian attacks on the seringais on the river Mutumparaná, two missionaries offering to help in the contact were sent there" (Indian Museum, microfilm 43, sheet 487). On December 10, 1951, Francisco Meireles sent a letter to Royal Taylor, giving him permission to take part in the expedition. The group set out from the headwaters of the Ribeirão in January 1952, traveling the Mutumparaná and Formoso rivers until reaching the Jaci-Paraná River. According to Royal, the Indians they were trying to contact were the Wari', but no contact was made.

While the SPI imposed some restrictions on the work of the missionaries, it also clearly relied on these enthusiastic volunteers for sensitive and dangerous tasks. Moreover, the SPI considered the conversion of the Indians

to Christianity an important step toward achieving its own goal: the transformation of the Indians into "citizens." A letter dated April 6, 1951, written
by the then head of the Ninth RI, Fernando Claro de Campos, to the SPI's
director, is an ode to the missionaries. According to de Campos, the NTM
"carries out extremely important social and religious work in our country
and neighboring regions." He adds that "spiritual assistance" to the Indians
(referring here to the recently contacted "Araras") is just as important as material assistance, and that the former could not be provided by the SPI. A
report by Francisco Meireles on the process of contacting the Wari', dated
August 17, 1962, when many of them were already living peacefully with the
whites, also clearly expresses this admiration for the work of the Protestant
missionaries. Speaking of the Tenente Lira post, he comments, "Were it not
for the humanitarian and highly effective collaboration of the Adventist [sic]
missionaries of Guajará-Mirim, whose entire work is devoted to helping the
savages, we sincerely believe [that] they would have already returned to
the forest. . . . The crops are planted by the Indians solely at the initiative of
the missionaries."

There were conflicts, however. After the pacification process was initiated
and missionaries began to live at the posts (occupying each of them in 1962),
there were frequent incompatibilities between themselves and the heads of
post, sometimes resulting in expulsion of the former. In his request to remove the missionaries in July 1967, one of these heads claimed they were
"compromising the post's work." In December 1961, soon after establishing
peaceful contact in the region of the Negro and Ocaia rivers, by then the only
area not contacted, the SPI directorate decided to suspend all missionary activities at the posts. Indeed this decision had probably already been taken in
1959, since in a letter sent to the head of the Ninth RI on November 24, 1959,
a member of the Ministry of Justice's Territorial Affairs Commission asked,
"Why were the American missionaries prohibited by the SPI when they have
been providing valuable assistance to the Indians [referring to the OroNao'
of the Whites, the only subgroup contacted at the time]?" He claimed to
have been informed that "children who die were eaten," and asked for a mission to be established in the area by the prelacy (Catholic Church) and for
the "New Tribes" to be allowed to continue its work (Indian Museum, microfilm 43, sheet 491).

Despite their expulsion, the missionaries were clearly needed to help the
Indians (materially). In January 1962, a missionary was asked to treat sick

people at the Tenente Lira post. In March the same year, at the Rio Negro–Ocaia post, one of the furthest from the town, there was just one boat, belonging to the missionaries, which transported sick people and SPI employees. The missionaries, for their part, provided frequent reports on their activities to the head of the RI and were always ready to assist the SPI, aiming to maintain good working relations.

Intermittently, the foreign nationality of most of the missionaries was raised as an issue, with any problems commonly being attributed to this fact. In August 1962, the head of a post wrote a letter complaining that the missionaries were failing to inform him about their activities, stating in closing that he would not be "subordinated to foreigners." Suspicion was also sometimes cast on the interests prompting these "Americans" (as they were usually called) to live in Brazil, more specifically in border areas rich in natural resources like this part of Amazonia.[4]

THE WORK OF THE CATHOLIC CHURCH

The first person connected to the prelacy of Guajará-Mirim who volunteered to encounter the "feared" Wari' was Father Mauro at the end of 1950, whose misadventure was related in chapter 3. His objective differed little from that of the NTM missionaries, since he left "to save the pagan Indians, bringing them into the Lord's flock" (*O Cruzeiro* [illegible date]). But while he shared their intentions, he lacked the missionaries' training and acted as a martyr.

Dom Roberto Gomes de Arruda—the bishop and later the emeritus bishop of Guajará-Mirim until his death in 2003—claimed that, much earlier than the 1950s, Dom Rey, who became bishop in 1932, had insisted (possibly with the SPI and local authorities) on the urgent need to pacify the Wari':

Ah, he insisted much, much earlier [than 1950] as the town was constantly surrounded by Indians. . . . The railroad construction, for example, faced numerous problems because of the presence of the Indians, who sometimes tried to defend themselves or their region and destroyed part of the work. For this reason—I never read this anywhere, but various people told me that it is documented—they had to electrify some areas of track, electrocuting Indians so they didn't destroy the work completed during the day. . . . And in the final years especially, almost daily, at least two or three times a week, people arrived at the hospital with arrow wounds. . . . There was always people there ready to pull arrows from victims' bodies or treat the arrow wounds. (Dom Roberto 1993)

I cannot say to what extent the prelacy tried to participate in the first contacts with the Wari'. Whatever the case, after the episode involving Father Mauro, the Catholics only acted again in 1961 in the pacification of the region of the Negro and Ocaia rivers, when missionaries from the NTM, allied with the SPI, had already established peaceful contact with the OroNao' of the Whites (1956). By then, they were living close to the Doutor Tanajura post, having launched contact expeditions along the Laje and Negro rivers.

While clashes between the NTM and the prelacy were frequent,[5] there were also divergences within the SPI concerning missionary activity in general. The SPI's directorate acted more cautiously and imposed greater restrictions on the presence of NTM missionaries, although, in the specific case of the Wari', the head of the Ninth RI openly supported the mission for some time and remained unsympathetic to the Catholics, refusing the prelacy's offer of help for the Indians. In a letter sent to Father Roberto Gomes de Arruda (later bishop) on May 9, 1962, he gives thanks for the offer, adding that he would "prefer not to accept the interference of lay or religious folk, whether Brazilian or foreign." At the time in question, the NTM missionaries were living and working at the SPI posts.

The inconsistencies within the SPI not only related to the missionary presence but also to the purpose of their work. In August 1963, the director of the SPI, Lieutenant Colonel Moacir Ribeiro Coelho, authorized Father Roberto Gomes de Arruda to "work with the Indians of the Ribeirão, on the condition of respecting their moral principles and customs." In December 1967, in a report requested by the SPI director on the situation of the villages, the then head of the Ninth RI wrote, "The religious teachings are in Christianity, administered by Catholic priests and Protestant missionaries. These religious practices have spontaneously helped to dissuade them from their macabre rituals."

In 1963, when most of the Wari' had ceased warring with the whites and depended in some form on them (for medical treatment, food, and manufactured goods), the prelacy tried to gain a firmer foothold among the Indians.

It had already taken an active part in the pacification of the region of the Negro and Ocaia rivers in 1961, and now, after some months of treating sick people from the Ribeirão River with the direct permission of the minister of agriculture, it attempted to establish a kind of mission in the same area. In contrast to the NTM missionaries, who worked as collaborators and indeed subordinates to the SPI, the prelacy wished to act with complete autonomy. This stance obviously led to the SPI's rejection of the prelacy's request for an area of 400 hectares on the Ribeirão to build a "hospital, school, headquarters, craft workshop, and church."

Following a definitive refusal in 1965, the prelacy accepted the offer from a civil organization in Guajará-Mirim—the Sociedade São Judas Tadeu, made up of Franciscans from the Third Order Regular (a community to which various priests from the prelacy belonged)—of a plot of 32,000 hectares situated on the shores of the Guaporé River, slightly above the confluence with the Mamoré, near the small town of Surpresa, in order to establish an agricultural school for students from the region (fig. 17). However, they set as a condition that the project for implanting the school be deferred and the area used primarily to receive sick Wari' who went to the city for help.

The first group, composed of twenty OroWaramXijein and OroMon Indians, disembarked in Sagarana on November 17, 1965, accompanied by Fathers Bendoraites and Roberto Gomes de Arruda (fig. 18). There were no houses or any other kind of facility, and work began as soon as a suitable site was chosen for the buildings. Only Father Roberto remained with them for a time, later joined by Father Michel, a carpenter who helped in the work. However, the administration was soon taken over by a young Bolivian, appointed by Father Bendoraites, who used violent methods to "civilize" the Wari'. It is important to note that this area was not part of the territory known and used by the Wari', and that they perceived this relocation as a punishment for having killed whites, and as a strategy employed by whites to avoid new attacks, since the Wari' lack of knowledge of the surrounding area meant they had nowhere to escape.[6]

The activities at Sagarana, like all the other works of the Guajará-Mirim prelacy (today a diocese), are sustained by donations from church members, many of them subscribers to the magazine Lettres d'Amazonie, published in Paris and dedicated exclusively to news on the diocese's activities. According to Dom Roberto (personal communication, 1993), a French NGO called Cooperation, supported by the Catholic Church, assumed responsibility for sending a workforce at the request of the diocese.

17. The Guaporé River, seen from Sagarana, 2005.

18. A view of Sagarana, 2005.

PUBLIC OPINION

The conflicts between Indians and whites worsened in the 1940s and became much more intense in the following decade. Seringais and cultivated plots were abandoned out of fear of the mounting number of Indian attacks and the effects of this tension adversely affected the region's economy.

Faced with heavy losses, the rubber bosses and other powerful locals acted in two ways. First, they pressed the government to invest in pacifying the Indians. According to the SPI's reports, in April 1951 the federation of rubber bosses "supported" the creation of an SPI attraction post on the upper Jamari River where various seringais were located. In September 1957, the governor of Rondônia intervened directly, requesting measures from the SPI to pacify the Wari' (the pacification work had already started), on the grounds that the constant Indian incursions were "disrupting the work of rubber tappers on the Pacaás Novos and Ouro Preto rivers." In March 1959, the Guajará-Mirim Trade Association requested action from the SPI following the death of a rubber tapper who had been attacked by Indians on the upper Laje River. In July 1961, the Banco de Crédito do Amazonas gave money toward the pacification of the Wari'.

Second—and simultaneously—the rubber bosses, who were also the owners of local trade, took their own initiatives, organizing the so-called punitive expeditions to intimidate and exterminate the Wari'. As Dom Roberto explained to me:

> "They then organized armed groups for what they called 'clearing the area.' This clearance involved destroying all of the villages, killing everyone they met."
>
> "Did the government know or was the action organized by private groups?" I asked.
>
> "By private groups. But who didn't know? If the entire population knew, how could the government not know? It was generally approved. Nobody could find a solution to the problem, right? Terrible massacres. The whites arrived, armed groups, at dawn. They then machine-gunned the village." (Dom Roberto 1993)

The massacres were indeed public knowledge and appeared in the newspapers:

> A wide variety of stories were created about the Indians in question, always depicted as the scourge of the Rondônia wilds. But everything

suggests that these stories were designed to justify attacks periodically made on their malocas by rubber tappers from Guajará-Mirim, who slaughtered women and children. The rubber tappers used machine guns acquired in Bolivia and hired professional Indian hunters. The incursions against the Pacaás Novos numbered in their dozens and aimed to capture lands rich in Brazil nut and rubber trees. (*Alto Madeira*, January 6, 1962)

The NTM missionaries also knew of the expeditions organized against the Wari'. According to the missionary Royal Taylor, around 1956 the SPI inspector in Guajará-Mirim was "pressured" to pacify the Indians, and "others were already invading the malocas on their own account." This was when the missionaries offered to attempt peaceful contact on the left shore of the Pacaás Novos: "The inspector was a very amicable man. He had the support of the government and we offered him the staff. Three or four men went from the SPI, while the mission sent Joe Moreno, Abraham Koop, and Richard Sollis" (Royal Taylor 1994).

According to Dom Roberto, they already knew of the attacks planned on the Indian malocas. One time, therefore, the bishop Dom Xavier Rey was able to intercede with the organizers, asking them to allow time for the prelacy to attempt peaceful contact with the Indians attacking the Pacaás Novos region:

> "This was when on December 8, 1960 the Indians captured—and this you know—a boy who was traveling from Guajará to Iata [close to Lage]. . . . The Indians surrounded him at the base of the mountains—he was going by bicycle—and killed him there. Only the trunk was found. The Indians had cut off his legs and taken them. The body was riddled with arrows. There's a photo and everything. This ended up stoking the hatred in Guajará. An expedition to exterminate the remaining Indians was immediately organized. That was the decision in Guajará: to finish off every last Indian, leaving no one. And the bishop, knowing about this plan, pleaded with the organizers of this punitive expedition."

> "Who were the organizers?" I asked.

> "The rubber bosses, and all the men from Guajará."

> "Including Manuel Lucindo?" I asked.

> "Manuel Lucindo and the other one, the Greek, Manussakis. Manussakis was in control of the Ouro Preto area. He had an interest in this. From what Dom Rey told me—I didn't see this—Manussakis alone had forty armed men in the forest, just to locate the Indian settlements and not

leave a single survivor. They didn't leave one child. They had to liquidate everyone."

"This was in the 1960s?" I asked.

"Until 1960, or 1961, the start of 1961. So, faced with the organization of this punitive expedition, the bishop intervened and asked the expedition leaders to stay put while he contacted the governor, who at the time was Alvarenga Mafra, to see if something could be done." (Dom Roberto 1993)

As we shall see, the outcome of this episode was the governor's dispatch—without the SPI's knowledge—of the SPI officer Fernando Cruz to help the prelacy in an expedition to the region of the Negro and Ocaia rivers. But before this group had left, the SPI and the NTM missionaries had already achieved peaceful contact with the Wari' on the left bank of the Pacaás Novos River and those from the area of the Laje River.

Having shown the climate reigning in Guajará-Mirim, which drove the whites to the massacres and the attempts to pacify the Indians, I now wish to turn to the episodes of contact themselves, when the Wari' decided to approach the whites peacefully. I shall start at the beginning—if one exists—sticking to the chronology of the attempts to contact the Wari', since much of what happened in each new encounter is explained by what happened earlier.

CHAPTER 9

The Widening River

Contact with the OroNao'

of the Whites

Jamain Xok Tain, a man from the OroNao' of the Whites subgroup, told me that before the spi contact team began work on the Doutor Tanajura post in 1955, the site was the center of a seringal belonging to Manussakis. The Wari' left their swiddens on the Dois Irmaos River and headed to Tanajura to make war and obtain tools.

> The elders summoned us to leave on a war expedition. At this time they were still angry with the whites. We left Towi [name of swidden] and traveled to Tanajura. The Wari' wanted metal tools. . . . It was very far. We slept three nights. Very far! "Let's fetch tools!" One of the elders prepared the bundle of babassu leafstalks [ritual fire for war], which one man would carry under his arm. . . . We reached Tamajain and caught fish. The women stayed there before turning back. . . . We ate fish and roasted a spider monkey. It was roasting when we heard shots fired by whites on the big river [Pacaás Novos] at Tanajura. We thought, "They're still there! Let's go!" We weren't afraid. We arrived at Pitop. There was no path. They hadn't yet cleared a path [between Tanajura and Pitop]; they hadn't suspended the tools yet. . . . We heard the sound [of a boat] arriving from upriver. . . . It came from the seringal on the headwaters of the We Turu [Da Gruta] River. This is the one we shot at. The Wari' stayed on the creek, those who shot, because I didn't shoot. . . . Just one died. . . . The whites fired their guns. The elders shouted with joy. They ran. They arrived at Pitop; they

drank the water from the creek. "We shot him!" Just one died. (Jamain Xok Tain 1994)

Expeditions like this occurred whenever the Wari' wanted tools, which seems to have been often. One day, arriving at the upper sources of Pitop Creek, they found tools suspended in the trees, tied with lianas: "The tools were suspended at Pitop. They hung up many on the Pitop headwaters. The tools were suspended for the first time at Pitop. . . . So we arrived at Pitop and there were the tools hanging from trees [mimics the Wari' eagerly cutting the lianas and taking the tools]" (Jamain Xok Tain 1994).

The whites had cleared a wide path from Pitop to Tanajura, but at first they only left the tools at Pitop. Royal Taylor states that Tanajura was a former seringal, abandoned after Indian attacks. The missionaries had helped construct the post from the start along with various SPI employees (Josias Batista, Antônio Barros, and perhaps Ostílio, according to Royal), including Saul Monteiro, an Indian from another ethnic group.[1]

> The first step was to clear the forest to a distance out of arrow range. Abraham [Koop] made a house for Barbara [a missionary who lived at Tanajura for many years] in 1955. He and the Bolivians built it. There was a outpost formerly belonging to the seringal, which the team must have used at the start of contact. There was a lockable room and an open area. . . . First they cleared a path to the forest. They saw traces of Indians and started to leave presents. This was in 1956. After a few days they returned to where the presents had been left. The first time the lianas had been cut. The Indians had taken nothing and left crossed arrows as if to say: don't pass this point. The third or fourth time, the Indians took the presents and as a joke left stale maize cake and pot shards hanging from the lianas. This was when they [the whites] relaxed and began leaving presents closer to the post.[2] (Royal Taylor 1994)

Curiously, all the Wari' present at the time insist that they always took the tools. "The Wari' didn't leave the tools. The Wari' were really excited with the tools. They never left them. The Wari' like tools. Even the small ones. They took them all, all of them. . . . People discovered: 'The whites suspend tools.' The Wari' said, 'We want them too!' Because of the tools nobody was ever still [meaning they traveled continually to Pitop]. 'Let's go!'" (Jamain Xok Tain 1994).

They also found the idea strange that they would have left stale maize cake and other things in place of the tools. However, an episode recounted by Oroiram led me to believe that the missionaries had misinterpreted what they had seen. Oroiram said that one time when the missionaries were coming up the Dois Irmãos River in a motor boat, his father saw them from afar and yelled, "The whites are coming!" The Wari' dropped everything they were carrying, including maize cake, and ran. "When they returned to find the things they'd dropped, they saw that the whites had left tools next to the maize cake." Equivocations like this are frequent on both sides when we compare the whites' accounts with those of the Wari'.[3]

The presents were placed ever closer to the Tanajura post. "The tools were no longer at Pitop. They were on another creek. They stopped leaving them at Pitop. They put them downriver, closer to their house. . . . The whites had a clear view of the Wari' arriving. The Wari' approached very slowly to take the tools since they were in the whites' field of vision. They took them and ran away. Some were afraid and stayed behind without taking any tools. Others went. 'Let's approach really slowly!' " (Jamain Xok Tain 1994).

One day, the Wari' arrived at Tanajura and found no tools on the path. When they arrived at the whites' house, they found it empty and sent Tem We, then a boy, and his brother to go inside and take the tools.

> "The white man has left," we said to ourselves. We approached their house and entered. As it was raining heavily, the white man didn't hear us. He was inside his mosquito net. "Hey, hey!" [shouts of the white man]. . . . When I passed him, he stabbed me [with a knife]. . . . Our fathers had remained outside: "If he emerges, we'll shoot him. The white man got our son!" But he didn't come out; he stayed inside. (Tem We 1994)

Tem We left the house and managed to reach the forest where the others were. Bleeding heavily, he was carried to his village, but first they spent a while at Pitop waiting for the other men to return. They had stayed close to the house to shoot the white man if he emerged. According to Royal, Tem We had actually been stabbed by Saul, an Indian from another ethnic group, who, alone in the house, had been startled by the Indians entering and reacted. The missionaries were in town buying supplies. After this episode, Saul refused to stay at the post any longer. Learning of the event, the missionaries imagined that the Indians had become hostile again, so they decided to travel to them for the first time, traveling up the Dois Irmãos River by boat (they had journeyed upriver before to clear the route, since the river was densely overgrown).

At that moment the Wari' were planning a revenge raid to kill the whites who had injured Tem We. While they headed toward Tanajura, the missionaries were journeying up the Dois Irmãos River to meet them.

> So Parap [Tem We's father] said, "I'll shoot whites for my son! I'll avenge him!" "Let's go," everyone said. There were many Wari'. They slept in the forest and drank maize drink. "Let's go!" Women went too. They stopped at Tom Tan. "Let's go, let's make war!" But they [the whites] had already arrived. They [the Wari'] arrived at Komi Tatam and heard the noise of the motor. The whites beached the boat at the Tokon Me port. From there they took the path and walked. . . . They [the Wari'] crossed the river and watched in hiding. The one who generated Jimain Jiparaí arrived [Parap], he approached and fell in the river. My brothers said, "Let's shoot whites!" They [the whites] were happy. They whistled. Perhaps they were Indians who had already been civilized [wijam wari']. Then they left. They had suspended tools. We took all of them. "Let's go after them! Let's shoot them!" . . . Just as they sat down in the motor boat . . . Parap shot. He struck one man's hat. The arrow knocked off the hat [sound of whites shouting]. They tried to hit his foot but failed. (Jamain Xok Tain 1994)

According to Oroiram, it was Manim who hit the missionary's hat (Abraham's): "There were many whites. All of their arrows missed. The late ones[4] failed to hit [the whites]. The whites started the outboard motor. Manim ran and knocked off the hat [of one of them]. They didn't fall. They simply went away" (Oroiram 1993).

Royal Taylor, who took no part in the encounter, recalled the version of the missionaries who were present:

> The Dois Irmãos River was very overgrown, full of channels. Very swampy and very difficult. The first time they went by canoe fitted with an outboard motor: Abraham, Moreno, Richard Sollis, and the SPI staff. They cleared the way and on the next trip, tied up the canoe, walked, and arrived at an abandoned maloca. They left presents at the maloca. The Indians set an ambush and started to shoot. Everyone ran backward, while Abraham sat down watching, even taking some arrows as craftwork samples. The others yelled for him to start the motor. This was in 1956. They all ducked down with him clutching the motor. Later I asked [the Indians] whether

they had been shooting to miss, because their aim was so bad. [They] said they had been shooting for real. It was God's protection. God only takes when he wants to. (Royal Taylor 1994)

This "magical" protection of the missionaries against the arrows became a kind of legend not only for the missionaries but for the converted Wari' too. I asked Jamain Xok Tain, then a Christian, "Why did the Wari' arrows miss, or more exactly, why did the whites not fall?"

Had the whites not believed in God. . . . They believed: Moreno, Abraham, Richard, the late Saul, Lucindo Preto. . . . They started the motor and left. People shot from other positions. The arrows ran out and the whites hadn't fallen. And they weren't far away, the Dois Irmãos is a small river. They opened the motor full-throttle and disappeared. "The whites escaped! They didn't fall, they didn't fall!" They saw all the arrows in the water: "You're women! They weren't far away." (Jamain Xok Tain 1994)[5]

According to Royal Taylor, the whites only made these two journeys up the Dois Irmãos River, the first time just to clear the way. They were preparing for another trip—including a protective mesh for the canoe, revealing their own suspicions that they had escaped the previous time by pure chance—when the Indians appeared at the Tanajura post. However, the Wari' insist that the whites approached by river other times to leave tools.

How many encounters actually took place remains uncertain. According to Tem We, it was raining during this period and the maize had just finished ripening, suggesting that these events took place between January and February 1956. Whatever the case, the Wari' did not make direct contact with the whites until May of the same year, which is when the SPI documents first mention an approach by them—twenty men—to the post (the episode when Tem We was stabbed is not mentioned). Inspector Francisco Meireles visited Tanajura in July 1956, when the Indians were handed "gifts." His message about the encounter concludes, "The region's most warlike tribe has entered pacification phase."

Royal Taylor, speaking of this first peaceful approach to the post, estimates that it occurred at the end of 1956.

When they first appeared at the post, they ventured as far as the clearing and shouted. They shouted and the men cautiously walked toward the Indians. They reached the middle of the clearing, stuck two poles into the ground, placed objects on them, and walked away, back to the house.

The Indians merely watched. The men emerged from the house with their arms raised, showing they were unarmed, and waited for the Indians, who eventually came to receive the presents from the missionaries. . . . The Indians then began to visit the post regularly. (Royal Taylor 1994)

Before this, Oroiram states, a group had reached the post looking for tools. Close to the house they saw a domestic pig ("a strange white-lipped peccary") and tried to chase it away by firing arrows. When the SPI employee, Josias, looked out to see what was happening, the Wari' fled. Reaching a safe distance, they shouted, "Give us axes!" "What?" asked Josias, who was carrying a small shotgun. The Wari' returned to their village without any tools. Sometime later, they returned to Tanajura again in search of tools and decided to "call the whites" ("we call them," they say), judging that these whites had no wish to kill them.

> "Later we decided to visit them again. 'Give us tools!' 'What?' They took a basket full of tools, two men carrying it either side."
>
> "Did they leave it on the path?" I asked.
>
> "No, they handed them over to us. 'Ha, ha, ha, ha' [laughter of the whites]. They got us. They patted the shoulders of the Wari' affably. 'Ha, ha, ha, ha.' They gave us shorts." (Oroiram 1993)

> We asked, "Give us tools!" The whites didn't hand us them. They hung the tools up and the Wari' went to fetch them. Josias approached carrying an axe tied to a branch to give to Maxun Kworain, who retreated, walking backward, until he stopped and took the axe. Josias embraced him and laughed. The whites had asked the Wari' to leave their bows on the ground. All of them took axes and on returning home told their coinhabitants, "We touched their bodies!" (Manim 1993)

Those returning from a tool-gathering excursion would say, "Don't be afraid, the whites aren't killing anyone!" But the Wari' remained apprehensive and even when they spent the day at Tanajura they returned to the forest to sleep.

> We called them. "We arrived! We came to fetch tools," they said to them [in Wari']. I think it was the *caboclos* [*oro caboco*], Saul, who understood, not the whites. Did you meet Saul? He died. Saul knew. He was the one who called, "Come, come!" . . . I'm not sure, he said something like "Come

19. Wari' entering a house accompanied by a white man.
Probably Ribeirao during the first half of the 1960s.
(Photo by Geraldo Mendonça da Silva)

back tomorrow!" We returned [home]. . . . We didn't trust the whites. . . .
We were really scared of them. It seemed they would kill us. We returned
home. After a long period away, they came. Saul paddling the canoe, with
Josias. "We've arrived, everyone!" they yelled. "Wow!", we said to them.
"Let's go!" and so we went in the canoe with them. (Tem We 1994)[6]

According to Oroiram's account of the first encounter, after bringing a
basket full of tools, the whites offered them strange foods such as salt, sugar,
and coffee. The Wari' spat out everything, even the bananas, "which were too
strong-smelling for us." From then on, they began to visit the post frequently
(figs. 19, 20, 21, and 22).

They visited the post by day and slept at Pitop. So the bartering process
began. This interested the Indians. They went away, spent a couple of
months in the forest and suddenly returned. . . . Women also came [on
their third visit, when Royal was already at the post]. They were already

20. Wari' youths. Probably Ribeirão during the first half of the 1960s.
(Photo by Geraldo Mendonça da Silva)

too used to receiving things. . . . If someone saw the Indians arriving, they would shout, "Here come the Indians!" They ran across the clearing. They would take all the clothing and plates. So, when they caught sight of the Indians, the missionaries ran to collect everything. . . . The Indians themselves resolved to wear clothes on visiting the post; they liked to imitate civilized folk. Later they began to visit the post naked to receive clothing. They didn't take the metal tools so they would receive more. (Royal Taylor 1994)

Despite refusing foods they disliked, the Wari' were from the outset amazed by the quantity of food and the generosity of the whites, who treated them like visiting kin, hunting and fishing for them: "We ate a lot of game: peccary, peccary, peccary; fish, fish. The whites were really good, they killed game and gave it to us" (Jamain Xok Tain 1994).

Some people became jealous over these whites, demanding the same type of fidelity and privileges expected from generous kin: "Many people were jealous and said, 'These are our whites!' Or as the late Wem Parawan said, 'These are my sons' whites!' " (Oroiram 1993).

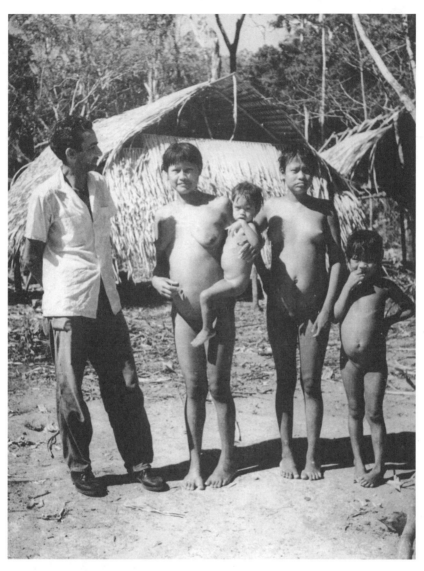

21. The photographer Geraldo Mendonça da Silva with Wari' women and children. Probably Ribeirão during the first half of the 1960s. (Photo by Geraldo Mendonça da Silva)

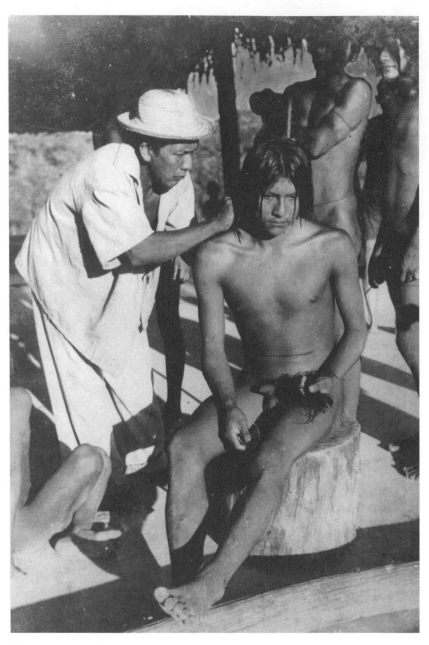

22. Cutting a young man's hair. Probably Ribeirão during the first half of the 1960s. (Photo by Geraldo Mendonça da Silva)

ENEMY POISON

Amid this abundance, when they were still highly excited about these enemies (as they continued to call them) who acted so unusually, the diseases arrived. The Wari' sneezed, coughed, and came down with fever and diarrhea. Alarmed, they returned to their villages and stayed there until they died or recovered. When the whites saw them sick at the post, they tried to give them injections, but they were "afraid of the needle" and fled. Many refused to swallow the medicines, believing they were being poisoned. Interestingly, though, they always sought out the whites again, even after spending long periods away from the post.

> "Everyone was coughing from the disease. 'Come here, we'll give you injections!' The Wari' were afraid. 'Let's go, let's leave the whites here!' We went away. We crossed a stretch of river. My true maternal grandmother, Orowao Memem, died. I was very sick too. The next day, we continued. We stopped at Komikon Towarao. . . . My grandfather's son, Watakao Koxi, died. We continued. We crossed. . . . Ton Pan died, Wem Xao's wife. . . . They buried her."
>
> "Why didn't they eat her?" I asked.
>
> "There weren't people [enough for the funeral]. . . . She died. We dug and dug and buried her. Tokorom Mip arrived with his mother. 'You're dying from the whites' diseases!' he said. 'Yes, we're dying!' 'Get walking!' But we couldn't walk. My brothers couldn't walk. Tokorom Mip carried my older brother. . . . We arrived at Tain Mixem and stopped. People there, our coinhabitants, knew that we were sick and came [to help]. . . . There were the *wari'-wijam* too [referring to the *caboclos* who worked for SPI, who apparently followed them]: Manelzinho, the late Saul, Noel. . . . So they arrived. Parap was angry: 'Let's shoot them!' They [the *wari'-wijam*] were afraid and turned back. They no longer wanted to stay there and left for Tanajura. They were worried about being shot. . . . We stopped carrying our kin, there were so many people. We carried on. We crossed Tamajain. . . . At Xikin my older brother died. And Jimon died at Xat Jama. Two of my older brothers died. We reached Tokon Kopakao. Our house. We slept. After a long time, I recovered, Afonso's mother too [his first wife]. We all recovered. Then the airplane arrived. It didn't land, it just circled overhead. People died. At Tokon Kopakao, Tokon OroMc, Ton Pin. This is why they died. The strange liquid from its motor fell to earth. . . . When the airplane left, people became sick. They all died."

"What was the sickness?" I asked.

"Coughing, a lot of coughing. Orowao Xikwa's mother died there, Maxun Horok's mother, my older brother, Maxun Hon, my older sister, another older sister, another older sister, my older brother Hwerein Hota, my father Urutao, my older brother Hwerein Mo Pin, Orowao Memem. Many Wari'. They all died."

"Did you eat the dead?" I asked.

"I don't know, we didn't follow them. Had we not been sick ourselves . . . I know Orowao Memem was burned, because we saw it."

"Why didn't you eat them?" I asked.

"Had we been well . . . Had there been more people . . . Orowao Memem was completely burned. They didn't eat him. After a long, long time, they [the Wari'] became angry again: 'Let's shoot them!' Because of the white people's disease. But the anger passed. We went to him [the white man] and said, 'You poisoned us!' He said, 'No, it was the other whites, the Bolivians. The Bolivians poisoned you.' 'Really?' 'Really. Come back and stay here with us. Needles are good. Your people didn't listen to me. If I pierce you with a needle, you'll get better. Come quickly!'" (Jamain Xok Tain 1994)

Apparently the Wari' on the left bank of the Pacaás Novos were unfamiliar with these diseases, or at least failed to attribute them to contacts with these enemies, unlike the groups on the other bank, who prior to pacification had already linked some diseases to the whites. Moreover, these OroNao' were isolated from the other Wari', protecting them from the pathogenic agents transmitted by people from other subgroups. This contrasted with the Oro-Nao' on the right shore, who sickened after encountering the OroWaram, a group more exposed to white diseases.

"We stayed and stayed and then decided to go. 'Let's go!' We didn't take his things; we took flour only. The late Saul gave it to us. . . . We arrived home and stayed. We left him and soon began to die."

"Did you know about white diseases?" I asked.

"No, we didn't think there was any sickness. . . . 'The whites poisoned us! The whites poisoned us!' 'Let's go!' They died on the way. . . . The fire ate all of them. Xatoji's mother died [his first wife], one died, then another. . . . 'Let's go, let's go again!' [to Tanajura]. This was when an airplane arrived, circling us. When it went, the deaths started. The liquid fell from it. Everyone died. I was the one who cut up the corpses."

"Could the corpses be eaten?" I asked.

[Laughing] "We sucked out the brains. We burned [the rest]."

"Did fear of the white disease stop you from eating them?" I asked.

"Had we been less thin . . . There was no meat on us, we were pure bone . . . Everyone died, almost nobody was left. Then the whites arrived: 'You're all going to die!' And they injected us. . . . He said to us, 'Let's go!" And they lead us away. The whites took us to Tanajura. They gave us medicines. Some others died, then it stopped." (Oroiram 1993)

Royal Taylor gave his version of the episode:

They caught diseases and took them to the forest. We had to make mercy trips to the forest to help them. It was malaria and pneumonia. We took injections to the upper Dois Irmãos River. . . . From 1957 to 1959, we treated them at the post; they spent a few days there and returned. We would go after them in the forest. Until their third or fourth contact, they always withdrew at night to sleep in the forest. Later they began to sleep in the mosquito net of Josias Batista, the head of the post. They were already shivering from malaria when they left. We did everything we could to stop them returning to the forest. We began to make boat trips upriver to treat them. . . . Josias went to town one time and returned to the post with chicken-pox unawares. The Indians slept with him in the same mosquito net. Later they left for a couple of months. On returning, they said that an airplane had flown over the village and many people had gotten stiff necks and died. In 1958 we had an outbreak of measles at the post, when eighty to one hundred Indians stayed at the post for treatment. It was at this time that the first family, that of Parap, Tem We's father, settled at the post. During the measles epidemic, we did twenty-four-hour shifts. We worked day and night, and there was just one death. Dr. Duarte, a military doctor, helped us out. . . . Two or four months after Parap, other families started to arrive, perhaps to be nearer the treatment. This was when malaria was introduced. After contact with colds, they caught pneumonia with every change in the weather. (Royal Taylor 1994)

According to Conklin (1989, 101–3; 2001, 50), the postcontact epidemics here spread more slowly and less acutely in comparison with the other Wari' subgroups. The diseases did not strike everyone at the same time, but gradually, meaning that the OroNao' could try different responses. Conklin argues that this was a consequence of the gradual way in which the Wari' approached the whites, visiting the post and then staying away for months, a pattern maintained for around two years. The group's survival rate was also higher because when the postcontact epidemics occurred (influenza, measles, whooping cough, malaria, mumps), they received a reasonable level of medical care, as during the measles outbreak. Nonetheless, even for these OroNao', the epidemics had a devastating effect, causing an unusually high number of consecutive deaths among them.

SOME DATES

Before examining the contact with the OroNao' of the Whites in more depth, we can quickly list the dates (table 3) recorded in the SPI documents from 1956 through 1960.

Table 3. Timeline: 1956–1960

YEAR	MONTH	
1956	May	Twenty Wari' men arrive at the Tanajura post.
	July	Francisco Meireles visits the post and the Indians are handed presents.
	August	Eighteen Indians visit Tanajura post.
	October	Four visits by the Wari'. They take the presents, leaving decorated arrows and a hat painted with annatto.
	November	Francisco Meireles visits the post.
1957	January	Indians stay at the post for a few days. Flu epidemic quickly treated. Those well enough return to the village, a walk of twelve days from the post.
	May	Josias goes to the maloca. Counts three malocas with twenty-five men, twenty-three women, and fifty-six children.
	July	Indians arrive asking for presents.
	October	Post occupied by an army corporal and five soldiers to prevent journalists from infiltrating the area in search of Lieutenant Furtado (reported as captured by the Indians).
	December	Frequent Wari' visits. People from Guajará-Mirim arrive to meet the "famous Indians" and bring presents. Total Indians assisted: 104; 11 die from mumps.

Table 3 (*continued*)

YEAR	MONTH	
1958	February	Flu epidemic.
	March	Sick, the Indians return to their villages. The head of the post accompanies them with medicines. Indians given a lot of shirts, trousers, shorts, and belts.
	April	Indians still visiting, now with women and children. Already living closer to the post, about one day's journey away.
	May	Josias spends a fortnight at the maloca.
	June	Flu and malaria. No Indians living at the Doutor Tanajura post, but they visit the post and allow visits to their village.
	July	Seventy-nine Indians visit.
1959		In 1959, some Indian huts built next to the Tanajura post. The Indians decide not to make a swidden after seeing the large swidden at the post.
	February to April	Malaria, flu, and diarrhea. Six die, despite medicines. Visit by recently pacified Indians.
1960	January	Sixty-seven recently pacified Indians visit; fifty-seven return and ten stay at the post. All of them catch flu.

WE WANT PEOPLE FOR OURSELVES

The Wari' spent many decades refusing any peaceful contact with the whites. At a time when groups from the Laje region were still hostile, taking presents and returning to the forest, the OroNao' on the left bank of the Pacaás Novos decided to visit the house of the whites—who "seemed to like" them and "call them" (terms used by the Wari')—to ask for more metal tools. Despite the illnesses, attributed to poisoning by the whites, they remained on peaceful terms with the latter, returning to the post when cured to stay with these enemies. "Sometimes we asked the Indians, 'Why don't you kill us all?'" Royal Taylor told me. "They must have blamed us for their many deaths.

Perhaps it was the conveniences of civilization, knives and so on, or the fact that contact would be with us or the other whites who would kill them. We didn't know how to ask this" (Royal Taylor 1994).

My own questions are slightly different: Why did they decide to approach at that moment? Why were the OroNao' from the left bank the first to approach, and not the Wari' from other subgroups?

Conflict between Indians and whites worsened considerably in the 1950s and local society pressured the SPI to increase its efforts to pacify the Indians haunting the region. This was when the NTM missionaries arrived in Guajará-Mirim, eager to meet uncontacted Indians, and proposed to help the SPI make contact with the Wari'. The site chosen to begin this joint work was the Doutor Tanajura post. Although I cannot be certain, presumably the rubber bosses on the Pacaás Novos and Ouro Preto rivers, at whose confluence the post was established, had sufficient influence to persuade the SPI to begin work there.[7] The missionaries gave this team an unusual profile: an eager disposition with almost no concern for their own safety. The way in which they planned the different stages of approach was decisive, likewise their actions at moments of crisis, when, for example, they decided to journey up the Dois Irmãos River after the stabbing of Tem We, in search of the Indians who, they knew, would now be wary of their intentions. Trained in linguistics, they quickly learned a basic Wari' vocabulary, traveling to the Moré, in Bolivia, for this purpose.

For the OroNao' of the Whites, many factors were in play. Although their area had suffered fewer incursions than the other groups—whose lands were heavily occupied[8] and who even so remained uncontacted—they may still have been under heavy attack from the whites, provoking a desire to end the war. Additionally, the SPI employees, who acted without the help of the missionaries at the Lage and Ribeirão posts, may have had less success in convincing the Indians of their friendly intentions. Perhaps they hung too few tools in the trees, or lacked sufficient courage and concern for self to move closer to their villages and leave more presents. However, we know of contact attempts in other areas, and the Indians of the Ribeirão tell of trips made to the whites' house to take the tools left hanging there. This suggests that the OroNao' of the Whites did indeed act differently from the others, who, under heavier pursuit, possessed even more objective reasons for seeking peaceful contact with the whites. Hence some aspect of the life of these OroNao' during the period before pacification must serve to explain why their situation differed from that of the other Wari', causing them to "call" the whites.

The clearest difference is the isolation experienced by this Wari' subgroup compared to the others, a situation that had already lasted three decades. As we saw, until almost the end of the nineteenth century, the OroNao' of the Whites had lived on the affluents of the right shore of the Pacaás Novos River, along with the other OroNao' constituting a single subgroup. Apparently, the left bank was sporadically frequented during hunting expeditions. Shortly before the turn of the century, a group composed of OroNao' families (and a few OroEo and OroAt) decided to clear swiddens on the Dois Irmãos River, an affluent of the left shore of the Pacaás Novos. Various people say that the definitive crossing occurred because these families could no longer stand the bat bites, which even caused deaths. Another man claimed, though, that they actually fled from the attacks by whites. Those who crossed continued to communicate with those on the right shore until sometime between 1920 and 1930, when crossing the river became impossible due to the intense traffic.[9] They became isolated from the rest until 1961, when some of the group joined the teams establishing peaceful contact with the groups on the Laje and those who were living in the region of the Negro and Ocaia rivers.

According to the latter people, the difficulty in communicating between the different shores was caused by an episode highly reminiscent of the Nanananana myth. In the past, they say, the Pacaás Novos River was not as wide as it is today, but was a small creek, allowing the women to fish there using weirs. One day, the women were fishing and saw someone cross the river. It was the "spirit of the water" (*jami kom*). That night there was a downpour and by morning the river was so wide it could no longer be crossed with ease. They began to do so only in the dry season, using a bridge made from tree trunks. But the most important outcome of the widening of the Pacaás Novos was that it now allowed the whites to penetrate into Wari' territory, since their motor boats had been unable to navigate on the previously narrow river.

The OroNao' of the Whites have another explanation for the widening of the river. They also associate the event with the whites' incursion, but here the cause/effect relation appears inverted. For them, the whites were directly responsible for the widening of the river as they gradually "ate" the shores with their metal tools and outboard motors. But as the other OroNao' claim, it was the increasing use of the river by the whites—a fact related to the unusual increase in the quantity of water—that provoked the isolation of the OroNao' on the left bank for almost thirty years.

Separated, the group missed their kin from the other side. Some informants state that the latter ventured as far as the shores of the Pacaás Novos River but lacked the courage to traverse it. Those who did so discovered on arriving on the left bank that the lost group had moved inland and could no longer be found: part of the group lived on the Dois Irmãos River and its affluents, while the other part had headed toward the Novo River. Presumably, though, the loss must have been considerably higher for the group that became isolated, especially since they found themselves without foreigners who could function as a support for their experience of difference. They would have been forced, therefore, to discover alterity among their own, among coinhabitants, normally considered consanguinal kin. I had asked them whether, when they were isolated, they had ceased holding intergroup festivals. "No," they replied: different villages invited each other, even for *huroroin'*, the most complex festival, which most clearly marks the position of foreigners. Whatever the solution, its sociological cost was certainly high.

Even so, my claim that the OroNao' experienced their isolation as a lack of foreigners would be more difficult had they not resorted to a kind of replica of the Nanananana myth to explain the broken contact with the other subgroups.[10] As we have seen, the myth deals precisely with the isolation of a group of people, likewise the result of an excess of rain after the passage of the "spirit of the rain" (becoming a "spirit of the water" in the myth of the widening river). This isolated group leaves in search of people and meets an enemy people with whom they immediately forge an alliance, enabling the reconstitution of a society composed of different subgroups. The isolated OroNao' reenacted this myth at the moment of contact in two forms. The first was "appearing to the whites," "calling them," after making sure that their intentions were friendly and that they themselves wanted people, namely the Wari'. The interesting factor—lending further strength to the argument—is that despite perceiving these friendly intentions in the past, as we saw in chapter 3, the Wari' decided to remain at war. But they were not isolated then. The generous whites came to be seen as potential foreigners, since this was how the latter category was realizable at that moment. The Wari' did not offer them daughters in marriage, as Nanananana did, but demanded presents, just as they do with foreigners at the end of festivals. The whites, for their part, acted appropriately by being generous, offering a lot of food, and meeting the requests for presents without delay. A kind of fortuitous meeting of interests or actions ensued, reminiscent of the episode of Captain Cook's arrival in Hawaii analyzed by Sahlins (1981): each side acts in a way that meets the other's expectations without knowing their respective motives and ideas.

The second form in which the myth became reenacted involves the relationship between the Wari' themselves. As we shall see in the following chapters, the OroNao' of the Whites saw the alliance with the whites as an opportunity to reestablish contact with their lost kin. Soon after pacification, they no doubt became aware of the whites' curiosity concerning the rest of the still uncontacted Wari', perceiving that they would enable them somehow to meet their lost kin and foreigners. Indeed, a short while after agreeing to live with the whites—which happened around 1959 after a long period of coming and going—they took an active part in the teams organized to contact the other Wari'. The first to be approached were those living in the Laje region. Once again the Nanananana myth became realized: the OroNao' of the Whites' narration of the encounter with the OroWaram repeats, almost word for word, the episode when Nanananana encounters the enemy people and presents himself as kin. The fact that the Wari' set off to encounter their other kin so soon after contact may well have interrupted their effort to transform the whites into foreigners (which, according to the Oropixi' myth, is what the whites were before becoming as they are today). But the Wari' may have also always wanted to keep them as enemies, even if coinhabitants. After all, they never offered their women to the whites. I return to this question later.

While the sociological facts are striking, an important material dimension is continually emphasized by the Wari': they needed axes, urgently. When the Pacaás Novos River was closed, the Wari' say, metal axes were still fairly rare among the group on the left bank, and the axe stones brought from where the OroEo lived—the only source, as we saw, being located at Kit at the right shore of the upper Negro River—could not be replaced when they eventually broke. While the other subgroups continued to visit Kit to obtain stones when the prized metal axes were unavailable, the only choice for the isolated Wari' was to embark on a war expedition to the Pacaás Novos River in search of tools.

In conclusion, I argue that, despite the exceptional involvement of the NTM missionaries in the pacification process and the attacks from whites suffered by the OroNao' at that moment, the decisive factor pushing them toward the whites was their sense of isolation. Certainly, had it not been for the insistence of the contact team in proving their friendly intentions to the Wari', the Indians, however desperate, would not have approached, primarily since they had no wish to die. The isolation had generated problems of two different kinds—material and sociological—whose solution was urgent, prompting the Wari' to accept, for the first time, particular whites as coin-habitants, relinquishing their war with them.

This is an interesting point. Around the start of the twentieth century, when the whites contacted the Wari', the latter were thirsty for enemies and had no wish to give up war, despite perceiving the friendly intentions of some of the whites. Half a century later, they saw themselves losing the war and, to a certain extent, losing themselves. Faced by analogous situations—whites who gave presents and wanted peace—they acted in different ways, seeking foreigners among the enemies and foreigners through the enemies, since the whites led them to the groups with which they had lost contact. We can summarize this by affirming that the historical moment determined the shift in priorities, the importance given to different types of relation, and, in some ways, a renewal of the categories of "foreigner" and "enemy."

CHAPTER 10

"The Enemy Says He's OroNao'"

Contact with the OroWaram,

OroWaramXijein, and OroMon

THE OROWARAM

The OroNao' of the Whites say that soon after going to live with the whites they were asked to help search for their kin, to "get them" and "make them stop." Tem We, a member of this subgroup, gave the following account:

"The OroWaram were at war. We had arrived [to live with the whites] and for a while nothing happened. Then Moreno [a NTM missionary] arrived: 'Get to your people [*win ma'*] and make them stop,' he said. 'Just like we made you join us. Find your people and bring them too.' They were shooting the whites. . . . We went via the Ouro Preto River, looking for the OroWaram hereabouts [Tem We was speaking from the Lage post]. . . . We searched and searched but found nobody."

"You went by boat?" I asked.

"By boat along the Ouro Preto. We didn't see any Wari'. So Moreno came up and said, 'No, the Wari' are near the whites on the mountain road. They killed a child, a white woman's son.' 'Okay, let's go.'"

"You went as far as the headwaters and encountered no Wari'?" I asked.

"Yes. When they said they'd killed a white boy [in the mountains], we came back to Tanajura and slept. We went to Guajará." (Tem We 1994)

According to Tem We, the team that ventured up the Ouro Preto comprised the missionaries Moreno and Royal, Tem We himself, and his brother Jimain Jiparai. Tem We was more than likely referring to the excursion in

1959 to the right shore of the Ouro Preto River (an OroWaram area), which, the SPI report states, included these missionaries, pacified Indians from Tanajura, and SPI agents.[1] Tem We added that they were still traveling when they learned about the boy who was killed, prompting their return to the Tanajura post at the mouth of the Ouro Preto. From there they journeyed to Guajará-Mirim and then set out by truck along the road linking the town to Porto Velho, passing through the mountains where the body had been found close to the Lage post. I am unsure who took part in this second expedition, or whether it corresponds to the expedition undertaken in April 1960 that is also recorded in the SPI documents. Participating in the latter expedition were Josias Batista (SPI), Royal Taylor (NTM), and Indians from Tanajura, who journeyed to kilometer 13 of the highway between Porto Velho and Guajará-Mirim to attempt contact with the Indians attacking the area—again unsuccessfully.

A new expedition was organized, following the tracks of warriors who had shot a woman. This time they almost reached the uncontacted Indians. Tem We, who participated in all of these expeditions, gave this account:

" 'Let's go! Where did they shoot the woman?' 'Here,' they said. Moreno arrived: 'Let's go! Follow the Wari' tracks!' 'Let's go!' [the OroNao' replied]. We followed the tracks left by P. [who had shot the woman] as he escaped. We slept. The next day my older brother, Tokorom Mip, killed a guan. . . . We walked and walked and stopped to sleep. The following day: 'Let's go!' We walked and walked and discovered their path. 'Here's their swidden! Maybe they're there!' But they'd already left. . . .

We circled the area. We searched and searched. 'They fled! Let's go!' We drank coffee and ate bread until full. 'Search for your people properly!' Moreno exclaimed angrily. 'The Wari' are eating the whites!' he said. . . . 'Let's go!' We crossed a small affluent. Manim [OroNao'] said, 'I'm going to drink water!' We walked and walked. And then he yelled. We had found Worao. Manim shouted, 'I've found Wari'!' He [Worao] fired an arrow skyward [in Tokon Towa swidden]. . . . We cried, 'Don't shoot! We're not enemies [*wijam*], we're OroNao',' we said to him, to no avail."

"Were you wearing western clothing?" I asked.

"No, we'd removed all our clothing. 'Take off your clothes when you meet your people so they won't run away,' they said. . . . 'Let's go!' [the OroNao' said]. 'They've gone already!' Just one red macaw and some maize beer remained. They'd fled. They were afraid. 'Perhaps the whites have come to kill us,' they thought. 'They left!' [the OroNao' said]. 'We'll return soon,' Moreno said. 'Your people don't want to be followed. They'll kill us,' he added. 'Really?' we said. We ran back and at dusk stopped to sleep. A truck was already waiting. They [the whites] looked after us. We returned to where they'd killed the boy." (Tem We 1994)

How did the OroWaram experience this situation? According to Ko'um, a man from this subgroup (fig. 23), some warriors had departed for the town of Guajará-Mirim to kill whites, and P. had shot a woman who had left her house to fetch water. At that moment, added Ko'um (who had taken no part in the expedition), Tokorom Mip, Jimain Jiparai, Tem We, and the late Wem Kap and Wem Kakami (OroNao' of the Whites) were already in Guajará. Those who had killed the woman fled and the OroNao' followed them by truck. They knew the whites were surrounding them when, at night, they heard the *kopu* hawk, which signals enemies are approaching. They decided to flee. "They retreated some way but the whites soon approached. They re treated further and the whites approached." Finally they arrived home at the Tokon Horok shouting, "We killed an enemy!" They entered reclusion, ly-ing down in the men's house, sealed by a leaf screen. They heard the *kopu* hawk again, which provoked consternation: "Let's go, let's escape from the enemy! Let's go to Om Pijain." The women separated maize kernels to take and everyone left for Tokon Towa. On arriving they called the inhabitants to flee with them. Everyone went except Xowam, Mon Min, and Orowao Pan Naran, who would follow later. When Xowam and Mon Min went to bathe, the former saw the enemies approach. Mon Min, who had taken his bow, fired an arrow. This was when the OroNao' began to shout that they were not enemies. From the viewpoint of the OroWaram, however, Manim was carrying a shotgun and had every intention of killing them. Ko'um's account continued:

"Xowam was walking when he saw them: 'They're coming!' It was Manim, old Manim. Manim, Jamain Jiparai, Tokorom Mip, and Tem We. 'We're go-ing to get you!' Manim said [or thought]. 'No you won't!' [said or thought the OroWaram]. 'I'll get you with this gun!' said [or thought] Manim.... 'We'll kill you! We'll kill you!' ... He had a shotgun. He wanted to kill the Wari' with a shotgun. [Mon Min shot an arrow.] 'Don't shoot! We came. We're not enemies, we're OroNao'!' ... Had he [Mon Min] recognized

23. Ko'um. Rio Negro–Ocaia 1987. (Photo by Beto Barcellos)

this haircut... The Wari' left their hair long, like yours used to be [referring to me]."

"Tokorom Mip had cut his hair?" I asked.

"Yes. He'd removed his clothing. His body seemed Wari', but his hair was different."

"They weren't using clothes?" I asked.

"No. Had they called [the Wari'] with clothes, they might have fled. Xowam was very young still. 'Don't shoot! We're OroNao'! We're Oro-Nao'!' Xowam looked and ran to join his people. 'Let's go, let's flee from the enemy!' [Sound of gunshot.] That's why we were scared."

"Did Moreno go too?" I asked.

"I think Moreno stayed at Tokon Horok [the first abandoned village]. I think they said to the OroNao': 'Run to look for the Wari'!' The whites stayed put. The whites stayed in the village and the Wari' said, 'Let's find them!' They reached the swidden and waited. 'I'll kill you, I'll kill you,' said [or thought] Manim. So the Wari' fled. They [the OroWaram] met on the path and shouted, 'The enemy is coming!' The enemy said, 'We're OroNao'.' . . . They [the OroWaram] fled and hid behind a trunk. They thought they would shoot them [with the shotgun]. 'Let's shoot them!' They waited and waited until the sun began to set. They reached Om Pijain. The big river was close and they [the fleeing OroWaram] came to me: 'The enemy's arriving! The enemy says he's OroNao'. At Tokon Horok!' 'Really?!' So we thought: 'Let's go there and shoot them!' They [the enemies] hung up tools in the houses. When the OroWaram arrived, the Oro-Nao' had already gone, leaving the tools. . . . Looking at the ground, they saw they had taken the path toward Tokon Horok. They arrived there and found everyone had left. But the houses were there; they hadn't burned them as the whites usually did."

"Did you think they might not be whites, then?" I asked.

"No. We thought they really were whites. They hung [the tools] in front of the men's house. Hoes for weeding, scythes. 'Let's go to them!' [the OroWaram said]. . . . We walked and walked, following them. When close, we returned. We decided to drink maize. Some stayed in Om Pijain and others in Tokon Horok." (Ko'um 1993)

According to Ko'um, the OroNao' left. Time passed. One day an airplane flew over Om Pijain and Tokon Horok. Soon after, the OroNao' (and the whites) returned, this time by boat along the Laje River. This was when they captured a woman called Ariram. Tem We said that the new expedition left almost immediately after returning from the excursion when they were nearly struck by Mon Min's arrow. They visited the spot where the child had been killed and from there headed upriver on the Laje. Juvêncio, the head of the Tenente Lira (now Lage) post, located the trail left by the fleeing OroWaram. Midway on the river, they disembarked and proceeded on foot, following the tracks. On the path, one of the SPI agents, Augusto, fell into a trap—and then something interesting happened. While the accounts thus far give the impression that the Wari' were mere assistants on the expedition, receiving orders from the whites and unhesitatingly obeying them, their response to this event clearly reveals an enormous interest in encountering their people.

> It seems Wari' were there; Juvêncio had already seen [them]. "Really?!" we said. "Let's go!" We slept. The next morning: "Let's go!" With Juvêncio, Augusto, who's now dead. "Here's their trail," they said to us. "Really?!" We slept. "Let's go!" . . . We pushed the motor onto dry land and followed their trail. We walked and walked. The Wari' had stuck bamboo arrow tips on the path, poisoning it. . . . They made a hole and buried the blades, hiding them as if they weren't there. . . . We, Wari', all passed by and continued. When Augusto stopped, he fell, he didn't see them. He bled profusely. The whites called us repeatedly. [The whites on the expedition said,] "Look at Augusto! The enemies [meaning the OroWaram] set a nasty trap with bamboo, the Wari'.[2] Stay with Augusto!" they said. "No, we're the ones who will get our people [*win ma'*]," we told him. (Tem We 1994)

Royal and perhaps one or more SPI employees stayed behind to look after the injured man, while the OroNao' and the missionaries Moreno and Richard followed the trail. Approaching the Om Pijain swidden village, the missionaries decided to wait in the nearby forest. Following the missionaries' advice, the OroNao' undressed and, laden with axes and machetes, headed toward the village. Later they discovered that a man called Wao Taran was hidden in a tree overlooking the path and saw them pass by. They came across a trail leading to the river and saw that the women—no men were in the village at that moment—had gone to bathe, save for one woman who was busy crushing maize at home. The OroNao' decided to hide near this trail and wait for the women to return to their houses and capture them. "After a while, the women who had gone bathing returned. 'They're coming, younger brother!' Tokorom Mip said, 'Look!' 'Get them!' They were coming. They were still approaching when my younger brother, Tokorom Mip, grabbed one of them [by the arm]" (Tem We 1994).

Ko'um (OroWaram) told his version:

I was at Horonain Xitot. Those who captured [the women] headed toward the village. A man, now dead,[3] looked down at the path and saw: "Enemies! The enemy will kill my children!" And he ran away. They [the women] heard and began to rush out of the water. They ran. There was a large sweet potato plantation. Tokorom Mip remained hidden. The whites stayed in the forest further away. Ariram was walking and as she looked back they grabbed her. "The enemy caught me!" Ariram exclaimed. "Don't shout! We're not enemies, we're OroNao'!" Tokorom Mip said. "Let go of me!" she exclaimed. "I'll go home and sit down." "Don't let go of her! She might escape!" they said to each other. "Let's go!" And they went ahead, pushing her. They arrived at her house and asked, "Where's your husband?" They wouldn't have spoken like that, in Wari', had they been enemies [the narrator reflects]. "We're OroNao'! I'm Tem We, I'm Jimain Jiparai, I'm Wem Kap." She trembled heavily. They'd scared her. . . . "If the men arrive, tell them not to shoot." They gave her tools. She took two axes. They sat down together. "My daughter's father went that way," she said. "Let's talk properly." They talked and talked. As they chatted, A'ain [Ariram's husband] came back. When he saw them, he thought they were enemies. "Oh no, the enemy captured my daughter's mother!" He cried. "The enemy will kill my daughter's mother!" He retreated a short distance and cried. "I was numb with rage," A'ain said. "If my daughter dies, I may die too." He put down his arrows and went to his wife. "If the enemy sees me, he will kill me too. That way I'll die with my daughter." They [the OroNao'] looked back and saw him. "Is that your husband?" "Yes, that's my husband, my daughter's father!" They held him. "Don't be afraid of us, we're OroNao'! No, we're not lying, we're OroNao'. The whites don't know how to speak properly [makes unintelligible sounds]." "Really?!" [exclaimed A'ain]. "Take a tool!" He took one. They talked at length. "Orowao Memem is our mother's name. This here is our older brother [or mother's brother, aji'], Wem Kap. The other one, Xijan, stayed there." "Wow!" [exclaimed A'ain]. (Ko'um 1993)

The rest of Tem We's account—who unlike Ko'um was present during this encounter—contains some important details:

" 'Let me go! I'm going to speak to my children's father! I'll speak to him and perhaps I'll come back.' 'No, stay here!' 'Let me go, let me go!' 'Talk to your husband,' we said to her. Her husband had gone hunting. We yelled for A'ain. We yelled and yelled. 'Come here, A'ain! Come here!' We called and called without reply until finally he came, bringing a lot of arrows. . . . 'No, older brother [*aji'*].' We called him older brother right away, as though kin."

"So you didn't really know him, then?" I asked.

"No. We called him older brother for no reason. 'No, older brother, we're not enemies.' " (Tem We 1994)[4]

Perceiving that A'ain and Ariram were afraid, the OroNao' decided to sleep in the forest near Om Pijain and return the next day. Before going, they explained that the whites had asked them to search for them and persuade them to stop warring.

According to Tem We, the OroNao' met up with the whites back in the forest and told them about the peaceful encounter with the OroWaram. The next day, the whites told the OroNao' to return to the village. On arriving they found a lot of people, many OroWaram coming from other villages to see this "*wijam* who says he's Wari.' " But not everyone was friendly, despite A'ain's explanations.

"They're not enemies," A'ain said. They had come to speak to A'ain during the night. "They're not enemies, they're our grandchildren [*winaxi'*] on our grandfather [*jeo'*] Oronkun's side. . . ." Some people liked us and others wanted to kill us, wanted to shoot us. . . . Those who liked us didn't think we were enemies. But some wanted to kill us. We were very afraid. (Tem We 1994)

Ko'um's version differs slightly but confirms the OroWaram hostility. Soon after the first conversations, he said, the OroNao' took A'ain to where Moreno was hidden in the forest.

"The whites don't know how to speak properly; he stayed there. Moreno is up in the tree. The white man is here. When you see him, call him" [said the OroNao']. "Okay," said A'ain. They went there. Bees surrounded him. He came down. They said to Moreno, "Here's a Wari', Moreno! The Wari' is good, Moreno!" . . . Moreno held him, "Don't fear me" [imitates Moreno laughing]. . . . He had hung up some tools. He cut one down and gave it to A'ain. (Ko'um 1993)

I asked Ko'um if they had come to shoot the outsiders and he confirmed that "some people wanted to shoot," despite A'ain's explanations. They said, "They're not OroNao', they're whites!" The OroNao' returned to Om Pijain the next day accompanied by the whites. The encounter with the rest of the Wari' was riddled with ambiguities: on the one hand, those who arrived were friendly because they wanted tools; on the other hand, they wanted to kill enemies.

> The boat came and stopped. "Axes, axes!" we exclaimed. Paton shouted, "Let's kill the enemy!" . . . The river was already high. Genival was at the prow. Moreno was handling the motor. They [the OroNao'] shouted, "We came!" Afraid, Genival stopped the canoe and jumped out, running away. The OroNao' disembarked: Tokorom Mip, Tem We, Jimain Jiparai, and Wem Kap. "We came!" The whites looked on. . . . "The whites aren't angry, they like us. Stop shooting the whites," said Wem Kap. "Talk to the whites!" The whites stared. We took tools. "Let's go, let's see the houses," Richard [a missionary] said to us. "Let's go!" . . . We arrived at the village. The whites sat down. We spoke at length between ourselves. Moreno had no idea what we were saying. (Ko'um 1993)

According to Tem We, the OroWaram asked the OroNao' to sing the music (*tamara*) of the ancient ones in this first large encounter. However, Ko'um claimed this took place in the subsequent encounter when the contact team, including the OroNao', returned after a few days absence (having gone to call Juvêncio, the head of the post, and the missionary Frederick). They sang and danced. The women offered the visitors maize beer. The Oro-Nao' asked the OroWaram to make a trough of beer for them so they could return as guests of a *huroroin'* festival. According to Ko'um, "They said: 'Let's head to Guajará. We'll fetch our wives and come back.' . . . The late Wem Kap lied to us. [Imitating the OroNao' accent:] 'Chop down a trunk. Let's drink. If I die from the beer, you can have sex with my wife. You can have sex with her until satisfied. You'll satisfy yourselves with my wife'" (Ko'um 1993).

The OroNao' left with the whites and failed to return for the festival. According to Ko'um, the OroWaram "became anxious" and decided to visit the Tenente Lira post. Arriving, they asked for tools and returned to their houses saying that the whites were crazy giving presents to them. Parap, an Oro-Waram man, said that after waiting in vain for the OroNao', someone had the idea of visiting the Tenente Lira post "to call the whites." The others liked his suggestion and decided to accompany him.

" 'Let's go too,' we said. And we appeared to the whites at the old post."

"Why did you want to go?" I asked.

"We wanted to arrive [at the whites]."

"Why did you want to arrive?" I asked.

"We didn't want the whites to continue killing us [in the villages]. They went and killed OroMon too. . . . We went to call him at the old post. We called repeatedly and Genival appeared. . . . He killed fish for us. We ate a lot." (Parap 1994)

Apparently this group spent some days at the post. According to Parap, they obtained tools and soon returned to their villages. Moreno and Royal subsequently arrived at Tokon Mere by boat, distributed tools, and told them to stay there, to make a swidden, and to stop killing the whites. Ko'um said that this encounter at Tokon Mere included some OroNao' men and their wives: "They said, 'These are our wives.' The women said, 'We're not enemies, we're Wari'! Listen to how we speak. The whites don't know how to talk properly.' The next day, Royal arrived: 'Right people! Stay here. I'm going to inject you all.' I think the sickness was Royal's curse. 'The sickness will arrive,' he said" (Ko'um 1993).

THE OROWARAMXIJEIN

Before the epidemics spread, the OroNao' and the whites had already asked the contacted Wari' to tell the OroWaramXijein and OroMon that the whites were friendly, and to stop killing them and come to receive metal tools. A dense network formed with various people communicating the news to different villages. The testimony of Nowi, an OroWaramXijien man staying among the OroWaram as a festival guest at the moment of contact, is interesting. His own local group was being so heavily pursued by the whites that they no longer made swiddens. Some men had visited the OroWaram at Kao Pin Xi Ni Tamara for a *tamara* festival: notably, they were still holding festivals despite the instability of continually fleeing from the whites' attacks. Shortly after the festival, his father-in-law went there to take his daughter Orowao, Nowi's wife, who accompanied her father. This was when "the Oro-Nao' who found us returned again," Nowi recalled. Having already heard of the arrival of these strangers, they had decided to shoot them, but were dissuaded by Paton (OroWaram).

"They're *wari'-wijam*. They say they're OroNao'. 'Our grandfather was called Mawi. Hwerein Powam was our grandfather's name. They were our ancestors long ago.' And I insisted, 'Let's shoot the enemy!' And we went. Mon went too. And then the enemies called us."

"Who were they?" I asked.

"Tokorom Mip, Jimain Jiparai [here the OroNao' are called *wijam*].... They spoke clearly to us: 'We're not *wijam*, we're OroNao'.' 'Really? We were going to shoot you!' [the OroWaramXijein said]. They drank our maize beer. They drank and drank, and called us: 'Let's go!' We arrived [at Tokon Horok] and cooked capuchin monkey. 'Let's kill them. They were the ones who hunted us. Let's kill them with knives!' [the OroWaramXijein thought]. But Paton said to me: 'They're good.' So we put our knives down." (Nowi 1994)

Nowi left to inform his coinhabitants, who were heading toward the upper Laje. Others did the same and news of the arrival of whites who said they were OroNao' spread among the Wari'.

They had already gone throughout the forest. "The enemies are good! The enemies say they are OroNao'! They are really good!" "Really? Let's go!" And they arrived. We arrived. . . . "Let's call the enemy!" So we went to the Lage post. We arrived and yelled, "We arrived!" The enemies replied, "Hey, did you arrive?" They cut down papayas and gave them to us. "Sleep here!" We slept. The next day we left for home and began to die. The sickness got us. We died, died, died. We stayed put in one spot. They gave us injections. (Nowi 1994)

How did other OroWaramXijein experience this moment? Tem Wito, an OroWaramXijein man, said that Nowi was responsible for informing them. He had arrived in their village announcing, "The enemies are saying, 'We're OroNao'!'" Afterward he went to other villages and on returning called them to go to the whites. Meanwhile, a white man (a regional inhabitant, not a member of the pacification team) had killed Harein's younger brother. They continued until reaching "OroWaram land" at the mouth of the Laje. The whites were there along with many Wari'.

Ton Pan, an OroWaramXijein woman, said that her local group was then living on the headwaters of the Ribeirão, escaping from the whites who were hunting them down. Paulo, an OroNao' man unknown to them, had arrived shouting, "Don't be afraid. We're not enemies, we're OroNao'." They ran away and wept, fearful of dying. Domingos, an Indian from another indigenous group who worked for the SPI, accompanied Paulo, along with other OroNao'. Finally they answered their call and went to the village where they obtained metal tools. They then carried on to Domingos's house on the headwaters of the Ribeirão. They slept just one night there and were already sick by the following day. Afterward the OroNao' called them to go to the Ribeirão post (Major Amarante, downriver), where they met many OroMon who had gone there directly.

Nawakan, an OroWaramXijein man, also said that Nowi had told them the news. Nowi had arrived at Xat Araji, where he lived, and said, "The Oro-Waram are saying that the enemies are their kin!" Alarmed, they fled to the Laje's headwaters. According to Moroxin Pik, an OroWaramXijein woman, Nowi's phrase on encountering them was, "The enemies are saying they're our kin! Let's go to meet them!" They went but were unable to approach the whites very closely as they became afraid. Orowao Tata, an OroWaramXijein man, was also in flight on the headwaters of the Ribeirão. Paulo, an OroNao' man, approached them and shouted, "Your coinhabitants, the OroWaram, have already arrived." They received tools. The women there took the initiative of going, seduced by reports of abundant food: "Let's go! We should already be eating lots with them!" Paulo confirmed, "Your coinhabitants are eating lots there!" They arrived at the Major Amarante post, but the Wari' had gone: the OroWaram had all traveled to the Tenente Lira post.

THE OROMON

The news spread rapidly and the OroMon, who lived further upriver, learned about the events at the same time as the OroWaramXijein. Part of the group headed to Tokon Horok, the OroWaram village mentioned earlier, and from there to the Tenente Lira post. Another part arrived at the Ribeirão River where, according to Pan Kamerem (OroWaramXijein) there were three houses belonging to whites who welcomed them. At the mouth lived José Dias, the head of the Major Amarante post; upriver, close to the present-day location of the Ribeirão post, was the house of Domingos (SPI); at the source of the river lived Aldenir (a Makurap Indian) and Baitá (an "Aruá" Indian).[5] Jimon (OroMon) stated that Ko'um, the OroWaram man responsible for the accounts transcribed above, had gone to meet them at a salt lick on the Laje

River where they had gone to hunt tapir. He had said, "The enemies caught the OroWaram. The enemies aren't thinking properly [are crazy]. We took tools. The enemies said, 'We're OroNao', we're OroNao.'" They then went to Tokon Horok and from there to the Tenente Lira post: "That was when they killed a cow for us. We ate the cow and stayed there. So the sickness got us."

I asked Jimon whether they had returned home: "No. The whites had killed many of us in the forest. So we stayed here."

Orowao Powa (OroMon) said that Pa' Tokwe Uru, also OroMon, had gone to call on them on the Laje headwaters where they had fled from the whites. He had already visited the OroWaram and arrived saying, "The enemy turned into Wari' [*wari' pin na wijam*, where *pin* signifies "completely" and *na* indicates the third person singular]." They then went to Tokon Horok, where many people were gathered. From there, Orowao Powa was asked to join the team that would leave to attempt peaceful contact with the OroNao', OroEo, and OroAt living on the Negro and Ocaia rivers.

Harein (OroMon) said that his local group was then living near the headwaters of the Mutumparaná River. They made no swiddens because they were surrounded by whites and continually on the run. Nowi had arrived saying, "The enemy said, 'I'm OroNao.' They sing *lumuru.*" They did not follow Nowi: "We weren't persuaded." Soon after Harein's sister was killed by whites, and Wem Tawinain arrived to call them: "The enemy who is our coinhabitant is good!" They decided to go with him: "We wanted tools. 'Let's get tools from their whites!' . . . We went to the Ribeirão River. We obtained tools and left. The other Wari' said to us, 'You should all come here for good.' 'Really?' . . . We went to the forest, to the mountains. . . . Eventually we reached the Ribeirão" (Harein 1993).

All of them went to the Major Amarante post and from there to the Tenente Lira (Lage) post, after an OroMon man called them, claiming there was no disease at the latter. However everyone became sick and decided to return to the forest.

Jamain Tokwam (OroMon) said that when they were found by Nowi, they were living on the run from whites, on the small creeks, affluents of the upper Laje. According to Jamain Tokwam, Nowi had arrived saying, "'The enemy visited us. The enemies appear to be saying, "We are foreigners" [*tatirim*].' 'What are their names?' [the OroMon asked Nowi]. 'Tem We, Jamain Jiparai. "We're Wari'," the enemies said. "I'm Tem We," the enemy said. "I'm Tokorom Mip," the enemy said'" (Jamain Tokwam 1994).

Jamain Tokwam added that the OroNao' actually looked like enemies: their hair was cut. Tired of being pursued, they decided to go with Nowi. They reached the OroWaram swidden village of Tokon Horok. From there they continued to the Tenente Lira post, already becoming sick en route. On their arrival, Royal Taylor gave them injections and they ended up staying.

THE EPIDEMICS

Among the OroWaram, OroWaramXijein, and OroMon—and on the Negro and Ocaia rivers, as we shall see—the new diseases spread very quickly. The spi documents provide some information on the epidemics. Peaceful contact with the OroWaram occurred in April 1961 and in May of the same year the head of the Tenente Lira post, Juvêncio, sent a request for medicines to treat contacted Indians living 3 kilometers from the post. He states that six people had already died of "pneumonia, flu, and fever." The documents dated from June and July also mention the epidemics, one of them adding that the Indians were being treated in the forest by a nurse. According to Von Graeve (1989, 55), a few days after first contact, more than two hundred Indians had succumbed to flu and fever. The OroWaramXijein and OroMon, recent arrivals at the Major Amarante post, some 286 people in all (58), sickened after being visited by train passengers from the Madeira–Mamoré railroad who had decided to stop there to "have a look at the famous Pakaa-Nova.... This proved fatal; almost immediately the Indians contracted influenza. The most vivid impression of the episode was supplied by the post's Indian agent, José Dias: 'a continuous roar of coughing that came from the Indian camp'" (58).

I lack any detailed accounts from the Wari' of this region concerning the diseases; like the OroNao' of the Whites, though, they returned to their villages in alarm when they became ill, remaining there for some time. Those who recovered went after the whites again. But this was not the general rule. While some people continued to come and go, others immediately stayed with the whites, occupying villages close to the attraction posts. There they received treatment and reestablished themselves. Conklin (1989, 101–3) states that those treated were generally cured; the mortality rate was very high only among those who fled and ended up dying in the forest. As I mentioned earlier, Conklin notes that the illnesses spread much more quickly along the Laje, Ribeirão, Negro, and Ocaia rivers because contact in these

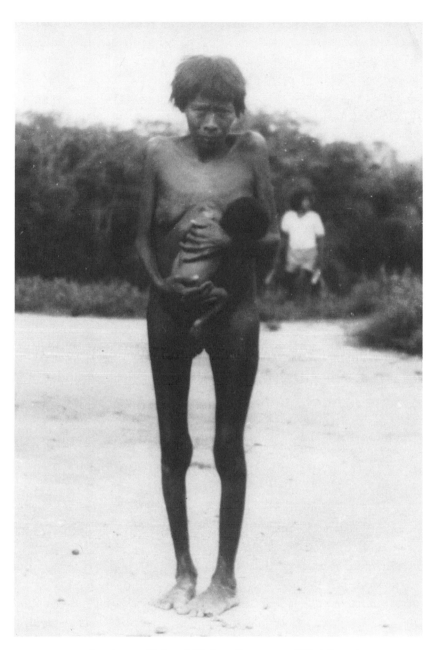

24. A woman with her child, just after contact. Ribeirão, 1962.
(Archive of the Guajará-Mirim Prelacy)

25. A woman carrying maize in a basket. Probably Ribeirão during the first half of the 1960s. (Photo by Geraldo Mendonça da Silva)

26. Women wait with their children. Probably Ribeirão during the first half of the 1960s. (Photo by Geraldo Mendonça da Silva)

regions included the participation of other Wari'. Thus while the OroNao' of the Whites gradually approached the Tanajura post, generally in exclusively male expeditions, the Indians from other areas were visited directly in their villages, meaning that women and children also had contact with the outsiders relatively quickly (figs. 24, 25, 26, and 27).

THE RESISTANT OROMON

While most of the Indians came and went, seldom if ever remaining far from the whites, a group of OroMon families left the Tenente Lira post at the end of 1961, escaping the flu outbreak, and were only encountered again eight years later. They were the last group of isolated Wari'. Two men from this group provided testimonies, one of them recorded, which I reproduce below.

Harein (OroMon) was initially reluctant to live near the whites. Finally he decided to go to live at the Major Amarante (now Ribeirão) post, and from there went to the Tenente Lira (Lage) post, in search of a place free of

27. A Wari' woman carrying her child in a bark sling. Probably Ribeirão during the first half of the 1960s. (Photo by Geraldo Mendonça da Silva)

diseases. But the move was in vain. Alarmed by the flu outbreak at the Lage post, he returned to the forest, far from the whites.

"'Let's get away from the whites!' We returned. . . . We went to the forest, far away, to the mountains. There is [land for] a swidden there, on the land bordering the mountains. . . . We stayed for many years. We had children there. That's where Wem and Ko'um were born . . . Just two children were born in the mountains. . . . Many whites came, looking for land. They came from all sides. Our land was in the middle. . . . They came up the Ouro Preto, from every direction. . . ."

"Were you afraid?" I asked.

"Yes, we were. 'Let's escape from the whites again!' We returned to Ko-jain [a swidden located on a left-bank affluent of the middle Laje River]. We cleared swiddens. We were angry still. 'Let's kill enemies!' we said to each other. . . . They had already killed my younger sister on the Laje. 'Let's kill enemies!' 'Let's!' Orowao Powa, I, and all the other coinhabitants who have now died. . . . We appeared to a woman [they shot her], the one I mentioned earlier. The whites from there found out. They took the arrow to Guajará. We stayed and stayed and those now dead arrived. . . . At Ko-jain. Antônio Costa [of the SPI] along with Wari', and a Makurap *caboclo*, Aldenir. The Wari' [who went to call them] included my younger brother, Maxun Hat, Xin Xoi, Wao Tok Am, the late father of Orowao, Maxun . . . These were the people who went to call us. They appeared to us. Orowao Powa went to harvest maize. . . . We stayed in the forest [the entire group had gone in search of bamboo for arrows and Orowao Powa separated from the rest to return quickly to the swidden to fetch maize]. They encountered Orowao Powa. . . . He fled, thinking the whites had come to kill him. 'I think the whites want to kill me!'"

"Did they wear clothes?" I asked.

"The Wari' who went to call us wore clothing. We had none. The Wari' who gathered us and made us arrive wore clothing. They shouted: 'It's us! Don't run! It's us!' . . . They called us back. We arrived back at the village [Kojain]. There were lots of knives. Not large ones, small ones. Orowao Powa came to say, 'I met our people. Our people, with the whites, they called me.' 'Let's go,' we said. We arrived at Kojain. There was a house and maize. They gave us small knives with small handles. . . . We slept two nights at Kojain. . . . 'Let's go,' said Antônio Costa. We came."

"Why did you immediately accept the whites' command? Why didn't you stay?" I asked.

"We accepted quickly. We were afraid of dying. The whites could have killed us. There was no more land. There were whites everywhere. The land where we were living was small."

"Did you think of your kin who were already living with the whites?" I asked.

"We thought of them too. 'Let's go!' we said. We slept. The next day we went. We arrived at the headwaters of the Ribeirão. The late Domingos was already there along with many Wari'. Domingos gave us injections. The next day, the late Antônio Costa said, 'I'm going to Guajará.' He went to Guajará to speak with the leader there. He told Antônio Costa to call us, which he did. So we left for the Ribeirão [Major Amarante post]." (Harein 1993)

A truck went to fetch them at the post, carrying clothes. They proceeded to Guajará and from there directly to Sagarana, the headquarters of the Catholic mission. Soon after arriving, a measles epidemic struck them and various people died.

Orowao Powa told me that he had decided to live far from the whites after participating in the expedition to contact the Wari' on the Negro and Ocaia rivers. From there he returned to Tokon Mere, an OroWaram swidden, and then fled, afraid of the white diseases. His older brother had already gone, saying, "Let's get far away from the whites. They're no good!" They went to Komikon Kap, on the headwaters of the Ouro Preto, and cleared a swidden there. According to Orowao Powa, the first to leave were Harein and his wife, Pakao, the daughter of To'o Xiri and the sister of Orowao Powa; To'o Xiri and her husband, Jimon Kotowa; Harein's father, Pa Tokwe Uru, and his wife, Moroxin Jori; and Xijan, the son of Pa Tokwe Uru's sister. Orowao Powa, his wife, Jap, his older brother Wao Pixoi and the latter's wife, To'o Xak Wa, all met up with them later.[6]

Orowao Powa stressed that the period in the forest had been essential for them to cure themselves from the diseases. He had argued with one of those who came to call them back: "Why did you come to call us? There are diseases there." As I emphasized previously, this is an interesting point: the Wari' at first did not connect the white medicines with curing the epidemics; being cured was seen to involve moving away from the focus of contamination. In fact, as we saw, these OroMon were taken from Major Amarante to

Sagarana and died shortly afterward. Why did they accept when the whites called them the second time? They were under less pressure compared to the first contact, since they had cleared swiddens and had not suffered a single death in the eight years they remained in isolation. On the contrary, they were the ones who provoked the whites by attacking them. According to Orowao Powa, they killed two people over this time, and not just one woman as Harein recounted.

The answer to this question is not found in the accounts of the isolated OroMon but in the testimonies of a small group of OroEo and OroAt who decided to accept the call of the whites some years later. I examine this case in more detail later: for now, I simply note that these OroEo and OroAt felt extremely isolated and it was their wish to live in society that led them to accompany the kin who called them to live with the whites. The OroMon apparently remained isolated for longer because their group was larger, the kinship relations between its members enabling a kind of miniature society: parents, parents-in-law, siblings, and siblings-in-law. In contrast, the OroEo/OroAt group comprised just one couple, their children, and the husband's unmarried brother.

The extreme isolation experienced by the remaining uncontacted groups reveals the key role played by this factor in their eventual decision to live near the whites. At one end of this spectrum we have the OroNao' of the Whites who also became isolated, though not from their own choosing. Like the smaller groups, they wanted people: they wanted to live in society, not merely among their own kin. But did this apply to the OroWaram, Oro-WaramXijein, and OroMon as a whole?

WHO IS THE ENEMY?

What led the members of these subgroups, who continued to have contact with foreigners and even hold festivals, to finally accept the call of the whites? One obvious reason, made explicit by themselves, is the fact they were surrounded by whites and forced to hide from them. However, this persecution had already been intense in 1959 and 1960, and yet they had been little inclined to accept peaceful contact with the expeditions made in these two years. In 1959, NTM missionaries, accompanied by OroNao' from Tanajura, joined an SPI expedition attempting contact in the Laje River region. This failed to encounter any Indians. In April 1960 another expedition was undertaken, also involving contacted Wari', again without success. In May the same year, the head of the Tenente Lira post was attacked by Indians and the reports show that throughout 1960 the Wari' alternated between approaching to take presents and armed attacks. Peaceful contact was only achieved in April the following year, after the episode in which Mon Min tried to shoot the expedition's members.

Obviously their pursuit by whites meant the Wari' distrusted any that approached; they had no means for differentiating the good from the bad. Neither could they differentiate their own kind among the whites, since as well as accompanying the latter like coinhabitants, their hair was cut strangely and some even wore clothing. Contact only occurred when the OroNao' of the Whites had the chance to talk with Ariram and tell her they were not enemies but OroNao' who had separated a long time ago. It is worth examining this moment closely since it involved two groups who saw the situation from different perspectives. We can begin with the viewpoint of the Wari' who arrived with the whites.

As we saw in the previous chapter, the OroNao' of the Whites decided to approach peacefully, largely because they were isolated and desired new people. This conclusion derived from noting the association made between the flood myth and the widening of the Pacaás Novos River, and the apparent reenactment of this myth at the moment of contact with the OroWaram. Like Nanananana's family, the OroNao' of the Whites became isolated due to an excess of water. They subsequently left in search of people. The OroNao' approached the whites, possibly with the idea of making them foreigners, and soon discovered that these enemies could take them to the true foreigners, the other Wari'. So eager were they in this encounter that, as I showed above, they disobeyed the whites—to whom they had thus far appeared submissive—when Augusto injured himself in a trap and they decided nonetheless to proceed without delay to meet their kin.

In the myth, Nanananana discovers signs of people and hides in wait to see who appears. In the reference version (chapter 6), a group of women approach and he grabs one of them by the arm. She cries and he tries to calm her, asking her to call her fellow villagers. In other versions, the captured people, men, call Nanananana "enemy." Explaining that he is not an enemy, he calls the strangers "brothers" by classifying his daughters as "our (inclusive) daughters." In the historical event, the OroNao' hide and wait for the women to pass by, grabbing one of them by the arm. She cries and they claim they are not enemies but Wari', OroNao', and prove they are kin by citing the names of shared ancestors.

Table 4. Nanananana and Pacification

NANANANANA	PACIFICATION
Old woman, spirit of the rain, appears, provoking floods.	Old woman, spirit of the water, appears, widening the river.
The excess of water leaves a man without sons-in-law.	The excess of water leaves a group without foreigners.
Man departs in search of sons-in-law.	Men depart in search of foreigners.
He encounters an enemy group and transforms them into kin.	They meet enemies whom they try to transform into foreigners (the whites) or succeed in doing so (the other groups).
Reconstitution of Wari' society: the subgroups separate.	Reconstitution of Wari' society: the subgroups mix.

Again I emphasize that myth and event are related as a series of logical transformations,[7] not as historical events that become blurred. The Wari' knew they were living through a different kind of situation and never claimed that these outsiders were mythic personae. For the purposes of analysis, this observation allows us to consider pacification as a new version of the Nanananana myth (table 4).

Like any historically determined new version, modifications occurred. Nanananana, on meeting these *wari'-wijam* (as the OroWaram sometimes refer to the OroNao' of the Whites), offers them his daughters in marriage in order to ensure the reproduction of his small group. The OroNao' did not offer women to the OroWaram, first because there were no women among them at that moment, but especially because the reproduction that interested them was that of society as a whole. They wanted foreigners: rather than offering women in marriage, therefore, they offered their women as prey of the hosts of a *huroroin'* festival. Even so, many marriages eventually occurred. The association between affines (here, sons-in-law) and foreigners, clearly visible when we compare the versions, has been highlighted throughout this book. The last item in the above schema reveals an important transformation occurring with pacification, illustrating Sahlins's thesis (1985) concerning the historical dimension of any structure. As we shall see below, one of the outcomes of pacification was the mixture of members of different subgroups at the SPI posts. Over time, the category "foreigner" became redefined and the subgroups once again separated.

Comparison with the myth also shows that, for the OroNao' of the Whites, the OroWaram were not simply Wari' but occupied the position of enemies, just like those whom Nanananana encountered and quickly transformed into affines through marriage. Being Wari' means living and eating together, sharing festivals, and exchanging women. Those who rupture these exchanges become enemies, since "enemy," as we have seen, is a position rather than a category; if and when exchanges are reestablished, the enemies become Wari' again.

Turning to the OroWaram viewpoint, it is surprising that despite noting that the OroNao' spoke their language, recited the names of common ancestors and, in some cases, sang the *tamara* music, they classified them as enemies/whites rather than Wari'. This is revealed by the announcements made by the OroWaram who went to tell the others of the events: "The enemy is saying, 'I'm OroNao',' " "The OroNao' are saying the enemies are their kin!" and "The enemy turned into Wari' [*wari' pin na wijam*]." Did the OroWaram really fail to perceive the difference between the whites and the OroNao', after talking to them, merely because they were accompanied by whites and cut their hair differently? Once again, the answers are various and complementary.

First, as I discussed earlier, for the Wari', coinhabitants (*win ma'*) are effectively kin since they are consanguinized by physical proximity. Living together with the whites, eating with them and sleeping in the same place, means establishing kinship ties, which, from the OroWaram viewpoint (unaware that the OroNao' had not married the whites), had happened to the OroNao'. In a sense, therefore, the OroNao' had indeed transformed into white enemies and were indistinguishable from the others, apart from the unusual fact of claiming they were Wari'. Moreover, if the OroNao' were Wari', as evinced by their language, music, and names, they were also more typical enemies than the whites, precisely through being former Wari' who, like Oropixi', went away and lost contact with their own people. Hence the meaningful enemy is one whose origin can be traced directly to Wari' society and can be reincorporated by the latter, as occurred with the OroNao' of the Whites.

This helps explain various details. Wari' accounts of the encounter practically ignore the presence of the whites, turning the event into a meeting between Wari' who see each other as enemies. Confirming this idea, the OroWaram attributed the violent intentions to the OroNao' rather than the whites, claiming that an OroNao' man was carrying a shotgun and wanted to kill them.

Accusations like this against the cited OroNao' man are fairly common in the accounts of contact. Wao Tok Am, an OroKaoOroWaji man, told me that before contact the OroNao' of the Whites killed the OroMon with guns. The whites told them to make peaceful contact and they took the opportunity to shoot. Paletó, who was present during this conversation, added that the OroNao' differed from the whites due to their violent behavior.

> They stayed after shooting. The true enemies [*iri wijam*, meaning the whites] shoot and then disappear quickly. Not the Wari'. They wait to see whether they will call the others. The next day, we went to cut up the dead and they were still there. The dead swelled up and only then did they leave. They seemed to be Wari'. We said, "Had the enemy gone away quickly . . . They seem like Wari'. The former OroNao' perhaps." . . . "Why does the enemy pursue us so relentlessly? They can't be enemies, they must be Wari'. The enemy was never like that. He attacked us just once and went away." . . . "The enemy isn't like that, he doesn't keep pursuing the Wari'." (Paletó 1995)

According to Paletó, peaceful contact was only made possible by the intervention of the missionaries, who did not allow the Wari' to be killed and who kept watch on the OroNao' during the expeditions.

Hence, the OroWaram's failure to recognize the OroNao' as Wari' cannot be attributed to a lack of close observation or attention to details. Another code is at work: the enemy is a partial stranger rather than a total one, someone who was once Wari' and can become so again. As in several versions of the Oropixi' myth, the OroNao' of the Whites, in rejoining the others, or bringing the others to join themselves, revert to being Wari', coinhabitants and kin.

Clearly things had changed, though. Although they all became coinhabitants again, they also turned into coinhabitants of the whites by living alongside them. This point is essential and renders the analysis more complex. Were everything simple—had the Wari' merely wished to approach their kin, reconstituting their social organization precisely as it had been before the invasion of the whites—they would have returned to the forest and their villages, distancing themselves from these enemies in order to sustain a warfare relation with them. Arguably the Wari' were aware that they could no longer live in the same way, since more and more whites were invading their lands and killing them with powerful weapons. Nonetheless, the uncontacted OroMon managed to remain isolated for years without suffering a single death. Other smaller groups who had returned to the villages soon came back to live near the whites, claiming there were insufficient people to live in the forest and they felt alone. In other words, most Wari' groups actively chose to live with the whites, rather than simply being forced to under pressure.

Whenever I asked the Wari' why they had not returned to the forest, remaining close to the whites instead, they replied that they had stayed in order to live rather than die as victims of diseases. However, the same informants also sometimes declared that they cured themselves in the forest, rather than at the posts where they had been contaminated. But instead of staying where they were after recovering, they returned in search of the whites. Why? Certainly the abundance attracted them. They always mentioned how much they ate, the cattle killed for them, and the presents they received. But they also said that they were ordered to work, to harvest poaia (*Polygala angulata*) and rubber, and to make collective swiddens. Indeed, the way they describe the period immediately following contact leads me to believe that they accepted the orders of the whites without hesitation, as though they had no option. Clearly other questions were also involved and the Wari' desire to live with the whites was more structural than circumstantial. A consideration of this point is left for the conclusion.

CHAPTER 11

The Great Expedition

Contact with the OroNao', OroEo,

and OroAt on the Negro

and Ocaia Rivers

Each stage of contact with the Wari' comprised a unique moment: not only was each subgroup—or set of subgroups occupying a particular region—living through specific historical experiences, but the groups meeting each other were also different. While the OroNao' of the Whites approached the whites directly, and the OroWaram were met by unknown people claiming to be Wari', the OroNao' of the right bank of the Pacaás Novos River initially interacted with people from a group they already knew—the OroMon—and with the OroNao' of the Whites, whom they had never seen. So the first contact took place between Wari' and whites, the second between two Wari' groups unknown to each other, enemies in a sense, and the third between Wari' and known Wari', foreigners. Like the encounter with the OroWaramXijein and the OroMon, the encounter of the OroEo and OroAt with the whites was mediated by their coinhabitants, very often kin, who went to the villages to tell people that the whites were approaching.

The encounters with the OroNao' of the right bank and with the OroEo and OroAt are the best documented by myself; as well as working more intensely with the Wari' of the Negro River during my field research, I also had the chance to conduct lengthy interviews with Dom Roberto Gomes de Arruda, one of the protagonists of this phase of contact, and with some members of the OroNao' of the Whites subgroup and an OroMon man who also took part.

I should make it clear that, from a nonindigenous viewpoint, practically my only sources concerning the expedition I shall describe are two interviews with Dom Roberto (1993 and 1995) and an article written by himself for the magazine *Lettre d'Amazonie* (1970). Apart from Valdemar "Kabixi," an Indian who had lived with the whites for a long time and whom I interviewed on the subject, I was unable to find anyone else who participated in this encounter; indeed many had already died. However, our primarily interest here is the view of the different Wari' groups involved. The correlations and contrasts between their different perspectives—and between these and the viewpoint of the whites, represented by Dom Roberto—form the main substance of this chapter.

PREVIOUS ATTEMPTS

As we saw in chapter 3, the OroNao' who inhabited the right shore of the Pacaás Novos, recall that the three attempts at peaceful contact were made by the whites before the establishment of contact properly speaking. The first of these occurred around 1920 when various women were taken from the Panawin swidden and later returned with a cargo of presents and diseases. The other two attempts occurred later and were limited to airplanes flying over Tokon Torowakan around 1940 and Pin Karam several years later. Some informants claim that all three attempts were led by Francisco Meireles, an SPI officer.

Some time passed without any new approaches being made.[1] In the middle of 1960, the SPI and the NTM missionaries, helped by the recently pacified OroNao' of the Whites, undertook an expedition to the Negro River to try to establish friendly contact with the region's Indians,[2] who continued to attack the whites, especially the rubber tappers living in the area. Simultaneously, they attempted to contact the groups occupying the basin of the Laje River and its affluents.

I have little information about this expedition and am unsure how many journeys were actually made. An SPI document, dated August 1960, indicates preparations for another trip (unmentioned in any later documentation) and reports that all that had been located was an abandoned village with no mention of encountering Indians. In this document, Domingos Araújo, an SPI employee, requests axes and machetes to "attract the Indians on the Ocaia River," whose village had been visited, he wrote, "by our OroNao' Indians accompanied by two American missionaries."

The missionary Royal Taylor confirmed that the NTM had attempted contact on the Negro River and revealed that this venture had been suddenly interrupted by the expedition led by Fernando Cruz and supported by the

Catholic Church of Guajará-Mirim, discussed shortly below: "We wanted to make contact on the Laje, on the Negro River, just like at Tanajura, slowly and very calmly, only approaching when there was no flu. This was the error of the hasty contact of Fernando Cruz, bringing everyone. The mission had already begun contact on the Negro River" (Royal Taylor 1994).

When I asked Dom Roberto—the former bishop of Guajará-Mirim, a priest at the time, who participated in the expedition led by Fernando Cruz—about this prior attempt at contact, he recalled an interesting fact forgotten by Royal Taylor: the Wari' had sunk the boat used by the missionaries and SPI employees. "They had been on the Negro River, as far as the mouth of the Ocaia River, and there they even lost a boat. They journeyed upriver in the screened boat, fully armored to protect them from the arrows. And there, while they seemingly took a small boat and traveled partway up the Ocaia, the Indians boarded the boat left at the river mouth, where the river is deep, and sank it. When they returned, the boat had disappeared" (Dom Roberto 1993).

If this really happened   very possible, since I have heard various mentions of a boat sunk in this region—it is clear that, like the Wari' of the Laje, the inhabitants of this region were also disinclined to approach the whites, even after seeing them arrive with presents and apparently with no intention to attack. Whatever the case, no kind of encounter, even indirect, appears to have taken place, since neither the expedition members nor the Wari' of the Negro River reported seeing each other. However, A'ain Kaxun, an OroNao' man from this area, stated that a year before the Fernando Cruz expedition (of May–June 1961), the Wari' had found metal objects, like small gourds, hanging in Koxain village, but had no idea who had left them. These may have been presents left by the missionaries, who had visited the region in August 1960. The village found on the Ocaia could well have been Koxain. The OroNao' of the Whites—who, according to the SPI document, participated in this contact attempt—failed to mention the journey with the NTM missionaries during my interviews with them about contact on the Negro and Ocaia rivers.

ORGANIZING THE EXPEDITION

In early 1961, the situation in the Guajará-Mirim region was dramatic with the population terrified and outraged by the Wari' attacks. Peaceful contact with the OroWaram had yet to take place and people had been shot on the

outskirts of town. In the area formed by the right bank affluents of the Pacaás Novos, where the OroNao', OroEo, and OroAt lived, the main victims
were rubber tappers. Apparently, the SPI and the missionaries opted to concentrate their contact attempts on the Laje area, perhaps due to its relative
proximity to the town. Indeed in April that year they succeeded in pacifying
the OroWaram. Meanwhile, the conflicts continued in the other area and
intensified to the point where, according to Dom Roberto, the rubber bosses
decided to organize an expedition to exterminate these Indians.

Dom Xavier Rey, then the bishop of Guajará-Mirim, learned of this expedition and according to Dom Roberto tried to prevent it at all costs. Clearly
bothered by the alliance between the SPI and the fundamentalist missionaries, and possibly seeing the chance for the Catholic Church to gain access
to the Indians of the region, Dom Rey turned directly to the governor of
Rondônia state, Alvarenga Mafra.

President Jânio Quadros, aware of events, asked the SPI director Colonel Tasso de Aquino to send someone immediately to head a pacification
expedition, bypassing the middle echelons of the SPI, including the head
of the Ninth SPI Regional Inspectorate (RI), Alberico Soares Pereira. This
was when the SPI officer Fernando Cruz arrived in Guajará-Mirim: "To head
the expedition called 'Governor Mafra' in this territory, Colonel Tasso de
Aquino appointed a former employee with a thorough knowledge of indigenous customs, Inspector Fernando Cruz, who received direct instructions
from the president, Jânio Quadros, and from his boss, Colonel Aquino" (*O
Imparcial*, May 21, 1961).

According to Dom Roberto,

> In May, right at the start of May 1961, Fernando Cruz arrived. He held a
> meeting in Guajará with the traders. But unfortunately he brought much
> talk and few resources, in financial terms, since his aim was to obtain funds
> there in Guajará from the traders. Only he was perhaps a little too hard-
> line in his approach. He said to the traders, "Give me the money needed
> for this work or I'll denounce you as Indian killers." The locals calmly re-
> plied, "Fernando, we're all willing to help, only you must understand the
> following: the SPI always promised and never delivered. It has debts with
> all of the traders here; it has never paid anyone. So we can't just dish out
> money blithely either." (Dom Roberto 1993)

Fernando Cruz's only support came from the rubber boss—and renowned
Indian killer—Manuel Lucindo, who took him by boat to the Negro River.

On the way, they stopped at the Tanajura post where some of the already contacted OroNao' of the Whites lived, and from where Fernando Cruz took "two or three Indians to help him in the work. This was in May 1961. It was not yet an expedition, but Fernando's attempt to undertake some preliminary research" (Dom Roberto 1993). I know little about this "research trip," but it apparently lasted no more than a few days. According to Dom Roberto, Fernando Cruz returned to Guajará, though some of those accompanying him, including the Wari', remained on the Negro River awaiting his return.

According to Dom Roberto, Fernando Cruz, on returning to Guajará, tried to get round the impasse by holding a new meeting in which he claimed that he had already contacted the Indians, hoping this ruse would allow him to obtain the necessary funds: "He held a meeting with the Guajará rubber bosses rather than the traders. Only he failed to realize that the rubber bosses and traders were one and the same. So the same men turned up at the meeting." The rubber bosses said that his word was not enough and that release of any funds would depend on showing them the Indians: "Bring these newly contacted Indians here for us to see. We want to see and touch them, and verify that it's true. . . . Otherwise we won't believe you" (Dom Roberto 1993).

The newspaper *O Imparcial* gives a different version of the relation between Fernando Cruz and the local powerful men: "In concluding this report, we should point out that this is the first time in the history of pacifying the Indians that an expedition has received the full support of . . . rubber bosses and the public as a whole, and this we can attribute to the work of Inspector Fernando Cruz, who since his arrival has obtained an accord with everyone, explaining the situation, showing the real interest of the president, Jânio Quadros, and the [SPI] director, Tasso de Aquino" (*O Imparcial*, May 21, 1961, p. 1).

In Dom Roberto's version, Fernando Cruz, faced with the difficulties imposed by the rubber bosses and traders, abandoned the work and before leaving visited the bishop to explain the situation.

On the evening of May 18, 1961, he went to the prelacy, knowing that this expedition attempt had been made at the bishop's insistence. So, intending to explain his decision, he appeared at the prelacy for a meeting with Dom Rey. I was there too. . . . Fernando declared, "The people here don't want to help, they don't care, and I've no means of continuing the work. So I've already booked my return and tomorrow I leave for Brasília, I'm leaving." Faced with this dilemma, Dom Rey assembled all of the priests, who were already on the premises, and proposed, "This is the situation: we can't agree to the massacre. We know that if Fernando Cruz abandons the work, the expedition to wipe out this people will go ahead. We can't agree to this. So even if we have to sell this prelacy, sell the church, sell everything, we must undertake this pacification. We can't agree to the annihilation of this people. So let's see what we can do." Everyone agreed that everything possible had to be done. But how? Nobody knew. Then Dom Rey said to Fernando, "We cannot allow the massacre of this people; if the prelacy assumes responsibility for the contact work to save them, will you agree to work with us? Forget the government and the SPI: let's save the Pakaa Nova people." (Dom Roberto 1993)

This was how the prelacy became involved in the expedition. As its representative, the church sent the then Father Roberto, who left his work as a teacher in the interior of São Paulo to place himself at the disposal of the bishop, Dom Rey. Events unfolded very quickly since on May 20, 1961, just two days after the meeting between Fernando Cruz and the bishop, the expedition left Guajará-Mirim for the Pacaás Novos River, and from there to the Negro River, in a large boat owned by the Sistema de Navegação do Guaporé. As a result, preparations were made hastily, both in terms of purchasing supplies—bought on credit by the prelacy, according to Dom Roberto—and recruiting the team. This haste was explained not only by the imminence of an armed attack against the Indians but also because the river levels would soon be too low for navigation by large boats. Notably this expedition completely ignored the local SPI, and according to Dom Roberto (*Lettre d'Amazonie*, n. 33, 1970, 6), the head of the RI, Alberico Soares Pereira, did everything possible to impede the voyage. Naturally they wanted to leave as soon as possible and we can surmise that a religious conflict was also in play: this was the prelacy's chance to curtail the activities of the NTM missionaries—with whom Inspector Alberico maintained a close alliance—among the Wari'. This became more clearly apparent later with the visit of that inspector, accompanied by a missionary, to the expedition's encampment on the Negro River.

Most of the expedition members were apparently recruited in the street. A news report published by *O Imparcial*, dated May 21, 1961, states that the expedition included the SPI officer Gilberto Gama—who either arrived from Brasília or was already working in the region—and Rui Figueiredo, from the newspaper *Diários Associados*, along with another forty men. According to the newspaper, everyone was carefully examined by army doctors and a dentist. But in reality there was no time for any medical checks, as Valdemar "Kabixi," who took part in the expedition, told me. He added that the rubber boss Manuel Lucindo allowed several of his men to take part in the team: "Alexandre Peres, Miguel Lara, as I recall. Manuel de Brito. I know he sent a large contingent of people to help in the expedition. The people from Tanajura went (the OroNao' of the Whites), as well as those who Fernando Cruz managed to assemble. In all, there were sixty 'civilized' people on this expedition" (Valdemar 1993).

As well as people, the boat set out laden with supplies: food for the expedition members and presents for the Indians.

"We knew that the Pacas Novos River level falls during the dry season. Navigation would become impossible. And the forecast was a minimum of six months, or more, to attempt contact. We had no idea where we would be heading. So we had to take supplies for at least May to January, when the rains would arrive, the river level would rise, and we could return to Guajará. So Dom Rey bought enough food for this period and the number of men who . . ."

"And presents for the Indians?" I asked.

"Yes. Axes, scythes, and tools. Also, well, Fernando Cruz believed greatly in glass things. Trinkets. There was enough." (Dom Roberto 1993)

THE JOURNEY

The boat's departure was watched by the Guajará-Mirim authorities and a large crowd. Given the infamous ferocity of the Wari', everyone was extremely doubtful about the success of the expedition.

I can't say I wasn't scared . . . Look, to give you an idea: when we set out from Guajará's port, on May 20 [1961], at about three in the afternoon, a crowd turned up on the shore. There was the judge, the mayor, the boat company commander: all of Guajará's authorities were there. Dom Rey. People could be heard saying: poor folk, not one of them will return. It's a suicide expedition. We left with this impression. Who knew? What Indians there had met any of us? How would we communicate with them? Nobody knew. None of us knew a word of the people's language. (Dom Roberto 1993)

That night the boat arrived at the Tanajura post on the Pacaás Novos. They asked the head of the post, Josias Batista, to allow some of the already contacted OroNao' men to assist the expedition. A report by Josias, dated June 30, indicates that thirty-six Indians from Tanajura accompanied Inspector Fernando Cruz to help establish contact on the Negro River. According to Dom Roberto, however, Josias received orders from Inspector Alberico to avoid any collaboration with the expedition and not release any Indians.

> It was Josias who told us, "Look, I can't let anyone go because I've been given orders to the contrary, indeed threatened with dismissal if I help you. But there are some families along the river, on the seringal of Dona Chiquinha and others, especially those living along the river shore. These people don't depend on us, so, if they agree to travel upriver with you, I'm not responsible." So we set off there. We arrived at this seringal, disembarked and contacted these people; they accepted. There were three families: husband, wife, and some children; not many children, but a few. In any case, ten people in total. We took all of them in the boat, since we couldn't leave the women there on the shore. (Dom Roberto 1993)

The Wari' families set off with a boat full of unknown whites to meet people whom they knew existed but had not seen for a long time. As in the pacification on the Laje River, the desire of these OroNao' to be in contact with whites and to use their resources to encounter other Wari' is surprising. As we shall see, the same happened later with the OroWaram, OroWaram-Xijein, and OroMon who agreed to accompany Gilberto Gama, traveling with him from the Laje for the Negro River.

An article by Dom Roberto on the Negro River contact, written in 1970, evokes the Wari's almost uncontained desire to travel with the whites. On arriving at Dona Chiquinha's seringal, Fernando Cruz asked to speak to a man called Rui Caxi, whom he presumed to be the chief of the Indians based there. Fernando invited him to "help us contact the wild Indians," but he refused, saying he no longer trusted whites. Fernando then demonstrated his authority over his men, shouting at them and promising that anyone who mistreated any Indian would be shot. This, Dom Roberto wrote, was enough to convince Rui Caxi of the seriousness of these whites and agree to the invitation. What most interests us, though, is what ensued: "Ten minutes later, all of the Indians, including the women, were on the boats. Inconsolable with this mass exodus, which deprived her of an extremely cheap 'workforce,' Dona Chiquinha begged Fernando, already on his boat, to leave her at least one Indian woman. 'Choose,' replied Fernando. But none wished to remain" (*Lettre d'Amazonie*, n. 33, 1970, 6).

During a second meeting with Dom Roberto, in 1995, I took the chance to ask him directly about the Wari''s ready acceptance of the invitation to travel up the Negro River. He replied, "They immediately agreed to go. The whites wanted to leave the women, but all of them had to go together. They were excited!"

Xijan, an OroNao' of the Whites man who accompanied Fernando Cruz, described the invitation in his account of the Negro River expedition, revealing that their interest had been to meet those he called "our people."

"'Let's go, let's see the Wari,'" the whites said to us. 'Okay!' we replied."

"Why didn't you refuse?" I asked.

"We wanted to gather together and bring back our people." (Xijan 1995)

On May 23, the large boat reached the Boa Vista ranch, close to the mouth of the Negro River and from there turned back. The expedition members journeyed up the Negro River in small canoes, transporting the supplies in small batches. After a series of forest encampments, on May 26 they reached an abandoned house at a former seringal on the left shore of the Negro River, a short distance below the mouth of the Ocaia.[3] They made this their base camp, naming it the Dom Rey Camp. The Wari' did not stay with the whites—I am unsure who made this choice—and built their houses about 100 meters from the base. In his article of 1970, Dom Roberto mentions an interesting occurrence on the first night they were camped in the forest. The OroNao' of the Whites sang, apparently *tamara* music, revealing their wish to turn the whites camped there into foreigners, at least momentarily. "Before we slept, the Indians on the expedition offered us a serenade of singing and dancing, to which we were invited and which we accepted much to their joy" (*Lettre d'Amazonie*, n. 33, 1970, 7).

On May 27, Bishop Dom Rey arrived at the base camp and reported that the SPI inspector Alberico was furious about the expedition, organized as though he did not exist. Two days later, they were visited by the mayor of Guajará-Mirim and a telegraphist who brought an antenna for the radio. Dom Roberto explained to me that during this time he had asked some OroNao' of the Whites to travel to Koxain, the abandoned village already located. The Indians refused to go, saying they were afraid of attacks from the "wild Indians," confirming that there was a climate of war. This will become evident in the accounts of Manim (from the OroNao' of the Whites' group) and the OroNao' of the right bank. While the OroNao' of the Whites wanted to encounter foreigners—"our people," as Xijan said—they knew that, at least initially, they would be meeting enemies. Their allies at that moment—those with whom they related as foreigners—were the whites. We can also imagine that although the warfare encounter frightened them, it also excited them, especially since their alliance with the powerful whites meant that they were well armed for war.

On June 2, the course of events was suddenly changed with the unexpected arrival of Inspector Alberico, accompanied by the American missionary Moreno, the army doctor Duarte, and some OroNao' from Tanajura—including the son of Xijan, one of the expedition members. According to Dom Roberto, Alberico's intention was to interrupt the team's work and force them to return. However, all of the expedition members defended Fernando Cruz, forcing the visitors to withdraw "head between their legs" (*Lettre d'Amazonie*, n. 33, 1970, 10). Xijan's son told his father that Alberico had planned to go to the Laje River and, from there, cross the Ouro Preto River along with some already contacted Indians and reach the source of the Ocaia, contacting the isolated Indians before the expedition. It was only then that Fernando Cruz's team learned that the missionaries and the SPI had already established peaceful contact with the Indians of the Laje. Determined not to relinquish their superiority on the Negro River—and clearly revealing that their humanitarian and selfless concern for the Indians was mixed with political and religious competition with the NTM—Gilberto Gama, Fernando Cruz, and Dom Roberto returned to Guajará-Mirim with the idea of carrying out Alberico's plan before him.

Leaving Guajará-Mirim, Gilberto Gama headed to the Laje River, taking five men from the OroNao' of the Whites' group as interpreters (one of them Manim). There they met people from the OroWaram, OroWaramXijein, and OroMon subgroups who, learning about the expedition's objective, informed them that the Ouro Preto was untraversable at that time of year because the river level was still very high, and expressed their interest in traveling with them to the Negro River. Gilberto Gama therefore returned to Guajará-Mirim with around thirty Indians from the Laje, including men, women, and children: "The town's entire population lined up to see and embrace them. . . . Timid and wary at first, they quickly succumbed to the human warmth surrounding them and agreed to demonstrate their archery skills and dances" (*Lettre d'Amazonie*, n. 33, 1970, 10).

Dom Roberto told me that once in Guajará-Mirim they had to find a way of taking all of the Indians to the Negro River: "So from there we boarded all these people, all of whom wanted to journey upriver. We had to find a boat for all of them: women, children, everyone" (Dom Roberto 1993).

In the other interview, Dom Roberto provided more detail about this episode. Gilberto Gama, learning that it would be impossible to cross the Ouro Preto to reach the Ocaia by foot, had decided to return.

> "But then the entire group [of Indians from the Laje] insisted on taking part. . . . What could he do? Gilberto brought all of them to Guajará . . ."
>
> "Why did the Indians so quickly want to go? Why did they want to join the contact expedition?" I asked.
>
> "It's interesting. In principle, I would say they were all eager for this contact. That's my impression. Because faced by the threat [from whites] and everything . . . I don't know . . . it became a party for them." (Dom Roberto 1995)

Like the OroNao' of the Whites, the Wari' of the Laje were immediately enthused by the idea of encountering other Wari'. The difference is that the Wari' of the Laje had never at any moment broken their relations with the OroNao' of the right bank. For example, one of the OroMon men joining the expedition had lived with these OroNao' for a while, precisely at Koxain,[4] and had returned to his own lands just before the arrival of the whites for the contact on the Laje. Hence the Wari' of the Laje seem to have been motivated not by the desire to renew relations, like the OroNao' of the Whites, but simply to meet their kin, to use the "lift" provided by the whites to reach them quickly. The accounts also suggest that they liked the prospect of being able to give their kin coveted objects such as metal tools. This would allow them to greet the foreign Wari' in an advantageous position as givers of goods and allies of the whites, making them powerful and feared and enabling them to intimidate the foreigners who were, in fact, enemies who were tamed but always ready to attack.

This group left the Laje already contaminated by diseases, since the epidemics had started there. Those who were healthy may have been contaminated by the whites from Guajará-Mirim who went to visit them at the prelacy. They left the town for the Negro River without receiving any kind of medication. Documents of the SPI mention the health situation of the Indians who took part in the expedition. One of the documents, dated June 10, 1961, states that Gilberto Gama had returned from the Laje bringing twenty-two "wild Indians," including women and children, and that some of them were sick, probably from measles. It adds that more than 100 sick Indians had stayed in the malocas and that the next day Gilberto Gama would leave for the Negro River with the twenty-two Indians from the Laje. Eleven days later, eight of these Indians, by now ill, were forced to return to Guajará-Mirim.[5]

THE ENCOUNTER ACCORDING TO DOM ROBERTO
GOMES DE ARRUDA

On June 25, 1961, some expedition members left the base camp on the Negro River, heading toward the Ocaia with the intention of reaching the abandoned village that had already been located and named the "burned village," since two of its five houses had been razed. The Wari' name is Koxain. Here they found two large cylindrical stacks of maize and decided that they should make their definitive encampment in the village, given that the Indians would certainly return there to fetch the maize. The OroNao' of the Whites women and children, as well as the recently arrived OroWaram, OroWaramXijein, and OroMon families, remained at the Negro River camp where most of the supplies were stored. Fernando Cruz, Dom Roberto, Gilberto Gama, and Antônio Costa, with men from the OroNao' of the Whites, OroWaram, and OroMon, reached a spot on the right shore of the Ocaia River, below Koxain, and camped there, identifying the location as "Camp 26," a reference to the date on which the process of contact was initiated, the twenty-sixth of June.

From Camp 26, Dom Roberto and Antônio Costa, along with some Oro-Nao' men, journeyed up the Ocaia with the intention of clearing the river to allow the transportation of equipment in canoes. Close to Koxain, one of the Indians showed Dom Roberto leaves on the ground arranged as a seat, indicating that uncontacted Wari' had recently passed by. They followed the path taken by the Indians and discovered that it led directly to Koxain. Arriving there, they found the village empty.

> So we reached the village. Very cautiously, we entered. Nobody was there, but many people had passed through. He [the OroNao' of the Whites man] told me, "Judging by the volume of maize taken, a lot of people passed through today." Well, we didn't wish to wait there too, since it was risky. We took a little maize, ate, and then headed back to our camp. . . . On

arrival, I encountered Costa and another companion [who were] terrified, telling me, "Look, there are Indian tracks everywhere. We spotted on the shores of the river that they passed by a short while ago, since the water is still cloudy, but we couldn't see anyone." "Well, we're being followed then. But in that case, given that they haven't attacked us yet, they're probably not that aggressive. But let's clear the undergrowth here anyway and make our camp right here next to the river bank. The other side of the river is flooded. Nobody will arrive from the other shore because the water there is fairly deep. Let's stay by the shore." (Dom Roberto 1993)

The following day, Dom Roberto and the others returned to Koxain and hung up "a small new aluminum kettle that we brought, plus a new machete." They traveled along the shore of the Ocaia to where they had left the canoe. On arriving they met Gilberto Gama, who had come upriver to tell them what had happened that morning close to Camp 26.

Early morning they sent a canoe . . . Our arrangement was to have an Indian alongside always to be able to communicate. As we had various, each small group that left had to have an Indian in it. So Xijan, who's here at Sotério [present Wari' village], went with this group, if I'm not mistaken, The pilot was Joaquim [white] and at the prow was . . . I don't remember who . . . a young man . . . paddling. They were heading downriver and, some twenty or so meters from the camp, the tents, they heard. It was fairly dark still. They heard the twang of a bow from the other shore, the left bank of the river, and the whoosh of an arrow. Nobody knew who it was aimed at, so everyone ducked. Joaquim flung himself backward and [the arrow] hit him . . . in the left arm, I think. He grabbed the arrow and immediately fell in the water. . . . And then Xijan, [who was sitting] in front, stood up and began to shout to the assailants. They were startled, hearing someone speak their own language, claiming to be their brother, and so on, a friend. Scared, they gathered their bows and arrows, and ran. The Indians back in the nearby encampment—there were still two or three in the camp—heard the conversation, Xijan's shouting, and understood everything. Immediately they removed their clothes, dived into the water, swam across the river, and ran into the forest to try to encounter the others. He [Xijan] returned, then, with the canoe. . . . Our companions, the whites, said in alarm, "It's pigs, peccaries in the forest." But the Indians understood differently. Well, it was complete confusion. Fernando

Cruz and the rest of the group only understood what had happened after Xijan arrived and the other one presented the arrows. (Dom Roberto 1993)

According to Paletó—who was present at my second interview with Dom Roberto—eight men from the OroNao' of the Whites, as well as Orowao Powa and Orowao Noji, both OroMon, and the Canoé Indian Saul,[6] followed the uncontacted Indians. Dom Roberto then decided to clear a path from where they were staying to the Wari' trail leading to Koxain, facilitating the return of the group that had left in pursuit of the Indians. Late afternoon on the same day (June 26), Orowao Powa came back.

He arrived tired, the poor soul, bringing a disarmed bow, the string dangling from one end, and an arrow snapped in the middle, signifying the suspension of hostilities. He said, "Our entire group went to the others' village, where we talked, and the group sent this message for you to keep. Now . . . they're going to ask the chief to come here to talk to you. They'll only be able to arrive tomorrow afternoon, because the village is far and it will take them all of today to reach there, meaning they will only be able to arrive back here tomorrow late afternoon when the sun is low in the sky." We then understood that, firstly, the hostilities were suspended. This allowed us to relax a bit. Second, they wanted to come to meet us, so we would have to do something to make this contact easier. We therefore decided to go to the village. We sent Fernando Cruz the message along with the bow and arrow . . . I sent it to him that night. Early the next morning he set out with the group from downriver, all the canoes went. . . . So I took a large group of men, myself in the front with the compass, showing the way, and the others clearing the path. By midday we were in the village with the path more or less clear enough to transport our things there. We went there to await the chief on his way to talk to us. At about four in the afternoon our companions arrived first, informing us that the OroNao' chief was due to arrive shortly with his warriors. . . . Indeed, half an hour later we saw a line assembling there by a large clearing on the edge of the village facing the river. A line assembled there with ten to twelve men. Only I didn't know the custom either. I stood there looking, what was I supposed to do? . . . Well, the chief then called one of our group over to ask, "Who's your chief over there? We're here waiting." So they returned with the message and I went there, along with Fernando Cruz, and they showed us who the *taramaxikon* [leader, in Wari'] was. I went over to him and he immediately gave me the bundle of arrows and bow. I took them, not understanding the meaning of the gesture, but accepting them. I handed the bundle to the others, who placed everything in the tent. The other men made the same gesture, handing over all of their weapons. However, they kept some baskets filled with roasted meat and so on . . . but later placed everything on an old bed and regrouped. Well, they started to talk. So we attempted the first contacts, [the first] talks, in the afternoon, via interpreters. It was difficult. (Dom Roberto 1993)

Without qualified interpreters, the whites could only speculate as to what the Wari' were saying (fig. 28). Dom Roberto's description of this moment is interesting:

At first we tried Costinha, Antônio Costa, as an interpreter, but he understood nothing of what Jamain To U was saying. So we called Maxun . . . I don't remember now, but a companion from Tanajura, who had already lived with Costa for some time and understood him well. So, using two interpreters we managed to converse with Jamain To U. He came with two men. The others remained back with our group, while he brought two assistants who remained with him the whole time. We talked throughout the night. The first thing I asked him was permission to stay in the area. . . . After consulting with his companions, Jamain To U replied, "Look, you can stay here, but I can only see armed men. So you're not really displaying . . . You say that you come as friends to help us, to protect us, but I don't see any women or children. So you need to show us your families, your women and children, bring them here. Then you'll show us that you trust us. Only then can you enter our villages, not before. We won't accept that." . . . Well, since we had the Indian women and children at the camp downriver, we immediately sent for their families to come by canoe. They brought them, meaning that all the doors were immediately opened. I also asked him for some guides and companions to help us visit all of the villages, spreading our message of peace. His reply was, "You haven't got the legs for that." And indeed we later discovered it was impossible. "But," he said to me "contact your white chief to ensure that there are no more attacks against us. If they stop, the question of hostilities is over. Now I'll send people to all the OroWari' villages for you. Be reassured, I just need ten days . . . He counted on his hand: *pi'am, pi'am, pi'am* . . . [sleep one night, another, another], *maho'* [enough]. Ten days, or ten sleepovers, and

28. Wari' men with brand-new necklaces. Rio Negro area, 1961.
(Archive of the Guajará-Mirim Prelacy)

he would have contacted all the villages and there would be no more problems with Indian attacks. (Dom Roberto 1993)

THE ENCOUNTER ACCORDING TO THE ORONAO' OF THE
WHITES AND AN OROMON MAN

Xijan, a man from the OroNao' of the Whites subgroup, who was in the ca-
noe when Joaquim was shot with an arrow, began his account by saying that
Fernando Cruz had called him to accompany them to "the OroWaram," after the latter had already established peaceful contact with the whites. From
there they returned to Guajará and proceeded to Tanajura and the Negro
River. For Xijan, the purpose of the journey to the Laje was to summon "the
OroWaram" (a category in which he includes the OroWaramXijein and the
OroMon who arrived in the OroWaram villages to see the whites). As he
continued his account, it became clear that, in his view, the Laje trip preceded the great expedition to the Negro River undertaken in the boat of the
Sistema de Navegação do Guaporé.

Fernando had called us, along with the OroWaram: "Let's go, let's see Wari'." We agreed. We arrived at Tanajura. There were many of us. . . . Arriving at the Negro River, we disembarked from the big boat, which then turned back. The supplies stayed. We unloaded everything and took a 12HP [motor]. . . . We journeyed part way up the river and slept. There was a house built by whites on the Negro River and the leader [Fernando Cruz] told us to stay there. . . . After a while there, Fernando said, "Let's see Wari'." "Okay," we replied. We went. We reached the Ocaia. . . . There we found the OroNao"s maize [at Koxain]. . . . No people; they'd fled. Just the maize. We slept. . . . Elsewhere, on the other shore, the OroNao' who attacked us were sleeping. . . . Well, the next day, the leader [Fernando] told us to hunt. . . . Early in the morning, he sent me off. We went. I paddled behind with Joaquim in the prow. A'ain Kaxun and A'ain Xit Kao Tokwe [the two men who fired the arrows] were already there. They were in the water, very close to ourselves. They struck Joaquim and he fell in the water. I stood up and shouted, "Why are you shooting us? We're OroNao'. Don't be afraid. Don't shoot me," I said to them. "We're not enemies! We're Oro-Nao'!" (Xijan 1995)

Discovering that Joaquim was still alive, Xijan took him to the nearby encampment. There Fernando Cruz told them to pursue the assailants.

"We saw just the bows that they'd left. 'Hurry,' the leader [Fernando] said. Fernando told us to remove our clothing so they would not be scared of us. I, the late Saul [Canoé], Manim, Orowao Toko Jai, and Paulo [all Oro-Nao' of the Whites] went."

"Was this when you encountered Jimon Pan Tokwe?" I asked. [Jimon Pan Tokwe was the first man to be encountered by the "pacifiers."]

"Yes, on the trail. He was running away in fright. Orowao Powa had gone with us too so that they'd recognize him. He had returned just recently from the Negro River area to his house. They were holding festivals. The OroNao' Ni Mon [as the OroNao' of the right bank are known] recognized Orowao Powa. (Xijan 1995)

Xijan's observation reveals the importance attributed to the presence of the Laje River Wari' in this encounter; in contrast to themselves, who had been isolated for decades, the people of the Laje were recognizable to the OroNao' of the Negro River. This may explain an apparent chronological mistake at the beginning of his account: according to Xijan, the trip to the Laje River to call the "OroWaram" to go to the Negro River (noting, incidentally, that Xijan himself took no part in the Laje contact) occurred before the start of the expedition, contradicting the information from Dom Roberto, the SPI documents, and various local news reports. In my view, aware of the importance of the presence of the Laje Wari' in establishing contact, Xijan considered that this episode of pacification did not begin without these Wari'. The contrast with Dom Roberto's description is interesting since, during my first interview, he simply omitted the Laje episode, emphasizing the expedition preparations and the encounter in the "burned village." Dom Roberto was clearly unaware that the OroNao' of the Whites and the OroWaram had a completely different relationship with the OroNao' of the right bank: for the former, they were almost enemies, given the time they had spent apart without contact; for the latter, they were foreigners, Wari', who could be easily recognized.

The episode of the arrow attack is essential for all of the Wari' informants. Furthermore, the OroNao' of the Negro River claim that the whites only managed to find them because they were able to follow the tracks of the men who attacked them. Manim's description is reminiscent of a war account, interspersed with allusions to dead animal prey. He assumed a role as an ally of the whites in opposition to the Wari', a kind of personal assistant to Fernando Cruz. He was also the only one to state openly that he carried a shotgun.

> The next day we went to Koxain on the Ocaia. Miguel, Jorge, and I killed a spider monkey. We slept rough and returned the following day. We killed a guan and ate it. The OroNao' [the uncontacted ones] were already approaching from another direction. Coming, coming. It wasn't even day yet and the leader Fernando said, "Go to the camp and fetch some food!" "Okay" [the Wari' replied]. Xijan, Valdemar "Kabixi" [who denied being in the canoe in his account], Joaquim. . . . They paddled. As they started paddling, Joaquim's arm was struck. . . . He [Joaquim] arrived, shaking heavily. They gave him an injection and medicine to drink. A lot of blood. It hurt. Fernando said to me, "Run to the Wari', Manim. Get the Wari'. The Wari' are arriving." "Okay" [Manim replied]. "Here's the munitions and the shotgun. Remove your shorts and shirt, remove everything." [Manim uttered the latter phrase in Portuguese.] I was left just in my skin. . . .

"Right. Let's go!" We followed them. They [the warriors] had dispersed. We saw only their footprints. (Manim 1993)

Continuing with his account, Manim provided his own version of the subsequent events, describing himself as the effective leader of this encounter, not only as the first person to speak to Jimon (all the other versions state that Jimon recognized and spoke to Orowao Powa [OroMon] first), but also as the organizer of the action.

We were arriving in the village and Jimon Pan Tokwe was running. He was a coinhabitant of Paulo [A'ain Kaxun] and A'ain Xit Kao Tokwe [the OroNao' who had shot the arrow]. He looked back and saw A'am Tara. We got him. A'am Tara and I. We spoke, "We're not enemies. I'm Wari'." "What kind of Wari' are you? What's your name?" "I'm Jimon Pan Tokwe." "Are you OroNao'?" [they asked Jimon]. "We're OroNao'. And you? What type of Wari' are you?" [Jimon asked]. "No, I'm OroEo, my father was OroEo. My father's childhood name was Jao. My father crossed to the other shore and married my mother." "My mother was OroNao'" [Manim said]. "Really? So you're my true kin" [Jimon said]. "Don't be afraid of me, stop trembling. I'm Wari'. This gun I'm carrying belongs to the whites." (Manim 1993)

Xijan's account of the encounter with Jimon emphasizes the presence of the OroMon man, Orowao Powa, who was recognized by Jimon. But Orowao Powa only participated in this first encounter. Having sickened, he returned from Koxain to the whites' camp and was the first to break the news of the peaceful contact. Although I lack his version of events, Dom Roberto's account (see above) puts words into his mouth, I think, by claiming that he said that the chief of the OroNao' would come the next day.

"We arrived at Koxain where their maize was stored. This was when Orowao Powa saw Jimon walking along the path. Jimon looked back. Orowao Powa shouted, 'It's him.' [So the OroNao' of the Whites spoke.] 'Don't be afraid of us, we're OroNao'. We too are true OroNao'. We arrived where the whites live. . . . We too are Wari', we're not enemies. The whites called us earlier; we appeared to them. They told us to do the same with you: "Call your people [win ma']," the whites said about you.' 'Really?' said Jimon. 'Here's an axe, and another.' We gave him axes. 'Let's go,' we said to him. We reached Koxain. There were still pans there that the late

Antônio Costa had hung up. 'Take them! Let's go!' we said to him. Those who had shot at us had fled in fear."

"Where did you go from there?" I asked.

"I think the name was Hwijimain Xitot [actually Terem Matam]. It wasn't far. We crossed the Ocaia, traveling up another river. . . . We arrived close to the house [village] and heard the sound of women crushing maize. Jimon told us to sit on a log and wait for him to speak to the others. (Xijan 1995)

Orowao Noji, an OroMon man present at the encounter with Jimon Pan Tokwe along with Orowao Powa, provided a brief account:

"I was the one who got them. Orowao Powa and I. Just two of us. [. . .] He was very scared, shaking. 'Don't be afraid of us!' He was really frightened."

"Did you look like whites?" I asked.

"We'd already been whites for a long time. We wore clothes." (Orowao Noji 1994)

According to Manim, on arriving at Terem Matam (he recalled the swidden's name clearly), Jimon wanted to enter the village straight away. Manim reminded him of the risks, once again demonstrating that, for Manim, they were at war: "I stopped and said, 'Jimon Pan Tokwe, I can't rush ahead. I'm going to sit down [before reaching the village] so they won't shoot me.' . . . 'Okay,' said Jimon" (Manim 1993).

The men from Terem Matam arrived at the spot where the Wari' were waiting and invited them to enter the village.

Nothing happened until we heard Jamain To U whistling. [Jamain To U was an OroMon man who was living with the OroNao'; he was Paletó's father-in-law]. Then they arrived bringing many arrows. They saw me. They stopped and I said to them, "Come here." They came toward me. "Don't be afraid of us. We're not enemies, we're Wari'. The gun I'm carrying belongs to the whites." "Let's go!" [the inhabitants of Terem Matam said, inviting them to enter the village]. We followed them and arrived. We stopped. "Let's fill the foreigners with maize beer!" said Jamain To U. He filled a pot of beer and we drank it. (Manim 1993)

From the visitors' point of view, they were quickly recognized as foreigners. Indeed, the residents of Terem Matam treated them as such, not only offering them maize beer but also asking them to sing and dance before doing the same.

> "As soon as we arrived, we said to them, 'Come, don't be afraid of us. We're Wari', we're OroNao'. The whites also called us a long time ago. We've been coinhabitants [win ma'] of the whites for ages. That's why we came to call you too. Our shotguns belong to the whites.' All of us had guns. We entered their house. They were afraid. We drank maize beer. Those who had shot at us [the two OroNao' men] still hadn't returned."
>
> "Did you dance tamara?" I asked.
>
> "Songs of the ancient ones. We told them to dance too. They danced. We slept there. Early the next day, we said to them, 'Let's get axes!'" (Xijan 1995)

Manim described in more detail the importance of the music in identifying the strangers as Wari'. Additionally, tracing the names of common kin enabled them to address each other by kin terms, an important gesture among the Wari'.

> The late Manim [one of the just-contacted OroNao'] asked, "What's your father's name?" "My father's childhood name was Jao. He went there [to the other shore of the Pacaás Novos] and began to be called Jimon Maram." "Wow, your father is my true kin! He's my father!" [said Manim]. . . . I drank maize beer until full. I spoke and spoke. When I'd finished, he [the other Manim] asked me, "Do you know how to sing too, my son?" "Of course I know how to sing! I'm Wari'! I'm not an enemy! We dance in our land!" [The narrator sings the music sung on the occasion.] . . . We sang everything and said, "Enough! Let's stop!" "Okay." So they formed a line to dance and sing. (Manim 1993)

Nevertheless, Manim did not feel at ease with these strangers, not even with the man claiming to be his classificatory father. Their efforts to convince the OroNao' they had just met that they were foreigners and kin reflected their awareness that the long period of isolation had transformed them into enemies. "I didn't sleep at all," Manim said. "I kept the shotgun by my side. . . . So my people wouldn't kill me. . . . Dawn came. They gave me maize drink. I spoke to Jamain To U: 'Let's get axes!' . . . We took the path" (Manim 1993).

Accompanying the visitors, some residents of Terem Matam traveled to Koxain, where the whites were already camped waiting for them.

We crossed the Ocaia [Koxain is on the other shore]. We said to them, "Don't be afraid of them. The whites aren't angry." We reached Koxain, where the leader [Fernando Cruz] was. "Here are the Wari'!" we said to him. He was content.... They ate and slept there. The next day, they said, "We're going!" They took many axes and returned home.... The whites were extremely happy. We said to them, "Tell the others to come to fetch axes!" "Okay!" (Xijan 1995)

Manim's account clearly reveals the extent to which he considered himself an ally of the whites. It also illustrates the difference between the way the event was seen by the whites (Dom Roberto) and by the OroNao' of the Whites. (As we shall see below, the OroNao' of the right bank perceived the situation even more differently.)

"We reached Koxain. There were lots of whites there, lots of Bolivians. We arrived. I shouted to Fernando, 'Fernando! I won!' [Manim used the Portuguese verb *ganhei*, as though winning a race: he claims to have been the first to bring the uncontacted Wari'.] There were many whites. I said to them: 'Don't be afraid of them [the whites].' 'Okay.' We sat down.... The OroNao' sat on a log."

"Were they carrying bows and arrows?" I asked.

"They put them down. They received axes, pans, machetes. Everyone took them.... The leader, Fernando, told me to ask the Wari' to sing.... They sang *tamara*.... 'We're on our way,' said the recently contacted OroNao' [the next day]. They took machetes, axes, and pans, and left. A few nights passed and then a large number of people [*wari'*] arrived."

"Did the women come too?" I asked.

"No. Just men." (Manim 1993)

THE ENCOUNTER ACCORDING TO THE ORONAO'
OF THE RIGHT BANK

Jimon Pan Tokwe was an OroWaram man who spent most of his life among the OroNao' of the right bank, eventually dying at the Negro–Ocaia village a few years ago. According to the accounts, he was the first inhabitant of the Negro River area to be encountered by members of the contact expedition. He recounted that his old maize was stored at Koxain (the "burned village"), close to the mouth of the Ocaia. At the time of contact he was living at Terem

Matam, located on an affluent of the right bank of the Ocaia called Tokwa Em, which joins the Ocaia just above Koxain.

One day, after they had finished clearing a swidden at Terem Matam, Jimon and some other men went to Koxain to fetch maize and saw metal objects suspended there: pans, machetes, and axes. They also saw footprints left by the boots of those who had left the tools. They took the objects and left quickly, afraid of being killed. Later, they returned to Koxain and found more objects hanging up.

On returning to Terem Matam, Jimon told everyone what he had seen: the villagers then decided to leave on a war expedition to shoot the whites. They headed toward Koxain, which was not far. On arrival, they spotted various signs of whites, such as boot prints, but also remains of maize cake and other signs typical of the Wari'. According to A'ain Kaxun, an OroNao' man of the right bank, they began to think that these white enemies might be the former OroNao' who had disappeared long ago. Paletó said that they also thought they might have been kin who had been taken by whites and never returned, such as the mother of Mo'am and other women, described in chapter 3. Perhaps they had finally come back: "They had lit a fire, woven baskets and sewn together leaves for maize cake. They made white maize flour. There were leftovers of maize. 'Hmm, are the whites like that? They seem like Wari'! Perhaps they are Wari'!' Perhaps the OroNao' have arrived. . . . But one thing alone made us think they were whites: a strong smell of clothing" (A'ain Kaxun 1993).

That day they slept in the forest, fearing that the whites could surprise them at Koxain. The next day they followed the intruders' tracks and heard the sound of a tree being felled. Then they heard someone shout a name: "A'am Tara!" the name of one of the OroNao' of the Whites who was there. This was followed by the typical Wari' reply to this kind of call: "Ha?" They again wondered about the identity of these people: " 'Hmm, are there enemies who call themselves A'am Tara?' So we said, 'Perhaps they're the former OroNao' " (Paletó 1995).

Obviously this interpretation may be have been made later, after discovering that those present were the OroNao' from the other shore of the Pacaás Novos. However, as we saw in earlier chapters, these OroNao' were effectively undergoing a process of "enemization" due to their long period of isolation. The doubts were not exactly over whether the intruders were whites or Wari', since it was clear that they were not full Wari', their kin or foreigners. What they were actually questioning was the ontology of these enemies-whites, since they perceived that they were enemies with something familiar about them. Given that the only Wari' who were being "enemized" were the OroNao' of the Whites—and those who had been abducted and had disappeared—they may well have made these observations during the encounter itself. The transformation of the OroNao' into enemies—and the enemies still left were the whites—was a possibility the Wari' probably considered right away. The flip side becomes clear in Manim's account cited above; armed with a shotgun, he says that he spent the night awake, afraid of being attacked.

The group of Terem Matam men hidden in the forest were stalking the whites-OroNao', waiting for the ideal moment to shoot them. A'am Tara (OroNao' of the Whites) would have been one of their victims, but he moved too quickly: "Then came A'am Tara, Antônia's older brother. The whites had told them to cut firewood. He came. 'Teu, teu, teu' [sound of wood being chopped]. He carried an axe. He was completely white, wearing clothes. He didn't look anything like the Wari'. He was fully dressed. He was white!" (A'ain Kaxun 1993).

A'ain Kaxun probably did not reach this conclusion merely because of the clothes, although clothing notably played an important role in the identification. Following Wari' logic, A'am Tara was white since, being neither kin or a foreigner, he could only be an enemy. Why else would he be in the company of their enemies? Every coinhabitant, as we know, is an equal.

The warriors were unable to attack that day and slept nearby. They were animated. Jimon Pan Tokwe recounted that at night they sang and danced, strumming their bows. The next day, they crossed the Ocaia again and waited. A lot of the men became frightened and abandoned the attack. Only the young A'ain Kaxun and A'ain Xit Kao Tokwe remained. At that moment, someone ordered the OroNao' of the Whites to leave in search of something (Xijan says they told them to hunt). They left by canoe.

> They came. Joaquim was in the middle. In the prow was Xijan, paddling. He was using a hat and good clothing. They approached . . . Xijan came into view. We stood up. We were going to shoot that Xijan, a tall enemy. Then A'ain Xit Kao Tokwe said to me, "Older brother, let's shoot the one in the middle without any clothes." I stopped pointing the bow in Xijan's direction. Xijan passed by and then another [also] in the middle [Xijan's son, according to Jimon] and then came Joaquim. My bow string caught A'ain Xit Kao Tokwe, who was also aiming to shoot, meaning I missed and

29. A'ain Kaxun (Paulo) makes a rubber drum using an aluminum
pan as its base. Rio Negro–Ocaia, 2003.

the arrow hit here [on the arm]. A'ain's arrow only cut [the air]. Had A'ain
been lower down I would have struck him [Joaquim] here [in the chest]
and he would have died quickly. The arrow only cut him. . . . He held on
to the canoe hull [screening himself] so I couldn't shoot again. He cried
from the sting of the wound in the cold water. We fled. . . . The OroNao'
[of the Whites] whistled to us, shouting, "Uuuu, we're Wari', we're Wari'.
We're OroNao'!" We understood nothing. (A'ain Kaxun 1993) (fig. 29)

The warriors ran to join the other men waiting some distance away. They
thought they had killed the enemy. They waited a while for the whites to
leave so they could enter their houses and take the tools.

During this interval, Xijan stopped shouting and went to the encampment where the leader Fernando Cruz was located. He told them to leave
immediately in pursuit of the uncontacted Wari'. "'Run after them. Get your
people quickly!' the leader said" (A'ain Kaxun 1993). "'Get the Wari'!' said
the leader [Fernando Cruz]. 'Don't shoot them. Just get them!'" (Jimon
1995).

When he stood up, A'ain Kaxun saw the enemies approaching, many of
them armed with guns. He decided to run away. The enemies ran after him,
following his footprints.[7] At that moment, Jimon explained, he slipped in

mud and fell, meaning he lost touch with the others, who continued on to Koxain and waited for him. Meanwhile, Jimon took another path leading to Koxain and met Orowao Powa, an OroMon man: "I entered the forest. Then Orowao Powa arrived. 'I stopped there because of the enemy! He went to the village!' [said Jimon]. I thought it was one of my companions. He looked at me in surprise. He recognized me, but I didn't recognize him. 'It's me, my father. The whites called the OroNao'" (Jimon 1992).

Jimon described this episode in another interview:

> "I saw some leaves moving in the forest. I looked back and saw Orowao Powa. He saw me: 'Is it you, [classificatory] father?' 'It's me.' 'The Oro-Nao' of the Whites called us and brought us. We went to the whites. We came with them.' . . . His companions were waiting. He went to them and shouted, 'He's the one! Go!' My [classificatory] younger brother, Tem Paxi, my younger brother, Paton. They came. . . ."
>
> "Did you recognize them?" I asked.
>
> "Yes. They lived here." (Jimon 1995)

Paletó explained that Orowao Powa had lived for a long time among the OroNao'. He had eaten maize in Koxain and as soon as he returned to his land, "the whites got him." However, Jimon did not recognize the OroNao' of the Whites who approached later, saying, "I'm Xijan"; "I'm Manim. I'm OroEo. My father was called Jimon Maram." They gave him lots of machetes and axes. According to Jimon, the Wari' who had arrived were already coughing and sick, and asked to be taken to Terem Matam, the village where he lived. Close to the village, they stopped when Jimon heard the sound of his wives playing flutes. He asked the visitors to wait in the forest.

> Late in the afternoon, I heard my wives playing small flutes. They were doing this so we would kill game for them. "Sit here! They might be scared of you. I'll speak to them" [Jimon said to the visitors]. I left the OroNao' and went to them. Awo Kamip [a man of about fifty today] was a child. . . . I arrived. "Give me an axe, Father!" Awo Kamip said to me. I threw some . . . and said to them, "We shot the OroNao' of the Whites. I brought the Oro-Nao'. They don't look good. Their hair is cut strangely. They're waiting over there. Jamain To U [Jimon's brother-in-law] whistled. . . . They appeared. They arrived [in the village]. "Give them maize beer!" They drank it. At nightfall, Jamain To U told them to sing *tamara*. They sang and sang, then stopped. We talked among ourselves. "I'm OroEo," Manim said. "I'm

Xijan," Xijan said. They slept. Next day, they said, "We're going!" And I began to cough. The sickness had got me. "Let's get their axes!" [said the men of Terem Matam]. They took baskets. Those who were well said, "Let's get the whites' things!" They went. I stayed. The sickness didn't get me lightly. (Jimon 1995)

As soon as the OroNao' entered Terem Matam, Xiemain—Paletó's younger brother—ran toward a nearby creek where women and men were weir fishing, meeting them on their way back to the village. After telling them what was happening, the men decided to kill these intruders. One of the men was Paletó.

We were coming back. As we were arriving, Xiemain heard us playing flutes and went running to meet us. Your father [Paletó was addressing me] Manim [of the right bank] shouted, "Let's shoot the whites! They're crazy!" . . . Your father Manim and I rushed off. When we reached our port, where we go to bathe, we saw them. They were sitting in the men's house. They looked horrible with those haircuts. . . . "Come here," they said to me. I decided not to shoot them. I walked over. They said, "We're Wari'. We're OroNao'. Don't be afraid of us." (Paletó 1995)

Paletó added that the OroNao' had said, "We're completely white! We're coinhabitants [win ma'] of the whites!"—making a direct association between coinhabitance and identity. But they also said they were Wari' and soon started to trace common kin:

When my late mother arrived, she asked him [Xijan], "What's your mother's name?" "Toko Pi'am is my grandmother's name, my mother's mother" [Xijan replied]. "Hey! It's our mother! So I should call you sister's son! I would call your mother older sister," my mother said to Xijan. "Wow, you're my mother?" "Yes, I am!" He [Xijan] said to his sons, "This is your maternal grandmother, boys!" "Wow! Give us maize beer, maternal grandmother! Toast maize for us, maternal grandmother!" "Okay." My mother toasted maize and gave it to them. She gave them Brazil nuts. (Paletó 1995)

Paletó provided an interesting description of how Jamain To U, his father-in-law, asked the visitors to sing tamara: "Do you know how to sing? Perhaps you're whites!" Afterward, referring to Saul, a Canoé Indian (naked like the others), he asked, "And this one, doesn't he sing?" The OroNao' replied, "No, this one turned completely white."

Those who had shot Joaquim had yet to return. Hidden in the forest, close to Terem Matam, they heard voices and other sounds, and thought that the whites were celebrating killing the Wari'. Those from the house shouted to them, "A'ain Kaxun! You shot the OroNao'! . . . The OroNao' returned [from the opposite shore of the Pacaás Novos]!" They went to the water's edge cautiously, afraid that the warriors would mistake them for enemies and shoot. After the men left Terem Matam for Koxain, Jimon met the warriors: he told them that those they had wanted to kill were the former OroNao' and took them to Terem Matam. There they waited for the men to return from Koxain.

The latter had continued to Koxain with the specific objective, as Jimon expounded, of obtaining the metal tools being distributed by the whites. According to Paletó, the group included himself, Jamain To U, Wem Tawinain, Manim, and some boys: "There weren't many of us!" he said. As they were arriving, they heard a gunshot (a man from Koxain was hunting) and they became afraid. Xijan then decided to shoot in the air again to signal their approach.

> Xijan shouted, "I'm going to shoot for them [to hear]!" He took his shotgun. Manim gathered us: "Come quickly! Don't be afraid! He won't shoot you, he'll shoot over there." We covered our ears. "Stay still!" "Pou!" [sound of gunshot]. "Let's go," he said to us. We were carrying maize cake. They had asked us to make some to give to them. They like maize cake. . . . Your father Manim [of the right bank] carried a basket; Jamain To U carried another to bring back machetes. . . . "Don't be afraid of the whites," they said to us. "There are lots of them." We walked along the path. (Paletó 1995)

Paletó described the moment of entering Koxain (figs. 30, 31, and 32).

> We had almost arrived when Manim called to us: "Come here. They're going to shoot. They usually shoot when Wari' are caught." Manim gathered us and the OroNao' [of the Whites] fired. The people from the house shot too: "Pou! Pou! Pou!" "Don't be afraid!" "We're not afraid," we replied. "Come!" The priest was standing there. Fernando too. . . . They stood still, looking at us. We weren't feeling brave; we were scared of them. . . . We looked at the glasses covering their faces. "Come!" the white man said.

30. Dom Roberto Gomes de Arruda with three Wari' men.
The man on the far right is Jamain To U; the man in the
middle is Paletó (his son-in-law). Rio Negro area, 1961.
(Archive of the Guajará-Mirim Prelacy)

31. Dom Roberto Gomes de Arruda with the same three Wari'
men pretending to shoot arrows (Paletó in the middle).
Rio Negro area, 1961. (Archive of the Guajará-Mirim Prelacy)

32. The SPI officer Fernando Cruz with the same three men. The man on the far
right is Jamain To U; the one in the middle is Paletó. Rio Negro area, 1961.
Lettre d'Amazonie, n. 33, 1970.

"The whites are calling you" [the OroNao' of the Whites translated]. . . . We went across to Fernando. The OroNao' [of the Whites] said to us, "This is the leader." We spoke to him, "Are you well, leader?" "*Awi na, awi na*" [good, good], he said to us [in Wari']. We went over to the priest: "We're well [or: "we're good!"]." "Euo, euo, euo!" [priest's unintelligible speech]. . . . He embraced us. He was happy with us. "Stop doing that" [sound of bow firing an arrow]. "Stop shooting!" they're saying to you [the OroNao' of the Whites translated]. "It's over, leader!" [the OroNao' of the Whites reassured Fernando Cruz]. They took all of us by the hand and said, "Come! Sit here." He [Fernando] walked away to fetch axes. . . . All of us received them. . . . We slept. The next day, we left. (Paletó 1995)

Recalling Dom Roberto's claim that Jamain To U had presented himself as the chief and that the axes had been delivered to him, I asked Paletó whether Jamain To U alone had received the axes.

"We all received them. I, Jamain To U, Wem Tawinain, Manim."

"Did Jamain To U act as a leader?" I asked.

"No, he wasn't the leader. The whites were happy with all of us. . . . They gave us axes, machetes. I took an axe, then another, and stopped. If I'd taken a basket . . . Only Jamain To U had one. They gave him lots. They gave and gave. . . . Manim had a basket too and he took away a lot. We could only take what we could carry in our hands. (Paletó 1995)

Jamain To U was taken to be the chief because he craved tools and took the initiative, placing them in his basket, leading the whites to surmise that he would distribute them among his people like a chief. Precisely the opposite happened. On arriving back at Terem Matam, meeting the warriors who had by now returned, Jamain To U refused to give them any of his tools. He said, "They're my tools." The men said, "We got them from the whites. These whites of the OroNao' are not thinking straight!"

Paletó also denied that they had talked all night when they stayed for the first time at Koxain, contradicting Dom Roberto. "We lay down and slept," he told me.

When they returned to Terem Matam and told everyone about the surfeit of tools among the whites, the other men wanted to go. A'ain Kaxun said that they had initially been frightened, presuming that the whites would avenge the attack on Joaquim. The OroNao' of the Whites came to call him, telling him not to be afraid and that the whites wanted to see him. He went. When he arrived, they led him to meet Joaquim, who treated him as a "younger brother."

> "I reached the whites. 'How are you?' [phrase spoken in Portuguese], the whites asked. 'You shot your older brother,' they told me. At night, he arrived, carrying his arm in a sling of red cloth. 'Where's my brother?' [Joaquim asked]. 'Here's your younger brother!' 'Ah! How are you?' he asked me. 'You shot me, younger brother. Look at your arrow [wound] here! It hurt a lot, younger brother. I'm not angry with you anymore.'"
>
> "But you didn't understand what he was saying, did you?" I asked.
>
> "No, I didn't. The OroNao' told me what he was saying." (A'ain Kaxun 1993)

A'ain Kaxun added that he never returned to Terem Matam. He stayed at Koxain and "became used" to the whites. He said that after a while the Wari' who had been at the "Dom Rey Camp" on the Negro River arrived. Later all of the OroNao' of the right bank gradually arrived.

According to Paletó, the people from Terem Matam and Hwijimain Xitot arrived. I asked him whether there were any other villages inhabited by the OroNao' at that time and he replied that the OroNao' were few in number, many of them having been killed by the whites: "We weren't many. If the whites hadn't killed so many of us . . . It's only now, after we came to live near the whites, that we have become many. Look how many people there are!"[8]

SICKNESS

Those who went to Koxain and returned to Terem Matam became ill and contaminated the others. As I mentioned earlier, Jimon quickly perceived the state of health of the OroNao' and OroMon who approached him, and he felt ill when the OroNao' were still at Koxain. Paletó had the following to say about the diseases:

> As soon as I arrived, the fever began. "I've got a fever!" Jamain To U was also feverish. Everyone had fever. . . . The next day, the OroNao' [of the Whites] came: "Come quickly!" They rounded us up and took us back [to Koxain]. . . . Everyone went. My mother, Xin Tao, A'ain Tain, and Orowao Pijiman stayed. . . . They were reluctant. "We don't want to go! We'll stay near the maize!" All of them became ill and died. I went so that my children would live. Xijan [OroNao' of the Whites] had said to me, "Run

with our daughters, younger brother!"... "Let's go!" Jamain Jiparai [Oro-
Nao' of the Whites] said to me. He pushed me forward. "My throat is hurting! I'm going to die!" [Paletó said].... Had we been able to walk.... The
whites came and carried us along the path. We arrived at Koxain where we
received injections. We were afraid of the injections. "We don't want any
needles!" The OroNao' said, "Look! This is what enabled us to stay alive."
We saw [the OroNao' of the Whites took injections so they could see]....
I was brave. They pierced me, pierced my backside. They pierced To'o Xak
Wa [Paletó's wife]. Syrup for our coughing. We started dying as soon as we
arrived. (Paletó 1995)

According to Dom Roberto, the flu outbreak began after the SPI inspector Alberico's second visit to the encampment, bringing contaminated
people, about ten days after the first encounter with the OroNao' on the
Ocaia River.

[Alberico] went to the Ocaia. They spent a night there and, unfortu-
nately—they didn't know, I've no wish to blame anyone, it was an accident—the pilot or, who knows, one of his companions must have had flu.
And our Indians are very curious. As we were at peace, they began to arrive, to visit. Just one night spent there, and that was it: contamination.
Within a few days practically the whole tribe was suffering from flu. Then
the problem became really serious. (Dom Roberto 1993)

Clearly, though, the first large wave of alien pathogenic agents appeared
earlier: if not with the members of the Fernando Cruz expedition, then certainly with the Indians of the Laje, since they left there already sick. According to Dom Roberto, the outbreak of diseases was expected, but the number
of Indians inhabiting the region was underestimated: "We had initially calculated a population of around three hundred people. But with Jamain To
U's information, we concluded that the tribe numbered approximately three
thousand in total" (Dom Roberto 1993).

Undoubtedly this calculation was exaggerated: judging by the genealogical data, the OroNao' population, combined with that of the OroEo and
OroAt, did not exceed 300 people.[9] But whatever the case, the problem was
the lack of medication. Dom Roberto, in 1995, recounted that he had returned to Guajará-Mirim to try to obtain new supplies but had to wait until
the start of August. On August 8 he and his companions embarked for Ocaia
with "the medications and more provisions, milk, maize flour."

Despite the high number of deaths, particularly among those who refused to go to Koxain or returned quickly to their villages, those who received treatment were soon cured. A'ain Kaxun said he arrived at Koxain and
decided to stay primarily because the OroNao' of the Whites warned them
that they would die should they return to their villages. Along with the fear
of diseases, people also stayed at Koxain because of the good treatment they
received: the whites ordered the OroNao' of the Whites and the Wari' of the
Laje to clear swiddens and hunt for them. Additionally, supplies arrived directly from Guajará-Mirim. A'ain Kaxun mentioned an airplane that landed
at Koxain bringing, among other things, an enormous box of jerked beef. For
the OroNao' of the Negro River, even those who were sick, the experience
may well have reminded them of visiting kin in other villages, when they
were generously fed by their hosts.

> The whites said to me, "Stay with the Wari' and hunt for them so they
> can eat and live." . . . I killed capuchin monkey and they ate. . . . Antônio
> [Costa] gave them injections. They ate. I never stopped. Every day I went
> hunting. We never tired of walking. I found peccaries and killed them:
> one, two, three, four. (Manim 1995)

> Only we cleared swiddens, the ones who had got [contacted] them. They
> [the uncontacted Wari'] didn't plant anything. We planted for them. . . .
> They told us to hunt for them too. "Kill fish for them!" So we did. (Orowao
> Noji 1994)

> Koxain was a large swidden, a large swidden belonging to the whites.
> We didn't plant anything. They planted for us. It was good. "Plant for the
> Wari'!" [the whites said]. (Paletó 1994)

Those who suffered most from the epidemics in this region were not the
OroNao', who were treated relatively quickly, but the OroEo and the OroAt
who became contaminated simultaneously with the former, but remained in
the forest, far from the whites and their medicines.

CONTACT WITH THE OROEO AND OROAT

Soon after the expedition reached Terem Matam, a man called Maxun
Taparape traveled to the OroEo and OroAt villages to tell them what had
happened and call them to fetch the abundant metal tools. Paletó said that

his coinhabitants suggested he should go. A'ain Kaxun claimed that it had been the whites and the OroNao' of the Whites who told them to advise the other Wari' living in the region. However, everyone is unanimous in stating that Maxun Taparape acted improperly, since he arrived shouting nonsense and terrified the Wari'.

> He traveled far, all the way to Kit [at the right shore of the upper Negro River]. He walked and walked. He arrived among the Wari' and yelled nonsense, shaking a machete. . . . He should have said, "Our coinhabitants shot the enemy. Former OroNao'." He should have told them, "Let's go! There's a lot of sickness. Let's go so you'll survive." The OroEo would have said, "Okay!" And would have gone. [But] he shouted, imitating the whites: "The whites are with us! The whites are with us!" He waved the machete. "We fled," the OroEo said. "We were afraid of Maxun." He spouted nonsense and they fled. (Paletó 1995)

> Maxun Taparape arrived shaking the machete in the air and yelling, "We've turned completely into whites!" The Wari' fled shouting, "The white man has gone mad. Let's shoot him!" And they fled into the forest. Then Maxun Taparape became afraid and said, "It's me, Maxun Taparape. There is a lot of white disease, you're going to die! Let's drink their medicines." The Wari' declined to go. He slept with the OroEo and the next day a group accompanied him to Koxain. (Tokohwet, OroEo woman)

> He arrived playing with a machete, pretending he was going to attack: "I'm white! I'm going to kill you!" The OroEo [named] Wao Omiji grabbed an arrow ready to shoot. Then Jimon O [Maxun Taparape's other name] said his name so they would recognize him. He went away after just one day and left a machete. . . . The OroEo had just killed whites on the Pacaás Novos and were still in reclusion. Two days later the sickness began. (Oronkun, OroEo man)

Some OroEo men went to Koxain, took tools, and returned. There they became contaminated and spread the disease to others. However, one informant claimed that Maxun Taparape was already feverish when he visited the OroEo and OroAt. This happened around the end of June: it was only at the end of August that the pacification team decided to go to the OroEo and OroAt villages to distribute medicines. Most people were already dead.

Oronkun, an OroEo man who was about fifteen at the time, said that the sickness had begun at Pakun, a village close to Komi Pixik, where he lived. When some men from Komi Pixik went to visit those from Pakun, they encountered one person dead on the path and saw vultures. Oronkun calculates that they found more than twenty people dead in the village. The group returned to Komi Pixik by nightfall, already feeling ill. Oronkun said that he and his older brother had been the only ones not to sicken and they had tried to feed the sick by hunting, fishing, and making maize drink. His mother died, her body eaten by vultures, and he had cried alone, since those still alive were too sick to manage to cry (the ritual song).

The OroEo tried to escape the diseases by fleeing to villages ever further from the whites, a response found among the Wari' in general, as we have seen.

> I was at home and Wao Xin To [one of the OroEo men who went to Koxain] arrived back from Koxain. He had stayed a while there, but didn't like the whites and decided to return. . . . The same day that Wao Xin To arrived, the fever started at night. "Let's run!" As soon as we entered the forest, Maxun Horok died. . . . We fled from the disease. We left the corpse there and carried on. . . . We had no maize; we fled without thinking. In the middle of the river, Pixon's father died. We burned him and carried on. We wanted to reach somewhere with healthy people. In the middle of the night Orowao Tata and Wem Pato died. They'd been sleeping together. They died quickly, like sorcery victims [jami makan]. Ki'Moi, OroMon, and Orowao Kukui also died. So we decided to return to Komikon Wam [the village they had left] because nobody remained. (Xi Waram, OroEo, 1993)

As occurred elsewhere, the survivors were too feeble to carry the sick or even provide adequate funerals for the dead. The dead were not eaten, not so much from fear of being contaminated by strange diseases, but because the living were almost dead, too weak to fetch the enormous quantity of firewood needed to roast a corpse—and there were dozens of them—or even to weep and eat. They were also socially disorganized, in flight, without swiddens. Sometimes they managed to bury a body, preventing its consumption by vultures.

After some of the recently contacted OroNao' men had been cured, they accompanied the whites and the other Wari' to the OroEo and OroAt villages where they knew many people lived, now probably sick. The OroEo and OroAt knew these men well since the subgroups had been in close contact in recent times.

> "We hadn't been there long and I had already fattened. Only To'o Xak Wa [his wife] was very ill. So the priest said to me . . . and your older brother, Hwerein Pe e', also said, 'Let's search for the OroEo!' . . . We went. We arrived at Hwijimain Xitot, where Pariri was. 'Our older brother is alive!' We had looked for him everywhere in the forest. . . . He told us, 'Our children's mother died!' 'Really? If only you had visited the whites earlier . . .' 'No, we're very afraid of these whites of yours.' " (Paletó 1995)

Hwijimain Xitot is located in OroAt territory but was occupied by Oro-Nao' people who had settled upriver to escape the whites. From there, the team trekked for a few more days through the forest, arriving at the area known as Kit. There they set up a kind of base camp where the whites waited for the sick. According to Dom Roberto, the Wari' who accompanied them warned that the OroEo and OroAt would probably be alarmed were the whites to enter the villages. The Wari' men removed their clothing and left in search of people. Close to Kit they killed game with a shotgun: later, Paletó said, they discovered that one of the local inhabitants, Mijain Wiri, had heard the shot and, aware of the arrival of the OroNao' of the Whites at Koxain, had thought: "The whites [wijam] who are OroNao' have arrived . . . I'll shoot them!"

Most of the survivors, extremely ill, were found in the forest rather than the villages: "We reached people who said they were dying. . . . They were in the forest. 'We're going to stay in the forest so we can survive! So we can recover from the diseases' [the sick people said]. This is the Wari' way: someone sickens and goes to the forest to cool his body [from the fever, the main sign of a serious illness]. They are afraid to be sick at home. They flee" (Paletó 1995).

Dom Roberto confirmed this had been the case: "They were in the forest, lost there. I didn't find one at home. The houses were abandoned. They were lying on the ground in the forest" (Dom Roberto 1995).

The sick were carried by the Wari' to Kit where they received medication (fig. 33): "So by afternoon a lot of people were already there. Almost everyone was carried. They brought a few at a time. Some arrived on foot. . . . So we began to medicate them. Antônio Costa and someone else. We did the rounds. They moaned all night. . . . After these injections, they began to

33. A sick person being carried. Rio Negro area, 1961 or 1962.
(Archive of the Guajará-Mirim Prelacy)

respond quickly and the next day were already much better" (Dom Roberto 1995).

This moment was when many of the OroEo and OroAt, especially the women, first saw the whites of the expedition. The recently contacted Oro-Nao' calmed them by saying—as the OroNao' of the Whites had said to themselves—that although the whites looked strange, they were good and had no hostile intentions. Judging by Paletó's account, the OroNao' of the right bank acted precisely like the OroNao' of the Whites when persuading the sick to take injections: " 'I don't want it, I don't want the thorn!' [the sick people said]. They hid their arms. Hwerein Pe e', I think it was, said, 'Look, the whites are going to pierce me!' They injected him. 'Look, it doesn't bleed. That's all. It'll make you live!' " (Paletó 1995).

They stayed for around three days at Kit and, when the sick were better—recovery was seemingly rapid with the antibiotics—they went to Hwijimain Xitot and from there to Koxain, and later to the central encampment on the Negro River, where there were more provisions and plentiful fish. Fernando Cruz and a group of Wari' men and women headed in another direction: from Kit they journeyed toward the Pacaás Novos River, aiming to reach the seringal of Manuel Lucindo and show him that peaceful contact had been achieved.

> "Don't be afraid of the Wari'. They're your coinhabitants. Make them your kin" [Fernando said to the whites on the seringal]. . . . Fernando said, "I came!" "Wow!" They ran toward us. "Look at the new Wari' who've just arrived, who shot you here. They're my Wari'. If you see them around when they come here to fish, don't shoot them." "Wow!" "Paint me with annatto!" the whites said. "Okay," the [Wari'] women replied. They painted them. The strange whites laughed. (Paletó 1995)

After telling the river dwellers encountered en route about the pacification, they arrived at the "Dom Rey Camp" on the Negro River where they left some of the women. They continued toward Guajará-Mirim where Fernando wanted to show off the recently contacted Wari'. On the way, at the mouth of the Novo River, they met an OroNao' of the Whites man who lived separate from the others. He warned the OroNao' of the right bank of the danger they faced by accompanying the OroNao' of the Whites, confirming suspicions they had already been harboring. One informant, whose name I shall omit, told me: "He saw us. It was the first time that we had seen him. He said, 'Is it you?' 'It's us!' 'Why did you accept these people? The sons of

Xijan and Manim don't like you. They go about on the Novo River saying, "I hunted them with a gun. I killed them." That's what these people said about you. They killed you with guns.'"

Meanwhile at Koxain the Wari' came and went. Some OroEo died on the path to Koxain. Others, seeing the intensity of the sicknesses, returned to the villages for a while. According to Mijain, an OroEo man who was a child at the time, given the intensity of the epidemics and the number of deaths, Wao Xin To [OroEo] said to his children, "Let's all go the forest! After you've grown, we'll shoot the whites to avenge our kin." The adults decided to embark immediately on a war expedition: "Let's shoot the whites, chop them up, bring them, and eat them!" Since they had made no swiddens, due to being weak, disorganized, and in mourning, they also planned to steal food, especially nonbitter manioc, for later planting. A group of men and women therefore headed off to the Pacaás Novos headwaters and ended up reaching the outskirts of a seringal.

According to Xi Waram, also OroEo, two whites had run into them in the forest. Once their mutual fear had subsided, the Wari' realized that they had already seen these men at Koxain. Even so, they slept at some distance from them. One of the Wari' planned to shoot them but was dissuaded by his companions, who argued that they should also approach the whites, given that all the other Wari' had done so. They agreed to follow them to the seringal where they worked. The whites offered them food and clothing, and they ended up staying. They learned how to tap rubber, use guns, and, everyone says, enjoy life on the seringal. Game was abundant and they never went hungry. They accepted the goods given to them by the whites as presents, not as payment for the work they were performing. Some boys were taken to other sites to work. Toji stated that the rubber boss Nazozeno adopted him as a son and took him to live with his family in Guajará-Mirim. There Toji learned various trades, including training as a carpenter, builder, and mechanic. Mijain, an orphaned boy at the time, was adopted by Pedro, one of the men from Nazozeno's crew. Mijain told how he forgot the Wari' language and was forced to relearn it later. In Guajará, he had met Father Bendoraites, one of those responsible for the Sagarana colony where a few Wari' had already settled. He presented him to Mamxun Wi, an OroEo man, kin of Mijain, who invited him back to live among the Wari'. Mijain refused, "Because he called Pedro father and his wife mother." He decided to return to the Wari' only some time later after experiencing problems in Guajará-Mirim.

This was not a common scenario among the Wari', though. Part of the

OroEo group that reached the seringal immediately agreed to return to the Negro River when the SPI sent an OroNao' man to fetch them. While the material living conditions on the seringal exceeded their expectations, social life was lacking and they wanted to meet their own people again. This probably occurred at the start of 1963, since an SPI document from this year mentions the transportation of twenty-five OroEo Indians who had been living on Nazozeno's seringal. The others remained there by accident: they were on a hunting expedition when the boat came to fetch them and arrived days later to find that the boat had already left. They later returned one by one and by various routes to the Negro River, where they found the Wari' living at the recently created post (still active today, located near the mouth of the Negro) or in the various nearby villages.

WE WANT PEOPLE FOR OURSELVES

When Maxun Taparape told the OroEo and OroAt about the whites' arrival at Terem Matam, two OroAt brothers, one of them married to an OroEo woman and with children, decided not to approach these enemies under any circumstances. I had the chance to talk with one of these men, Jamain Tamanain, who today lives at the Rio Negro–Ocaia village.

> We heard about the whites, but we didn't like them. We detested them. . . .
> I remembered all my kin, all my coinhabitants, who had been murdered by the whites. "I don't want to approach the whites!" I hated them. "Let's live alone, with our children," my older brother said to me. "Okay," I replied. We went far away and lived alone. We stayed a long time . . . perhaps several years. We don't know how many years.[10] (Jamain Tamanain 1993)

Jamain told me that when Maxun Taparape arrived, he was clearing a swidden at Pakun. He had no wish to go to Koxain to obtain tools and ended up seeing the start of the epidemics: according to him, these began when Wao Xin To, an OroEo, returned from Koxain. It was as though a gale had swept through, he said, taking away the people (who had died). This was when they resolved to move far away from the whites and their diseases. Jamain already felt sick and weak. Initially they went to live at a swidden on the upper Ouro Preto. But there was no more maize and they planted just nonbitter manioc and sweet potato. They also used wild fruits as accompaniments to meat and fish. While living there, other Wari' said, they shot whites on the Ouro Preto River. After a while, they decided to meet their own people, but found only the bones of the dead on the trails. They trekked from one site to another, but encountered no one. They were all dead, they concluded.

One day, when they went to cut bamboo for arrows, they heard voices. Jamain was elated and decided to follow these people:

> I ran after them. My fear of the whites had vanished. "I'm going to see!" I went. I followed and followed. We slept . . . Late afternoon we met up with him, Jimon Pan Tokwe, and also Benedito, A'ain Towa [Wari' men who had left the Rio Negro–Ocaia village to harvest bamboo in the mountains]. When Jimon Pan Tokwe saw us, he said, "You're still here, younger brother?" "Yes, I am, older brother." "You survived?" "Yes." "Is your older brother alive?" [referring to Jamain's brother, Wao Tokori]. "Yes, he is." "Wow!" And Jimon Pan Tokwe wept. He wept on seeing us. (Jamain Tamanain 1993)

Jimon Pan Tokwe and his companions returned to the post—the current Negro–Ocaia post—and told the others about the encounter. Various people told me that they knew Wao Tokori and Jamain Tamanain were alive and had linked them to the incident of the white person shot on the upper Ouro Preto. Their close kin—Orowam, Hwerein Pe e', and Wao Xin To—went to fetch them by canoe.

Hwerein Pe e' emphasized that they did not practice agriculture, which for him was synonymous with not having any food: "They had nothing to eat! They had no maize or nonbitter manioc. They just supped [fruits]. They ate *kawop*, *topi*, and killed game" (Hwerein Pe e' 1995).

The most interesting aspect of this whole episode is how it provides an extreme case of a point already stressed a number of times here: the Wari' movement toward the whites was primarily a movement toward Wari' society and social life, which had been disrupted and even interrupted by the nonindigenous invasion. This is what happened with the OroNao' of the Whites and, to a lesser extent, all of the other Wari'. The episode was like a paradigmatic enactment of the flood myth (Nanananana), which I have already linked to the actions of the OroNao' of the Whites in approaching the whites. Jamain's words speak for themselves.

> "Why did you lose your fear of whites?" I asked.
>
> "I don't know. I didn't want to live alone anymore. I didn't want us to live alone. I wanted us to be many. We had no maize to drink. We ate only Brazil nuts and game. . . . We ate the meat accompanied with nonsense

food. I'll tell you [laughing]. We ate tapir meat with *nao* [a fruit]. We ate the meat with patauá too. When we had *pupunha*, we ate it with deer. We ate meat with babassu as well."

"Was that why you didn't want to stay there anymore?" I asked.

"Yes. We wanted to eat maize with our coinhabitants."

"Did you think all the Wari' had died?" I asked.

"Yes, all of them. Perhaps nobody was left. My older brother said only we remained. It was as though we were alone . . ."

"Did you like it when you arrived at the post?" I asked.

"I was happy because finally there were people for me. I was really happy. . . . My anguish evaporated. I stayed there." (Jamain Tamanain 1993)

Another interesting point is Jamain's association of life in society with agriculture in general, specifically maize cultivation, a topic explored in chapter 1. It is as though maize was impossible to grow not only because of the loss of seeds but also the lack of commensals. Maize cultivation typifies humanity and human beings live in society. Jamain Tamanain, laughing ashamedly when he told me how they ate meat with wild fruits (rather than maize, as one should), made me think that this is precisely what they thought: they were not living as people.

In his account, Hwerein Pe e' mentioned an important detail. During the three or four days that elapsed between the encounter with Jimon Pan Tokwe and the canoe journey to fetch the isolated group, one of the OroAt men, Wao Tokori, had made a rubber drum. He wanted to offer it to the Wari' when they arrived, so they could sing and dance. These isolated Wari' were clearly in search of something more than kin and more than emotional solace: they wanted a social life in all its complexity, as occurs in the festivals. While they wanted kin, they also wanted affines who could be confronted.

An interesting comparison can be drawn here with the group of OroMon who remained isolated for around eight years. As I commented in chapter 10, the big difference resided in the makeup of the two groups. The OroMon formed one large group with various couples, their children, and their in-laws. For better or worse, there was a nucleus, a kind of miniature society. The other group, however, was composed of just three adults; that is, one man, a couple, and the couple's children. Was it coincidence that the OroAt lost maize while the OroMon managed to keep it?

Although not everything went well for the OroAt when they arrived at the post—within a few days, one of the couple's children sickened and died, while the pregnant wife lost her child—even so they had no desire to return to their swiddens in the forest.

FURTHER THOUGHTS

The attempt to reconstruct (or recreate) these pacification episodes has more than one aim. Among other things, I wished to present a body of ethnographic material that strikes me as extremely rich, especially given the scant descriptions existing of events of this kind.[11] Possibly the reader may have found the description of each of the episodes overly long, but my intention was to allow the Wari' and the whites who took part in these events their own points of view.

The encounters between the Wari' and the whites are revealing in various senses. They highlight the symbolic schemas chosen to classify these unusual events and thereby reveal important aspects of Wari' thinking, especially in terms of their concept of alterity. The meaning of the categories "foreigner" and "enemy" set out in the first two parts of the book, based on an analysis of events that characterized life before pacification and a set of myths, acquires a new dimension in the episodes involving contact with the whites. The Wari' became embroiled in events where they were forced to classify, and rapidly, people and their behaviors, revealing the constitutive attributes of these categories in the process. If we conclude, based on myths and war accounts, that the enemy is ontologically Wari', the conception reigning during pacification that the OroNao' of the Whites were the most bloodthirsty, the enemies properly speaking, not only confirms this conclusion but also functions as a kind of prime example of it. It is as though the Wari' conceptual schema was presented to us as a caricatural portrait in which the use of a few striking features suddenly reveals the essential. How else could we have such a clear vision of the importance for the Wari' of the relation between foreigners, and that life in society means, above all, the relations between different people? The Wari' experience of pacification illustrates Albert's observations (1992, 152) on the importance of studies of contact for exposing the dynamic aspects of the "savage mind."

The accounts of pacification reveal that the associations between myth and event, as I have already shown in chapter 10, do not arise from an incapacity to perceive the particularity of historical events. The OroNao' narratives on the pacification of the OroWaram show that they considered themselves to be living through a new, specific moment. They did not perceive themselves as survivors of the flood, nor did they see tails on the OroWaram, like those characterizing the enemy group of Nanananana. Since both were Wari' and faced by an equivalent situation, it is understandable that the OroNao' and Nanananana acted in a similar way. As I observed in the introduction, the mythic account and the historical event were associated by the Wari' because they were able to be related logically. Both foreground a basic existential problem: the importance of life in society.

The accounts of pacification also reveal the conjunctural nature of structure evoked by Sahlins (1985, xiv). On the one hand, events are clearly interpreted on the basis of specific cultural premises. The agents of pacification, imbued with their own idea of the "savage mind," interpreted the left-over maize cake and objects abandoned by the Wari' as they fled as presents expressing a desire for peace. The Wari' as a whole thought that the whites left presents because they were probably very isolated, thirsty for people, and wanted to be approached and incorporated by the Wari'. The OroNao' of the Whites wanted strangers and this indeed was how they treated the other Wari' (despite seeing them as enemies too); the latter, for their part, initially related to them as enemies, precisely what they were transforming into after so many years of isolation and proximity to the whites. The pacification team on the Negro River, filled with ideas concerning the social organization of indigenous groups, managed to turn a selfish man, who carried a basket to take the largest amount of goods possible just for himself, into an authentic native chief. The Protestant missionaries turned themselves into a target for arrows by believing that God, a figure from their own myths, would protect them.

On the other hand, events have their own force, determining the specific form in which structure becomes realized. Although the Wari', or at least some of them, wished to reconstitute their society as they had known it before the invasion of whites, the movement toward them—who had no knowledge of the Indians' project—made the reestablishment of the older order impossible, or perhaps even undesirable.

Returning to questions raised at the end of chapter 10, if the Wari' were looking for foreigners, why did they not move away from the whites (some indeed did so) as soon as contact with the other subgroups was achieved? And why did they not incorporate the whites straight away as foreigners, marrying them (the Wari' always expressed distaste for this idea) and turning them into consubstantials? They opted to keep them as enemies (which is how they refer to whites in general even today), but at the same time they began to live close to them.

The motives leading them to live next to these enemies are manifold. Clearly the material goods attracted them, particularly since the whites proved to be exceedingly generous hosts: they offered food and gave many presents. Perhaps the Wari' also knew that failure to remain allied with the whites would mean that they would be unable to achieve the social life that they felt could be resumed. Excessive warfare was forcing them to live on the run in constant fear. Though they had not abandoned festivals, they were probably less frequent, especially since festivals are not held during mourning and they were losing their kin in large numbers.

Without wishing to minimize the practical conditions, I do not think that they explain everything. Did they become dependent on metal tools, sugar, and medicines, knowing that nothing would go back to how it was before? Were they disorganized and afraid following the deaths of more than half of their people? Yes in both cases. But why did they risk more deaths by approaching the whites and why do they say today that they are turning into whites? This is the theme of the conclusion.

Conclusion

MIXTURES: LIVING WITH THE ENEMY

Some years after pacification, the Wari' no longer lived in the named areas of their territory. They built their houses close to indigenous posts, located at sites deemed more accessible by the whites. However, apart from Sagarana, the SPI—and, later, FUNAI—posts were situated close to the territories formerly occupied. In these new villages, the Wari' became coinhabitants not only of whites and people from other indigenous groups but also of Wari' foreigners who had previously occupied other named areas. Here I do not mean to suggest that the Wari' never lived with foreigners in the past, or that a chaotic mixture of people was found at the posts. As we saw in chapter 1, a group of foreigners might decide to live in a named area associated with the territory of another subgroup, meaning that this area would become associated with the subgroup of its current inhabitants, or the foreigners may be subsequently incorporated by the local subgroup through marriage. Affinity was the means of incorporating not only enemies but also foreigners, who became coinhabitants and kin in the process. In terms of subgroup organization at the posts, I showed the tendency to settle at the posts closest to the group's original territories. So, for example, most of the OroNao', OroEo, and OroAt live at the Rio Negro–Ocaia post and nearby villages, while the Oro-Waram live at the Lage post and on its outskirts.

Living at the same location, the foreigners began to act as typical co-inhabitants, marrying among themselves, calling each other by kin terms, and sharing food. In sum, they gradually turned into consanguines, despite the completeness of this process being cast in doubt with each internal conflict, whose fault lines usually coincide with the limits of the subgroup. From this perspective, the Wari' today live in a tenser environment amid coinhabitants who are really foreigners, and relatives who are not really kin.

Despite being fixed around the FUNAI posts for most of the year, the Wari'
often move away for shorter periods in small groups composed of consanguines and real affines to live in other areas within their traditional territory.
These are the swidden villages, occupied for one or two weeks between August and October when they clear, burn, and sow the maize swiddens, and
for a few days in December and January to harvest the crop. In January and
February they also leave the posts for several weeks to collect Brazil nuts.
Until a few years ago, they also used to spend some days in the forest extracting rubber.

From the second half of the 1990s, the Wari', encouraged by FUNAI, began to disperse, inhabiting smaller villages at some distance from the posts,
though most of the population has remained at the latter. As we saw in chapter 1, therefore, some of those who occupied the Rio Negro–Ocaia post are
today distributed in another three settlements—Panxirop, Piranha, and
Ocaia—situated upstream on the Negro River in this order.[1] There are also
small local groups constituted by one or two families on the shores of the
Negro River, downriver of the post, a location the Wari' call Boca. In addition, FUNAI persuaded other families to occupy sites located on the borders
of the Lage Indigenous Area to help control illegal logging. The same process
of dispersion is occurring at the other posts. As in the swidden villages, in
these new areas people live among kin, plant maize close to home, and have
access to abundant game.

The problem with living near the posts is soil exhaustion: this makes cultivating maize more difficult and leads many families to plant bitter manioc,
a crop that requires less fertile soils. Part of the flour made from this manioc
is consumed and the rest sold in Guajará-Mirim. Because it provides a se-
cure way for the Wari' to obtain money to purchase the industrial products
they need—oil, sugar, soap, clothing, as well as DVD players—its cultivation is highly encouraged by FUNAI (see Leite 2007 for a recent analysis of
the new consumption habits of the Wari'). Flour has also become a kind of
local currency, used to pay for the produce acquired from visiting traders, or
even other Wari'. After distributing part of any large catch of fish to close kin,
people often sell the rest to the post's other inhabitants. The same usually
occurs when large game is caught, the meat sold for the same price charged
in Guajará-Mirim (fig. 34).

But flour is not the only source of money. Brazil nuts are very high priced
nowadays, and people try to collect as much as they can. Also, many people
receive regular salaries, either as teachers or indigenous health agents at the

34. A visiting trader at the Rio Negro–Ocaia village, 1987.

posts and some nearby villages, or through pensions (as rural workers, exempted from tax contributions). There is also the money that women receive for maternity leave, worth four minimum wages and generally paid in a single installment. Apart from these women, all those receiving salaries have current accounts at the Banco do Brasil in Guajará-Mirim.

While the Wari' living at the posts are planting less maize, they never cease lamenting this fact. Those who maintain the crop, grown at a sizable distance from the post, are heavily sought out by their kin. This is an important point. As we saw in chapter 1, for the Wari', maize is a sign of humanity: human beings, including animals with spirit, plant maize and drink beer. Life in the villages in contrast to life in the forest, when they kept away from the maize as it grew—was characterized by the presence of maize, the base for the drinks consumed during festivals and warfare reclusion. This would only be a problem, however, if the Wari' thought that they had really abandoned maize. According to them, the situation is no more than a temporary setback, since those who have not planted the crop might do so again at any time. This has indeed happened: those who have gone to live in smaller villages situated on fertile soils have immediately cleared a maize swidden close to the settlement.

Returning to the issue of living with strangers, the Wari' have also been incorporating people from other indigenous groups in similar fashion, seeking to turn them into affines and consanguinize them, as they do with foreigners. A minority at each post, these Indians marry with the Wari', eat their food, and adopt their language.[2] Previously called *wijam*, enemies, they are now classified as *wari'* in various contexts (see chapter 2), especially when wishing to differentiate them from the whites. Despite the efforts of FUNAI and the Catholic missionaries to nurture a pan-indigenous identity in which all the Indians are equally Wari' in contrast to the whites, the incorporation of enemies through marriage, physical proximity, and food sharing is inherent to Wari' culture. *Wari'* and *wijam* are above all positions, occupied by beings who are ontologically indistinct. A logical outcome of this single ontology is the conception that every enemy is originally a Wari' who, as we saw in earlier chapters, passed through a process of "enemization" caused by spatial distancing and a rupture in the exchange of festivals and women. From this perspective, "enemization" is a reversible process, requiring only geographical proximity and the reestablishment of marriages.

A good example of this process of incorporating enemies are the OroWin, a Txapakura group, possibly traditional enemies of the Wari', who survived the massacres of the whites, and were settled by FUNAI at the Rio Negro–Ocaia post, previously inhabited exclusively by the Wari'. After a while mixed marriages began to form, producing children through which the Wari' established kin ties with the OroWin. A Wari' woman told me that, following the death of an OroWin man, the Wari', though somewhat awkward at first, felt compelled to weep at the funeral, using teknonyms to refer to the deceased, treating him as a consanguine. The OroWin were in a process of incorporation or "warinization" when FUNAI transferred them to another post, São Luís, on the upper Pacaás Novos, about one day's journey from the Rio Negro–Ocaia post by outboard motor. The geographical distance will undoubtedly diminish the volume of matrimonial exchanges, but the OroWin left with Wari' children and grandchildren, which ensures continuing contact between them.

Nowadays the whites are the only ones to be persistently called *wijam*, enemies, meaning that today *wijam* is synonymous with white men and women. When the Wari' say the *wijam* are arriving, they are not predicting war but merely the arrival of a few whites to visit them or undertake some kind of work. They are enemies lacking the relation of warfare, which enables once unthinkable phrases to be pronounced, such as "I'm going to the *wijam*'s house to ask for fish hooks." Although whites became coinhabitants, they were not turned into affines and consubstantials like the other enemies.

This helps explain why the only kinship term I heard the Wari' use for un-known whites was "brother-in-law." As I observed in my analysis of the Pi-nom myth, brothers-in-law can be seen as enemies with whom one must live rather than make war. In contrast to the Tupinambá, who made their enemies into brothers-in-law in order to kill them, the Wari' make them into brothers-in-law because they do not kill them. The other enemies, those one wishes to—or can—incorporate into society, are turned into true brothers-in-law, given that affinity is the way of achieving this incorporation. But these incorporated affines are no longer called brothers-in-law, since they are rap-idly consanguinized by the exchange relations and commensality they begin to maintain with the Wari'. The white enemies could be called brothers-in-law precisely because this is what they are not.

By bringing the enemies to live alongside them, the Wari' lost the war. To-day war is no more than a threat—and a desire—or a symbolic war that does not produce killers. Let us examine the latent war with the whites first.

Two cases, both of which I witnessed, provide good examples. When I arrived in Sagarana in December 1993, I was quickly informed that the most knowledgeable man was away. Harein had just gone to spend a period at the Lage post, where his younger brother lives. Two days later I was surprised by Harein's reappearance in Sagarana. He explained that on arriving at the Lage post, he heard a rumor that the whites were going to kill all the Wari' of Sagarana. Worried about his family back home, he returned immediately. A similar case involved Awo Xohwara. He left early to fish one day and did not return until late at night. He had gone alone, and the Wari' of the Rio Negro–Ocaia post were extremely worried, gathering in his house. They sus-pected he had been killed by a certain white man and began to plan their revenge. Finally Awo Xohwara returned to general relief—and disappoint-ment. The latter case highlights an important point: if warfare is a desire, it is also a constant threat, insofar as today's *wijam* are coinhabitants who live alongside the Wari' and interact with them daily. The Wari' live without war but with the enemy.

Young men, however, have found a way of making war with the whites, which involves participating in the wars waged among the whites themselves. Some of them yearn to join the Brazilian army, supposing that this will take them to the battlefields, "to kill enemies!" as they say. But few are accepted and none of them has been "lucky" enough to take part in a war, where they would discover it involved something completely different from the warfare about which their fathers so often talk.

As well as this potential warfare, feared and desired, there is the actualization of symbolic warfare with the whites through shamanry. As killers, the shamans act in two forms. They track down their enemies via the wind—accompanied by animal spirits—and, invisible to their eyes, shoot them. The victims then sicken and die. A shaman once told me, "The whites of Guajará-Mirim think they're dying of diseases, but actually we're the ones killing them." They may also attack the whites in their visible animal form. A jaguar-shaman told me one day that he and two other shamans, his coinhabitants, killed a white man on the Ribeirão River this way. For the whites, it was merely a jaguar attack. Snake-shamans also attack in this form.

Even so, the war engaged in by shamans is not the same war pursued before pacification. After killing an enemy, the shamans do not enter reclusion, do not leave their hair to grow long, and do not fatten their women. They are not effectively killers and the place of the killers, important to the construction of male identity, has become vacated.

As well as killing whites, shamans are mediators in another war, the one between the Wari' and animal spirits. As we saw in chapter 2, the preferred prey of the Wari' are animals with spirit, which for this reason are also human, or more precisely, may also occupy the position of predators. They try to kill the Wari' with arrows, like enemies in warfare or like prey in hunting. At these moments, they are the *wari'*, the human beings, while the Wari' comprise their prey, *karawa*. This potential role reversal, also characteristic of the Wari' warfare with Indians and whites, is essential to the idea of humanity as a position related to the act of predation. Alternation between the positions of *wari'* and *karawa*, predator and prey, is a constitutive feature of the Wari' person. Although the Wari' are continually aware of their war with the animals, the shaman's activities are essential to making this real. Only the shaman with his special vision (that is, his double point of view) can see this war unfold and transmit "frontline" news to the Wari'. Having lost the relation with their other enemies, the Wari' were left with the animals to provide a way of maintaining the central aspect of their ontology: humanity as a position, ready to be occupied by different beings.

However, the importance of warfare—of real warfare—for the Wari' was not absolute. Although killing an enemy founded male identity and warfare functioned as an important mediative relation between men and women, we have also seen that hunting and warfare are equivalent activities. Indeed, the enemy's flesh—or his spirit-blood, which generated meat and fat—was offered to women like animal prey. Society did not appropriate any kind of symbolic wealth from the enemy, and the entire process was limited to a transformation of the killer's body. The enemy's spirit-blood made him fatter and more vigorous, which in turn augmented his capacity to swell his wife's belly with food and children. While the experience of warfare was important in terms of constituting Wari' men as killers, the same can be achieved through hunting, also a relation between subjects. Today men offer just animal meat to their wives. And this satiates them. As a woman from the Rio Negro–Ocaia settlement told me when I asked her if she liked her husband: "He keeps my belly full" (of food and children).

Among the Wari', the enemy position is incorporated via the shaman, not the killer. As well as acting as a killer and mediator in the war with animals, the shaman embodies the enemy position within the group, frequently passing through "altered states," which make the group vulnerable and allow the Wari' to experience the prey position and become aware of the humanity of animals. In this sense, the position of shamans is analogous to that of people from other indigenous groups who become their coinhabitants, though produced in reverse. While the other Indians are *wijam* "warinized" by marriage and physical proximity, shamans are *wari'* "wijamized" by enemies—the animals that shoot them and "animalize" their spirit. Both are classified as Wari' but represent a dangerously proximate alterity.

Returning to the questions discussed in part 2 ("In Myth"), I now wish to compare the postpacification mixture of the categories of consanguine, foreigner, and enemy, central to the social and existential dynamic of the Wari', with the mixture of worlds attributed in myth to the whites. According to the system of myths analyzed in previous chapters, whites were responsible for mixing earth and water, elements associated with the world of the living and the dead, respectively. At a generic level, we could say that the Wari' make a logical association between real worlds that must be kept apart—those of the living and the dead—and symbolic worlds, categories, and positions that must be kept apart (which does not mean that people or groups cannot move between them). However, it is tempting to identify further correlations between life today, as perceived by the Wari', and the consequences of mixing water and earth.

Various characteristics of the world of the dead provide us with an insight into why the Wari' today see the presence of this world in the world of the living. As we saw in chapter 2, recent arrivals in the world of the dead are welcomed with large quantities of maize beer offered by one of the world's inhabitants, Towira Towira, just like foreigners in a festival. We have also seen that offering fermented maize beer is a form of symbolic killing realized between foreigners. Those killed by maize beer become killers, while dead women dedicate themselves to making maize drink for their husbands. Despite containing an inversion, the transformation of maize beer victims into killers suggests an equivalence between warfare and festivals, and hence between enemies and foreigners, precisely one of the features of the world of the living after pacification. Indeed, even this inversion—the turning of victims into killers—can be associated with the increase in warfare during the period preceding pacification, when the victims of the Wari' began to kill them in large numbers. The world of the dead is also present through opposition: while it contains killers but no warfare, the world of the living today contains only a war without killers: that of the shamans and animals.

The mixtures are obviously relative. While the configurations of the categories of consanguine, foreigner, and enemy underwent variations, from a broader perspective the difference between them was preserved, highlighting the fact that they comprise intrinsically dynamic positions. Consanguines, foreigners, and enemies did not cease to exist, although they have not always been the same.

The episodes of pacification clearly demonstrate something that had already been made evident in the first two parts of the book: social life for the Wari' is not limited to the relation between consanguine kin. Foreigners, people who embody the position of affinity, are conceived as a necessary evil, and the encounter with the whites allowed them to verify this in various ways. I refer, for example, to the affliction caused by the lack of foreigners to the OroNao' of the Whites and smaller groups that went into isolation during pacification. The foreigner category is fundamental for the Wari', not only by embodying the alterity internal to society, but also by constituting a kind of link between the Wari' and their enemies. The latter are conceived to be ontologically identical to the Wari', former foreigners who moved away and ruptured the exchange cycle. To be reincorporated into society, it suffices for them to approach and remake the consubstantial ties through marriage. A prime example are the OroNao' of the Whites, who remained isolated for years and later returned to form part of the group.

The foreigner is thus the point of transition and transformation. Wari' society is conceived as a circumstantial entity: its composition inevitably varies with the passage of time, and this dynamic is the essence of the Wari' conceptualization of historical process. This also helps explain why the subgroups were maintained amid the many transformations occurring with pacification.

People began to live together at the FUNAI posts, but the division of society into subgroups was preserved.

If the category of "foreigner" is fundamental to enabling this fluidity, the same happens with the category of "enemy," which the Wari' have worked to preserve, despite losing the war. They insist on calling the whites—now their coinhabitants—enemies. But they also say that they are turning into whites. They have decided, therefore, not only to live with the enemy but to live as the enemy.[3]

METAMORPHOSES: LIVING AS THE ENEMY

Here I intend to answer the questions I raised in the introduction and at the end of chapters 10 and 11. Why did the Wari' opt to live with the whites when contact between the subgroups was already assured? Why did they risk more deaths during the postcontact epidemics to return to where the whites were? As I observed previously, material interests are only part of the explanation.

The Wari' decided to live with the whites without absorbing them as real affines through marriage, as they did with the OroWin, the Canoé, and the Karipuna man, who became their coinhabitants and learned their language. They insist on not marrying them and strongly criticize the few marriages between whites and Wari' that have taken place, some of them rapidly dissolved (see Kelly 2003, ch. 5, for the same point among the Yanomami). They also insist on classifying the whites as enemies, *wijam*, as they always did, although today they live alongside them and eat their food. So why do the Wari' want to live with the enemy? Moreover, why do they want to live as the enemy, claiming from time to time that "we're completely white" (*wijam pin urut*, where *wijam* means enemy, here specifically whites; *pin* means completely; and *urut* is the pronoun "we exclusive")?

In the introduction, I stressed the distinct way in which Amerindian peoples relate to difference, in contrast to our own, basing my argument on the analysis developed by Lévi-Strauss (1991) in *The Story of Lynx*. For Amerindians, difference is structural and needs to be maintained, while for us it is conceived as dangerous and tends to be eliminated. This at least partially explains the asymmetric nature of the first encounters between Indians and whites in the Americas: while the former were interested in dialogue, valorizing the invaders precisely because of their difference, the whites strived from the outset to civilize the Indians, trying to transform them into replicas of themselves and extinguish any hint of difference. I observed that this way of preserving difference was achieved in a peculiar form, since the Indians seemed to comply with the invaders' desire perfectly, imitating their gestures, using their clothing, and experimenting with their food.

I also emphasized in the introduction the singular nature of this transformation into an Other, which frequently lasted only a short time: the "savages" were soon back to their old customs. What was manifested, then, was a desire to experiment for a while, or in a way concomitant with native practices, a different way of being, attractive precisely because of its difference.

The Wari' relation with the whites seems to illustrate this process perfectly. They approached the whites by keeping them different, maintaining them as enemies. The other enemies with whom they began to live were, as we saw, "warinized" by living together and especially by marriage. They no longer offer a difference to be experimented with. The Wari' judged that this difference in relation to the whites could be preserved in some form and opted to do so, avoiding the definitive means of annulling it, namely through marriage.[4] I explain this point by taking the example of shamans, which not only illustrates the question of marriage but also the fact that the Wari' experience of the whites' way of being can be associated with shamans' experience of the life of the animals associated with them and which allow them to acquire a double viewpoint: just as shamans call themselves *wari'* and *karawa* (animal), likewise the Wari' today call themselves *wari'* and *wijam* (enemy and white). We can begin with the marriage of shamans.

The Wari' say that during the shaman's initiation, his animal affines offer him a girl, just as a Wari' boy was promised a newborn girl as a wife. From then on, he began to treat the parents and brothers of his future wife as real affines, offering them game, bows, and arrows. When the girl entered puberty (when her breasts became evident), the man would go to her village to fetch her, consummating the marriage. From then on, the Wari' say, they become consubstantial through the intimacy of day-to-day living, including the exchange of body substances through sex and physical proximity at night, and the sharing of food, meaning that they eventually acquire a single body.

Similarly, the shaman lives with his animal affines, walks and eats with them, but simultaneously remains at home, living with his Wari' relatives. When his wife (he may have more than one) enters puberty, his animal affines invite him to consummate the marriage through sexual relations and living together. If still young, the shaman attempts to postpone this step as long as possible, since he knows that his marriage implies his definitive transformation into an animal—or, from the Wari' perspective, his death. When Wan e', a peccary shaman, was old, the Wari' used to say that his animal-affines were calling him, saying it was time for him to consummate the alliance. When I returned to the Rio Negro–Ocaia post, already informed of the death of Wan e', whom I called father, people tried to comfort me with the reassurance that he was well: he had already been seen in his new home by another shaman, where he had established a new family with his animal wife. Recently, the elderly shaman Orowam related his weakness and constant illnesses to the call of the animals for him to effectuate the alliance: his two jaguar-wives were now young women, and he smiled in describing their jovial air and beauty. According to him, he could no longer postpone this marriage and his death (in this world). For Wari' shamans, marriage therefore presumes a definitive transformation, passing to the other side and abandoning one of their perspectives or one of their bodies.

My hypothesis is that contact with the whites enabled the Wari' to explore the possibility of living similarly to their shamans, experiencing a double point of view as whites and Wari' simultaneously. As it is with shamans, this experience is realized in their bodies. This point is analyzed below, where I shall try to show how the theory of Amerindian perspectivism developed by Viveiros de Castro (1996, 1998a, 1998b, 2002) and Lima (1995, 1996, 2005), and discussed briefly in chapter 2, affords new insights into what is conventionally called interethnic contact or, in the past, acculturation.[5]

As we saw in chapter 2, the Wari' locate what we conceive as identity or personality in their bodies, kwere- (a root always accompanied by a possessive suffix: kwere-his, kwere-our, etc.); an entity's way of being and acting is defined by its body. While all beings (including what we define as objects and natural phenomena) have a body, only some possess a spirit or soul, which the Wari' call jam (again, always accompanied by a possessive suffix). The latter beings include the Wari', enemies, and some animals, especially their favorite prey. The beings with jam- are, above all, those capable of transforming themselves, of actualizing their body in different forms, depending on the new relations that they establish (see too Vilaça 2005 and 2009b).

All beings with the capacity I have termed spirit, or soul, are thought to be human, wari', and are characterized by engaging in properly human practices: they live in houses, drink beer, hold festivals, and fight with their affines. However, these practices are actualized in different forms depending on the subject's perspective. Thus beer for the Wari' is a maize drink, while the jaguar's beer is the blood of its prey (and enemies) and the tapir's beer is composed of mud. While Wari' houses are made of palm straw and wooden trunks, jaguars live in caves. The Wari' explicitly relate these differences in perspective to differences in body: the jaguar's body is this way, they say. As I discussed in chapter 2, this phenomenon, common to diverse Amerindian peoples, has been dubbed "perspectivism" by Viveiros de Castro (1996, 1998a), who differentiates this idea from what we call relativism, which implies the notion of a single nature (universalism) apprehended by multiple outlooks or cultures. In perspectivism, however, there is no pregiven nature prior to the outlook: instead, this nature is constituted by the perspective itself. Thus the jaguar's perspective is no less true than that of the Wari'; they are equivalent: what the jaguar sees as drink is what the Wari' see as blood. This leaves us, then, with the idea of multiple natures and a single culture, a "multinaturalism" instead of our "multiculturalism" (Viveiros de Castro 1998a, 477–79).

To return to the shamans, the Wari' say that they transform into animals by the application of the animals' annatto and babassu palm oil on their bodies, by being bathed by them and, above all, by becoming their companions and commensals (see Vilaça 1992). This is an experience determined by the body, as the shaman Orowam said to me, "The jaguar is my true kin. My true body is jaguar. My true body has fur."

The idea that shamanic activity is characterized by bodily transformation is fairly widespread among Amerindians, very often expressed as the adoption of animal clothing. Examples include the Yagua of Venezuela, whose shamans use "magical clothing" that allows them to see underwater (Chaumeil 1983, 51); the Kogi of Colombia, for whom a mythic figure transforms into a jaguar on ingesting a hallucinogenic substance and puts on a jaguar mask, enabling him "to perceive things in a different way, in the way a jaguar sees them" (Reichel-Dolmatoff 1975, 55); the Baniwa of northwestern Amazonia, who sometimes describe the shaman's transformation into a jaguar as "putting on a cloak, the jaguar cloak" (Wright 1998, 82); and the Desana, among whom the use of pelts, masks, and other "disguises" characterizes the animals as animals and also enables shamans to transform into animals (Reichel-Dolmatoff 1975, 99, 115, 120, 124, and 125). Here rather than being fantasy costumes or disguises, clothes are forms of equipment that allow life to be experienced in another environment, like a diving suit, as Viveiros de Castro observes (1996, 1998a). According to Viveiros de Castro, commenting on the paraphernalia used in rituals, "We are dealing with societies which inscribe efficacious meanings onto the skin, and which use animal masks . . .

endowed with the power metaphysically to transform the identities of those who wear them, if used in the appropriate ritual context" (Viveiros de Castro 1998a, 482).

It seems to me, therefore, that there is no substantive difference between the animal clothing used by shamans and the body adornments and the manufactured clothes worn by Indians in contact with whites. Chaumeil's observation (1983, 157, n. 11) on the Yagua's resistance to adopting Western clothing dovetails with this idea: "because adopting white people's clothing is also, in a way, to become white."

It is important to stress that although they may function like items of equipment, clothes cannot be disassociated from a global context of transformation. Thus when the Wari' say that they are turning into whites, they explain that today they eat rice and pasta, use shorts, and wash with soap, just as a jaguar-shaman knows he is an animal when he has fur on his body, eats raw animals, and walks in the company of other jaguars. Clothing is a constitutive part of a set of habits that form the body (figs. 35, 36, and 37).

Carneiro da Cunha's observation (1998, 12) on the importance of journeys for the shaman's training in western Amazonia provides an interesting example of this idea. According to Carneiro da Cunha, today's Western-style journeys, involving distant travel and stays in different cities, are seen to be

35. The Rio Negro–Ocaia soccer team, 1987. (Photo by Beto Barcellos)

36. The school at the Rio Negro–Ocaia village, 1987.

37. Paletó, his grandchildren, and the author in front of the teacher's new house at Rio Negro–Ocaia, 2007. (Photo by Dušan Borić)

equivalent to the soul's journeys, in some contexts, such as among certain Pano groups, replacing traditional apprenticeship. As an example, Carneiro da Cunha cites the case of Crispim, a Jaminawa man who for decades was the most renowned shaman of the upper Juruá River and who had stayed in Ceará and Belém, where he had apparently studied. Carneiro da Cunha observes that the broader meaning of these journeys is to give shamans the chance to learn about the world of the whites. By uniting the global (that is, the viewpoint of the cities and the whites) with the local, Crispim became a translator, a mediator of the relation between different worlds, a core attribute of shamanic activity. But what exactly do these journeys involve and how do the apprentices "learn" about the white world? Carneiro da Cunha's description provides a lead: "People say that he was raised by a white godfather who took him to Ceará and, after a murder in which he had dirtied his hands, then to Belém, where he studied, before returning to the Upper Juruá" (Carneiro da Cunha 1998, 12).

What this description suggests is that, far from comprising primarily visual experiences (such as our own visits to museums and other places), journeys for Amazonian peoples involve the establishment of intense social relations and living (peaceful or otherwise) with people from these other worlds. This is precisely what some of the Wari' say in describing their trips to cities: they speak of the food shared with the whites, the physical aggressions, and living in close proximity in the same dwellings. It can be concluded, then, that learning here is acquired through bodily experience; indeed, I would even suggest that by constituting "bodily displacements," these visits to the cities are equivalent to shamanic journeys for the Pano.

It is paradoxical, therefore, that the so-called studies of interethnic contact involving Amerindian groups generally focus on the relation between sociocultural entities (groups, institutions, individuals as "social actors" or "historical subjects") and not on the relation between corporal aggregates. From the pioneering acculturation studies of the American culturalist school[6] to the studies inspired by Balandier's notion of the "colonial situation" (1951, 1971),[7] passing through the works of Darcy Ribeiro (1957, 1996 [1970]), emphasis is given to the encounter between entities defined a priori in terms of Western ontology, with a strong emphasis on the "representational" aspects of action and society. In this view, cultural features migrate from one society to another, as in acculturation studies, or concrete institutions and actors (though conceived in terms of "social roles") act as mediators of complex relations of confrontation between human groups perceived to be culturally distinct (without the meaning of this "culturally" being questioned), as in the studies of interethnic friction initiated by Cardoso de Oliveira in 1963 and continued, after successive reworkings, by his students (see Oliveira Filho 1988, 54–59).[8] What seems to be lacking in these analyses is greater attention to what the Indians say. How do they conceive this distinction between groups? How do they understand this contact? The wealth of ethnographic research available since the 1960s has shown that indigenous sociology is above all a "physiology," and that instead of "acculturation" or "friction," the key terms are transubstantiation and metamorphosis.

As an exemplary case of contact between Indians and whites thought of as an exchange of body substances, I cite the Peruvian Piro studied by Peter Gow (1991), who conceived of themselves today as "people of mixed blood." As an example of the contrast between acculturation and transubstantiation, we can examine two different perspectives on the Pataxó Indians: those of the ethnologist Eduardo Galvão and the Shavante Indian Mário Juruna. Galvão, in an article on cultural areas of Brazil written in the 1950s, claimed that the Indians of the Northeast, including the Pataxó of Bahia, were "mixed" and recorded the "loss of traditional cultural elements, including the language" (Galvão 1979, 225). In 1984, the Pataxó, threatened by farmers who were claiming their lands, alleging they were no longer authentic Indians, were visited by a committee headed by Mário Juruna, then a federal deputy, whose proposal was that they should abandon the lands. Expelled by the Pataxó, Juruna returned to the city, claiming that the reserve was "occupied mostly by *caboclos* and a mere half dozen Indians" (CEDI 1984, 293). The news report published in the *Folha da Tarde* (September 4, 1984) on the episode, which scandalized those defending indigenous rights, ended as follows: "Asked about the signs that had led him to question the authenticity of the reserve's Indians, [Juruna] replied, 'Indians don't have beards, moustaches, or chest hair'" (cf. CEDI 1984, 293; see too Conklin 1997, 727).

Here the "opening to the Other," which according to Lévi-Strauss (1991, 16) defines Amerindian thought, is a "physiological" opening. It is curious that although the native conception of society is not organic, in the sense given to this term by functionalism, a relation between body and society exists that, in the hurry to "de-organicize" society, modern processualist studies of contact have apparently failed to perceive (see Oliveira Filho 1988, 35 and 54). While society may not be an organism, in the sense of a set of functionally differentiated parts, it is a somatic entity, a collective body formed from bodies.[9] Located at diverse levels, the boundaries separating kin from nonkin, and the latter from enemies, are corporal. What the consubstantial group exchanges with other equally conceived units are substances: foods, semen, sweat, blood, and human flesh (see Gow 1991, 261 on the Piro; Seeger 1980, 127–31 on differentiating between corporation and corporality).

These ideas in mind, it is interesting to ponder the meaning for Amerindians of what we usually call tradition. In an article on the concept of tradition among the Akha (Burma/Myanmar), Tooker (1992) observes that for them the term *zán*, meaning "way of life," "way of doing things," "customs," "tradition," is conceived as a set of practices, a load that one carries in a basket. The idiom of tradition is, therefore, "exteriorizing" and opposes our idea of tradition as a set of internalized values to which one adheres, like a system of beliefs—an idea related to our own theological conception of culture (see Viveiros de Castro 1992a, 25).

Tooker begins her article by recounting the case of a Chinese family that decided to become Akha: "They moved into an Akha village, built an Akha-style house with an Akha ancestral shrine, took on an Akha genealogy, spoke the Akha language, *wore Akha clothes* and became Akha" (Tooker 1992, 800; my italics). Had they wished at any time to revert to being Chinese, it would have been enough to take the opposite path, as did an Akha couple who, after spending a few days in the city and becoming Christian, returned to the village, "reconverting" to Akha customs (799).

For Amerindians, I suggest, the idiom of tradition is also exteriorizing, but does not involve a load, a set of practices to be carried, because, as we have seen, human beings all have the same practices: they drink beer, live in families, and make war. The difference between them is given by their point of view, and this is determined by the body. Consequently, tradition is body, substance. It could even be said that, in a sense, tradition is internalized, not as a belief, as an attribute of the spirit, but as food, as body fluids, and as clothing that, along with affects and memory, constitute the body.

In an article on the transformation of the notion of culture among the Tukano of northwestern Amazonia, Jackson (1995, 18) abandons a "biological" notion of culture that, according to her, likens having a culture to the way animals have fur and claws, in favor of a more dynamic notion in which culture is like a jazz musician's repertoire; that is, something that happens as improvisation. While we can concur with Jackson, as with Conklin (1997), in questioning the imposition on Indians of an alien notion of authenticity, Jackson seems to have missed an essential point in the example she chooses, much as the relation between body and society escaped the critics of the "naturalized" model of society, as I noted earlier. Taken from the indigenous viewpoint, animal skin is itself essentially dynamic and hence somewhat inappropriate as a metaphor for fixed (genetic) attributes. As Århem (1993, 115) has shown in relation to another Tukano group, animals are held to be able to swap skin, transforming themselves into beings of other species. If "culture" becomes "nature," it becomes intrinsically mutable, just as the processualists would wish. It is not enough, therefore, to add a historical dimension to the old notion of culture; a radical shift of perspective is necessary—a shift only possible if we adopt the indigenous perspective.

In saying that they are "completely white," the Wari' do not mean that they are losing their tradition, or their culture, as we might think on seeing them drink manioc beer (which, they say, they learned from the Makurap Indians) or drink alcohol, eat manioc flour, use shotguns, and dance *forró*. Instead, they mean that they now have the experience of another point of view. Just as the jaguar-shaman can see blood as beer, the Wari' know that manioc flour is the whites' maize paste, or that *forró* is their *tamara*.

As Paletó taught me in Rio de Janeiro, it is necessary to know what the whites' beer is, what their war is, or their subaquatic world of the dead. While in relativism the idiom of translation is "culture," in Wari' "multinaturalism" (Viveiros de Castro 1998a) the idiom is "nature." During Paletó's first days in Rio (fig. 38), a friend invited us to his birthday party. As soon as we arrived, he offered us a drink, and Paletó accepted a glass of Coca-Cola. He downed it in one gulp, and our host, assuming he was thirsty or had liked the Coke a lot, immediately offered him another brimming glass, which Paletó drank again in one gulp. Only after the third or fourth glass, when Paletó began to belch, did it dawn on me that he was drinking the Coca-Cola like maize beer. Like the coincidences that unfolded in Hawaii and that increasingly confirmed the identification of Cook with Lono (Sahlins 1981, 1985, 1995), my friend behaved as a typical host at a Wari' festival: he offered ever more drink to his guest. Paletó, in the position of guest, not only had to down the glasses in one go, he had to accept each new glass offered to him. This is what he did and would have continued to do until vomiting (to drink more), had I not intervened by asking, "Do you want to stop drinking?" To which he replied, "Can I?" The maize beer festival of the whites involves downing Coca-Cola, but what matters is that it cannot be anything other than a beer festival.[10]

38. Paletó and Abrão preparing to leave Rio de Janeiro, 1993.
(Photo by Beto Barcellos)

We can therefore grasp why the Wari' want to continue to live with the whites. Once again, I stress that I am not suggesting that material questions are irrelevant to this choice; clearly, they want to be close to the whites' goods, their axes and the medicines for sicknesses that have become an indelible part of their lives, as well as DVD players, electronic keyboards, and the soccer matches and "fight films" on the televisions now present in the villages. But if they like this world so much, why not marry the whites and mix with them for good? Why insist on avoiding the really effective way, apart from predation, of consummating this transformation?[11]

In response, I would argue that the Wari' want to continue to be Wari' being whites, want the two things at the same time, both points of view. The other enemies, those whom they drew in, such as the OroWin, quickly became Wari'. This is the eventual outcome of the proximity completed by marriage: identity. The Wari', in my understanding, do not want to be equal to the whites: they want to keep them as enemies, preserving their difference without, though, ceasing to experience it. In this sense, they live today like their shamans: they have two bodies simultaneously, which often become merged. They are Wari' and whites, sometimes both at the same time, like their shamans when in trance. While the Wari' in the past had the indirect experience of another position, the enemy position, today they experience it directly in their bodies.

NOTES

INTRODUCTION

1 Translator's note: Serviço de Proteção ao Índio, which ran from 1910 to 1967.
2 Throughout this book, I use the term "whites" to refer to those whom the Wari'
   call simply "enemies" or "white-bodied enemies" in their own language, and
   "civilizados" in Portuguese.
3 Translator's note: Fundação Nacional do Índio (National Indian Foundation),
   set up in 1967 to replace the SPI.
4 For a discussion of the methodological and epistemological questions involved
   in the contextualization of historical documents in anthropological works on
   native peoples, see Fausto 1992, 381; Pompa 2003, 25–30; Rosaldo 1980, 17; Salomon 1999, 19–95; and Whitehead 1988, chaps. 1–5; 2003, vii–xx.
5 Confining myself to South America, I refer the reader especially to the mon-
   umental ethnohistorical work compiled in *The Cambridge History of the Native Peoples of the Americas*, vol. 3 (Salomon and Schwartz 1999). For tropical South America, key works include the collections edited by Carneiro da
   Cunha (1992), Viveiros de Castro and Carneiro da Cunha (1993), Franchetto
   and Heckenberger (2001) on the Upper Xingu, Whitehead (2003), and Fausto
   and Heckenberger (2007b), as well as the articles collected in *L'Homme* 126–28
   (1993). Some regions emerge as focal points for these kinds of analyses. This
   is the case of border regions, which, being a focus of disputes, as in the case
   of the Ecuadorian and Peruvian Andean foothills, known as Upper Amazonia,
   provide researchers with a larger abundance of records (see Taylor 1992, 213;
   1999; and Santos-Granero 1992a, 1992b). The same applies to the Guianas and
   the Caribbean, which have received the attention of numerous authors, including Rivière (1995, 2006a, 2006b), Grenand (1982), Hulme (1986), Whitehead
   (1988, 1999), Hulme and Whitehead (1992), Farage (1991), Dreyfus (1993), and
   Gallois (2005), among others.
6 As the author points out, an exception can be made in the case of the Guarani
   of the missions, since they were soon taught to read and write by the Jesuits and
   subsequently produced a number of written records (Salomon 1991, 41).

7 I should add that the earliest written documentation referring to the Wari' is sparse and somewhat imprecise, meaning we cannot be sure that it concerns the Wari' rather than other groups. I therefore decided not to invest in a direct study of these documents, almost always using secondary sources where necessary instead.

8 See too Franchetto 1992, 339–56; and Coelho de Souza 2001, 358–400.

9 Concerning this same region, there is also the book by the filmmakers Connolly and Anderson (1987), titled *First Contact: New Guinea's Highlanders Encounter the Outside World*, which was published as a complement to the film of the same name from 1983, itself based on footage recorded by Mick Leahy, an Australian gold prospector, in 1933.

10 Wachtel's book (1971) provides a classic example of this procedure. The Indians, the author observes, "perceived events through the prism of myth" (1971, 42). Other key examples include the cited works of Sahlins (1981, 1985, 1995) and the authors in the book edited by Schieffelin and Crittenden (1991b). For other instances, I refer the reader to the collections edited by Hill (1988b) and Carneiro da Cunha (1992), and to an article by the same author on Canela messianism (1986). Also interesting are the cited article by Teixeira-Pinto (2000) on the Arara view of the pacification process, the paper by Fausto (2002b) on the first encounters of the Parakanã (a Tupi-Guarani people) with whites, the analysis by Viveiros de Castro (2000b) of some indigenous narratives, and a text by S. Hugh-Jones (1988) on the reinvention of the Tukano origin myth. The latter is found in an issue of the journal *L'Homme* (106/7), titled "Myth and Its Metamorphoses," which contains other articles relevant to this topic.

11 For a demonstration of this point, see Sahlins 1995. On the proximities between mythical and historical accounts, see Lévi-Strauss 1981, 61; Ramos 1988, 229; Turner 1988, 198; and Gallois 1993, 22–24.

12 See Detienne 1981; Vernant 1980, 23; and Sahlins 1995, chap. 4, for comments on this topic.

13 Examples include some of the contributors to Hill 1988b, a work introduced by precisely this polemic: Chernela 1988; Dillon and Abercrombie 1988; Hill and Wright 1988; Roe 1988; and Turner 1988. Taken as a whole, the focal point of the criticisms made of Lévi-Strauss's work is his notion of cold and hot societies (see Charbonnier 1961, 44–45; also Lévi-Strauss 1976a, 36). I refer the reader to Bernand 1992, 412; Gow 2001, 14–15; Viveiros de Castro 1999, 150, n.43 and 168; and Fausto and Heckenberger 2007a, 14, for further commentary on this debate.

14 For other examples, see Instituto Socioambiental 2000, 16–54.

15 For an analysis of the empirical bases of indigenous magical thinking, see Fausto 2002b on the pacification of the Parakanã.

16 Obeyesekere is criticizing Sahlins's interpretation (1981, 1985) of this episode.

In reply, Sahlins agrees that European mythical thought exists. However, he criticizes Obeyesekere's inversion of roles, which he traces to the author's "irreproachable moral inspiration" (Sahlins 1995, 9). For Sahlins, "Obeyesekere's anti-ethnocentrism turns into a symmetrical and inverse ethnocentrism, the Hawaiians consistently practicing a bourgeois rationality, and the Europeans for over two hundred years unable to do anything but reproduce the myth that 'natives' take them for gods" (1995, 8), thereby reproducing "classic Occidental dualisms of logos and mythos, empirical reason and mental illusion" (1995, 6).

17 Seeking to explain the oscillation in the impacts caused by first contact for different peoples, Schieffelin, Crittenden, et al. (1991) observe in the final chapter of their book, titled "Historical Impact," that these encounters did not always lead to "profound cultural revaluations" (1991, 284) like those described by Sahlins in Hawaii. We are faced, therefore, by a diverging set of complexities related to the "processes involved when historical activities and cultural structures do not easily articulate with one another" (1991, 285).

18 See Gow 2001, 16–17 for similar comments; also Sahlins 1997.

19 See Clifford 1988, 344, also cited by Viveiros de Castro (1992a, 27; 2002, 195–96), Wagner (1975, 20–34), Tooker (1992), and Vilaça (1993, 1999b, 2000b). Also see Taussig (1993b) on the mimetic compulsion of indigenous Americans.

20 The violence unleashed with European invasion is a key theme in the so-called anthropology of warfare and violence. The theses developed in the pioneering works of Lévi-Strauss (1976b [1942]) on the relation between warfare and exchange, Florestan Fernandes (1970 [1952]) on warfare among the seventeenth-century Tupinambá, and Pierre Clastres (1997 [1977]) on violence and warfare in the South American lowlands were widely debated, but it was the work of Chagnon (1983 [1968]) on the intrinsic and violent nature of Yanomami warfare that proved the main inspiration for a discussion focused on the effects of the European invasion on native war patterns. For various aspects of this discussion, see Harris 1979, 1984; Albert 1989; Chagnon 1990; Ferguson and Whitehead 2000; Ferguson 1995; and Fausto 2001.

21 As for other Amazonian indigenous groups in general, see Viveiros de Castro 1986, 1992b, 1992c, 1993b, 2002; Carneiro da Cunha and Viveiros de Castro 1985; Fausto 2001, 2007b; and Vilaça 1992, 2000a, for analyses of specific ethnographic cases.

22 For an analysis of the relation between the increase in magical violence and the invasion of whites in the highland region of Guiana, see Whitehead 2002. The author explains this increase as an attempt to regain community control of the violence, which had reached previously unknown levels with the introduction of firearms (2002, 223). For a wider discussion of magical violence in Amazonia and other regions, see Whitehead and Wright 2004.

23 On the etiological conceptions of the Wari', see Conklin 1989. For other studies
    on the indigenous perception of white diseases, I refer the reader to Albert 1992
    on the Yanomami, and Buchillet 2000 on the Desana.

24 See Carneiro da Cunha 1986; Viveiros de Castro 1992a, 2002; Taylor 1993, 2007;
    Gow 1991, 2001, 2006; Severi 2000; Fausto 2007a; and Oakdale 2001. But forget-
    ting isn't the only factor. As Carneiro da Cunha and Viveiros de Castro (1985)
    reveal in their analysis of Tupinambá warfare and vengeance, there is also an
    active production of memory; in this case, of the deaths caused by enemies that
    must be avenged. For a broader discussion of social memory, see Halbwachs
    1968, 1994.

25 See Carneiro da Cunha (2007, xi) for a commentary on this inversion.

26 I should emphasize the point that the dehumanization of enemies (or of some
    of their aspects; see Fausto 2007b) took place with the predatory act, not prior
    to it. This maintains the difference highlighted earlier between Wari' warfare and
    the warfare practiced by whites, and the Wari' perception of a difference in the
    logic of warfare in the wake of the massacres, when they were treated as prey
    from the outset.

27 Sahlins (1997, 126) makes a similar observation: "The continuity of indigenous
    cultures consists of the specific ways through which they transform themselves."

28 Or as Whitehead puts it (2002, 246), "This is not to suggest that violence can be
    "deconstructed," or that with closer cultural contextualization it will be revealed
    as somehow less brutal and destructive."

29 In this book I have used the spelling Lage when citing the name of the post, and
    Laje when referring to the river.

30 Vilaça 1992.

1. THE FOREIGNER

1 Although there are clear similarities between the Wari' subgroups and this type
   of unit among other indigenous groups, such as the Pano *nawa* (Erikson 1990,
   79–84; 1996), the Nambikwara bands (Price 1972, 113–33) the Kulina *madiha*
   (Viveiros de Castro 1978, 18–23; Pollock 1985, 38–46), and the Kanamari *dyapa*
   (Costa 2007), I have opted not to draw comparisons here and refer the interested reader to these works instead.

2 Over the years, the experience of living together and the intermarriages have
   led to the OroNao' of the Whites gradually being incorporated into the other
   OroNao'. Today the Wari' as a whole usually refer to them precisely as they refer
   to themselves, simply OroNao'. Occasionally, though, the use of the residence
   site as a qualifier (OroNao' of the other shore, of Tanajura, of Santo André, etc.,
   or OroNao' of the Negro River) reveals the persistence of a difference within

the OroNao' subgroup. Despite these changes, here I have opted to maintain the designation OroNao' of the Whites, commonly used in the postpacification period examined here. Conklin (2001, 35–36) refers to them as the OroNao' of the Dois Irmãos area.

3 After harvesting, the maize was stored under the roofs of the houses, a practice that continues today in some locations.

4 Wari' houses nowadays imitate the houses of the region's nonindigenous population, with a double-pitched roof and stilt palm walls. Contemporary villages, built around the FUNAI buildings (called the post), have many more houses. The Rio Negro–Ocaia village, for example, had sixty-three houses in January 2002, and another six others scattered along the shores of the river, close to its mouth. Encouraged by FUNAI, the Wari' are currently looking to redisperse into smaller villages.

5 When fleeing from the whites in the middle of the 1950s, the OroNao' lived in OroAt swiddens at the Ocaia village.

6 Here it is worth recalling that in other contexts the Wari' depict themselves as inhabitants of a type of environment—the *xitot*—that contrasts with forest.

7 11°00′23″ S, 064°26′06″ W.

8 I take the opportunity to point out that the subgroups are not corporate groups like lineages or clans. Despite the Wari' Crow-type kinship terminology (with an Omaha equation), these are absent among the Wari'. For an analysis of the Wari' kinship system, see Vilaça 1995.

9 Conklin, however, explains that this is not a strict rule and that subgroup affiliation may vary over an individual's lifespan.

10 The Wari' say that the subgroup is a name: *wixixi*, "our name," as in the phrase "our name is OroNao'. " This does not mean that personal names are chosen from a repertoire specific to each subgroup, though some names are more closely associated with particular subgroups. For a discussion of Wari' proper names, see Vilaça 1992.

11 Variations in conception theories among informants from the same group have been reported by other Amazonian ethnographers. See C. Hugh-Jones (1979, 115) and S. Hugh-Jones (2001, 255) for the Barasana and Carneiro da Cunha (1978, 101) for the Krahó.

12 For an analysis of Wari' kinship terminology, see Vilaça 1992, 1995. The terminology is nonprescriptive and the consanguine kinship terms have no affinal content.

13 There is also the category of *wira*, a kind of formal friend, today fallen into disuse. The Wari' say that when someone arrived at a village (generally of another subgroup) and was unable to establish kinship relations with any of the inhabitants, one of the latter would treat the visitor as a *wira*. This type of relationship

could form between same or opposite sexes and involved companionship and an interdiction on sexual relations. The *wira* of the father and mother could be inherited by their children, and a *wira* could become consanguine kin over time. Today some older people can cite the names of some of their *wira* who are still alive, always foreigners, but I never heard the term used as a vocative, as was customary in the past.

14 Prescriptive affinity is absent among the Wari'. Real affines are necessarily distant kin, since marriage is prohibited between near kin, a common feature in Crow-type terminological systems. The prohibited kin positions are M, F, MZ, FB, MB, FZ, C, MZC, FBC, MBC, FZC, MZCC, FBCC, MBCC, FZCC, BC, ZC, DC, SC, BCC, ZCC, MM, MMZ, MMB, MF, MFB, MFZ, FF, FFB, FFZ, FM, FMZ, and FMB. This does not mean that the Wari' push these prohibitions to their limit, trying to marry the nearest possible kin. Preferential marriage takes place with a consanguine of a real affine and/or with an affine of a real consanguine, irrespective of the genealogical distance involved, as long as the union is not prohibited.

15 One myth tells that before the Wari' discovered the war club, adultery provoked an internal war in which bows and arrows were used, as against enemies.

16 For a brief description of Wari' festivals—with photos illustrating a *huroroin'* festival performed in 1986—see Conklin 2001, 41–45.

17 This is the ideal drink. When no maize is available, they offer drinks made from wild fruits or honey.

18 On hearing their guests arrive, the Wari' would exclaim, "Here come the frogs!"

19 In terms of preparation and presentation, various parallels can be drawn between fermented maize beer, the food offered in *tamara*, and the flesh of a dead person eaten in the Wari' funeral. This flesh was roasted after it had putrefied, the inverse of what happens with the maize beer, which "rots" after being cooked. In both cases, the preparation involved a kind of double cooking. Like the food offered in the *tamara* festival, the flesh of the deceased was divided into small pieces and eaten with chopsticks. Additionally, this flesh also induced vomiting and comprised an antifood. For a more extensive analysis of these parallels, see Vilaça 1992 and 2002a.

20 However, we need to consider the possibility of a positive connotation to the fact that the *huroroin'* guests are "less foreign." Since the distance of remote foreigners is more clearly defined, the nearest would be precisely those that need to be subject to a more radical process of alienation, as occurs in the *huroroin'* festival.

21 On the idea of affine-less affinity in Amazonia, see Viveiros de Castro 1993b, 167 and ff.

22 While *nem* and *namori* are both potential vocatives, informants always empha

sized the use of the former term. This is interesting because if the guests are "taking brothers-in-law," and the host men desire their wives, what can be concluded is that these men want their own sisters back, demonstrating a clear desire not to obtain these women per se, but to undo the alliance with the foreigners.

2. THE ENEMY

1 Note that enemy names are composed in the same way as Wari' subgroup names: a collectivizing prefix—*oro*—preceding a noun or verb. This corroborates the idea expounded in the myth that enemies originate from Wari' society, and that the process of "enemization" involves the transition from kin to foreigner.

2 For more information on the Txapakura-speaking peoples, see Leigue Castedo 1957; Lévi-Strauss 1948; Meireles 1986, 1989; Métraux 1948; Nimuendaju 1925, 1981; Nordenskiöld 1924; Peggion 1999; and Rydén 1942.

3 For detailed descriptions of these Indians, see Vilaça 1992, appendix 2.

4 Wem Parawan died at the Rio Negro–Ocaia village at the end of 2004.

5 Here the true enemies (*iri wijam*) are whites. The qualifier *iri* (true) is used here to differentiate them from indigenous enemies, simply *wijam*. At other times, the opposite occurs: the Indian enemies are called true enemies.

6 The Wari' do not usually employ the plural when referring to the enemy as a group.

7 Here the true enemies are the Indians in contrast to the whites.

8 Among the Wari', the death of the enemy is a precondition for the transformation of warriors into killers. Injuring without killing was ineffective: the enemy's spirit-blood would not enter the warriors, meaning they could not enter reclusion.

9 For the Wari', there was no difference between killing men, women, or children—all were equally enemies, *wijam*—although the enemy is usually referred to as a male. When they refer to an enemy's wife, they say enemy's female, just as one refers to the female of an animal. I return to this point later.

10 11°02'318" S; 64°51'594" W.

11 In other contexts the Makurap are classified as whites rather than Indians: I once asked a Wari' man whether the whites liked a particular Makurap man, who was married to a Wari' woman in Sagarana. He replied, "As if he were not white too." However, other people describing this massacre claimed it was carried out by rubber tappers from the Ouro Preto River.

12 Taussig (1993a, 113–16), in his study of the colonization of the Putamayo region, reflects on the impact of cannibalism in the Western imagination: "The allegations of cannibalism served not only to justify the enslavement of the

Indians by the Spanish and Portuguese from the 16th century onwards. They also nourished and expanded the repertoire of violence in the colonial imagination" (114).

13 This radically differentiates enemy meat from the flesh of a dead Wari', which was left to rot before being roasted on a grill; moreover, the latter's flesh was generally roasted and eaten at the same location. See Vilaça 2000a for a comparison between funerary and warfare cannibalism.

14 During the Wari' funerary rite, the dead group member is always eaten by non-kin, ideally affines. However, when explaining why kin do not eat the dead body, people emphasize not the risk of death but the impossibility of perceiving the dead kinsperson as a corpse (see Vilaça 1992, 1998, 2000a).

15 The idea of the dead enemy's blood penetrating the body of the killer is common in the South American lowlands (Albert 1985, 351, n.17 lists various groups; also see Lima 1995, 203–4 on the Tupian Juruna). Notably, this is the only context where the Wari' draw a clear association between spirit and blood, an association common among other Amazonian groups.

16 For the Wari', semen derives from blood.

17 The Wari' do not explicitly associate pregnancy and warfare reclusion. However, they do say that the killer, with a protuberant belly caused by the intake of fat, is just like a pregnant woman. See Conklin 1989, 239–44; 2001, 203.

18 This is another common feature in the South American lowlands. Among the Tupian Araweté, for example, the victim remains connected to the killer as a consubstantial, an appendix (Viveiros de Castro 1992c, 2002).

19 Nor do they capture material items that are later made into symbolic wealth, as among the Kayapó, who transformed manufactured objects into *nekretch* or ritual objects (Lea 1986; Turner 1992, 330; Gordon 2006).

20 Inversely, women are also conceived as an important medium of relations between the Wari' and their enemies, as we shall see in the Oropixi' and Nananananananananananana myths later. Here, the Wari' give their women to enemy men as a way of taming or "warinizing" them (also see Vilaça 1992).

21 According to Conklin's informants (2001, 32), only men ate the enemy's flesh.

22 This association is not exclusive to the Wari'. Killing, hunting, and sex are also closely associated for the Yanomami. People say playfully that a man who has sex, like a good hunter, enters a state of homicide (Albert 1985, 346, n.12; Taylor 2000, 314–16).

23 Here we need to note an inversion: though a victim, since he is "killed" by an excess of sour maize beer, the recently arrived dead man is identified as a killer.

24 See McCallum 1996 and Kensinger 1995 for a description of the concept of body among the Cashinahua. See Vilaça 2005 and 2009b for a critical analysis of anthropological studies of the body on the basis of Amazonian data. Also see

M. Strathern 2009; Lock 1993; Lock and Scheper-Hughes 1987; and A. Strathern 1999.

25 This list may vary according to the shaman (who can see the *jam-* of some beings and not others).

26 *Jam-* is also the form in which people act in dreams, modeled on the shamanic dream. During dreams, one's *jam-* may be captured by a sorcerer, animal, or ancestral figure, and taken to live with the captor. The Wari' usually claim not to dream at night, except for shamans. See Fausto 2001 on the Parakanã, who likewise state that only shamans have the capacity to dream.

27 This metamorphic capacity as a definitive trait of humans has been shown by Ingold in relation to the Ojibwa, though the latter do not associate it with the spirit: "For the Ojibwa this capacity for metamorphosis is one of the key aspects of being a person" (2000, 91).

28 M. Strathern (1992, 85) makes a similar observation in commenting on Haraway's critique of science.

29 This idea is not exclusive to the Wari'. Among the Piaroa, for example, predators are the prey of their prey (Overing 1995).

30 In the case of encounters with enemies, the Wari' killed by them are no longer recognized as Wari': they have become full enemies. Revenge is not conceived as "bringing back the blood of the dead kinsperson," as some Amerindian groups affirm.

31 Animals such as jaguars and tapirs may appear as Wari' to some people, especially children, in order to capture them. The incorporation of animal offspring as pets, treated as children by their owners, a practice common to many Amazonian groups (see Taylor 2000 on the Jivaro), was not practiced by the Wari', who had no animal pets before the contact with whites.

32 Likewise, the animals with spirit can transform into other animal species. Indeed, bearing in mind the identity between enemies and animal prey (see above), this capacity for animals to transform from one species into another may help explain the variation in the names of enemy groups in the war accounts. It is as though the limit between "species" was traversable for enemies too.

33 Viveiros de Castro (1986, 1992c) explores this theme in his analysis of Tupi-Guarani warfare.

3. THE WHITE ENEMY

1 Nowi (OroWaramXijein man, who is about seventy).

2 Jimon Pan Tokwe (OroWaram man, who would be about eighty-five today).

3 Hwerein Pe e' (OroNao' man, who is about seventy).

4 Watakao Oromixik (OroNao' man, who is about seventy).

5 When I asked whether this had made the husbands angry and vengeful—since extraconjugal relations are often a cause of fights—Paletó replied, "No, they weren't angry. They would have been angry had they been Wari', or if they had seen the whites." This implies that the Wari' did not hit their wives out of jealousy or a sense of betrayal, but out of anger for receiving a bad wife from their affines. Fights between couples are not related to the psychological fact of jealousy but to the social fact of affinity.

6 Cutting children in half with a machete seems to have been a recurrent practice among the whites who attacked the Wari'.

7 See Meireles 1986, 1989; Von Graeve 1989; Conklin 1989; Mason 1977.

8 Apparently neither were the Wari' linked to whites indirectly: they say that they never acquired metal tools or manufactured goods from other Indians.

9 Estimating the age of adult Wari', especially older people, is extremely difficult. The age that I attributed to some people during my doctoral fieldwork (1992–94) proved inadequate when, almost ten years later, I came to revise my estimates in preparation for the book. A margin of error of five to ten years probably needs to be allowed. The ages given here refer to 2004.

10 The collection *Pacificando o branco* (Albert and Ramos 2000) contains a wide range of ethnographic data on the cosmological classifications of the whites. The Wayana, for example, classify them as animalized enemies, while simultaneously associating them with supernatural beings (Van Velthem 2000, 64–67). For the Waiãpi, whites and blacks are human but different since guided by the shadow-soul, which possesses an inclination toward animality (Grenand and Grenand 2000, 155). The Cashinahua associate whites with the Incas, avaricious and cannibalistic mythological beings characterized by the strangeness of their bodies (McCallum 2000, 388). The Arara (Carib) associated the whites of the FUNAI Attraction Front with malevolent mythic spirits (Teixeira-Pinto 2000, 414, 418).

11 According to Meireles (1986, 166), the whites were differentiated from other peoples (other Indians) by their material culture (clothing and so on) and by "the perception of a more complex and disturbing difference: 'the white body.'" Although the Wari' do sometimes refer to whites as "white-bodied enemies," skin color is and was not, I think, the primary distinguishing feature. Indeed, many of the whites who contacted them, such as the rubber tappers from Northeast Brazil, were probably of mixed ethnicity (European, indigenous, and African in origin) and fairly dark-skinned themselves. Once when I asked a Wari' man whether the whites' skin color had amazed them, he replied that what had been visible was not their skin but their clothing.

12 The expression used is "*om na ximikon*," which translates literally as "he had no heart." For the Wari', the heart is the organ of reason.

4. THE WHITE ENEMY

1 In some other versions, the water disappears after a full storm (strong rain with wind) as Oropixi' threatens, and not simply a gale as actually occurs in this version.

2 Red flour is made from raw maize, crushed with a little water, and then roasted. It is used as an accompaniment for meat and fish, and to sweeten maize drink. White flour is drier, since the maize grains are roasted and crushed afterward without water; this was the type preferred for long journeys.

3 Maize was the main Wari' crop before they started living peacefully with the whites. Some people planted a small amount of sweet manioc close to the house, likewise cotton, which was used to make adornments, threads, and rope. They had no knowledge of bananas.

4 They did not use kin terms to address each other as is customary between brothers.

5 As we have seen, the Wari' use the same word—*wijam*—to refer to traditional enemies and to the whites. In Portuguese they differentiate whites by calling them "civilizados."

6 Also see Gonçalves's discussion (2000, 239) on jealousy among the Paresi, where pairs of brothers also comprise the maximal instance of identity but can be split by disputes over women. In the Wari' case, though, jealousy is not properly speaking the cause of the rupture, but the aggression between the brothers.

7 Although those in the village explicitly lack water, not food, various people comment on the hunger that followed Oropixi's departure. This hunger may be related to the impossibility of making maize drink, an important part of the daily diet. Indeed, in our reference version, the difference between the family that stored water and the family of Oripixi's brother (and the others) is marked by maize drink, which is only shared after they make up.

8 Lévi-Strauss (1991, 89) remarks that almost all South American indigenous peoples fear the birth of twins. As an exception, he cites the ancient Peruvians and some groups located in the sphere of influences of the high Andean civilizations, such as the Aymara and Mojo. In the eighteenth century, some Txapakura groups, including the Moré, who speak a language very close to that of the Wari', were settled in Jesuit missions that made up part of the complex of Mojo missions (Meireles 1989, 78–79).

9 Three Wari' myths begin in precisely the same way: the younger brother has sex with the wife of the older brother, who takes revenge. These are Oropixi' Hwijin, and the red macaws.

10 Françoise Héritier (1979) suggests another way of interpreting the sexual relation with the brother's wife. She argues that having sex with the brother's wife

is to have indirect carnal contact with the brother, which constitutes a form of "second-degree incest." The conjoining of two identical subjects generates a meteorological, biological, and social short-circuit. The interpretation is undoubtedly of some interest in the case of Oropixi' given that biological and social disorder effectively occurs with the (meteorological) lack of water. However, this analysis tends to emphasize the similarity between the brothers, considered identical, while Wari' thought stresses precisely the difference between them. Moreover, Héritier's hypothesis of "second-degree incest" cannot be applied to Wari' sisters, who can have sex with the same man without any problem.

11 In *The Raw and the Cooked* (1994), Lévi-Strauss, analyzing the Bororo myth of the bird-nester (M1)—a narrative displaying various similarities with the Wari' myth of the red macaws, which, like the myths of Oropixi' and Hwijin (see chapter 5), also begins with a younger brother having sex with the older brother's wife—calls attention to the fact that the punishment is inflicted on the person who desired revenge, and not the person who committed incest (in the Bororo myth, a son has sex with his mother and suffers the revenge of his father) (Lévi-Strauss 1994, 48). I was able to record a number of actual cases of splits between brothers after one of them had sex with the other's wife. Generally the betrayed brother physically attacks the other and, as in the Oropixi' myth, it is he, not the betrayer, who is condemned by the family group and wider society.

12 As I mentioned previously, three Wari' myths begin by telling of a younger brother who has sex with his older brother's wife: Oropixi', Hwijin, and the red macaws. The latter begins with the episode of the bird-nester that appears in the Bororo (M1) and Gê (M7) myths analyzed by Lévi-Strauss in *The Raw and the Cooked* (1994, 35–37, 66–67). In the Bororo myth, the boy is abandoned in the macaw nest by his father as punishment for having had sex with his mother. In the Gê myth, the boy is abandoned by his brother-in-law, who was angered after being struck by stones, which were in fact macaw eggs. In the Wari' myth, the younger brother is abandoned in the macaw nest by the older brother for having sex with the latter's wife. The Wari' choose the relation between brothers to initiate a conflict that in the Gê myth takes place between affines. This also occurs in a certain form in the Bororo myth, taking into account that, among the Bororo, father and son are from opposite, exogamic moieties that exchange women between themselves. In the Juruna myth containing the episode of the bird-nester, the conflict is between a father-in-law and his son-in-law, the latter being the one who is abandoned (Tânia Lima, personal communication, 1995).

5. THE FOREIGNER, THE DEAD

1 Among the Wari', the father's brother is terminologically identified with the genitor.

2 A brother when talking to another refers to his wives as "our wives."

3 The Wari' play this drum during *huroroin'* and *hwitop'* festivals in which hosts and guests, usually from different subgroups or villages, confront each other.

4 A vine or cloth is often tied around the forehead to alleviate headaches, including those caused by drinking maize beer.

5 The Wari' word I translate here as image is *jam-*. The smoke seen under the water is an image of the smoke enveloping the body roasted on the surface and accompanies the deceased's spirit. The latter, in turn, is a double or other of the roasted body.

6 Even having never killed anyone while alive, men become killers when they die, and the killers spend the period of reclusion lying on an assai fiber hammock, drinking maize drink and blowing this flute.

7 According to the Wari', a musical duel took place between Hwijin and the Orotapan. Those narrating this myth always sing the songs, which are difficult to translate. In other versions, this musical duel occurs when Hwijin first falls in the water, or, as in the OroWaram versions, at the end of the myth, when the Orotapan ascend to the surface intent on eating the Wari'.

8 Wem Paron was the Orotapan leader, the biggest of them.

9 Just like the Wari' dance in festivals, in files.

10 According to the narrator, the six-banded armadillo has large claws like those of the giant armadillo. It is also very strong.

11 Wem Paron's children call Hwijin "Father," suggesting the two had become brothers.

12 When he narrated this version of the myth, Paletó was staying at my house in Rio de Janeiro: a few days earlier we had visited the city zoo where he had seen an elephant.

13 The spirits of the Wari' dead, who live underwater in human form, transform into peccaries when they come to the surface. They become the prey of the living and, once their bodies have been killed and eaten, return to the subaquatic world to return later as peccaries once more, and so on forever. The spirits are immortal. See Vilaça 1998.

14 The fish were classified by two informants: Paletó, an OroNao', and his son Abrão, consulting the book *Catálogo de peixes comerciais do Baixo Rio Tocantins* (Santos, Jegu, and de Merona 1984). The reader will spot various problems in this classification: its purpose is merely to enable a better understanding of the myth. For example, the trahira fish is identified by informants on other occasions as *Erythrinus erythrinus* (*wam* in the Wari' language). Fish and any other unidentified animal or plant species are cited in the text by their Wari' names.

15 As this woman was childless at death, she had probably had her children under the water: the spirits of the dead can also marry and have children.

16 Decoration used by the Wari' in festivals.

17 Hwijin was acting as a Wari' shaman, removing from the prey the attributes associated with humanness and making them edible.

18 Eating a consanguine is autocannibalism and provokes death. In funerals, desolate kin often wanted to eat the deceased in order to die. In a relatively recent episode (1990s), an old man bit the tongue of his dead grandson during the funeral, wishing to provoke his own death.

19 The connection between beer and devouring/cannibalism is clearly manifest in the festivals held between subgroups. For an analysis of this point, see chapter 1 and Vilaça 1992, 203.

20 This evokes the episode of the myth of Lynx in which the hero was remade by his wife from a small piece of bone leftover after his body was cooked (Lévi-Strauss 1991, 22–23).

21 For a more general discussion of perspectival vision, see Viveiros de Castro 1996, 1998a, 1998b, and 2002. For its elaboration among the Juruna, see Lima 1995, 1996, and 2005, and, among the Wari', Vilaça 1999b, 2000a, and 2005.

22 Though living on the river's shore rather than its bottom, Oropixi' is a water being like Hwijin. Narrating these myths to me, one man classified both Oropixi' and Hwijin as "water spirits." Oropixi' has active control over the water; he is the "water owner," as another informant affirmed. Some versions suggest that Oropixi' merges with water: his departure and return are represented by a storm.

23 The contemporary developments of Wari' Christianity force me to complexify this association between creation and the establishment of differences. In some ways, it is as if the difference has been taken too far, to the point where ontological categories, such as *wari'* and *karawa*, have lost their perspectival nature.

6. THE ENEMY

1 The hero is called Nanananana because of a linguistic peculiarity, a kind of stutter: he finishes his phrases repeating the sound "na."

2 As the Wari' lacked the technique to produce fire, its loss obliged a village's inhabitants to search for it elsewhere.

3 Boys sleep in the men's house from the age of eight or nine until marriage.

4 As I mentioned earlier, *oro* is a collectivizing prefix; *karakat* means to break, to act wrongly, to be ugly, and, according to the missionaries, to sin.

5 Although these individuals are called "other people" (*xukun wari'*) in the reference version, they are called "enemies" (*wijam*) in most versions.

6 Wari' discourse states that the children produced by white men and Wari' women are white. However, at issue is not the relation between two groups but the contact of Wari' women with isolated white individuals. Furthermore, these

relations are usually based on short-term clandestine sexual relations rather than marriage. The Wari' typically condemn these relations with whites.

7. THE BROTHER-IN-LAW

1 I presented a version of Pinom, narrated by Paletó in October 1986, followed by a brief analysis of the myth, in Vilaça 1992, 237–46. The reader may also consult the versions presented by Meireles (1986, 413–21) and Conklin (1989, 577–83; 2001, 242–46).

2 As I mentioned in an earlier note, maize flour (made from red or white corn) is cooked over a fire.

3 Note that in the Hwijin myth, the Orotapan are beings who live underwater and devour the Wari'.

4 Among the Wari', a young girl was promised to the boy when still a baby, and after this point he referred to her as wife and to her mother as mother-in-law.

5 Lévi-Strauss (1991, 142 n.1) had already noted the attenuation of this motif among other groups.

6 Men also take part in this type of fishing occasionally, but, according to Paletó, only married men. In any event, the activity is prototypically female.

7 As well as being women, the living are raw (*nenekun*) compared to the dead, who are said to be cooked (*jam'*). This association is not limited to the empirical fact of roasting the corpse. For the Wari', rawness also has the sense of immature, green. Children and green fruits are raw. In a sense, therefore, the dead are more social beings compared to the Wari', just like adults compared to children. For the Araweté, the living are also associated with women and rawness (Viveiros de Castro 1992c).

8. THE MOTIVES OF THE WHITES

1 Indian Museum, microfilm 42, sheet 457. The other citations of SPI documents refer to reports, letters, radiograms, and other documents contained on microfilms 41, 42, 43, 44, and 45, available for consultation at the Indian Museum in Rio de Janeiro. I shall provide precise references only in the case of polemical information that could be contested.

2 In 1980 the Tenente Lira post was transferred to the site now occupied by the Lage post.

3 Not just the Wari' looked for tools. For many native groups, metal tools comprised a strong initial attraction for approaching the whites. On the Waiãpi, see Gallois (2000, 208) on industrial goods in general; on the Wayana, see Van Velthem (2000, 61); on the Xikrin, see Gordon (2006).

4 The Wari' also learned to call the missionaries "os americanos" (*oroamericano*, "people of the americanos") and soon after the first peaceful contacts began to differentiate them as a special type of white, foreigners (*tatirim*) in relation to Brazilians.

5 See the report by Mauro Leonel Jr. (1984) and the microfilms already cited.

6 The Wari' say they were taken to Sagarana despite being in good health and without knowing where they were going.

9. THE WIDENING RIVER

1 The only nonindigenous account I have concerning this phase of contact comes from Royal Taylor, since the process is only briefly mentioned in the SPI documents I was able to consult. The missionaries seem to have been the most active during contact, with the SPI agents virtually absent. The Wari' accounts also emphasize the missionaries' role. However, I realize that I may have reached a different conclusion had I been able to interview the SPI employees involved in the contact.

2 This is a secondhand report since Royal was not present during this phase, arriving at Tanajura a short time later, in May 1957, after the Wari' had approached the whites' house for the second time. According to Royal, the missionaries present at this time were Joe Moreno, Abraham Koop, and Richard Sollis.

3 For an analysis of the notion of equivocation as intrinsic to any Amerindian relational context, see Viveiros de Castro 2004.

4 The late ones were named as such because today they are already dead.

5 This excerpt also shows the relationship between warfare and the construction of the male identity: those who failed to hit the target were called "women."

6 This encounter may well have occurred much later when the Wari' had already become sick. It seems to match an SPI document dated May 1957, reporting that Josias journeyed as far as the "maloca" and counted three "malocas" with twenty-five men, twenty-three women, and fifty-six children.

7 Von Graeve (1989, 51) states that the rubber bosses, realizing that their punitive expeditions had failed to achieve the expected result, and fearful of traveling on the Pacaás Novos River where they could be attacked at any moment, began to negotiate with the NTM to resolve the impasse peacefully. It should be noted that the missionaries had already undertaken an expedition to the Jaci-Paraná River in 1951, backed by the SPI, but encountered no Indians.

8 I cannot go into much depth on the occupation of the Dois Irmãos River by rubber tappers, likewise the attacks suffered by the Wari' of this region, since my informants from this subgroup were few in number. However, some details suggest that their territory was not heavily occupied by the whites before pacifi-

cation. For example, until peaceful contact, they had never seen chickens, while the other Wari' were already very familiar with them. Additionally, they said that whenever they wished to encounter white enemies to kill, they had to travel for days to the Pacaás Novos River, which indicates that the whites remained at some distance from their villages. I never heard of massacres perpetrated by the whites, which the other Wari' like to describe in vivid detail before recounting their own war expeditions.

9 Von Graeve (1989, 50) cites Guerra's claim (1953) that around 1950 the Pacaás Novos was the most heavily occupied of the tributaries of the Mamoré and Madeira, numbering some 789 rubber tappers.

10 Although this version of the flood derives from the OroNao' of the right bank of the Pacaás Novos and not the group that became isolated on the left bank, I think it amounts to a reflection of the OroNao' as a whole on the split occurring within their subgroup. This comparison between the historical moment and the myth is further legitimated by the movements of the isolated OroNao' in relation to the whites, which clearly relate to episodes of the myth.

10. "THE ENEMY SAYS HE'S ORONAO'"

1 Tem We does not mention the presence of the SPI agent, but there certainly was one since the missionaries were not allowed to organize expeditions to contact isolated Indians by themselves.

2 Here the informant is correcting himself for having called the OroWaram enemies (*wijam*), which is precisely what they would be from the white's point of view.

3 Possibly referring to Wao Taran, who was in the tree.

4 The similarity to the Nanananana myth (chapter 6) is clear: a man approaches a woman, grabbing her firmly by the arm, and frightening her. He tries to calm her, saying he is not an enemy, before asking her to take him to the men.

5 I am unsure whether Aldenir and Baitá worked for the SPI at the time or whether they were merely rubber tappers who collaborated voluntarily out of an interest in the pacification of the Indians. Their names are not found in any SPI document. Both married Wari' women: Aldenir is still alive today, living with his wife and children, in Sagarana. Baitá died recently at the same settlement.

6 I provide this perhaps apparently unnecessarily extensive list of names to contrast this group, by its composition, with the isolated OroEo and the OroAt whom I discuss later.

7 Carneiro da Cunha 1986 provides an interesting analysis of this kind of transformation, relating the messianic movement of the Canela Indians, in 1963, to the myth describing the origin of whites.

11. THE GREAT EXPEDITION

1 The journey of the ethnologist Etta Becker Donner to the region, accompanied by SPI employees, in August 1954, was primarily intended to produce a survey of the area and locate villages. Members of the expedition do not seem to have made preparations for actual contact with isolated Indians, though they must have at least considered this possibility.

2 I should make one point clear. Until at least the end of the 1940s, the OroNao' on the right bank of the Pacaás Novos River lived mainly along the affluents of the Santo André and Da Gruta rivers, having left the Ouro Preto sooner than this. From roughly the beginning to the middle of the 1950s, fleeing from the whites, they abandoned the invaded areas and built their villages exclusively in the more protected Negro and Ocaia river region, in OroEo and OroAt territories. This explains why they were concentrated there when they encountered the whites.

3 Almost thirty years later the Wari' founded a village, called Ocaia II, on this same site.

4 Koxain is situated on the left bank of the Ocaia River and, therefore, in typically OroAt territory. As I said in a previous footnote, at this time the OroNao', by their own account, were living on OroAt and OroEo lands, fleeing the whites.

5 This information may be unreliable. If the Indians from the Laje had measles, for instance, an outbreak would have immediately occurred on the Negro River at the moment of contact. This did not happen.

6 Although it is not certain, this is probably the same Saul who took part in the initial contact with the OroNao' of the Whites, as related in chapter 9.

7 Teixeira-Pinto (2000, 413–14), analyzing the activities of the "Arara Attraction Front," observes that the Arara associated the pacification agents with malevolent spirits, which always appear in the form of enemies, because of the way they acted: "people emerging from various directions, following the steps of the Indians, locating the villages, waiting on paths, forcing the encounter." Their response was to flee and then attack.

8 Hwijimain Xitot is located far upriver in OroAt territory. It is very possible that when the whites arrived the remaining OroNao' were concentrated in no more than two villages located in OroAt territory.

9 Other authors studying the Wari' (Von Graeve 1989 and Conklin 1989) have calculated the total Wari' population, including all the existing subgroups, at around 1,000 people.

10 By my calculations, they lived in isolation for at least two years.

11 See the introduction.

CONCLUSION

1 In 2007 people left the Ocaia settlement after being threatened by whites who accused them of invading their lands.

2 At the Rio Negro–Ocaia post the only non-Wari' Indians are two Canoé women. At the Tanajura post there are also two or three Canoé women married to Wari' men and, perhaps, an OroWin woman in the same situation. A Karipuna man lived at the Lage post at the start of the 1990s; he was married to a Wari' woman. The only "post" to shelter a larger number of people from other indigenous groups is Sagarana, but they still form a minority in relation to the Wari'.

3 For a well-described example of the same transformation, see Kelly 2003, 113 for the Yanomami, who say, "Nowadays lots of us are becoming *napë*" (enemy/white).

4 Against the argument that they do not marry whites because the latter do not wish to marry them, I stress that, from the Wari' point of view, they are the ones who do not value these unions.

5 I explored this topic in 1996 in my doctoral thesis and have developed my analysis in subsequent publications (Vilaça 1996b, 1999b, 2000b); see also Viveiros de Castro 1999.

6 On the Tenetehara, see Baldus 1937 and Wagley and Galvão (1961); on the Terena, see Silva (1949); on the Terena and Caduveo, see Oberg 1949; and on the Rio Negro area, see Galvão 1957, 1979.

7 I cite in particular those produced by Cardoso de Oliveira (1963, 1964, 1967), Melatti (1967), Laraia and DaMatta (1967), and, more recently, by Oliveira Filho (1988).

8 For an excellent critique of these studies, see Viveiros de Castro 1999.

9 See this idea in Viveiros de Castro 2000a, 29, n.40. I emphasize once again that the body here is not only physical substance, but includes affects and memory, which for ourselves are usually conceived as attributes of the mind.

10 On this type of equivocation, I refer the reader to an article by Viveiros de Castro (2004), which is dedicated to the theme, and to the work of Kelly (2003, 2005) on the relations between the Yanomami and the whites.

11 See Kelly (2003, 136) for the same avoidance among the Yanomami.

BIBLIOGRAPHY

NEWSPAPERS

Alto Madeira, January 6, 1962.
O Dia, September 25, 1951.
Folha da Noite, November 21, 1951.
O Imparcial, January 1, 1961; January 8, 1961; May 21, 1961.
O Jornal, July 23, 1963.
Última Hora, December 27, 1961; January 15, 1962.

MAGAZINES

Brown Gold, [s.n.], 1945.
O Cruzeiro, [illegible date].
Lettre d'Amazonie, n. 33, 1970; n. 135, 1996.

ADDITIONAL SOURCE

Museu do Índio, Rio de Janeiro. Microfilms 41–45.

BOOKS, ARTICLES, AND DISSERTATIONS

Albert, Bruce. 1985. "Temps du sang, temps des cendres: Représentation de la mala-
die, système rituel et espace politique chez les Yanomami du Sud-Est (Amazonie
brésilienne)." Ph.D. diss., Université de Paris X (Nanterre).
———. 1989. "On Yanomami 'Violence': Inclusive Fitness or Ethnographer's Rep-
resentation?" *Current Anthropology* 30: 637–40.
———. 1992. "A fumaça do metal: História e representações do contato entre os
Yanomami." *Anuário Antropológico* 89: 151–89.
———. 1993. "L'or cannibale et la chute du ciel: Une critique chamanique de
l'économie politique de la nature." *L'Homme* 126–28: 349–78.

Albert, Bruce, and Alcida Ramos, eds. 2000. *Pacificando o branco: Cosmologias do contato no Norte-Amazônico*. São Paulo: Unesp/Imprensa Oficial do Estado; Paris: IRD.

Arhem, Kaj. 1993. "Ecosofia makuna." In F. Correa (org.), *La selva humanizada: ecología alternativa en al trópica húmedo colombiano*. Bogotá: Instituto Colombiano de Antropología/Fondo FEN Colombia/Fondo Editorial CEREC, 109–26.

Balandier, Georges. 1951. "La situation coloniale: approche théorique." *Cahiers Internationaux de Sociologie*, XI: 44–79.

Baldus, Herbert, 1937. *Ensaios de etnologia brasileira*. São Paulo: Companhia Editora Nacional.

Balée, William. 1989. "Cultura e vegetação na Amazônia brasileira." In W. Neves, ed., "Biologia e ecologia humana na Amazônia: Avaliação e perspectivas," *Boletim do Museu Paraense Emílio Goeldi*: 95–109.

Becker-Donner, Etta. 1954. "First Report on a Field Trip to Guaporé Region (Pacaas Novos)." In *Annals of the 31st International Congress of the Americanists* (São Paulo) 31(1): 107–12.

Bernand, Carmen. 1992. Review of J. Hill, ed., *Rethinking History and Myth: Indigenous South American Perspectives on the Past*. *L'Homme* 122–24: 412–13.

Bonilla, Lydie Oiara. 2007. "Des proies si desirables: Soumission et prédation pour les Paumari d'Amazonie brésilienne." Ph.D. diss., École des Hautes Études en Sciences Sociales, Paris.

Boyer, Pascal. 1990. *Tradition as Truth and Communication: A Cognitive Description of Traditional Discourse*. Cambridge: Cambridge University Press.

Buchillet, Dominique. 2000. "Contas de vidro, enfeites de branco e 'potes de malaria.' Epidemiologia e representações de doenças infecciosas entre os Desana do alto rio Negro." In Bruce Albert and Alcida Ramos, eds., *Pacificando o branco: Cosmologias do contato no Norte-Amazônico*, 113–42. São Paulo: Unesp/Imprensa Oficial do Estado; Paris: IRD.

Caravaglia, Juan Carlos. 1999. "The Crises and Transformations of Invaded Societies: The La Plata Basin (1535–1650)." In Frank Salomon and Stuart Schwartz, eds., *The Cambridge History of the Native Peoples of the Americas*; vol. 3; part 2, *South America*, 1–58. Cambridge: Cambridge University Press.

Cardoso de Oliveira, Roberto. 1963. "Aculturação e fricção interétnica." *América Latina* 6(3): 33–45.

———. 1964. *O índio e o mundo dos brancos*. Brasília: Editora UNB.

———. 1967. "Problemas e hipóteses relativos à fricção interétnica: Sugestões para uma metodologia." *Revista do Instituto de Ciências Sociais* 4(1): 41–91.

Carneiro da Cunha, Manuela. 1978. *Os mortos e os outros*. São Paulo: Hucitec.

———. 1986. *Antropologia do Brasil: Mito, história, etnicidade*. São Paulo: Brasiliense/Edusp.

———, ed. 1992. *História dos índios do Brasil*. São Paulo: Fapesp/SMC/Companhia das Letras.

———. 1998. "Pontos de vista sobre a floresta amazônica." *Mana: Estudos de Antropologia Social* 4(1): 7–22.

———. 2007. Foreword. "Whose History and History for Whom?" In Carlos Fausto and Michael Heckenberger, eds., *Time and Memory in Indigenous Amazonia: Anthropological Perspectives*, xi–xiv. Gainesville: University Press of Florida.

Carneiro da Cunha, Manuela, and Eduardo Viveiros de Castro. 1985. "Vingança e temporalidade: Os Tupinambás." *Journal de la Société des Américanistes* 71: 191–217.

CEDI (Centro Ecumênico de Documentação e Informação). 1984. *Povos indígenas no Brasil/84. Aconteceu Especial* 15. São Paulo.

Chagnon, Napoleon. 1983 [1968]. *Yanomamö: The Fierce People*. Fort Worth: Holt, Rinehart and Winston.

———. 1990. "On Yanomamö Violence: Reply to Albert." *Current Anthropology* 31: 49–53.

Charbonnier, Georges. 1961. *Entretiens avec Claude Lévi-Strauss*. Paris: René Julliard/Plon.

Chaumeil, Jean-Pierre. 1983. *Voir, savoir, pouvoir: Le chamamisme chez les Yagua du Nord-Est péruvien*. Paris: Éditions de l'École des Hautes Études en Sciences Sociales.

Chernela, Janet. 1988. "Righting History in the Northwest Amazon: Myth, Structure, and History in an Arapaço Narrative." In Jonathan Hill, ed., *Rethinking History and Myth: Indigenous South American Perspectives on the Past*, 35–49. Urbana: University of Illinois Press.

Clastres, Pierre. 1997 [1977]. *Archéologie de la violence: La guerre dans les sociétés primitives*. Paris: L'Aube.

Clifford, James. 1988. *The Predicament of Culture: Twentieth-Century Ethnography, Literature, and Art*. Cambridge, Mass.: Harvard University Press.

Coelho de Souza, Marcela. 2001. "Virando gente: Notas a uma história aweti." In Bruna Franchetto and Michael Heckenberger, ed., *Os Povos do Alto Xingu: História e Cultura*, 358–400. Rio de Janeiro: Editora da UFRJ.

Conklin, Beth Ann. 1989. "Images of Health, Illness, and Death among the Wari' (Pakaas Novos) of Rondônia, Brazil." Ph.D. diss., University of California at San Francisco and Berkeley.

———. 1997. "Body Paint, Feathers, and VCRs: Aesthetics and Authenticity in Amazonian Activism." *American Ethnologist* 24(4): 711–37.

———. 2001. *Consuming Grief: Compassionate Cannibalism in an Amazonian Society*. Austin: University of Texas Press.

Connolly, Bob, and Robin Anderson. 1987. *First Contact: New Guinea's Highlanders Encounter the Outside World*. New York: Viking Penguin.

Costa, Luiz Antonio. 2007. "As faces do jaguar: Parentesco, história e mitologia entre os Kanamari da Amazônia Ocidental." Ph.D. diss., PPGAS/Museu Nacional/ UFRJ, Rio de Janeiro.

Damatta, Roberto. 1970. "Mito e antimito entre os Timbira." In Claude Lévi-Strauss, Roberto Cardoso de Oliveira, and Júlio César Melatti, eds., *Mito e linguagem social*, 77–106. Rio de Janeiro: Tempo Brasileiro.

Descola, Philippe. 2005. *Par-delà nature et culture*. Paris: Gallimard

Detienne, Marcel. 1981. *L'Invention de la mythologie*. Paris: Gallimard.

Dillon, Mary, and Thomas Abercrombie. 1988. "The Destroying Christ: An Aymara Myth of Conquest." In Jonathan Hill, ed., *Rethinking History and Myth: Indigenous South American Perspectives on the Past*, 50–77. Urbana: University of Illinois Press.

Dreyfus, Simone. 1993. "Os empreendimentos coloniais e os espaços públicos indígenas no interior da Guiana Ocidental (entre o Orenoco e o Corentino) de 1613 a 1796." In Eduardo Viveiros de Castro and Manuela Carneiro da Cunha, eds., *Amazônia: Etnologia e história indígena*, 19–41. São Paulo: NHII/USP/Fapesp.

Erikson, Philippe. 1990. "Les Matis D'Amazonie." Ph.D. diss., Université de Paris X (Nanterre).

———. 1996. *La griffe des aïeux: Marquage du corps et démarquages ethniques chez les Matis d'Amazonie*. Paris: Peeters.

Farage, Nádia. 1991. *As muralhas dos sertões: Os povos indígenas no rio Branco e a colonização*. São Paulo: Paz e Terra/Anpocs.

Fausto, Carlos. 1992. "Fragmentos de história e cultura tupinambá: Da etnologia como instrumento crítico de conhecimento etno-histórico." In Manuela Carneiro da Cunha, ed., *História dos índios no Brasil*, 381–96. São Paulo: Fapesp/ SMC/Companhia das Letras.

———. 2001. *Inimigos fiéis: História, guerra e xamanismo na Amazônia*. São Paulo: Edusp.

———. 2002a. "Banquete de gente: Comensalidade e canibalismo na Amazônia." *Mana: Estudos de Antropologia Social* 8(2): 7–44.

———. 2002b. "The Bones Affair: Indigenous Knowledge Practices in Contact Situations Seen from an Amazonian Case." *Journal of the Royal Anthropological Institute* 8: 669–90.

———. 2007a. "If God Were a Jaguar: Cannibalism and Christianity among the Guarani (16th–20th Centuries)." In Carlos Fausto and Michael Heckenberger, eds., *Time and Memory in Indigenous Amazonia: Anthropological Perspectives*, 74–105. Gainesville: University Press of Florida.

———. 2007b. "Feasting on People: Eating Animals and Humans in Amazonia." *Current Anthropology* 48(4): 497–530.

Fausto, Carlos, and Michael Heckenberger. 2007a. "Introduction: Indigenous History and the History of the 'Indians.'" In Carlos Fausto and Michael Heckenberger, eds., *Time and Memory in Indigenous Amazonia: Anthropological Perspectives*, 1–43. Gainesville: University Press of Florida.

———, eds. 2007b. *Time and Memory in Indigenous Amazonia: Anthropological Perspectives*. Gainesville: University Press of Florida.

Ferguson, Brian. 1995. *Yanomami Warfare: A Political History*. Santa Fe, N. Mex.: SAR Press.

Ferguson, Brian, and Neil Whitehead. 2000. "The Violent Edge of Empire." In Brian Ferguson and Neil Whitehead, eds., *War in the Tribal Zone: Expanding States and Indigenous Warfare*, 1–30. Santa Fe, N. Mex.: SAR Press.

Fernandes, Florestan. 1970 [1952]. *A função social da guerra na sociedade Tupinambá*. São Paulo: Pioneira/Edusp.

Fernandes, Rubem César. 1980. "Um exército de anjos: As razões da Missão Novas Tribos." *Religião e Sociedade* 6: 129–66.

Franchetto, Bruna. 1992. "'O aparecimento dos caraíba': Para uma história kuikuru e alto-xinguana." In Manuela Carneiro da Cunha, ed., *História dos índios do Brasil*, 339–56. São Paulo: Fapesp/SMC/Companhia das Letras.

Franchetto, Bruna, and Michael Heckenberger, eds. 2001. *Os Povos do Alto Xingu: História e Cultura*. Rio de Janeiro. Editora da UFRJ.

Friedman, Jonathan. 1988. "No History Is an Island: A Review Essay." *Critique of Anthropology* 8(3): 7–39.

Gallois, Dominique. 1993. *Mairi revisitada: A reintegração da Fortaleza de Macapá na tradição oral dos Waiãpi*. São Paulo: NHII/USP/Fapesp.

———. 2000. "Nossas falas duras: Discurso político e auto-representação Waiãpi." In Bruce Albert and Alcida Ramos, eds., *Pacificando o branco: Cosmologias do contato no Norte-Amazônico*, 205–37. São Paulo: Unesp/Imprensa Oficial do Estado; Paris: IRD.

———, ed. 2005. *Redes de relações nas Guianas*. São Paulo: Associação Editorial Humanitas/Fapesp.

Gallois, Dominique, and Luís Donisete Grupioni. 1999. "O índio na Missão Novas Tribos." In Robin Wright, ed., *Transformando os deuses: Os múltiplos sentidos da conversão entre os povos indígenas no Brasil*, 77–129. Campinas: Editora da Unicamp.

Galvão, Eduardo. 1957. "Estudos sobre a aculturação dos grupos indígenas do Brasil." *Revista de Antropologia* 5(1): 67–74.

———. 1979. *Encontro de sociedades*. Rio de Janeiro: Paz e Terra.

Gonçalves, Marco Antonio. 2000. "A Woman between Two Men and a Man between Two Women: The Production of Jealousy and the Predation of Sociality amongst the Paresi Indians of Mato Grosso (Brazil)." In Joanna Overing and Alan Passes, eds., *The Anthropology of Love and Anger: The Aesthetics of Conviviality in Native Amazonia*, 235–51. London and New York: Routledge.

Gordon, César. 2006. *Economia selvagem: Ritual e mercadoria entre os índios Xikrin-Mebêngôkre*. São Paulo: Editora da Unesp/Isa/Nuti.

Gow, Peter. 1991. *Of Mixed Blood: Kinship and History in Peruvian Amazonia*. Oxford: Clarendon.

———. 1996. "River People: Shamanism and History in Western Amazonia." In Nicholas Thomas and Caroline Humphrey, eds., *Shamanism, History and the State*, 90–113. Ann Arbor: University of Michigan Press.

———. 2001. *An Amazonian Myth and Its History*. Oxford: Oxford University Press.

———. 2006. "Forgetting Conversion: The Summer Institute of Linguistic Mission in the Piro Lived World." In Fenella Cannel, ed., *The Anthropology of Christianity*, 211–39. Durham: Duke University Press.

———. 2007. " 'Ex-Cocama': Transforming Identities in Peruvian Amazonia." In Carlos Fausto and Michael Heckenberger, eds., *Time and Memory in Indigenous Amazonia: Anthropological Perspectives*, 194–215. Gainesville: University Press of Florida.

———. 2009. "Christians: A Transforming Concept in Peruvian Amazonia." In Aparecida Vilaça and Robin Wright, eds., *Native Christians: Modes and Effects of Christianity among Indigenous Peoples of the Americas*, 33–52. Farnham, Surrey, UK and Burlington, Vermont, U.S.: Ashgate.

Grenand, Pierre. 1982. *Ainsi parlaient nos ancetres: Essai d'ethnohistoire Wayapi*. Paris: Orstom.

Grenand, Pierre, and Françoise Grenand. 2000. "Em busca da aliança impossível: Os Waiãpi do Norte e seus brancos (Guiana Francesa)." In Bruce Albert and Alcida Ramos, eds., *Pacificando o branco: Cosmologias do contato no Norte-Amazônico*, 145–78. São Paulo: Unesp/Imprensa Oficial do Estado; Paris: IRD.

Grotti, Vanessa. 2007. "Nurturing the Other: Wellbeing, Social Body, and Transformability in Northeastern Amazonia." Ph.D. diss., Trinity College, University of Cambridge.

Guerra, Antônio Teixeira. 1953. "Observações geográficas sobre o território do Guaporé". *Revista Brasileira de Geografia* 15(2): 221.

Guss, David. 1989. *To Weave and to Sing: Art, Symbol, and Narrative in the South American Rain Forest*. Berkeley: University of California Press.

Halbwachs, Maurice. 1968. *La mémoire collective*. Bibliothèque de Sociologie Contemporaine. Paris: Presses Universitaires de France.

———. 1994. *Les cadres sociaux de la mémoire*. Paris: Albin Michel.

Harris, Marvin. 1979. "The Yanomamö and the Causes of War in Band and Village Societies." In M. L. Margolis and W. E. Carter, eds., *Brazil, an Anthropological Perspective: Essays in Honor of Charles Wagley,* 121–32. New York: Columbia University Press.

———. 1984. "A Cultural Materialist Theory of Band and Village Warfare: The Yanomamö Test." In Brian Ferguson, ed., *Warfare, Culture, and Environment,* 11–140. New York: Academic Press.

Héritier, Françoise. 1979. "Symbolique de l'inceste et de sa prohibition." In Michel Izard and Pierre Smith, eds., *La fonction symbolique,* 209–43. Paris: Gallimard.

Hill, Jonathan. 1988a. "Introduction: Myth and History." In Jonathan Hill, ed., *Rethinking History and Myth: Indigenous South American Perspectives on the Past,* 1–17. Urbana: University of Illinois Press.

———, ed. 1988b. *Rethinking History and Myth: Indigenous South American Perspectives on the Past.* Urbana: University of Illinois Press.

Hill, Jonathan, and Robin Wright. 1988. "Time, Narrative, and Ritual: Historical Interpretations from an Amazonian Society." In Jonathan Hill, ed., *Rethinking History and Myth: Indigenous South American Perspectives on the Past,* 78–105. Urbana: University of Illinois Press.

Hugh-Jones, Christine. 1979. *From the Milk River: Spatial and Temporal Processes in Northwest Amazonia.* Cambridge: Cambridge University Press.

Hugh-Jones, Stephen. 1988. "The Gun and the Bow: Myths of the White Man and Indians." *L'Homme* 106–7: 138–58.

———. 2001. "The Gender of Some Amazonian Gifts: An Experiment with an Experiment." In Thomaz Gregor and Donald Tuzin, eds., *Gender in Amazonia and Melanesia: An Exploration of the Comparative Method,* 245–78. Berkeley: University of California Press.

Hulme, Peter. 1986. *Colonial Encounters: Europe and the Native Caribbean 1492–1797.* London: Routledge.

Hulme, Peter, and Neil Whitehead, eds. 1992. *Wild Majesty: Encounters with Caribs from Columbus to the Present Day.* Oxford: Clarendon Press.

Ingold, Tim. 2000. *The Perception of the Environment: Essays in Livelihood, Dwelling and Skill.* London: Routledge.

Instituto Socioambiental (ISA). 2000. *Povos indígenas no Brasil, 1996–2000.* São Paulo: Instituto Socioambiental.

Jackson, Jean. 1995. "Culture Genuine and Spurious: The Politics of Indianness in the Vaupés." *American Ethnologist* 22: 3–27.

Kelly, José Antonio. 2003. "Relations within the Health System among the Yanomami in the Upper Orinoco, Venezuela." Ph.D. diss., Darwin College, University of Cambridge.

————. 2005. "Notas para uma teoria do 'virar branco.'" *Mana: Estudos de Antropologia Social* 11(1): 201–34.

Kensinger, Kenneth. 1995. *How Real People Ought to Live: The Cashinahua of Eastern Peru.* Illinois: Waveland Press.

Krenak, Ailton. 2000. "O eterno retorno do encontro." In Instituto Socioambiental (ISA), *Povos indígenas no Brasil, 1996–2000*, 45–48. São Paulo: Instituto Socioambiental.

Kuikuro, Kujame/Atahulu. 2000. "O aparecimento dos caraíba." In Instituto Socioambiental (ISA), *Povos indígenas no Brasil, 1996–2000*, 31–33. São Paulo: Instituto Socioambiental.

Laraia, Roque, and Roberto Damatta. 1967. *Índios e castanheiros: A empresa extrativa e os índios do médio Tocantins.* São Paulo: Difusão Européia do Livro.

Latour, Bruno. 2000. *Jamais fomos modernos: Ensaio de antropologia simétrica.* São Paulo: Editora 34.

Lea, Vanessa. 1986. "Nomes e 'nekrets' Kayapó: uma concepção de riqueza." Ph.D. diss., PPGAS/Museu Nacional/UFRJ, Rio de Janeiro.

Leigue Castedo, Luis. 1957. *El Itenez salvaje.* La Paz: Ministerio de Educación y Bellas Artes.

Leite, Mauricio. 2007. *Transformação e persistência: Antropologia da alimentação e nutrição em uma sociedade indígena amazônica.* Rio de Janeiro: Editora Fiocruz.

Leonel, Mauro Jr. 1984. *Relatório de avaliação das comunidades Oro-Uari, Macurap e Canoé da Área Indígena Sagarana.* AESP/FUNAI.

Lévi-Strauss, Claude. 1948. "Tribes of the Right Bank of the Guaporé River." In Julian Steward, ed., *Handbook of South American Indians*, vol. 3. Smithsonian Institution, *Bulletin* 143: 371–79.

————. 1976a. "O campo da antropologia"; "Como morrem os mitos." In *Antropologia Estrutural 2.* Rio de Janeiro: Tempo Brasileiro (Biblioteca Tempo Universitário, 45).

————. 1976b [1942]. "Guerra e comércio entre os Índios da América do Sul." In Egon Schaden, ed., *Leituras de Etnologia Brasileira*, 325–39. São Paulo: Companhia Editora Nacional.

————. 1981. *Mito e significado.* Lisbon: Perspectivas do Homem, Edições 70.

————. 1991. *Histoire de Lynx.* Paris: Plon.

————. 1994 [1964]. *The Raw and the Cooked.* London: Pimlico.

Lévy-Bruhl, Lucien. 1996 [1927]. *L'âme primitive.* Paris: Quadrige/PUF.

Lima, Tânia. 1995. "A parte do Cauim: Etnografia juruna." Ph.D. diss., PPGAS/Museu Nacional/UFRJ, Rio de Janeiro.

————. 1996. "O dois e o seu múltiplo: Reflexões sobre o perspectivismo em uma cosmologia tupi." *Mana: Estudos de Antropologia Social* 2(2): 21–47.

————. 2002. "O que é um corpo?" *Religião e Sociedade* 22(1): 9–19.

————. 2005. *Um peixe olhou para mim: O povo Yudjá e a perspectiva*. Rio de Janeiro e São Paulo: Editora Unesp/Isa/Nuti.

Lock, Margaret. 1993. "Cultivating the Body: Anthropology and Epistemologies of Bodily Practice and Knowledge." *Annual Review of Anthropology* 22: 133–55.

Lock, Margaret, and Nancy Scheper-Hughes. 1987. "The Mindful Body." *Medical Anthropology Quarterly* 1(1): 6–41.

Mason, Alan. 1977. "Oronaó Social Structure." Ph.D. diss., University of California-Davis.

McCallum, Cecilia. 1996. "The Body That Knows: From Cashinahua Epistemology to a Medical Anthropology of Lowland South America." *Medical Anthropology Quarterly* 10(3): 347–72.

————. 2000. "Incas e Nawas: Produção, transformação e transcendência na história Kaxinawá." In Bruce Albert and Alcida Ramos, eds., *Pacificando o branco: Cosmologias do contato no Norte-Amazônico*, 375–98. São Paulo: Unesp/Imprensa Oficial do Estado; Paris: IRD.

Meireles, Denise. 1986. "Os Pakaas-Novos." Master's thesis, University of Brasília.

————. 1989. *Guardiães da fronteira: Rio Guaporé, século XVIII*. Petrópolis: Vozes.

Melatti, Júlio César. 1967. *Índios e criadores: A situação dos Krahó na área pastoril do Tocantins*. Rio de Janeiro: Instituto de Filosofia e Ciências Sociais da Universidade Federal do Rio de Janeiro.

Métraux, Alfred. 1946. *Myths of the Toba and Pilagá Indians of the Gran Chaco*. Philadelphia: American Folklore Society.

————. 1948. "Tribes of Eastern Bolivia and the Madeira Headwaters: The Chapacuran Tribes." In Julian Steward, ed., *Handbook of South American Indians*, vol. 3, Smithsonian Institution, *Bulletin* 143: 397–406.

Nimuendaju, Curt. 1925. "As tribus do Alto Madeira." *Journal de la Société des Américanistes de Paris* 17: 137–72.

————. 1981. *Mapa Etnohistórico de Curt Nimuendaju*. Rio de Janeiro: IBGE/Fundação Nacional Pró-Memória.

Nordenskiöld, Erland. 1924. "The Ethnography of South-America Seen from Mojos in Bolivia." *Comparative Ethnographical Studies* 3.

Oakdale, Susan. 2001. "History and Forgetting in a Indigenous Amazonian Community." *Ethnohistory* 48(3): 381–401.

Oberg, Kalervo. 1949. *The Terena and the Caduveo of Southern Mato Grosso*. Smithsonian Institution Institute of Social Anthropology Publication 9. Washington, D.C.: U. S. Government Printing Office.

Obeyesekere, Gananath. 1992. *The Apotheosis of Captain Cook: European Mythmaking in the Pacific*. Princeton, N.J.: Princeton University Press.

Oliveira Filho, João Pacheco. 1988. *"O nosso governo": Os Ticuna e o regime tutelar*. São Paulo: Marco Zero/MCT/CNPQ.

Overing, Joanna. 1995. "Who Is the Mightiest of Them All? Jaguar and Conquistador in Piaroa Images of Alterity and Identity." In James Arnold, ed., *Monsters, Tricksters, and Sacred Cows*, 50–79. New World Studies. Charlottesville: University Press of Virginia.

Peggion, Edmundo. 1999. "Os Torá." Available at http://www.socioambiental.org.

Pio Correa, Manoel. 1926. *Dicionário das plantas úteis do Brasil e das exóticas cultivadas*. Rio de Janeiro: Ministério da Agricultura, Indústria e Comércio.

Pollock, Donald. 1985. "Personhood and Illness among the Culina of Western Brazil." Ph.D. diss., University of Rochester, Rochester, New York.

Pompa, Maria Cristina. 2003. *Religião como tradução: Missionários, Tupi e Tapuia no Brasil Colonial*. Bauru: Edusc.

Price, David. 1972. "Nambiquara Society." Ph.D. diss., University of Chicago.

Ramos, Alcida. 1988. "Indian Voices: Contact Experienced and Expressed." In Jonathan Hill, ed., *Rethinking History and Myth: Indigenous South American Perspectives on the Past*, 214–34. Urbana: University of Illinois Press.

Reichel-Dolmatoff, Gerardo. 1975. *The Shaman and the Jaguar*. Philadelphia: Temple University Press.

Ribeiro, Darcy. 1957. "Culturas e línguas indígenas do Brasil." *Educação e Ciências Sociais* (Rio de Janeiro) 2(6): 1–102.

———. 1996 [1970]. *Os índios e a civilização: A integração das populações indígenas no Brasil moderno*. São Paulo: Companhia das Letras.

Rivière, Peter. 1995. *Absent-Minded Imperialism: Britain and the Expansion of Empire in 19th-Century Brazil*. London: Tauris Academic Studies.

———, ed. 2006a. *The Guiana Travels of Robert Schomburgk 1835–1844*. Vol. 1, *Explorations on Behalf of the Royal Geographical Society 1835–1839*. Series 3, vol. 16. London: Ashgate for the Hakluyt Society.

———, ed. 2006b. *The Guiana Travels of Robert Schomburgk 1835–1844*. Vol. 2, *The Boundary Survey 1840–1844*. Series 3, vol. 17. London: Ashgate for the Hakluyt Society.

Robbins, Joel. 2004. *Becoming Sinners: Christianity + Moral Torment in a Papua New Guinea Society*. Berkeley: University of California Press.

Roe, Peter. 1988. "The Josho Nahuambo Are All Wet and Undercooked: Shipibo Views of the White Man and the Incas in Myth, Legend, and History." In Jonathan Hill, ed., *Rethinking History and Myth: Indigenous South American Perspectives on the Past*, 106–35. Urbana: University of Illinois Press.

Rosaldo, Renato. 1980. *Ilongot Headhunting: 1883–1974; A Study in Society and History*. Stanford, Calif.: Stanford University Press.

Rydén, Stig. 1942. "Notes on the Moré Indians, Rio Guaporé, Bolivia." *Ethnos* 7(2–3): 84–124.

Sahlins, Marshall. 1981. *Historical Metaphors and Mythical Realities: Structure in the Early History of the Sandwich Islands Kingdom.* Association for the Study of Anthropology in Oceania, Special Publications 1. Ann Arbor: University of Michigan Press.

————. 1985. *Islands of History.* Chicago: University of Chicago Press.

————. 1995. *How "Natives" Think: About Captain Cook for Example.* Chicago: University of Chicago Press.

————. 1997. "O 'pessimismo sentimental' e a experiência etnográfica: Por que a cultura não é um 'objeto' em via de extinção (parte 1)." *Mana: Estudos de Antropologia Social* 3(1): 41–73.

Salomon, Frank. 1999. "Testimonies: The Making and Reading of Native South American Historical Sources." In Frank Salomon and Stuart Schwartz, eds., *The Cambridge History of the Native Peoples of the Americas*; vol. 3, part 1, *South America*, 19–95. Cambridge: Cambridge University Press.

Salomon, Frank, and Stuart Schwartz, eds. 1999. *The Cambridge History of the Native Peoples of the Americas.* Vol. 3, *South America.* Cambridge: Cambridge University Press.

Santos, Geraldo, Michel Jegu, and Bernard de Merona. 1984. *Catálogo de peixes comerciais do Baixo Rio Tocantins.* Manaus: Eletronorte/Inpa.

Santos-Granero, Fernando. 1992a. *Etnohistoria de la Alta Amazonia. Siglo XV–XVIII.* Quito: Abya-Yala.

————, ed. 1992b. *Opresión colonial y resistencia indígena en la Alta Amazonía.* Quito: Flacso/Abya-Yala/Cedime.

————. 2007. "Time Is Disease, Suffering, and Oblivion: Yanesha Historicity and the Struggle against Temporality." In Carlos Fausto and Michael Heckenberger, eds., *Time and Memory in Indigenous Amazonia: Anthropological Perspectives*, 47–73. Gainesville: University Press of Florida.

Sartre, Jean-Paul. 1966. *Being and Nothingness: A Phenomenological Essay on Ontology.* Trans. and with an introduction by Hazel F. Barnes. New York: Washington Square Press.

Schieffelin, Edward. 1991. "The Great Papuan Plateau." In Edward Schieffelin and Robert Crittenden, eds., *Like People You See in a Dream: First Contact in Six Papuan Societies*, 58–87. Stanford, Calif.: Stanford University Press.

————. 1995. "Early Contact as Drama and Manipulation in the Southern Highlands of Papua New Guinea: Pacification as the Structure of the Conjuncture." *Comparative Studies in Society and History* 37(3): 555–80.

Schieffelin, Edward, and Robert Crittenden. 1991a. "Introduction." In Edward Schieffelin and Robert Crittenden, eds., *Like People You See in a Dream: First Contact in Six Papuan Societies*, 13–43. Stanford, Calif.: Stanford University Press.

————, eds. 1991b. *Like People You See in a Dream: First Contact in Six Papuan Societies*. Stanford, Calif.: Stanford University Press.

Schieffelin, Edward, Robert Crittenden, et al. 1991. "Historical Impact: Southern Highlands Epilogue." In Edward Schieffelin and Robert Crittenden, eds., *Like People You See in a Dream: First Contact in Six Papuan Societies*, 257–92. Stanford, Calif.: Stanford University Press.

Seeger, Anthony. 1980. *Os índios e nós: Estudos sobre sociedades tribais brasileiras*. Rio de Janeiro: Campus.

Severi, Carlo. 2000. "Cosmologia, crise e paradoxo: Da imagem de homens e mulheres brancos na tradição xamânica kuna." *Mana: Estudos de Antropologia Social* 6(1): 121–55.

Shapiro, Judith. 1981. "Ideologies of Catholic Missionary Practice in a Postcolonial Era." *Comparative Studies in Society and History* 23(1): 130–49.

Silva, Fernando Altenfelder. 1949. "Mudança cultural terena." *Revista do Museu Paulista* 2: 271–379.

Smith, Pierre. 1980. "Positions du mythe." In *Le temps de la réflexion* 1: 61–81. Paris: Gallimard.

Staden, Hans. 1974. *Duas viagens ao Brasil*. São Paulo: Itatiaia/Edusp.

Strathern, Andrew. 1999. *Body Thoughts*. Ann Arbor: University of Michigan Press.

Strathern, Marilyn. 1992. *Reproducing the Future: Anthropology, Kinship, and the New Reproductive Technologies*. Manchester: Manchester University Press.

————. 2009. "Using Bodies to Communicate." In Helen Lambert and Maryon McDonald, eds., *Social Bodies*, 148–69. New York: Berghahn Books.

Taussig, Michael. 1993a. *Xamanismo, colonialismo e o homem selvagem*. Rio de Janeiro: Paz e Terra.

————. 1993b. *Mimesis and Alterity: A Particular History of the Senses*. New York: Routledge.

Taylor, Anne-Christine. 1992. "História pós-colombiana da Alta Amazônia." In Manuela Carneiro da Cunha, eds., *História dos índios do Brasil*, 213–38. São Paulo: Fapesp/smc/Companhia das Letras.

————. 1993. "Remembering to Forget: Identity, Mourning, and Memory among the Jivaro." *Man* 28: 653–78.

————. 1999. "The Westerns Margins of Amazonia from the Early Sixteenth to the Early Nineteenth Century." In Frank Salomon and Stuart Schwartz, eds., *The Cambridge History of the Native Peoples of the Americas*; vol. 3, part 2, *South America*, 188–256. Cambridge: Cambridge University Press.

————. 2000. "Le sexe de la proie: Représentations Jivaro du lien de parenté." *L'Homme* 154–55: 309–34.

————. 2007. "Sick of History: Contrasting Regimes of Historicity in the Upper Amazon." In Carlos Fausto and Michael Heckenberger, eds., *Time and Memory in Indigenous Amazonia: Anthropological Perspectives,* 133–68. Gainesville: University Press of Florida.

Teixeira-Pinto, Marnio. 2000. "História e cosmologia de um contato: A atração dos Arara." In Bruce Albert and Alcida Ramos, eds., *Pacificando o branco: Cosmologias do contato no Norte-Amazônico,* 405–29. São Paulo: Unesp/Imprensa Oficial do Estado; Paris: IRD.

Todorov, Tzvetan. 1983. *A conquista da América: A questão do outro.* São Paulo: Martins Fontes.

Tooker, Deborah. 1992. "Identity Systems in Highland Burma: 'Belief,' Akha Zan, and a Critique of Interiorized Notions of Ethno-religious Identity." *Man* 27: 799–819.

"Traditions et récits sur l'arrivée des Européens en Amérique." 1992. *Recherches Amérindiennes au Québec* 22 (2–3).

Turner, Terence. 1988. "History, Myth, and Social Consciousness among the Kayapó of Central Brazil." In Jonathan Hill, ed., *Rethinking History and Myth: Indigenous South American Perspectives on the Past,* 195–213. Urbana: University of Illinois Press.

―――. 1992. "Os Mebengroke Kayapó: História e mudança social de comunidades autônomas para a coexistência interétnica." In Manuela Carneiro da Cunha, ed., *História dos índios no Brasil,* 311–38. São Paulo: Fapesp/Companhia das Letras/ SMC.

―――. 1993. "Da cosmologia à história: Resistência, adaptação e consciência social entre os Kayapó." In Eduardo Viveiros de Castro and Manuela Carneiro da Cunha, eds., *Amazônia: Etnologia e história indígena,* 43–66. São Paulo: NHII/ USP/Fapesp.

Van Velthem, Lúcia. 2000. " 'Feito por inimigos': Os brancos e os seus bens na representação Wayana do contato." In Bruce Albert and Alcida Ramos, eds., *Pacificando o branco: Cosmologias do contato no Norte-Amazônico,* 61–83. São Paulo: Unesp/Imprensa Oficial do Estado; Paris: IRD.

Vernant, Jean-Pierre. 1980. "Le mythe au réfléchi." In *Le temps de la réflexion* 1: 21–25. Paris: Gallimard.

Vilaça, Aparecida. 1989. "Comendo como gente: Formas do canibalismo wari' (Pakaa Nova)." Master's thesis, PPGAS/Museu Nacional/UFRJ, Rio de Janeiro.

―――. 1992. *Comendo como gente: Formas do canibalismo wari'.* Rio de Janeiro: Editora UFRJ/Anpocs.

―――. 1993. "Claude Lévi-Strauss: História de Lince." *Caderno Idéias* 3. *Jornal do Brasil* (Rio de Janeiro), September 18 (Review).

―――. 1995. "O sistema de parentesco wari.' " In Eduardo Viveiros de Castro, ed., *Antropologia do Parentesco: Estudos Ameríndios,* 265–319. Rio de Janeiro: Editora UFRJ.

———. 1996a. "Cristãos sem fé: Alguns aspectos da conversão dos Wari' (Pakaa-Nova)." *Mana: Estudos de Antropologia Social* 2(1): 109–37.

———. 1996b. "Quem somos nós: Questões da alteridade no encontro dos Wari' com os brancos." Ph.D. diss., PPGAS/Museu Nacional/UFRJ, Rio de Janeiro.

———. 1997. "Christians without Faith: Some Aspects of the Conversion of the Wari.'" *Ethnos* 62(1–2): 91–115.

———. 1998. "Fazendo corpos: Reflexões sobre morte e canibalismo entre os Wari' à luz do perspectivismo." *Revista de Antropologia* 41(1): 9–68.

———. 1999a. "Cristãos sem fé: Alguns aspectos da conversão dos Wari' (Pakaa-Nova)." In Robin Wright, ed., *Transformando os deuses: Os múltiplos sentidos da conversão entre os povos indígenas do Brasil*, 131–54. São Paulo: Editora da Unicamp.

———. 1999b. "Devenir autre: Chamanisme et contacte interethnique en Amazonie brésilienne." *Journal de la Société des Américanistes* 85: 239–60.

———. 2000a. "Relations between Funerary Cannibalism and Warfare Cannibalism: The Question of Predation." *Ethnos* 65(1): 83–106.

———. 2000b. "O que significa tornar-se Outro? Xamanismo e contato interétnico na Amazônia." *Revista Brasileira de Ciências Sociais* 15(4): 56–72.

———. 2000c. "O canibalismo wari.'" In Joaquim Pais de Brito (coord.), *Índios, nós*. Exhibition catalogue. Lisbon: Museu Nacional de Etnologia.

———. 2002a. "Making Kin out of Others in Amazonia." *Journal of the Royal Anthropological Institute* 8(2): 347–65.

———. 2002b. "Missions et conversions chez les Wari': Entre protestantisme et catholicisme." *L'Homme* 164: 57–79.

———. 2003. "'Big Brother Wari': Os efeitos da idéia de Deus em uma cosmologia perspectivista." In Annals of the 51st International Congress of Americanists, July 14–18, Santiago, Chile.

———. 2005. "Chronically Unstable Bodies: Reflexions on Amazonian Corporalities." *Journal of the Royal Anthropological Institute* 11(3): 445–64.

———. 2006. *Quem somos nós: Os Wari' encontram os brancos*. Rio de Janeiro: Editora UFRJ.

———. 2009a. "Conversion, Predation, and Perspective." In Aparecida Vilaça and Robin Wright, eds., *Native Christians: Modes and Effects of Christianity among Indigenous Peoples of the Americas*, 147–66. Farnham, Surrey, UK and Burlington, Vermont, U.S.: Ashgate.

———. 2009b. "Bodies in Perspective: A Critique of the Embodiment Paradigm from the Point of View of Amazonian Ethnography." In Helen Lambert and Maryon McDonald, eds., *Social Bodies*, 129–47. New York: Berghahn Books.

Viveiros de Castro, Eduardo. 1978. *Os Kulina do Alto Purus—Acre: Relatório de viagem realizada em janeiro-fevereiro de 1978*. Brasília: FUNAI.

————. 1983. "Hierarquia e simbiose em questão." Review essay of Alcida Ramos, *Hierarquia e simbiose: Relações intertribais no Brasil. Anuário Antropológico* (Rio de Janeiro) 81: 252–62.

————. 1986. *Araweté: Os deuses canibais.* Rio de Janeiro: Anpocs/Jorge Zahar.

————. 1992a. "O mármore e a murta: Sobre a inconstância da alma selvage." *Revista de Antropologia* 35: 21–74.

————. 1992b. "Apresentação." In Aparecida Vilaça, *Comendo como gente: Formas do canibalismo wari'*, xi–xxiii. Rio de Janeiro: Editora UFRJ/Anpocs.

————. 1992c. *From the Enemy's Point of View: Humanity and Divinity in an Amazonian Society.* Translated by Catherine Howard. Chicago: University of Chicago Press.

————. 1993a. "Histórias ameríndias." *Novos Estudos* 36. São Paulo: Cebrap.

————. 1993b. "Alguns aspectos da afinidade no dravidianato amazônico." In Eduardo Viveiros de Castro and Manuela Carneiro da Cunha, eds., *Amazônia: Etnologia e história indígena,* 149–210. São Paulo: NHII/USP/Fapesp.

————. 1996a. "Os pronomes cosmológicos e o perspectivismo ameríndio." *Mana: Estudos de Antropologia Social* 2(2): 115–43.

————. 1996b. "Le meurtrier et son double chez les Araweté (Brésil): Un exemple de fusion rituelle." *Systèms de Pensée en Afrique Noire* 14: 77–104.

————. 1998a. "Cosmological Deixis and Amerindian Perspectivism." *Journal of the Royal Anthropological Institute* 4(3): 469–88.

————. 1998b. "Cosmological Perspectivism in Amazonia and Elsewhere." Simon Bolívar Lectures. Department of Social Anthropology, University of Cambridge.

————. 1999. "Etnologia brasileira." In Sergio Miceli, ed., *O que ler na ciência social brasileira (1970–1995),* 109–223. São Paulo: Sumaré/Anpocs/Capes.

————. 2000a. "Atualização e contra-efetuação do virtual na socialidade amazônica: O processo de parentesco." *Ilha* 2(1): 5–46.

————. 2000b. "Os termos da outra história." In Carlos Alberto Ricardo, ed., *Povos indígenas no Brasil (1996–2000),* 49–54. São Paulo: ISA.

————. 2001. "Gut Feelings about Amazonia: Potential Affinity and the Construction of Sociality." In Laura Rival and Neil Whitehead, eds., *Beyond the Visible and the Material: The Amerindianization of Society in the Work of Peter Rivière.* New York: Oxford University Press.

————. 2002. *A inconstância da alma selvagem.* São Paulo: Cosac Naify.

————. 2004. "Perspectival Anthropology and the Method of Controlled Equivocation." *Tipití* 2(1): 3–22.

Viveiros de Castro, Eduardo, and Manuela Carneiro da Cunha, eds. 1993. *Amazônia: Etnologia e história indígena.* São Paulo: NHII/USP/Fapesp.

Von Graeve, Bernard. 1989. *The Pacaa Nova: Clash of Cultures on the Brazilian Frontier.* Peterborough, Ont.: Broadview Press.

Wachtel, Nathan. 1971. *La vision des vaincus: Les indiens du Perou devant la conquête espagnole, 1530–1570*. Paris: Gallimard.

Wagley, Charles, and Eduardo Galvão. 1961 [1949]. *Os índios Tenetehara: Uma cultura em transição*. Rio de Janeiro: Serviço de Comunicação do Ministério da Educação e Cultura.

Wagner, Roy. 1975. *The Invention of Culture*. Englewood Cliffs, N.J.: Prentice Hall.

Whitehead, Neil. 1988. *Lords of the Tiger Spirit: A History of the Caribs in Colonial Venezuela and Guyana, 1498–1820*. Dordrecht: Foris Publications.

———. 1999. "The Crises and Transformations of Invaded Societies: The Caribbean (1492–1580)." In Frank Salomon and Stuart Schwartz, eds., *The Cambridge History of the Native Peoples of the Americas*; vol. 3, part 1, *South America*, 864–903. Cambridge: Cambridge University Press.

———. 2002. *Dark Shamans: Kainamà and the Poetics of Violent Death*. Durham: Duke University Press.

———. 2003. "Introduction." In Neil Whitehead, ed., *History and Historicities in Amazonia*, vii–xx. Lincoln: University of Nebraska Press.

Whitehead, Neil, and Robin Wright, eds. 2004. *In Darkness and Secrecy: The Anthropology of Assault Sorcery and Witchcraft in Amazonia*. Durham: Duke University Press.

Wolf, Eric. 1982. *Europe and the People without History*. Berkeley: University of California Press.

Wright, Robin. 1998. *Cosmos, Self, and History in Baniwa Religion: For Those Unborn*. Austin: University of Texas Press.

INDEX

APARECIDA VILAÇA is an associate professor of social anthropology in the Graduate Program in Social Anthropology (PPGAS) of the Museu Nacional, Universidade Federal de Rio de Janeiro, Brazil. She is the author of *Comendo como gente: Formas do canibalismo Wari'* (1992) and coeditor of *Native Christians: Modes and Effects of Christianity in the Americas* (2009).

DAVID ROGERS is a freelance translator and an anthropologist with research experience in southern Amazonia.

Library of Congress Cataloging-in-Publication Data
Vilaça, Aparecida
[Quem somos nós. English]
Strange enemies: indigenous agency and scenes of encounters in Amazonia/Aparecida Vilaça ; translated by David Rodgers.
p. cm.—(Cultures and pratice of violence)
Originally published in Portuguese: Brazil: Editora UFRJ, 2006.
Includes bibliographical references and index
ISBN 978-0-8223-4556-5 (cloth : alk. paper)
ISBN 978-0-8223-4573-2 (pbk. : alk. paper)
1. Pakaasnovos Indians—History. 2. Pakaasnovos Indians—Social life and customs. 3. Indians of South America—Brazil.
I. Title. II. Series: Culture and practice of violence series.
F2520.1.P32V5713 2010
981'.01—dc22
2009044001